Thucydides, Harold North

Thucydides. Book V.

Edited on the Basis of Classen's Edition

Thucydides, Harold North

Thucydides. Book V.
Edited on the Basis of Classen's Edition

ISBN/EAN: 9783337179175

Printed in Europe, USA, Canada, Australia, Japan

Cover: Foto ©Thomas Meinert / pixelio.de

More available books at **www.hansebooks.com**

SERIES OF GREEK AUTHORS

EDITED UNDER THE SUPERVISION OF

JOHN WILLIAMS WHITE AND THOMAS D. SEYMOUR.

THUCYDIDES

BOOK V.

EDITED

ON THE BASIS OF CLASSEN'S EDITION

BY

HAROLD NORTH FOWLER

INSTRUCTOR IN HARVARD UNIVERSITY.

BOSTON:
PUBLISHED BY GINN & COMPANY.
1888.

Entered, according to Act of Congress, in the year 1888, by
JOHN WILLIAMS WHITE AND THOMAS D. SEYMOUR,
in the Office of the Librarian of Congress, at Washington.

TYPOGRAPHY BY J. S. CUSHING & CO., BOSTON.

PRESSWORK BY GINN & CO., BOSTON.

INTRODUCTION.

THE fifth book of Thucydides presents other and greater difficulties of interpretation than those which precede. In order to judge of these difficulties correctly, and, so far as possible, to overcome them, it is necessary to examine the nature and composition of the entire book.

The division of the whole extant history into eight books, is doubtless due not to Thucydides himself, but to later grammarians. See Introd. to Book I. p. 54. The purpose of this division was merely to resolve the work into a series of nearly equal parts, so that a comprehensive view of the whole should be made easier, and yet the connexion should not be destroyed. The general observations and preliminary notices which precede the narrative of the war itself naturally formed the first book; the two main parts of the history, the account of the Archidamian war and that of the Sicilian war, remained to be divided symmetrically. This division was determined less by the contents than by the mere length of the narrative. The Archidamian war, which lasted for ten years, was divided into periods of three years, each of which occupied one book, and the tenth year was left over for the beginning of the fifth book, which was completed by the observations of the historian upon the period of some six years during which the peace of Nicias lasted. The connected narrative of the Sicilian war occupied a space about equal to two of the preceding books, and books six and seven were formed out of it.

The contents and character of the two parts thus combined to form the fifth book, are, however, essentially dissimilar. In the first part the narrative of the great war between Athens and Sparta is continued; in the second the various political intrigues and complications among the greater and smaller states of Greece, which led to the decisive conflict at Mantinea, are described. But these details are given with such minute accuracy concerning every phase of successful or unsuccessful intrigues and negotiations, the personal motives of individuals (of Pleistoanax and Nicias in c. 16; of Alcibiades in c. 43; 45; 46; of Agis in c. 71) are so carefully depicted, such a lively interest in Spartan affairs and customs is repeatedly expressed (in c. 34 § 2; 36 § 1; 66 § 2; 72 § 2; 75 § 3), an interest evidently arising from fresh impressions, that one cannot fail to observe a marked departure from the ordinary style of the author. On the other hand one not infrequently misses the ease and smoothness of expression which one might desire, and that sometimes in passages of special importance (as in c. 36 § 2; 49; 59; 65 § 3; 69 § 2; 71 § 2; 82 § 2 ff.). or short remarks, inserted where they have no special connexion, arouse rather than satisfy the desire for further explanation (cf. c. 31 § 6; 32 § 1; 35 § 1; 36 § 2: 38 § 4; 39 § 1; 51 and 52).

The simplest explanation of these unusual phenomena which present themselves to the attentive reader of the fifth book seems to be that offered by Classen:[1] "Though I am convinced that the whole work was written in the shape in which we have it after the conclusion of the Peloponnesian war, and that Thucydides was called away from life when engaged in the last revision and combination of the portions which he had noted down and sketched in outline from the beginning of the war, yet I do not believe that all parts of the work received an equally thorough review. I think that the masterly introduction, which makes our first book, was first completed with the full knowledge of the disastrous result of the twenty-seven-years war; that then the history of the ten-years war, and the Sicilian expedition, for which it is likely that the results of laborious inquiry were already at hand more or less perfectly worked out, received their final touches; and that after this, before the thread of the narrative was taken up again with the Ionic-Decelean war, the intervening period of the εἰρήνη ὕπουλος was described."

During this period the chief opponents abstained, as Thucydides says, from direct hostilities against each other's territory (ἀπέσχοντο μὴ ἐπὶ τὴν ἑκατέρων γῆν στρατεῦσαι, c. 25. 12), but in the light of sub-

---

[1] In his Introd. to Book V. p. 2 f. This has already been given in the Introd. to Book I., but is repeated here to preserve the connexion. For other views on this subject and for references, see Introd. to Book I. p. 20 ff.

sequent events the so-called peace appeared as an integral part of the whole war, and was consequently so treated by the historian. The description of this period constitutes by far the greater part of the fifth book. This description is very closely connected with the narrative of the last events of the ten-years war (the battle at Amphipolis and the interrupted expedition of the Lacedaemonians to Thrace, see c. 13); but still the change in style, the most striking points of which have been mentioned above, appears even in the description of the feelings at Athens and Sparta which led to the peace, and of the negotiations which preceded the treaty.

The narrative of Books II., III., IV., and the first thirteen chapters of Book V., as well as that of Books VI. and VII., advances regularly and equally, and is based upon the careful use and arrangement of the observations and inquiries of the historian. But the study of the domestic and foreign intrigues and negotiations carried on among the states of Greece, and especially in Peloponnesus, imposed new methods upon him. Thucydides tells clearly enough how he succeeded in obtaining accurate information concerning those matters which naturally escape the notice of a distant observer: ξυνέβη μοι ... γενομένῳ παρ' ἀμφοτέροις τοῖς πράγμασι, καὶ οὐχ ἧσσον τοῖς Πελοποννησίων διὰ φυγὴν καθ' ἡσυχίαν τι μᾶλλον αἴσθεσθαι, c. 26. 24 ff. Doubtless only his long sojourn in Peloponnesus, to which these words refer, and his intercourse with influential men in the most important states, enabled him to give us the instructive account of the secret intrigues which preceded the fifty-years truce between Athens and Sparta, and especially of the subsequent complications which centred for the most part in Argos (c. 27–83).

At the same time the character of the work, as regards both its general tone and its contents, undergoes a change. In all other parts of the history, in the superb introduction in Book I. as well as in the lively narrative of the first ten-years war and in that of the second half of the war so far as it goes, we are made to feel that the entire sympathy of the author is with Athens, and that, even after he has been forced to leave his native country, Athens is still for him the central point of the story. In the account of the period of nominal peace this is all changed. Athens retires to the background behind the Peloponnesian states, which are seeking their own advantage in the troublous ferment of changing party intrigues. Only when the restless ambition of Alcibiades succeeds in bringing his native city into the Argive alliance, does Athens once more become prominent in the detailed account of the negotiations which preceded the treaty of alliance (c. 43–46). There is, however, one point of specifically Attic interest which Thucydides does not neglect, — the relations of the allies in Thrace; for οἱ ἐπὶ Θρᾴκης ξύμμαχοι οὐδὲν ἧσσον (in spite of the conclusion of the peace) πολέμιοι ἦσαν, c. 26. 13. Although no great events took place in Thrace, he gives nevertheless an accurate though brief account of every movement and change of side. These are the isolated remarks mentioned above (c. 31 § 6; 32 § 1; 35 § 1; 38 § 4; 39 § 1), which show that the Thracian Chalcidians seized every opportunity of freeing themselves more and more from the hated rule of Athens. An important expedition to Thrace which the Athenians had planned for the winter of 417–416 B.C. was not actually sent, owing to the defection of Perdiccas (see c. 83 § 4 and note).

On the other hand Thucydides takes pains to make the most complete use of the information he derived from trustworthy sources concerning external and internal events in Peloponnesus, and to communicate to his readers his newly acquired insight into conditions with which he had previously been less familiar. The information he received seems to have been embodied in his history very much as he originally recorded it, and this may account for the marked attention given to the institutions and conditions of Sparta. Instances of this are the account of the discipline of the Lacedaemonian army (in c. 66), which is elaborated with evident interest, the description of the great effect of the personal bravery of the Lacedaemonians in the battle of Mantinea (in c. 72. 8 ff.), and of their conduct after a battle (in c. 73. 22 ff.). These and similar passages seem like notes taken from personal observation or from conversation with eye-witnesses.

These portions of the book, when compared with the rest of the history, exhibit sometimes a less polished mode of expression, and sometimes, probably in consequence of a special striving after clearness, contain repetitions of similar words and phrases. Both defects are exemplified in the chapters which form the transition from the account of the last warlike events in the autumn of 422 B.C. to that of the negotiations for the peace in the spring of 421 B.C. (c. 14 ff.). The account of the return of the Lacedaemonian re-inforcements under Rhamphias closes at the end of c. 13 with the remark that they knew τοὺς Λακεδαιμονίους. ὅτε ἐξῄεσαν, πρὸς τὴν εἰρήνην μᾶλλον τὴν γνώμην ἔχοντας. At the beginning of c. 14 it is stated in the same words, which here apply to both parties, that Athenians and Lacedaemonians alike πρὸς τὴν εἰρήνην μᾶλλον τὴν γνώμην εἶχον. In these words we may recognize the joint by which the narrative of the internal and external reasons which increased the desire for peace in both places, and of the conclusion of the peace itself, is connected with the reports of the last warlike movements, which may have been noted some time before. Nor can it be denied that the narrative itself contains a number of unusual and incongruent expressions. It is not without reason that Julius Steup (Rhein. Mus. 25, p. 273–305) finds many difficulties and much to criticise in this account, but the radical doctrine of interpolations which he adopts is not necessary. With the exception of the passage in c. 15. 5, for which a certain emendation has not yet been proposed, and that in c. 16. 6, which Stahl has probably restored to its proper form, all difficulties can be overcome by a careful method of interpretation proceeding from the proper point of view. For particulars, see the commentary and the Appendix on c. 17. 6.[2]

[2] According to the view above expressed (see also p. 3), which is that of Classen, the dividing line between the narrative of the first ten-years war and the account of the unsettled period which began with the peace of Nicias is to be sought at the end of c. 13. Steup, *Quaest. Thuc.*, and Herbst, Philol. 1879, p. 503 (see also p. 434) put it at the end of c. 24. Kirchhoff, Sitzungsber. d. Berl. Akad. 1882, p. 937 ff. and 1883, p. 838, sets it at the end of c. 20. If, as seems most probable, the narrative of the ten-years war was written in the first place after 421 B.C., or even after 404 B.C., it would certainly be remarkable if the account of the treaties in c. 18 f. and c. 23 f., with which this part of the war ended, were not contained in it. Still Classen's reasons for marking the division after c. 13 as given above are not without weight. As this part of the book was doubtless re-written for the express purpose of hiding the point of division, it may be impossible to fix its position accurately.

By laying before his readers an account of the reasons for the change in the policy of Athens and Sparta, and by communicating to them the documents recording the peace and the alliance between the two states, the historian prepared the ground for the presentation of the new times and new events. It was natural that he should wish to prefix to this part of his work beside a brief statement of its contents, the proof of the intimate connexion between the two periods of war which are apparently separated by a peace of more than six years (but which form, in the eyes of the careful observer, one whole) as well as the evidence of his own fitness for the office of historian of this whole period, an office made materially easier for him by the events of his life. This he does in c. 25 and 26. Just as he begins the whole work by introducing himself to his readers, so here, where he begins the treatment of material different from that of the preceding books, Thucydides brings himself to our notice and seeks to awaken our confidence in his will and ability to furnish us a faithful picture of events.

If we now cast our eyes over the events of the following period of so-called peace which lasted somewhat more than six years (from c. 27 to 83), the chief impression we derive is this: that amid the political complications and bickerings which chiefly occupy this period (τὴν μετὰ τὰ δέκα ἔτη διαφοράν τε καὶ ξύγχυσιν τῶν σπονδῶν) the hand of a powerful leader is everywhere lacking. In all the more important states parties stand opposed to one another with methods of violence or intrigue, and their leaders are without personal authority or dignity. In Sparta the weak King Pleistoanax and his followers, who are driven by pitiful fear to strive anxiously for peace (see c. 17), are opposed to the Ephors Cleobulus and Xenares, who urge the continuance of the war (see c. 36. 7 ff.), and who find in King Agis a pliant but powerless instrument of their designs (see c. 54 ff.). In Argos the oligarchical and the democratic parties, encouraged, the one by Sparta, the other by Athens, contend with various success; but both are always ready to receive proposals of worse than doubtful character, and therefore afford Alcibiades welcome opportunities for ambitious intrigues and interference. Finally, in Athens we find in its full development that state of things which Thucydides describes in fitting terms in ii. 65. 41, in which the men who succeeded Pericles in the conduct of affairs ἴσοι αὐτοὶ μᾶλλον πρὸς ἀλλήλους ὄντες τοῦ πρῶτος ἕκαστος γίγνεσθαι ὠρέγοντο; and now especially the rising ambition of Alcibiades strove to gain the upper hand over the deliberate caution of the aged Nicias who longed for rest and quiet (see c. 43 ff.). To be sure, the historian, in accordance with his principle, shows us only so much of the internal movements of party strife as is necessary for the explanation of the position of Athens toward the other states, and gives full information only of the negotiations in the Athenian assembly which the cunning of Alcibiades so conducted as to bring about the conclusion of the treaty with Argos and her allies, in c. 97. But he shows with how little energy and consistency the external policy of Athens was conducted at this time and throughout the whole of this period. The troops which had been promised to aid the Argives came too late (see c. 59. 15) and in insufficient numbers (see c. 61. 1), so that the battle of Mantinea was not merely a defeat for the Argives, but inflicted heavy losses upon the Athenians as well (see c. 74. 9). The detailed narrative of the military operations which preceded this decisive battle, and of the external influences brought to bear upon them, presents a picture which reflects little credit upon Argives or Lacedaemonians (see especially c. 58; 60; 64; 65 f.), and something of the indecision and uncertainty to be observed in the movements of the troops seems to have passed over into the narrative of the historian. Repeated revision might have infused greater clearness into these passages, and their obscurity must be ascribed in part to the carelessness of copyists, as is often remarked in the commentary; but the comparative want of precision in the narrative is due in great measure to its sympathetic reproduction of the vacillating course of events themselves.

It is deserving of special notice that Thucydides, before turning in the following book to the narration of the Sicilian expedition, with which the second great period of war begins, employs with great art and care a device not elsewhere to be found, in order to place in the proper light the spirit which then governed the policy of Athens. After it has been determined that the independence of the last of the Cyclades, the Doric Melos, must be destroyed by violence or voluntary submission, the leaders of the Athenian besieging force engage in a dialogue with the representatives of the besieged inhabitants, in which they express with undisguised openness the doctrine of the right of the stronger and the motives of naked self-aggrandizement, in accordance with which they reject every petition for indulgence and clemency (c. 85–113). And the theoretical justification of the method of brute force is immediately followed by its execution. The fifth book closes with the fall of the bravely defended town and the cruel punishment of its inhabitants. From this last part of the book a ray of light is cast forward upon the prevailing character of the second chief period of the Peloponnesian war.

From this summary it appears that the fifth book is, as regards by far the greater part, a well-planned connecting link between the two chief portions of the great history, just as the period of uncertain peace was itself recognized by the historian as an integral part of the great Peloponnesian war. For the attentive reader there remain, to be sure, some inequalities in the style of the narrative, some difficulties in expression, which can be entirely done away with only by repeated consideration and study. Yet with all its defects the fifth book affords us a no less clear and satisfactory insight into the events of which it treats, than the other extant parts of this immortal work.

The remainder of Classen's introduction is taken up with a sharp discussion and severe criticism of Müller-Strübing's *Aristophanes und die historische Kritik*, Leipsic, 1873. This writer believes that Thucydides, if not actually guilty of falsehood, at any rate habitually suppresses part of the truth, especially in matters connected with Athenian politics. His opinion is based mainly upon a theory that the real ruler of Athens and the Athenian empire in the fifth century B.C. was the minister of finance (ὁ ταμίας τῆς κοινῆς προσόδου or ἐπιμελητὴς τῆς διοικήσεως), who was elected once in four years. This election was naturally of the very highest importance, so that one cannot wonder if the strife of parties was very violent in Athens once in four years, even to the extent of interfering with her external policy and the conduct of her wars. Now Thucydides nowhere mentions the ταμίας τῆς προσόδου nor the disturbance caused by these elections: consequently the uncertain conduct of the Athenians, especially during the period treated in the fifth book, is left unexplained, although it was the duty of Thucydides to explain it by giving us full information concerning the elections of this all-important functionary. This, however, according to Müller-Strübing, he intentionally neglected to do on account of his own political position or affiliations. Müller-Strübing does not prove that the ταμίας τῆς προσόδου existed in the fifth century B.C., and there appear to be sufficient reasons for believing that the office was a later creation,[3] so that this theory falls to the ground. Müller-Strübing's explanation (p. 400 ff.) of the peculiarly vacillating and undecided conduct not only of the Athenians, but also of Argives and Lacedaemonians, in the summer of 418 B.C. (see c. 56—61) is based entirely upon this theory, and therefore need not be controverted in detail. The second point which requires special mention because of its bearing upon the character of Thucydides as historian of the period succeeding the peace of Nicias, is the discussion (p. 426 ff.) of Thracian affairs, with special reference to c. 83 § 4. According to Thucydides the only important military operation of the Athenians in Thrace after the loss of Amphipolis in the autumn of 424 B.C. was the attempt to recapture that town, which ended with the death of Cleon in November of 422 B.C. Not until 417 B.C. did the Athenians prepare to send a powerful expedition to protect their Thracian interests, and that expedition was given up on account of the defection of Perdiccas (see c. 83 § 4). Müller-Strübing thinks that the Athenians had had a large force in Thrace under the command of Demosthenes ever since 420 B.C., and that Thucydides is therefore consciously

---

[3] U. Köhler, in his essay *zur Geschichte des delisch-attischen Bundes*, in the Abhdln. d. Berl. Akad. 1869, says: "It is yet to be proved that this finance-office existed at all before the archonship of Euclides." Fellner, Sitzungsber. d. Wien. Akad. XCV. (1879) p. 382, says: "In my opinion the essays which have lately appeared have proved conclusively the impossibility of the existence of a superintendent of the finances (ἐπιμελητὴς τῆς διοικήσεως) before Euclides," after which he advances further arguments for his opinion. See also M. Fränkel in the third edition of Boeckh's *Staatshaushaltung d. Athener*, notes 269 and 277.

suppressing the truth. The main argument for this view is drawn from an inscription recording expenditures made from the treasury of Athens in the years 418 to 414 B.C. The inscription, which is very fragmentary, was first published by Rhangabé, *Ant. Hell.* No. 119, and afterwards by Boeckh, *Staatshaushaltung* II., p. 29 ff. with numerous restorations. It is now also published by Kirchhoff, *C. I. A.*, I., 180–183, and by Müller-Strübing, Rhein. Mus. 1878, p. 83 ff. In two places Boeckh read στρατηγοῖς τοῖς ἐπ' Ἠϊόνος τοῖς μετὰ Δημοσθένους, from which it would appear that Demosthenes was at this time (418 B.C.) in command of forces at Eion. But the letters upon the stone are in one case only ος τοῖς μετὰ Δημοσθένους, and in the other, according to Lolling's careful reading of the original, ΛΟΣ (*i.e.* γος) τοῖς μετὰ Δημοσθένους with the remains of either a P or a B before γος. The most probable restoration for both passages is, then, τοῖς ἐς Ἄργος τοῖς μετὰ Δημοσθένους. (So Fränkel in the third edition of Boeckh's *Staatshaushaltung*, II., p. 24, N. 4, and p. 25, N. 2.) In spite of this Müller-Strübing, Rhein. Mus. 1878, p. 83 ff., still maintains that Demosthenes was general in Thrace at this time, but brings forward no new arguments to support this opinion now that the inscription has failed him.

The other passages in *Aristophanes und die historische Kritik* which affect the interpretation of the fifth book of Thucydides are referred to in the commentary, for in spite of its fundamental error Müller-Strübing's book contains much which is instructive and valuable.

THUCYDIDES V.

* Ol. 89. 2; B.C. 422, Mar.

1 Τοῦ δ' ἐπιγιγνομένου θέρους * αἱ μὲν ἐνιαύσιοι 1
σπονδαὶ διελέλυντο μέχρι Πυθίων· καὶ ἐν τῇ ἐκεχειρίᾳ οἱ
Ἀθηναῖοι Δηλίους ἀνέστησαν ἐκ Δήλου, ἡγησάμενοι κατὰ
παλαιάν τινα αἰτίαν οὐ καθαροὺς ὄντας ἱερῶσθαι, καὶ
5 ἅμα ἐλλιπὲς σφίσιν εἶναι τοῦτο τῆς καθάρσεως, ᾗ πρότερόν
μοι δεδήλωται ὡς ἀνελόντες τὰς θήκας τῶν τεθνεώτων
ὀρθῶς ἐνόμισαν ποιῆσαι. καὶ οἱ μὲν Δήλιοι Ἀτραμύττειον
Φαρνάκου δόντος αὐτοῖς ἐν τῇ Ἀσίᾳ ᾤκησαν, οὕτως ὡς

THE TENTH YEAR OF THE WAR. Chaps. 1-24.

1. *The Athenians for religious reasons drive the Delians from their island.*

2. αἱ σπονδαὶ διελέλυντο: the truce was at an end, but no warlike operations are recorded until Cleon led the expedition to Thrace, after the Pythian festival (Metageitnion, Ol. 80, 3, *i.e.* Aug., 422 B.C.). See App. — ἐκεχειρίᾳ: here and in c. 2. 2; 49. 14, the *truce* in consequence of the festival. See App. — **4.** ἱερῶσθαι: pf. pass., depends upon ἡγησάμενοι. It refers to the purification and consecration of Delos which had taken place four years before (*cf.* iii. 104). The Athenians now thought that the Delians had at that time been consecrated (again) to Apollo when they were not yet entirely purified and cleansed from an ancient pollution; that is, that the re-consecration had taken place too soon. But besides (καὶ ἅμα), they thought that the manner of purification (by removal of the coffins) had not been sufficiently thorough. — **5.** ᾗ πρότερόν μοι δεδήλωται: upon this depends the indir. disc. ὡς ... ἐνόμισαν ποιῆσαι: "In which I have before related that they believed," etc. See App. — **7.** ποιῆσαι: inf. aor. after ἐνόμισαν, refers to past time like νομίσαντες ... ποιήσασθαι in vii. 17. 9: *they believed that in removing the coffins they had acted rightly.* GMT. 23, 2; H. 854. — Ἀτραμύττειον (not -τιον; here and in viii. 108. 19 with Vat.): an important place on the coast of Mysia, near the foot of Mt. Ida. — **8.** Φαρνάκου: Pharnaces was at that time still satrap on the Hellespont. He was succeeded in this office by his son Pharnabazus. *Cf.* viii. 6. 3. — ὥρμητο: with ellipsis of οἰκῆσαι. So we might say *as each man chose*. *Cf.* ii. 67. 10; iv. 48. 26; 74. 4; viii. 23. 2.

The expulsion of the Delians is regarded by Boeckh (Abh. d. Berl.

2 ἕκαστος ὥρμητο. Κλέων δὲ Ἀθηναίους πείσας ἐς τὰ ἐπὶ Θράκης χωρία ἐξέπλευσε * μετὰ τὴν ἐκεχειρίαν, Ἀθηναίων μὲν ὁπλίτας ἔχων διακοσίους καὶ χιλίους καὶ ἱππέας τριακοσίους, τῶν δὲ ξυμμάχων πλείους, ναῦς δὲ τριάκοντα. σχὼν δὲ ἐς Σκιώνην πρῶτον ἔτι πολιορκουμένην καὶ προσλαβὼν αὐτόθεν ὁπλίτας τῶν φρουρῶν, κατέπλευσεν ἐς τὸν Κωφὸν λιμένα τῶν Τορωναίων, ἀπέχοντα οὐ πολὺ τῆς πόλεως. ἐκ δ' αὐτοῦ, αἰσθόμενος ὑπ' αὐτομόλων ὅτι οὔτε Βρασίδας ἐν τῇ Τορώνῃ οὔτε οἱ ἐνόντες ἀξιόμαχοι εἶεν, τῇ μὲν στρατιᾷ τῇ πεζῇ ἐχώρει ἐς τὴν πόλιν, ναῦς δὲ περιέπεμψε δέκα ἐς τὸν λιμένα περιπλεῖν. καὶ πρὸς τὸ περιτείχισμα πρῶτον ἀφικνεῖται, ὃ προσπεριέβαλε τῇ πόλει ὁ Βρασίδας ἐντὸς βουλόμενος ποιῆσαι τὸ προά-

Akad., 1834, p. 6 ff.) and Curtius (*Hist. of Greece*, III. p. 200) as an unjust and tyrannical measure. But perhaps the scrupulousness in matters of religion which is expressed in the beginning of the treaty of peace (iv. 118. 1), and which caused the Delians to be brought back the very next year (c. 32. 4), was really the motive of the action of the Athenians.

2. *Cleon goes with fresh troops to the coast of Thrace, where the siege of Scione still continues, and attacks Torone by land and sea.*

1. Ἀθηναίους πείσας: some persuasion appears to have been needed to induce the Athenians to begin the war again after the truce of the preceding winter.

5. σχὼν ἐς: *steering to*. Cf. Hdt. vi. 92. 6, ἔσχον ἐς τὴν Ἀργολίδα χώρην. — Σκιώνην ἔτι πολιορκουμένην: the beginning of this siege is mentioned in iv. 131. The Athenians had built a wall of circumvallation and left a guard, but their main force had been withdrawn. Cf. iv. 133. 15. — **6.** αὐτόθεν . . . τῶν φρουρῶν: refers to the guard left at Scione, the ἐπ' αὐτῇ φυλακή of iv. 133. — **7.** Κωφὸν λιμένα: see App. — τῶν Τορωναίων: *in the territory of the Toronaeans*. The harbour of Torone is not mentioned until 11.

8. αἰσθόμενος ὑπ' αὐτομόλων: an exceptional const., αἰσθόμενος being treated as if it were διδαχθείς. The more natural prep. would be παρά, not Krüger's ἀπό. For this unusual use of ὑπό, see on i. 130. 3, ὧν ἐν μεγάλῳ ἀξιώματι ὑπὸ τῶν Ἑλλήνων. Kühn. 442, 1, 2 a. — **9.** οἱ ἐνόντες: of the garrison, as iv. 104. 2; viii. 84. 14. A freq. use of ἐνεῖναι. — **10.** τῇ πεζῇ: epexegetical addition to στρατιᾷ. Cf. i. 95. 11, ὑπὸ τῶν Ἑλλήνων τῶν ἀφικνουμένων; iii. 54. 4. — ἐς τὴν πόλιν: *against the city*. Cf. ii. 18. 2, ἀφίκετο ἐς Οἰνόην. — **11.** ἐς τὸν λιμένα: see App.

12. τὸ περιτείχισμα: Brasidas had united the suburb with the city (ἐντὸς

στειον, καὶ διελὼν τοῦ παλαιοῦ τείχους μίαν αὐτὴν ἐποίησε
3 πόλιν. βοηθήσαντες δὲ ἐς αὐτὸ Πασιτελίδας τε ὁ Λακε- 1
δαιμόνιος ἄρχων καὶ ἡ παροῦσα φυλακὴ προσβαλόντων
τῶν Ἀθηναίων ἠμύνοντο. καὶ ὡς ἐβιάζοντο καὶ αἱ νῆες
ἅμα περιέπλεον ἐς τὸν λιμένα περιπεμφθεῖσαι, δείσας
5 ὁ Πασιτελίδας μὴ αἵ τε νῆες φθάσωσι λαβοῦσαι ἐρῆμον τὴν πόλιν καὶ τοῦ τειχίσματος ἁλισκομένου ἐγκατα-
ληφθῇ, ἀπολιπὼν αὐτὸ δρόμῳ ἐχώρει ἐς τὴν πόλιν. οἱ δὲ 2
Ἀθηναῖοι φθάνουσιν οἵ τε ἀπὸ τῶν νεῶν ἑλόντες τὴν
Τορώνην καὶ ὁ πεζὸς ἐπισπόμενος αὐτοβοεὶ κατὰ τὸ δι-
10 ῃρημένον τοῦ παλαιοῦ τείχους ξυνεσπεσών. καὶ τοὺς μὲν
ἀπέκτειναν τῶν Πελοποννησίων καὶ Τορωναίων εὐθὺς
ἐν χερσί, τοὺς δὲ ζῶντας ἔλαβον καὶ Πασιτελίδαν τὸν ἄρ-

ποιήσας, cf. i. 62. 3; ii. 83. 5; vii. 5. 14) by breaking down the old wall on this side, διελὼν τοῦ παλαιοῦ τείχους, and building a new one to enclose city and suburb alike. This is the περιτείχισμα ὃ προσπεριέβαλε τῇ πόλει. — 14. καὶ διελὼν κτέ.: the rel. pron., which would here be in a new case (dat.) must be supplied from the preceding ὅ. G. 156, N. Usually a dem. or pers. pron. is introduced, as in i. 74. 8; 122. 14; ii. 4. 24. II. 1005. — τείχους: gen. of the whole depending upon an unexpressed word denoting the part broken down, as in ii. 75. 24. G. 168, N. 2; Kühn. 416, 1, N. 2. — αὐτήν: agrees in gender with the pred. noun and refers to city and suburb.

3. *Cleon takes Torone in spite of the brave resistance of the inhabitants, who are treated with great severity. The Boeotians take Panactum, an Attic border fort.*

1. Πασιτελίδας: *Pasitelidas*. *Cf.* iv. 132. 19, where he is called Epitelidas. See note *ad loc.* — ἐς αὐτό: into this

advanced περιτείχισμα, which (6 and 17) is called simply τείχισμα, and from which he afterwards (7) retires into the city. — **3.** ἐβιάζοντο: pass., as in i. 2. 4; iii. 94. 10. — **4.** See App. — **5.** φθάσωσι λαβοῦσαι: equiv. to πρότερον λάβωσι. G. 279, 4; H. 984.

7. οἱ δὲ Ἀθηναῖοι οἵ τε ἀπὸ τῶν νεῶν καὶ ὁ πεζός: *cf.* ii. 95. 5; iii. 13. 19. With these two subjs. distributing οἱ Ἀθηναῖοι agree respectively the two partics. ἑλόντες and ξυνεσπεσών, the latter being limited by ἐπισπόμενος, while both belong with φθάνουσιν. G. 279, 4; II. 984. — **9.** αὐτοβοεί: which is generally used in connexion with ἑλεῖν (ii. 81. 21; iii. 113. 29; viii. 62. 8), is here joined with ξυνεσπεσών which practically implies ἑλών. *Cf.* iii. 74. 8, αὐτοβοεὶ κρατήσειεν, and viii. 71. 12, αὐτοβοεὶ λήψεως οὐκ ἂν ἁμαρτεῖν. — τὸ διῃρημένον: (*cf.* c. 2. 14) the breach made by Brasidas in the old wall. — **12.** ἐν χερσί: *in actual battle*. *Cf.* c. 10. 40; iii. 66. 10; iv. 96. 14; 113. 6; vi. 70. 1. A similar expression is

χοντα. Βρασίδας δὲ ἐβοήθει μὲν τῇ Τορώνῃ, αἰσθόμενος δὲ καθ' ὁδὸν ἑαλωκυῖαν ἀνεχώρησεν, ἀποσχὼν τεσσαρά-
15 κοντα μάλιστα σταδίους μὴ φθάσαι ἐλθών. ὁ δὲ Κλέων καὶ οἱ Ἀθηναῖοι τροπαῖά τε ἔστησαν δύο, τὸ μὲν κατὰ τὸν λιμένα, τὸ δὲ πρὸς τῷ τειχίσματι, καὶ τῶν Τορωναίων γυναῖκας μὲν καὶ παῖδας ἠνδραπόδισαν, αὐτοὺς δὲ καὶ Πελοποννησίους καὶ εἴ τις ἄλλος Χαλκιδέων ἦν, ξύμ-
20 παντας ἐς ἑπτακοσίους, ἀπέπεμψαν ἐς τὰς Ἀθήνας· καὶ αὐτοῖς τὸ μὲν Πελοποννήσιον ὕστερον ἐν ταῖς γενομέναις σπονδαῖς ἀπῆλθε, τὸ δὲ ἄλλο ἐκομίσθη ὑπ' Ὀλυνθίων ἀνὴρ ἀντ' ἀνδρὸς λυθείς.

Εἷλον δὲ καὶ Πάνακτον Ἀθηναίων ἐν μεθορίοις
25 τεῖχος Βοιωτοὶ ὑπὸ τὸν αὐτὸν χρόνον προδοσίᾳ. καὶ ὁ

ἐς χεῖρας ἰέναι, to come to blows. Cf. ii. 3. 21; iv. 72. 15, ἐλθεῖν ἐς χεῖρας; 96. 7.
14. ἀποσχών: denotes at once actual distance (definitely expressed by τεσσαράκοντα μάλιστα σταδίους) and his failure to attain his end (which is negatively expressed in μὴ φθάσαι ἐλθών, cf. c. 25. 12). With the last phrase, cf. ii. 77. 19, ἐλαχίστου ἐδέησε διαφθεῖραι, where, however, μή is omitted. GMT. 95, 2 and N. 1; H. 1029. *He was only about forty stadia removed from getting there before (the Athenians).*
19. εἴ τις ἄλλος Χαλκιδέων: stands in opposition to the αὐτούς, i.e. the men of Torone (cf. Hom. A. 4), who were also Chalcidians. The Athenians were esp. angry with those who had formerly been their allies. — **ξύμπαντας**: as in iv. 129. 15, *all together*, expressing the sum total. — **21. αὐτοῖς**: i.e. the Athenians. Dat. of interest, as in i. 48. 9, Κορινθίοις δὲ τὸ μὲν δεξιὸν κέρας αἱ Μεγαρίδες νῆες εἶχον; 89, 15, ἐπειδὴ αὐτοῖς οἱ βάρβαροι ἀπῆλθον; 101. 6, οἱ Εἵλωτες αὐτοῖς ἀπέστησαν; iv. 42. 20 iv. 67. 24. G. 184, 3; H. 771. — τὸ μὲν Πελοποννήσιον, τὸ δὲ ἄλλο neut. sing. used as a collective noun Cf. ii. 45. 5; iii. 39. 29, πέφυκε . . ἄνθρωπος τὸ μὲν θεραπεῦον ὑπερφρονεῖν τὸ δὲ μὴ ὑπεῖκον θαυμάζειν; iv. 61. 19 πέφυκε γὰρ τὸ ἀνθρώπειον ἄρχειν μὲ τοῦ εἴκοντος, φυλάσσεσθαι δὲ τὸ ἐπιόν — **ἐν ταῖς ... ἀπῆλθε**: *were set free in th treaty;* cf. c. 18. 35. The expressio refers at once to the clause in th treaty and its execution. — **22. ἐκομίσθη**: *were carried away in exchange* Cf. i. 113. 14. — **23. ἀνὴρ ἀντ' ἀνδρὸ λυθείς**: ἀνήρ is here in partitive par tic. appos. with τὸ ἄλλο. Cf. ii. 103 4, τούς τε ἐλευθέρους ἄγοντες, οἳ ἀνὴ ἀντ' ἀνδρὸς ἐλύθησαν. Kühn. 406, 8 N. 11.
24. Πάνακτον: Panactum was a fortified place (τεῖχος) east of Eleu therae and nearly north of Phyle close to the Boeotian frontier. On it further fortunes, see c. 39, 40, 42.

μὲν Κλέων φυλακήν καταστησάμενος τῆς Τορώνης ἄρας περιέπλει τὸν Ἄθων ὡς ἐπὶ τὴν Ἀμφίπολιν.

4 Φαίαξ δὲ ὁ Ἐρασιστράτου τρίτος αὐτὸς Ἀθηναίων πεμπόντων ναυσὶ δύο ἐς Ἰταλίαν καὶ Σικελίαν πρεσβευτὴς ὑπὸ τὸν αὐτὸν χρόνον ἐξέπλευσε. Λεοντῖνοι γὰρ ἀπελθόντων Ἀθηναίων ἐκ Σικελίας μετὰ τὴν ξύμβασιν 5 πολίτας τε ἐπεγράψαντο πολλοὺς καὶ ὁ δῆμος τὴν γῆν ἐπενόει ἀναδάσασθαι. οἱ δὲ δυνατοὶ αἰσθόμενοι Συρακοσίους τε ἐπάγονται καὶ ἐκβάλλουσι τὸν δῆμον. καὶ οἱ μὲν ἐπλανήθησαν ὡς ἕκαστοι· οἱ δὲ δυνατοὶ ὁμολογήσαντες Συρακοσίοις καὶ τὴν πόλιν ἐκλιπόντες καὶ ἐρημώ10 σαντες, Συρακούσας ἐπὶ πολιτείᾳ ᾤκησαν. καὶ ὕστερον πάλιν αὐτῶν τινες διὰ τὸ μὴ ἀρέσκεσθαι ἀπολιπόντες ἐκ

27. ὡς ἐπὶ τὴν Ἀμφίπολιν: i.e. to get it away from Brasidas. For the account of the capture of Amphipolis by Brasidas, see iv. 105 f.

4. *Phaeax is sent from Athens to Sicily, and tries without much success to form a coalition of the other Sicilian Greeks against the Syracusans.*

1. Φαίαξ: at that time one of the most noted Athenians. Cf. Plut. Alc. 13, where he is mentioned as a rival of Alcibiades. — τρίτος αὐτός: with two others. Cf. i. 46. 7; viii. 35. 3; Δωριεὺς ὁ Διαγόρου τρίτος αὐτός.

3. Λεοντῖνοι γὰρ κτέ.: continuing to 16, a short account of Sicilian affairs, since the time when they were last mentioned in iv. 65. — 4. ἀπελθόντων Ἀθηναίων: in the summer of 424 B.C., after Hermocrates had brought about the peace among the Sicilian Greeks. See iv. 65. — 5. πολίτας τε ἐπεγράψαντο: *they enrolled new citizens* in order to strengthen the democratic party, and for their benefit a new division of land was to be made. — τὴν γῆν ἀναδάσασθαι: cf. ἀναδασμὸς

γῆς, Hdt. iv. 159. 8, and the Attic oath of the heliasts, Dem. xxiv. 149.

6. αἰσθόμενοι: with no expressed obj., refers to what precedes. Cf. i. 95. 22, οἱ δὲ αἰσθόμενοι ἀπῆλθον; 118. 9; 126. 21; 131. 1; 134. 1; ii. 25. 8; iii. 22. 22; iv. 67. 8, and often. — 8. ἐπλανήθησαν ὡς ἕκαστοι: *they* (i.e. the δῆμος) *were scattered in every direction*. The aor. referring to continued action in the past because this is regarded as a single historical event. GMT. 19, N. 2; H. 822 c. Cf. i. 6. 7; 8. 3; ii. 2. 2; iv. 56. 2. The ellipsis after ὡς ἕκαστοι is to be supplied from ἐπλανήθησαν. — 9. Συρακοσίοις, Συρακούσας: see App. — ἐκλιπόντες καὶ ἐρημώσαντες: the fact that the city was left without inhabitants is emphasized. — 10. ἐπὶ πολιτείᾳ ᾤκησαν: *they settled* (aor.) *there upon the assurance of citizenship*. Cf. i. 13. 5, ἐπὶ ῥητοῖς γέρασι πατρικαὶ βασιλεῖαι; iii. 114. 14, ξυμμαχίαν ἐποιήσαντο ἐπὶ τοῖσδε. The dat. with ἐπί expresses the condition upon which anything is done.

11. ἀρέσκεσθαι: *being contented*,

τῶν Συρακουσῶν Φωκαίας τε τῆς πόλεώς τι τῆς Λεοντίνων χωρίον καλούμενον καταλαμβάνουσι καὶ Βρικιννίας ὃν ἔρυμα ἐν τῇ Λεοντίνῃ. καὶ τῶν τοῦ δήμου τότε ἐκπεσόντων οἱ πολλοὶ ἦλθον ὡς αὐτούς, καὶ καταστάντες ἐκ τῶν τειχῶν ἐπολέμουν. ἃ πυνθανόμενοι οἱ Ἀθηναῖοι τὸν Φαίακα πέμπουσιν, εἴ πως πείσαντες τοὺς σφίσιν ὄντας αὐτόθι ξυμμάχους καὶ τοὺς ἄλλους, ἢν δύνωνται, Σικελιώτας κοινῇ ὡς Συρακοσίων δύναμιν περιποιουμένων ἐπιστρατεῦσαι, διασώσειαν τὸν δῆμον τῶν Λεοντίνων. ὁ δὲ Φαίαξ ἀφικόμενος τοὺς μὲν Καμαριναίους πείθει καὶ Ἀκραγαντίνους, ἐν δὲ Γέλᾳ ἀντιστάντος αὐτῷ τοῦ πράγματος οὐκέτι ἐπὶ τοὺς ἄλλους ἔρχεται, αἰσθόμενος οὐκ ἂν πείθειν αὐτούς, ἀλλ' ἀναχωρήσας διὰ τῶν Σικελῶν ἐς Κατάνην, καὶ ἅμα ἐν τῇ παρόδῳ καὶ

with and without dat. *Cf.* c. 37. 19; ii. 68. 7. — **ἀπολιπόντες ἐκ**: as in iii. 10. 8, ἀπολιπόντων ὑμῶν ἐκ τοῦ Μηδικοῦ πολέμου. Kühn. 447 c. — 12. **τῆς πόλεως τι χωρίον**: apparently a suburb of Leontini, the name of which points to a connexion with the Ionic Phocaea (see Holm, *Gesch. Sicilicus*, I. p. 198), while the fortress of Bricinniae was prob. at a greater distance from the city, though in the Leontine territory (ἐν τῇ Λεοντίνῃ. Holm, II. p. 9). — 14. **ὅν**: agrees with the pred. ἔρυμα. *Cf.* i. 10. 1. (G. 135, 3, N. 4; H. 610; Kühn. 369, 3. 15. **ὡς αὐτούς**: *i.e.* to join them. — **καταστάντες**: *i.e.* after they had established themselves and made preparations for defence. *Cf.* i. 59. 7; ii. 1. 3; iv. 75. 8. — 16. **ἐκ τῶν τειχῶν**: *from the* (two) *fortified places.* — **ἐπολέμουν**: *they carried on war* against the Syracusans. The impf. denotes the condition of hostility, not definite events. — **ἃ πυνθανόμενοι κτέ.**: returns to the beginning of the chap. — 17. **εἴ πως**...

διασώσειαν κτέ.: *in case they should persuade, etc., and so save the* δῆμος. An idea of purpose is implied as an apod. The whole is equiv. to a clause expressing intention. GMT. 53, N. 2; H. 907. — **τοὺς ... ξυμμάχους**: referring to the conditions which existed before 424 B.C. (iv. 65). See iii. 86. — 19. **κοινῇ**: with ἐπιστρατεῦσαι, the motive for a joint campaign being the continual (pres. partic. περιποιουμένων) aggressions of the Syracusans. 22. **ἀντιστάντος αὐτῷ τοῦ πράγματος**: *since his undertaking did not prosper*. As in c. 38. 20, ὡς δὲ ἀντέστη τὸ πρᾶγμα, in accordance with the well-known meaning of πράσσειν, *undertake*, or *carry on an undertaking*. *Cf.* i. 128. 13, τὰ πρὸς βασιλέα πράγματα πράσσειν; iv. 1. 4, ἔπραξαν δὲ τοῦτο οἱ Συρακόσιοι. — 24. **αἰσθόμενος**: see App. — 25. **διὰ τῶν Σικελῶν**: the Sicels in the country behind Syracuse. — **ἐν τῇ παρόδῳ**: on the march from Gela to Catana. This also goes to

ἐς τὰς Βρικιννίας ἐλθὼν καὶ παραθαρσύνας, ἀπέπλει. ἐν δὲ τῇ παρακομιδῇ τῇ ἐς τὴν Σικελίαν καὶ πά- λιν ἀναχωρήσει καὶ ἐν τῇ Ἰταλίᾳ τισὶ πόλεσιν ἐχρημά- τισε περὶ φιλίας τοῖς Ἀθηναίοις, καὶ Λοκρῶν ἐντυγχάνει τοῖς ἐκ Μεσσήνης ἐποίκοις ἐκπεπτωκόσιν, οἳ μετὰ τὴν Σικελιωτῶν ὁμολογίαν στασιασάντων Μεσσηνίων καὶ ἐπαγαγομένων τῶν ἑτέρων Λοκροὺς ἔποικοι ἐξεπέμφθη- σαν καὶ ἐγένετο Μεσσήνη Λοκρῶν τινα χρόνον. τούτοις οὖν ὁ Φαίαξ ἐντυχὼν [τοῖς κομιζομένοις] οὐκ ἠδίκησεν· ἐγεγένητο γὰρ τοῖς Λοκροῖς πρὸς αὐτὸν ὁμολογία ξυμβά- σεως πέρι πρὸς τοὺς Ἀθηναίους. μόνοι γὰρ τῶν ξυμμά- χων, ὅτε Σικελιῶται ξυνηλλάσσοντο, οὐκ ἐσπείσαντο

prove that Bricinniae lay some distance inland from Leontini.

5. *Phaeax, after negotiations with several cities of Italy, returns to Athens.*

1. τῇ παρακομιδῇ καὶ ἀναχωρήσει: the two corresponding nouns with but one art., as in i. 120. 10, **τὴν κατακομι- δὴν καὶ πάλιν ἀντίληψιν**, and ii. 64. 27. — **2. ἐχρημάτισε**: λόγους προσήνεγκε, Schol. This is used in like manner of conducting public business in c. 61. 6; i. 87. 17. With the dat., here only. Of the conduct of money matters, the mid. χρηματίζεσθαι is used in vii. 13. 13. — **3. φιλίας τοῖς Ἀθηναίοις**: *cf.* i. 63. 9, τοῖς Ποτειδαιάταις βοηθοί; iii. 66. 17; iv. 23. 4. The dat. depends upon the verbal force of φιλίας (G. 185; H. 765 a) in spite of the fact that φιλέω takes the acc. Kühn. 424, 2. — **4. ἐκπεπτωκόσιν**: the attrib. partic. is not infrequently put by Thuc. after its subst. when the latter is further limited by other words. *Cf.* i. 11. 19; 90. 6; and often. Perhaps, however, Cobet (Mnem. 14, p. 4) is right in omitting ἐποίκοις as a gloss. — **τὴν Σικελιωτῶν ὁμολογίαν**: the terms of this agreement between Athens and the Sicilians (424 B.C.) are given in iv. 65. — **5. στασιασάντων Μεσση- νίων**: Messene was disturbed by factions from its foundation to the latest times. See vi. 4. 24 ff., and A. Holm, *Gesch. Siciliens*, I. p. 198 ff. — **6. τῶν ἑτέρων**: doubtless the Ionic portion of the population, which had been subjected by Anaxilas (vi. 4. 34 ff.). These people, from the moment of their first appearance in Sicily, had had dealings with the Epizephyrian Locrians (Hdt. vi. 23). — **ἐξεπέμ- φθησαν**: *i.e.* by the Locrians to Messene in accordance with the invitation (ἐπαγαγομένων). — **7. καὶ ἐγένετο**: joined to the rel. clause in loose grammatical connexion. *Cf.* c. 2. 14.

8. [τοῖς κομιζομένοις]: see App. — **9. ἐγεγένητο γάρ**: on his way to Sicily, Phaeax had made a preliminary arrangement with the Locrians, who had hitherto been averse to the Athenian alliance.

11. οὐκ ἐσπείσαντο: *they made no treaty*, wishing to be free to take advantage of any opportunities which

Ἀθηναίοις, οὐδ' ἂν τότε, εἰ μὴ αὐτοὺς κατεῖχεν ὁ πρὸς Ἰπωνιέας καὶ Μεδμαίους πόλεμος, ὁμόρους τε ὄντας καὶ ἀποίκους. καὶ ὁ μὲν Φαίαξ ἐς τὰς Ἀθήνας χρόνῳ ὕστερον ἀφίκετο.

6 Ὁ δὲ Κλέων ὡς ἀπὸ τῆς Τορώνης τότε περιέπλευ- 1 σεν ἐπὶ τὴν Ἀμφίπολιν, ὁρμώμενος ἐκ τῆς Ἠιόνος Σταγείρῳ μὲν προσβάλλει Ἀνδρίων ἀποικίᾳ καὶ οὐχ εἷλε, Γαληψὸν δὲ τὴν Θασίων ἀποικίαν λαμβάνει κατὰ κράτος. καὶ πέμψας ὡς Περδίκκαν πρέσβεις, ὅπως παραγένοιτο 2 στρατιᾷ κατὰ τὸ ξυμμαχικόν, καὶ ἐς τὴν Θρᾴκην ἄλλους παρὰ Πολλὴν τῶν Ὀδομάντων βασιλέα, ἄξοντας μισθοῦ Θρᾷκας ὡς πλείστους, αὐτὸς ἡσύχαζε περιμένων ἐν τῇ Ἠιόνι. Βρασίδας δὲ πυνθανόμενος ταῦτα ἀντεκάθητο 3 καὶ αὐτὸς ἐπὶ τῷ Κερδυλίῳ· ἔστι δὲ τὸ χωρίον τοῦτο Ἀργιλίων ἐπὶ μετεώρου πέραν τοῦ ποταμοῦ, οὐ πολὺ ἀπέχον τῆς Ἀμφιπόλεως, καὶ κατεφαίνετο πάντα αὐτόθεν,

might be offered them, such as the occurrences at Messene above referred to. — 12. οὐδ' ἂν τότε: sc. ἐσπείσαντο.
— 13. Ἰπωνιέας καὶ Μεδμαίους: see App.
6. Cleon and Brasidas collect reinforcements, and take up positions opposite one another near Amphipolis.
1. τότε: refers to c. 3. 27. τότε often refers in this way to a time which is supposed to be well known to the reader. Cf. i. 101. 8; iii. 69. 2; iv. 46. 5; v. 4. 14; and see on i. 101. 8. — 2. Σταγείρῳ (Strabo vii. frg. 35 and Steph. Byz. have Στάγειρα): north of Acanthus, on the Strymonian Gulf. Cf. Hdt. vii. 115. 6. The birthplace of Aristotle. St. now reads here and in c. 18. 25 (not iv. 88. 9) Στάγιρος, acc. to the inscriptions. — 4. Γαληψόν: between the Strymon and the Nestus. Cf. iv. 107. 12; Diod. xii. 68; Strabo, vii. 35; Steph. Byz. s.v.
6. κατὰ τὸ ξυμμαχικόν: the alliance had been renewed, iv. 132. 2.
— 7. τῶν (with Vat. for τὸν) Ὀδομάντων: cf. ii. 101. 12. This tribe is mentioned by Hdt. vii. 112. 7. Its home was apparently in the plain between Strymon and Nestus. — ἄξοντας: with Linwood (Jahrbb. 1862, p. 200) for ἄξοντα, for this intention must be ascribed to the envoys, not to the foreign chief. — μισθοῦ: gen. of price, as in iv. 124. 22; vii. 25. 34. G. 178; H. 746; Kr. Spr. 47, 17, 3. Cf. Ar. Ach. 144. — 9. Ἠιόνι: cf. iv. 106. 17 and 18. — ἀντεκάθητο καὶ αὐτός: refers to ἡσύχαζε (sc. ὁ Κλέων) of the preceding line.
10. Ἀργιλίων: in the territory of Argilos, but on the right bank of the

ὥστε οὐκ ἂν ἔλαθεν αὐτὸν ὁρμώμενος ὁ Κλέων τῷ στρατῷ, ὅπερ προσεδέχετο ποιήσειν αὐτόν, ἐπὶ τὴν Ἀμφίπολιν, 15 ὑπεριδόντα σφῶν τὸ πλῆθος, τῇ παρούσῃ στρατιᾷ ἀναβήσεσθαι. ἅμα δὲ καὶ παρεσκευάζετο Θρᾷκάς τε μισθω- 4 τοὺς πεντακοσίους καὶ χιλίους καὶ τοὺς Ἠδῶνας πάντας παρακαλῶν, πελταστὰς καὶ ἱππέας· καὶ Μυρκινίων καὶ Χαλκιδέων χιλίους πελταστὰς εἶχε πρὸς τοῖς ἐν 20 Ἀμφιπόλει. τὸ δ' ὁπλιτικὸν ξύμπαν ἠθροίσθη δισχίλιοι 5 μάλιστα καὶ ἱππῆς Ἕλληνες τριακόσιοι. τούτων Βρασίδας μὲν ἔχων ἐπὶ Κερδυλίῳ ἐκάθητο ἐς πεντακοσίους καὶ χιλίους, οἱ δ' ἄλλοι ἐν Ἀμφιπόλει μετὰ Κλεαρίδου ἐτε- 7 τάχατο. ὁ δὲ Κλέων τέως μὲν ἡσύχαζεν, * ἔπειτα ἠναγκά- 1 σθη ποιῆσαι ὅπερ ὁ Βρασίδας προσεδέχετο. τῶν γὰρ 2 στρατιωτῶν ἀχθομένων μὲν τῇ ἕδρᾳ, ἀναλογιζομένων δὲ

Strymon. — 11. οὐ πολύ: about 20 stadia. — 13. αὐτόν: Cl. and one Ms. for αὐτόθεν, the repetition of which is useless. This renewed mention of Brasidas makes his intention in occupying Cerdylium more prominent, and makes the connexion of the following προσεδέχετο and παρεσκευάζετο easier. (St. and Schütz, with three Mss., omit αὐτόθεν.) — 14. ἐπὶ τὴν Ἀμφίπολιν ... ἀναβήσεσθαι: explaining the preceding ὅπερ ... ποιήσειν. Cf. iii. 59. 18, ὅπερ ἀναγκαῖον ... τοῖς ὧδε ἔχουσι, λόγου τελευτᾶν. — 15. τῇ παρούσῃ στρατιᾷ: without waiting for his expected reinforcements.
16. Θρᾷκας τε κτέ.: to be taken with παρακαλῶν, not with παρεσκευάζετο, which is used abs. as often elsewhere. Cf. ii. 11. 22; iii. 46. 9; vii. 34. 4; viii. 10. 4. The τε ... καί admits of no other const., and, moreover, the opposition between τοὺς Ἠδῶνας πάντας and the definite number of the other Thracians is made

more evident in this way. — 18. Μυρκινίων: Myrcinus, also an Edonian city, had been for some time in alliance with Brasidas. Cf. iv. 107. 9.
21. ἱππῆς Ἕλληνες: to distinguish them from the Edonians of 18. — τούτων: part. gen. It depends upon the obj. of ἔχων implied in ἐς πεντακοσίους καὶ χιλίους. About 1500 of these. — 23. μετὰ Κλεαρίδου: he was stationed at Amphipolis. Cf. iv. 132. 19. — ἐτετάχατο: this form (or the pf. τετάχαται) occurs also in iii. 13. 18; iv. 31. 7; vii. 4. 34. G. 118, 5, N.; 119, 3; H. 464 a.
7. *Cleon is forced by the impatience of his men to march out and reconnoitre.*
1. ἔπειτα: after ἔπειτα, when μέν precedes, δέ is sometimes found, and sometimes not; examples of both uses are about equally numerous. Here the Mss. omit δέ.
3. τῇ ἕδρᾳ: like ii. 18. 19, τῇ καθέδρᾳ, τῇ προσμονῇ, Schol. Cf. Hdt. ix. 41. 4. — τῶν στρατιωτῶν ἀναλογιζομέ-

THUCYDIDES V. 7.

τὴν ἐκείνου ἡγεμονίαν, πρὸς οἵαν ἐμπειρίαν καὶ τόλμαν μετὰ οἵας ἀνεπιστημοσύνης καὶ μαλακίας γενήσοιτο καὶ οἴκοθεν ὡς ἄκοντες αὐτῷ ξυνῆλθον, αἰσθόμενος τὸν θροῦν καὶ οὐ βουλόμενος, αὐτοὺς διὰ τὸ ἐν τῷ αὐτῷ καθημένους βαρύνεσθαι ἀναλαβὼν ἦγε. καὶ ἐχρήσατο τῷ 3 τρόπῳ, ᾧπερ καὶ ἐς τὴν Πύλον εὐτυχήσας ἐπίστευσέ τι φρονεῖν· ἐς μάχην μὲν γὰρ οὐδὲ ἤλπισέν οἱ ἐπεξιέναι οὐδένα, κατὰ θέαν δὲ μᾶλλον ἔφη ἀναβαίνειν τοῦ χωρίου, καὶ τὴν μείζω παρασκευὴν περιέμενεν, οὐχ ὡς τῷ ἀσφαλεῖ, ἢν ἀναγκάζηται, περισχήσων, ἀλλ' ὡς κύκλῳ περιστὰς βίᾳ αἱρήσων τὴν πόλιν. ἐλθών τε καὶ καθίσας 4 ἐπὶ λόφου καρτεροῦ πρὸ τῆς Ἀμφιπόλεως τὸν στρατόν, αὐτὸς ἐθεᾶτο τὸ λιμνῶδες τοῦ Στρυμόνος καὶ τὴν θέσιν

νων: cf. οἱ στρατιῶται ἀνελογίζοντο, viii. 83. 10, where the expression is used in the same sense as here. — 4. τὴν ἐκείνου ἡγεμονίαν: proleptic. Cf. i. 23. 26, αἱ δ' ἐς τὸ φανερὸν λεγόμεναι αἰτίαι αἵδ' ἦσαν ἑκατέρων, ἀφ' ὧν λύσαντες τὰς σπονδὰς ἐς τὸν πόλεμον κατέστησαν; ii. 21. 3, μεμνημένοι καὶ Πλειστοάνακτα ὅτε ἐσβαλὼν ἐς Ἐλευσῖνα ἀνεχώρησε. — πρὸς οἵαν ... μετὰ οἵας: the pron. is repeated with the same effect of emphasis as in vii. 75. 37. The opinion of Thuc. about Brasidas as well as Cleon remains the same, even after Cleon's success at Pylos. See on iv. 28. 24 and 39. 11, and Introd. to Book I., p. 45. — 5. ἀνεπιστημοσύνης: does not occur elsewhere in Thuc. The adj. occurs in ii. 89. 31, and freq. elsewhere. — 6. οἴκοθεν: placed first in its clause, even before ὡς, for emphasis. Cf. i. 77. 4 ff. — ξυνῆλθον: corresponds to ἐξῆλθε, c. 8. 7. See App. — καθημένους: remaining inactive, as in iv. 124. 24. See App.

9. ᾧπερ ... εὐτυχήσας ἐπίστευσέ τι φρονεῖν: (the manner) by which he had been successful at Pylos, and thus had acquired confidence in his own wisdom (φρονεῖν τι as in ii. 53. 19, ἀπολαῦσαί τι, to have some enjoyment), i.e. his method of reckless attacks. — 11. κατὰ θέαν: to reconnoitre. Cf. c. 9. 10; 10. 8; vi. 31. 5. Const. with τοῦ χωρίου, i.e. Amphipolis. — 12. καὶ τὴν μείζω κτἑ.: καί is the confirmation of what precedes: "and in fact (ii. 2. 26; iv. 1. 9) he was waiting for the reinforcements (mentioned in c. 6. 5 ff.), not that he might gain the victory (περισχήσων as in vii. 105. 4) without risk if he should be forced to fight (ἢν ἀναγκάζηται, sc. μάχεσθαι), but with the intention of forcing the town to surrender by surrounding it." — 14. βίᾳ αἱρήσων: take by force of arms. This is merely opp. to ὁμολογίᾳ παραστήσασθαι, acquire by agreement, and does not mean take by storm. See on i. 102. 7. — ἐλθών τε: and accordingly he went. Expressing conse-

τῆς πόλεως ἐπὶ τῇ Θρᾴκῃ ὡς ἔχοι, ἀπιέναι τε ἐνόμιζεν, 5
ὁπόταν βούληται, ἀμαχεί· καὶ γὰρ οὐδὲ ἐφαίνετο οὔτ'
ἐπὶ τοῦ τείχους οὐδεὶς οὔτε κατὰ πύλας ἐξῄει, κεκλημέναι τε ἦσαν πᾶσαι. ὥστε καὶ μηχανὰς ὅτι οὐκ ἀνῆλθεν
ἔχων ἁμαρτεῖν ἐδόκει· ἑλεῖν γὰρ ἂν τὴν πόλιν διὰ τὸ
8 ἐρῆμον. ὁ δὲ Βρασίδας εὐθὺς ὡς εἶδε κινουμένους τοὺς 1
Ἀθηναίους, καταβὰς καὶ αὐτὸς ἀπὸ τοῦ Κερδυλίου ἐσέρχεται ἐς τὴν Ἀμφίπολιν. καὶ ἐπέξοδον μὲν καὶ ἀντίταξιν 2
οὐκ ἐποιήσατο πρὸς τοὺς Ἀθηναίους, δεδιὼς τὴν αὑτοῦ
5 παρασκευὴν καὶ νομίζων ὑποδεεστέρους εἶναι, οὐ τῷ
πλήθει (ἀντίπαλα γάρ πως ἦν), ἀλλὰ τῷ ἀξιώματι (τῶν
γὰρ Ἀθηναίων ὅπερ ἐστράτευε καθαρὸν ἐξῆλθε, καὶ Λη-

quence. τε is here not a correlative of καί. — 17. ἐπὶ τῇ Θρᾴκῃ: in respect to the surrounding Thracian country. An indefinite description of its situation as i. 105. 6, ἐπ' Αἰγίνῃ; ii. 86. 11, ἐπὶ τῇ Ῥίῳ; vi. 2. 6, ἐπὶ τῇ θαλάσσῃ. St. omits these words as an interpolation.
17. ἀπιέναι τε ἐνόμιζεν: not to be separated by any stronger punctuation from what precedes. He examined the situation at his leisure, and believed that he could go away without a battle whenever he chose. — 18. οὔτ', οὔτε: used as if both belonged to one verb, ἐφαίνετο, although ἐξῄει is irregularly added in the second clause. — 20. ὥστε καὶ ... ἐδόκει: i.e. he was even sorry that he had not brought his storming machines with him. — οὐκ ἀνῆλθεν: refers to ἀναβαίνειν, 11. See App. — 21. ἑλεῖν ἄν: sc. ἐδόκει. His thought was ἕλοιμι ἄν or perhaps εἷλον ἄν. GMT. 53; H. 964.
8. *Thereupon Brasidas re-enters Amphipolis, and determines to attack the Athenians in two divisions commanded respectively by himself and Clearidas.*

2. καὶ αὐτός: these words indicate reciprocity in the movements of the two parties. Brasidas returned to the city which Cleon had approached. *Cf.* c. 7. 8 ff. εὐθὺς ὡς εἶδε κινουμένους τοὺς Ἀθηναίους is the natural consequence of κατεφαίνετο πάντα αὐτόθεν in c. 6. 12.
4. δεδιὼς τὴν αὑτοῦ παρασκευήν: οὐ θαρρῶν τῇ ἰδίᾳ παρασκευῇ, Schol. His force consisted mainly of mercenaries. *Cf.* iv. 80. 22. — ὑποδεεστέρους: refers in accordance with frequent usage to παρασκευήν (G. 138, N. 3; H. 615 a), and is therefore not to be changed (with Portus) to ὑποδεέστερος. — 6. ἀντίπαλα: without reference to a definite subj. *Cf.* i. 7. 8; ii. 56. 4; iii. 88. 4; iv. 117. 13. — ἀξιώματι: almost with the meaning of *excellence, efficiency* (τῇ δυνάμει, Schol.); but their reputation, with the respect arising from it, is also expressed by this word. — 7. καθαρόν: οὐχὶ συγκλύδων οὐδὲ ἐπικούρων, ἀλλ' αὐτῶν τῶν πολιτῶν, Schol. *Cf.* χρηστοῖς καταλόγοις ἐκκριθέν, vi. 31. 28. Similarly Hdt. i. 211. 3 and iv. 135. 10, τὸ κα-

μνίων καὶ Ἰμβρίων τὸ κράτιστον), τέχνῃ δὲ παρεσκευάζετο ἐπιθησόμενος. εἰ γὰρ δείξειε τοῖς ἐναντίοις τό τε 3
10 πλῆθος καὶ τὴν ὅπλισιν ἀναγκαίαν οὖσαν τῶν μεθ' ἑαυτοῦ, οὐκ ἂν ἡγεῖτο μᾶλλον περιγενέσθαι ἢ ἄνευ προόψεώς τε αὐτῶν καὶ μὴ ἀπὸ τοῦ ὄντος καταφρονήσεως.
ἀπολεξάμενος οὖν αὐτὸς πεντήκοντα καὶ ἑκατὸν ὁπλίτας, 4
καὶ τοὺς ἄλλους Κλεαρίδᾳ προστάξας, ἐβουλεύετο ἐπιχει-
15 ρεῖν αἰφνιδίως, πρὶν ἀπελθεῖν τοὺς Ἀθηναίους, οὐκ ἂν
νομίζων αὐτοὺς ὁμοίως ἀπολαβεῖν αὖθις μεμονωμένους,
εἰ τύχοι ἐλθοῦσα αὐτοῖς ἡ βοήθεια. ξυγκαλέσας δὲ τοὺς 5
πάντας στρατιώτας καὶ βουλόμενος παραθαρσῦναί τε καὶ
τὴν ἐπίνοιαν φράσαι ἔλεγε τοιάδε·

9 "Ἄνδρες Πελοποννήσιοι, ἀπὸ μὲν οἵας χώρας ἥκο- 1

θαρὸν τοῦ στρατοῦ. Plut. *Aem. P.* 8, αὐτῶν τῶν Μακεδόνων ἀρετῇ καὶ ἡλικίᾳ τὸ καθαρώτατον. — **Λημνίων καὶ Ἰμβρίων**: Attic cleruchi, often mentioned together as trusty followers, iii. 5. 5; iv. 28. 18; vii. 57. 8. — 8. **τέχνῃ**: *by artifice. Cf. c.* 18. 16. Const. with ἐπιθησόμενος, which is fut. partic. without ὡς expressing purpose after παρεσκευάζετο. Similarly ii. 91. 8; vi. 54. 18; vii. 17. 2; viii. 59. 2.
10. **ἀναγκαίαν οὖσαν**: *barely sufficient*, such as had been obtainable under the circumstances. *Cf.* vi. 37. 17. A similar use of the superl. occurs in i. 90. 21; 82. 10. — 12. **αὐτῶν**: objective gen. referring to Brasidas's own forces. ἄνευ προόψεως αὐτῶν is equiv. to εἰ μὴ αὐτοὺς προΐδοιεν. What follows carries out the same idea, the emphasis upon the consequence which was to be avoided being made stronger by the use of μὴ ἀπὸ instead of ἄνευ (for similar phrases, *cf.* i. 91. 28; iii. 40. 28, 30; iv. 130. 26; vii. 15. 12; 70. 40). καὶ μὴ ἀπὸ τοῦ ὄντος καταφρονήσεως is equiv. to καὶ

εἰ μὴ τοῦ ὄντος (*i.e.* their real weakness which would then appear) καταφρονήσειαν. "If he showed his weakness to the enemy, he thought he should be less likely (οὐ μᾶλλον for ἧττον) to gain a victory than if they did not see his forces and learn to despise them." This explanation is adopted from that of Schütz, Ztschr. f. d. Gymn. Wesen 12, p. 406, and St., *Symbola Philologorum Bonnensium*, p. 387 f.
14. **προστάξας**: προστάσσειν, *hand over to*, *place under the command of. Cf.* vi. 42. 8, κατὰ τέλη στρατηγῷ προστεταγμένοι. — 16. **ἀπολαβεῖν**: *cut off*, *get into his power*, as in ii. 90. 20; iv. 14. 19. — 17. **τύχοι ἐλθοῦσα**: equiv. to τύχῃ ἔλθοι.
19. **φράσαι**: *tell accurately. Cf.* i. 145. 4 and note; iii. 42. 10 and note.

9. Speech of Brasidas to his Troops.

It is sufficient to remind you briefly that you are Dorians opposed to Ionians.
§ 1. *Next listen to my plan: we must surprise the enemy while they are off*

μεν, ὅτι ἀεὶ διὰ τὸ εὔψυχον ἐλευθέρας, καὶ ὅτι Δωριῆς
μέλλετε Ἴωσι μάχεσθαι, ὧν εἰώθατε κρείσσους εἶναι, ἀρκείτω βραχέως δεδηλωμένον· τὴν δὲ ἐπιχείρησιν ᾧ τρό- 2
5 πῳ διανοοῦμαι ποιεῖσθαι διδάξω, ἵνα μή τῳ τὸ κατ' ὀλίγον καὶ μὴ ἅπαντας κινδυνεύειν ἐνδεὲς φαινόμενον ἀτολμίαν παράσχῃ. τοὺς γὰρ ἐναντίους εἰκάζω καταφρονήσει 3
τε ἡμῶν καὶ οὐκ ἂν ἐλπίσαντας ὡς ἂν ἐπεξέλθοι τις αὐτοῖς ἐς μάχην, ἀναβῆναί τε πρὸς τὸ χωρίον καὶ νῦν ἀτά-
10 κτως κατὰ θέαν τετραμμένους ὀλιγωρεῖν. ὅστις δὲ τὰς 4
τοιαύτας ἁμαρτίας τῶν ἐναντίων κάλλιστα ἰδὼν καὶ ἅμα
πρὸς τὴν ἑαυτοῦ δύναμιν τὴν ἐπιχείρησιν ποιεῖται μὴ

their guard and not expecting an attack. Wise use of the mistakes of others is the surest means of success. § 2-5. I, with my chosen troops, will attack their centre. Then you, Clearidas, in the moment of their confusion, will fall upon them with the rest of our forces; and if all do their duty, as I expect, then all will be sure of perpetual freedom from the yoke of Athens. § 6-9. I myself will prove that I can not only advise, but act. § 10.

2. ὅτι: namely; explanatory, in the particularization of what precedes. ὅτι . . . ἐλευθέρας (sc. ἥκομεν ἀπὸ χώρας) bridges over the transition from the interr. οἷας to ὅτι Δωριῆς, etc. — τὸ εὔψυχον: the noblest expression for manly courage. Cf. ii. 39. 7. — Δωριῆς, Ἴωσι: the same distinction of races is expressed with the same pride in i. 124. 5; vi. 77. 11; vii. 5. 17. —
3. ἀρκείτω δεδηλωμένον: corresponds nearly to the Lat. monuisse sufficiat. But the partic. modifies the double subj. of ἀρκείτω, ἀπὸ μὲν οἷας κτέ. and ὅτι Δωριῆς κτέ. GMT. 112, 2, N. 1.
4. τὴν δὲ ἐπιχείρησιν: const. with ποιεῖσθαι, although this has at the head of the sent. almost an abs. posi-

tion. See on i. 33. 16; 32. 18. — 5. ἵνα μή τῳ τὸ κατ' ὀλίγον κτέ.: lest our exposing ourselves in detachments and not all together seem poor tactics and cause discouragement to any one. See App.
8. καὶ οὐκ ἂν ἐλπίσαντας ὡς ἂν ἐπεξέλθοι: and since they would not have expected that anybody could (possibly) come out against them. οὐκ ἂν ἐλπίσαντας is equiv. to ὅτι οὐκ ἂν ἤλπισαν. ὡς with ἐλπίζειν, also in viii. 54. 4. — 10. κατὰ θέαν (cf. c. 7. 11) τετραμμένους: τετραμμένος πρός (or, as here, κατά) is the proper expression for a predominant inclination in one direction to the neglect of other things. See on ii. 40. 4. Cf. ii. 25. 11; 51. 13; vii. 73. 16. ἀτάκτως is to be taken with τετραμμένους as well as ὀλιγωρεῖν, which last is used abs. ("be careless"), as in ii. 62. 20; vi. 91. 40.
11. καὶ ἅμα: καί connects the adv. modifier πρός (cf. i. 6. 15; 10. 8) τὴν ἑαυτοῦ δύναμιν with the partic. ἰδών, which also limits the meaning of the verb. — 12. ποιεῖται: indic. in general prot. GMT. 51, N. 3. — μὴ ἀπὸ τοῦ προφανοῦς μᾶλλον κτέ.: προφανοῦς is in the same const. with ἀντιπαραταχθέντος, "not so much with regard

ἀπὸ τοῦ προφανοῦς μᾶλλον καὶ ἀντιπαραταχθέντος ἢ ἐκ
τοῦ πρὸς τὸ παρὸν ξυμφέροντος, πλεῖστ᾽ ἂν ὀρθοῖτο· καὶ 5
15 τὰ κλέμματα ταῦτα καλλίστην δόξαν ἔχει ἃ τὸν πολέμιον
μάλιστ᾽ ἄν τις ἀπατήσας τοὺς φίλους μέγιστ᾽ ἂν ὠφελή-
σειεν. ἕως οὖν ἔτι ἀπαράσκευοι θαρσοῦσι καὶ τοῦ ὑπ- 6
απιέναι πλέον ἢ τοῦ μένοντος, ἐξ ὧν ἐμοὶ φαίνονται, τὴν
διάνοιαν ἔχουσιν, ἐν τῷ ἀνειμένῳ αὐτῶν τῆς γνώμης καὶ
20 πρὶν ξυνταθῆναι μᾶλλον τὴν δόξαν, ἐγὼ μὲν ἔχων τοὺς
μετ᾽ ἐμαυτοῦ καὶ φθάσας, ἢν δύνωμαι, προσπεσοῦμαι
δρόμῳ κατὰ μέσον τὸ στράτευμα· σὺ δέ, Κλεαρίδα, ὕστε- 7
ρον, ὅταν ἐμὲ ὁρᾷς ἤδη προσκείμενον καὶ κατὰ τὸ εἰκὸς
φοβοῦντα αὐτούς, τοὺς μετὰ σεαυτοῦ τούς τ᾽ Ἀμφιπο-
25 λίτας καὶ τοὺς ἄλλους ξυμμάχους ἄγων αἰφνιδίως τὰς
πύλας ἀνοίξας ἐπεκθεῖν καὶ ἐπείγεσθαι ὡς τάχιστα ξυμ-

to what is to be seen and to the forces which stand arrayed against one another." — **13. ἐκ τοῦ ... ξυμφέροντος**: *according to what is advantageous under the circumstances*.

15. τὰ κλέμματα: τὰ στρατηγήματα, Schol., from the specially Lacedaemonian expression κλέπτειν for military stratagems (*cf.* Xen. *Anab.* iv. 6. 11 ff., where κλέπτειν is used of taking a mountain by stealth). — **ἅ** (sc. κλέμματα): with ἀπατήσας, a sort of schema etymologicum or cognate acc., since κλέμμα ἀπατᾶν is equiv. to ἀπάτην ἀπατᾶν. — **16. ἄν**: for its repetition, *cf.* i. 36. 14; 77. 20; 136. 17; iv. 114. 21. St. denies that this is a repetition, because the first ἄν belongs to ἀπατήσας, the second to ὠφελήσειε. But ἀπατήσας is equiv. to εἰ ἀπατήσειε, of course without ἄν. GMT. 42, 3, N. 1.

18. τοῦ μένοντος: an excellent example of Thuc.'s liking for neut. partics. instead of infs. Equally striking is ἐν τῷ μὴ μελετῶντι, i. 142. 22, with which ἐν τῷ ἀνειμένῳ below may be compared. GMT. 108, N. 4. — **φαίνονται**: with a pers. subj. where we should expect ὡς φαίνεται, as in c. 75. 12, ἐδόκουν; c. 113. 3, δοκεῖτε. — **20. ξυνταθῆναι**: see App.

23. ἤδη προσκείμενον: *already engaged*, after the first attack has been made. — **24. τοὺς μετὰ σεαυτοῦ**: opp. to τοῖς μετ᾽ ἐμαυτοῦ, 21, the 2000 Peloponnesian hoplites of c. 6. 21 (less the 150 which Brasidas kept for himself, c. 8. 13). To these are added the Amphipolitans and other allies. — **τούς τ᾽ Ἀμφιπολίτας καὶ τοὺς ἄλλους ξυμμάχους**: must be joined without intervening punctuation to the preceding τοὺς μετὰ σεαυτοῦ. It is the less usual arrangement by which τε introduces the second member, and καί the third, as in i. 13. 5 f. — **26. ἐπεκθεῖν καὶ ἐπείγεσθαι**: the only case of the use of the inf. in the sense of the second pers. imv. in Thuc. G. 269; H. 957; Kr. 55, 1, 5. For the

μίξαι. ἐλπὶς γὰρ μάλιστα αὐτοὺς οὕτω φοβηθῆναι· τὸ 8
γὰρ ἐπιὸν ὕστερον δεινότερον τοῖς πολεμίοις τοῦ παρόντος καὶ μαχομένου. καὶ αὐτός τε ἀνὴρ ἀγαθὸς γίγνου, 9
30 ὥσπερ σε εἰκὸς ὄντα Σπαρτιάτην, καὶ ὑμεῖς, ὦ ἄνδρες
ξύμμαχοι, ἀκολουθήσατε ἀνδρείως, καὶ νομίσατε τρία
εἶναι τοῦ καλῶς πολεμεῖν, τὸ ἐθέλειν καὶ τὸ αἰσχύνεσθαι
καὶ τὸ τοῖς ἄρχουσι πείθεσθαι, καὶ τῇδε ὑμῖν τῇ ἡμέρᾳ
ἢ ἀγαθοῖς γενομένοις ἐλευθερίαν τε ὑπάρχειν καὶ Λακε-
35 δαιμονίων ξυμμάχοις κεκλῆσθαι, ἢ Ἀθηναίων τε δούλοις,
ἢν τὰ ἄριστα ἄνευ ἀνδραποδισμοῦ ἢ θανατώσεως πράξητε,

third pers. vi. 34. 55 f. is adduced, but with doubtful propriety.
27. μάλιστα αὐτούς: St. writes μάλιστ' ἂν αὐτούς; but this use of the aor. inf. without ἂν with ἐλπίς and similar words is very common. *Cf.* ii. 80. 11; iii. 3. 15; 32. 15; iv. 28. 28; 80. 3; vi. 87. 18; and see on ii. 3. 8. G. 203, N. 2; H. 948 a, 952.—
28. τὸ ἐπιόν: like τοῦ παρόντος and τοῦ μαχομένου neut. sing. in personal signification, as in ii. 45. 5; iii. 39. 29 f.; vii. 43. 44.
31. νομίσατε τρία εἶναι, τὸ τοῖς ἄρχουσι πείθεσθαι: see App. — 33. τῇδε τῇ ἡμέρᾳ: *cf.* ii. 12. 14, ἥδε ἡ ἡμέρα τοῖς Ἕλλησι μεγάλων κακῶν ἄρξει; Ar. *Pax*, 435, εὐχώμεσθα τὴν νῦν ἡμέραν Ἕλλησιν ἄρξαι πᾶσι πολλῶν κἀγαθῶν; Xen. *Hell.* ii. 2. 23; Plut. *Lys.* 15. In closest connexion with this stands only ὑμῖν . . . ὑπάρχειν depending upon νομίσατε: "be sure that on this day there awaits you either — or —." This alternative which belongs with ὑπάρχειν extends to the end of the period, in the first term with the subjs. ἐλευθερίαν and Λακεδαιμονίων ξυμμάχοις κεκλῆσθαι, in the second only with γενέσθαι and its predicates, Ἀθηναίων δούλοις and κωλυταῖς ἐλευθερώσεως τοῖς λοιποῖς Ἕλλησιν. The words καὶ δουλείαν χαλεπωτέραν ἢ πρὶν εἴχετε are an emphatic addition to Ἀθηναίων δούλοις (not to be joined with ὑπάρχειν) "and that in a harsher bondage than the old one." In consequence of this and the other inserted clause (ἢν τὰ ἄριστα . . . πράξητε) the regular connexion of Ἀθηναίων τε δούλοις with a following καί is interrupted, and instead of this we have the more emphatic τοῖς δὲ λοιποῖς κτέ. A similar case occurs in i. 11. 4 ff. The difficulty of the passage is increased by the fact that the second ἤ (35) is without any explanatory words corresponding to ἀγαθοῖς γενομένοις. Brasidas avoids saying κακοῖς γενομένοις or any words to that effect, but makes the consequences so much the more prominent by the expressions δουλείαν χαλεπωτέραν and κωλυταῖς ἐλευθερώσεως. For another understanding of the passage, see App.—
35. κεκλῆσθαι: pf. of recognized appellation: "bear the (honourable) name of allies of the Lacedaemonians." *Cf.* ii. 37. 4; iii. 82. 51. GMT. 18, 3 *b*, N.; H. 849. — 35. δούλοις: refers to being subjects of Athens, ἀνδραποδισμοῦ to actual slavery. —
36. ἢν τὰ ἄριστα . . . πράξητε: "even if you fare in the best possible way,

καὶ δουλείαν χαλεπωτέραν ἢ πρὶν εἴχετε, τοῖς δὲ λοιποῖς Ἕλλησι κωλυταῖς γενέσθαι ἐλευθερώσεως. ἀλλὰ μήτε 10 ὑμεῖς μαλακισθῆτε, ὁρῶντες περὶ ὅσων ὁ ἀγών ἐστιν, ἐγώ τε δείξω οὐ παραινέσαι οἷός τε ὢν μᾶλλον τοῖς πέλας ἢ καὶ αὐτὸς ἔργῳ ἐπεξελθεῖν."

10 Ὁ μὲν Βρασίδας τοσαῦτα εἰπὼν τήν τε ἔξοδον παρ- 1 εσκευάζετο αὐτὸς καὶ τοὺς ἄλλους μετὰ τοῦ Κλεαρίδα καθίστη ἐπὶ τὰς Θρᾳκίας καλουμένας τῶν πυλῶν, ὅπως ὥσπερ εἴρητο ἐπεξίοιεν. τῷ δὲ Κλέωνι, φανεροῦ γενομέ- 2 νου αὐτοῦ ἀπὸ τοῦ Κερδυλίου καταβάντος καὶ ἐν τῇ πόλει ἐπιφανεῖ οὔσῃ ἔξωθεν περὶ τὸ ἱερὸν τῆς Ἀθηνᾶς θυομένου καὶ ταῦτα πράσσοντος, ἀγγέλλεται (προυκεχωρή-

and are not sold as slaves or put to death." τὰ ἄριστα (adv.) πράσσειν, sup. of εὖ πράσσειν, which occurs in ii. 64. 8; vi. 75. 17.
39. μαλακισθῆτε: as in ii. 43. 27, ἀλγεινοτέρα γὰρ ἀνδρί γε φρόνημα ἔχοντι ἡ μετὰ τοῦ μαλακισθῆναι κάκωσις ἢ ὁ μετὰ ῥώμης καὶ κοινῆς ἐλπίδος ἅμα γιγνόμενος ἀναίσθητος θάνατος. — 41. ἔργῳ ἐπεξιέναι: opp. to παραινεῖν or simply λόγοις, as in i. 84. 16; 120. 27.
10. *Cleon, having heard of Brasidas's intention, tries to retreat to Eion before it can be carried out. But Brasidas, after a short address to his men, makes the attack as agreed, and Clearidas comes up at the right moment. The Athenian army is thrown into confusion, which soon becomes a rout. In the heat of pursuit, Brasidas is mortally wounded, while Cleon is killed in his flight by a Myrcinian peltast. The rest escape after heavy losses to Eion. Brasidas dies after receiving the news of the victory.*
1. τοσαῦτα: so much and no more, esp. after short speeches. Cf. ii. 12. 1; 72. 1 and 13; iii. 31. 1; 52. 14;

iv. 11. 1; vii. 49. 1. So Plat. Prot. 318 a, τοσοῦτος ὁ ἡμέτερος λόγος. — 2. Κλεαρίδα: Dor. gen. as i. 103. 6, Διὸς τοῦ Ἰθωμήτα; v. 25. 4, Πλειστόλα. — 3. Θρᾳκίας τῶν πυλῶν: acc. to Leake in the northeast side of the wall, on the road leading to Drabescus. See Weissenborn, *Hellen*, p. 156. — 4. εἴρητο: cf. 9. 22 ff. — ἐπεξίοιεν: after he had himself made his ἔξοδος, l.
4. φανεροῦ γενομένου: personal (as in c. 9. 18, φαίνονται), with the three parties. καταβάντος, θυομένου, πράσσοντος. The action of first (καταβάντος) was naturally noticed (aor.) by the Athenians as soon as it took place (c. 8. 2); how that of the other two was observed (θυομένου καὶ ταῦτα πράσσοντος, present with reference to γενομένου) is explained by ἐπιφανεῖ οὔσῃ ἔξωθεν (as in c. 6. 12, κατεφαίνετο πάντα αὐτόθεν). — 5. αὐτοῦ: sc. Βρασίδου. — 6. θυομένου: mid. used esp. of sacrifices made for the purpose of observing the omens. Cf. Hdt. v. 44. 13; vii. 167. 7; 189. 9; ix. 10. 13; 33. 2; 62. 5; Xen. *Anab*. ii. 2. 3; vi. 2. 9. This purpose accounts also for the

κει γὰρ τότε κατὰ τὴν θέαν), ὅτι ἥ τε στρατιὰ ἅπασα φανερὰ τῶν πολεμίων ἐν τῇ πόλει καὶ ὑπὸ τὰς πύλας 10 ἵππων τε πόδες πολλοὶ καὶ ἀνθρώπων ὡς ἐξιόντων ὑποφαίνονται. ὁ δὲ ἀκούσας ἐπῆλθε· καὶ ὡς εἶδεν, οὐ βουλόμενος 3 μάχῃ διαγωνίσασθαι πρίν οἱ καὶ τοὺς βοηθοὺς ἥκειν καὶ οἰόμενος φθήσεσθαι ἀπελθών, σημαίνειν τε ἅμα ἐκέλευεν ἀναχώρησιν καὶ παρήγγελλε τοῖς ἀπιοῦσιν ἐπὶ τὸ 15 εὐώνυμον κέρας, ὥσπερ μόνον οἷόν τ' ἦν, ὑπάγειν ἐπὶ τῆς Ἠιόνος. ὡς δ' αὐτῷ ἐδόκει σχολῇ γίγνεσθαι, αὐτὸς 4 ἐπιστρέψας τὸ δεξιὸν καὶ τὰ γυμνὰ πρὸς τοὺς πολεμίους δοὺς ἀπῆγε τὴν στρατιάν. κἂν τούτῳ Βρασίδας ὡς ὁρᾷ 5 τὸν καιρὸν καὶ τὸ στράτευμα τῶν Ἀθηναίων κινούμενον,

use of ταῦτα πράσσοντος referring to the sacrificial ceremonies mentioned in vi. 69. 10. — 8. τότε: he had just gone out for the reconnoissance mentioned in c. 7. 11. — ἅπασα: "it was evident that the troops were all collected." — 9. ὑπὸ τὰς πύλας ... ὑποφαίνονται: *under the gate* (in the space between the gate and the threshold) *they were seen a little*, i.e. as far as was possible (ὑπο-) in this way. So, too, πόδες ... ὡς ἐξιόντων refers to the forces drawn up in readiness to march. This all shows accurate observation on the part of the scouts. But see App.
11. ἐπῆλθε: i.e. he went nearer to see for himself. — 12. οἱ: with ἥκειν, like the dat. with ἐλθεῖν in i. 13. 12; 27. 1; 61. 1; 107. 27; iii. 70. 2; vi. 46. 12; vii. 73. 5; viii. 96. 1. Plat. *Prot.* 321 c. Cf. also vi. 96. 2. In all these cases the dat. is the 'obj. for which' coinciding with the limit of motion. — 13. φθήσεσθαι ἀπελθών: *that he would get away in time*, i.e. before being attacked. — 14. τοῖς ἀπιοῦσιν: the art. indicates the successive execution of the ἀναχώρησις as commands were given: hence Cl. with good Ms. authority writes παρήγγελλε (used esp. of military orders, cf. c. 58. 16; 71. 18; 73. 11) for παρήγγειλε. "To the departing troops, i.e. as the separate divisions started, the command was given to turn to the left upon the road to Eion" (St. omits τοῖς). The idea of gradual departure is also contained in ὑπάγειν. The emphatic connexion of the two verbs ἐκέλευεν and παρήγγελλε by τε ἅμα and καὶ gives an intimation of Cleon's efforts to hasten the departure, which in the following αὐτὸς ἐπιστρέψας τὸ δεξιὸν κτέ. lead to pernicious haste. — 15. ὥσπερ μόνον οἷόν τ' ἦν: sc. in order to reach Eion.
16. σχολῇ: see App. — 17. ἐπιστρέψας τὸ δεξιόν: in his impatience, he causes the right wing to turn and advance (cf. ii. 90. 18) before its proper turn, thereby exposing it to attack. — τὰ γυμνά: the unprotected side (iii. 23. 19; v. 71. 6), i.e. the right side, the left being covered by the shield.

20 λέγει τοῖς μεθ' ἑαυτοῦ καὶ τοῖς ἄλλοις ὅτι "Οἱ ἄνδρες ἡμᾶς οὐ μένουσι· δῆλοι δὲ τῶν τε δοράτων τῇ κινήσει καὶ τῶν κεφαλῶν· οἷς γὰρ ἂν τοῦτο γίγνηται, οὐκ εἰώθασι μένειν τοὺς ἐπιόντας. ἀλλὰ τάς τε πύλας τις ἀνοιγέτω ἐμοὶ ὡς εἴρηται, καὶ ἐπεξίωμεν ὡς τάχιστα θαρ-
25 σοῦντες." καὶ ὁ μὲν κατὰ τὰς ἐπὶ τὸ σταύρωμα πύλας καὶ 6 τὰς πρώτας τοῦ μακροῦ τείχους τότε ὄντος ἐξελθὼν ἔθει δρόμῳ τὴν ὁδὸν ταύτην εὐθεῖαν ᾖπερ νῦν κατὰ τὸ καρτερώτατον τοῦ χωρίου ἰόντι τροπαῖον ἕστηκε, καὶ προσβαλὼν τοῖς Ἀθηναίοις, πεφοβημένοις τε ἅμα τῇ σφετέρᾳ
30 ἀταξίᾳ καὶ τὴν τόλμαν αὐτοῦ ἐκπεπληγμένοις, κατὰ μέσον τὸ στράτευμα τρέπει, καὶ ὁ Κλεαρίδας, ὥσπερ εἴ- 7 ρητο, ἅμα κατὰ τὰς Θρᾳκίας πύλας ἐπεξελθὼν τῷ στρατῷ ἐπεφέρετο. ξυνέβη τε τῷ ἀδοκήτῳ καὶ ἐξαπίνης ἀμ-

---

20. ὅτι: often used to introduce a dir. quot. Cf. i. 137. 22; iv. 38. 16; viii. 53. 20.— 21. δῆλοι δέ: (not δή with Kr.) epexegetical, as in i. 46. 3; 55. 9; iii. 34. 1.— τῇ κινήσει: hints at a restless movement toward hasty departure, not toward meeting the enemy.— 24. ἃς εἴρηται: sc. ἀνοίγειν. He had chosen for his sally not the Thracian gate, but two others (τὰς ἐπὶ τὸ σταύρωμα). By τὰς πρώτας τοῦ μακροῦ τείχους τότε ὄντος an outer gate in the long wall built by Hagnon (iv. 102. 18) seems to be meant. This wall was afterwards destroyed. Changes made by the Lacedaemonians in the fortifications of Amphipolis are referred to in iv. 103. 18.

27. τὸ καρτερώτερον τοῦ χωρίου: the higher parts of the ground, which Cleon, acc. to c. 7. 15, had seized. Brasidas directed his attack against this point in order to strike at the main force of the Athenians while still undivided. — 28. ἰόντι: the dat. denoting the person in respect to whom the statement is made is used most freq. of parties. denoting motion, estimation, or judgment. Cf. i. 10. 34; 24. 1; G. 184, 5; H. 771 b. — 30. κατὰ μέσον τὸ στράτευμα: with προσβαλών.

31. τρέπει, καὶ ὁ Κλεαρίδας ἐπεφέρετο: the connexion is close. "Just as Brasidas was forcing the Athenians to retreat, Clearidas fell upon them." The impf. is used of contemporaneous action. — 33. ξυνέβη τε κτέ.: "and so it came to pass that by the unexpectedness and suddenness (of the attack) from both sides at once the Athenians were thrown into disorder." So ξυμβαίνειν of several events occurring at once in i. 29. 1; v. 14. 20; 37. 20; vii. 75. 7; viii. 64. 17; 82. 15. — καὶ ἐξαπίνης: pleonastic strengthening of ἀδοκήτῳ. The art. τῷ belongs with both. St. (Adn. Crit. VI.) takes it as consequence of ἀδοκήτῳ and connects it with θορυβηθῆναι, which, in

φοτέρωθεν τοὺς Ἀθηναίους θορυβηθῆναι· καὶ τὸ μὲν 8
35 εὐώνυμον κέρας αὐτῶν τὸ πρὸς τὴν Ἠιόνα, ὅπερ δὴ καὶ
προκεχωρήκει, εὐθὺς ἀπορραγὲν ἔφυγε. καὶ ὁ Βρασίδας
ὑποχωροῦντος ἤδη αὐτοῦ ἐπιπαριὼν τῷ δεξιῷ τιτρώσκεται, καὶ πεσόντα αὐτὸν οἱ μὲν Ἀθηναῖοι οὐκ αἰσθάνον- 9
ται, οἱ δὲ πλησίον ἄραντες ἀπήνεγκαν. τὸ δὲ δεξιὸν τῶν
40 Ἀθηναίων ἔμενε μᾶλλον· καὶ ὁ μὲν Κλέων, ὡς τὸ πρῶτον οὐ διενοεῖτο μένειν, εὐθὺς φεύγων καὶ καταληφθεὶς
ὑπὸ Μυρκινίου πελταστοῦ ἀποθνῄσκει, οἱ δὲ αὐτοῦ ξυστραφέντες ὁπλῖται [ἐπὶ τὸν λόφον] τόν τε Κλεαρίδαν ἠμύνοντο καὶ δὶς ἢ τρὶς προσβαλόντα, καὶ οὐ πρότερον ἐν-

view of the close connexion of cause and effect, seems inadmissible (in the new ed. St. omits καί). A similar connexion of two unlike adv. expressions occurs in iii. 4. 4 f., ἀπαράσκευοι καὶ ἐξαίφνης ἀναγκασθέντες πολεμεῖν.
35. τὸ πρὸς τὴν Ἠιόνα: which was already on the way to Eion in 15 f. — 37. ἐπιπαριὼν τῷ δεξιῷ: "pressing forward (ἐπι-) and turning against the right wing." Cf. i. 61. 3, ὡς ᾔσθοντο καὶ τοὺς μετὰ Ἀριστέως ἐπιπαριόντας.
38. πεσόντα αὐτόν: that he had fallen. The partic. aor. with αἰσθάνεσθαι to express what has happened immediately before is found in Thuc. only here and in viii. 102. 3. In the 24 other passages always partic. pres. or pf. In c. 30. 3, the partic. pres. stands in connexion with the partic. aor. where the difference between them is plainly marked. The part. is equiv. to ὅτι ἔπεσεν. — 39. τὸ δὲ δεξιὸν ἔμενε μᾶλλον: after the fall of Brasidas, by which the violence of the attack was diminished, the right wing, although hard pressed, still stood its ground for a while. Cleon, to be sure, who had (cf. 17) made an ill-advised movement with the right wing, and hoped to escape with the whole army (ἀπῆγε τὴν στρατιάν), took to flight immediately; but the hoplites, who had formed in close order (ξυστραφέντες, as in ii. 4. 23; iv. 68. 25; vi. 91. 6) where they stood, defended themselves bravely for a while, though on the one hand Cleon was urging them to retreat, while on the other Brasidas was attacking with the utmost vigour. See App. — 40. ὡς τὸ πρῶτον οὐ διενοεῖτο μένειν: as he had from the first had no intention of standing his ground, with reference to c. 7. 10. — 43. ἐπὶ τὸν λόφον: apparently interpolated to explain αὐτοῦ; for that αὐτοῦ must be understood as an adv. of place is evident from its position. It points expressly to the place from which Cleon had just fled. Some copier, thinking of c. 7. 15 ff., thought wrongly that the close order was formed ἐπὶ τὸν λόφον, and added this explanation of αὐτοῦ, but after ἀπῆγε τὴν στρατιάν, 18, it is not probable that they were still ἐπὶ λόφον καρτεροῦ of c. 7. 15. — 44. καὶ

45 ἔδοσαν πρὶν ἤ τε Μυρκινία καὶ ἡ Χαλκιδικὴ ἵππος καὶ οἱ πελτασταὶ περιστάντες καὶ ἐσακοντίζοντες αὐτοὺς ἔτρεψαν. οὕτω δὴ τὸ στράτευμα πᾶν ἤδη τῶν Ἀθηναίων φυ- 10 γὸν χαλεπῶς καὶ πολλὰς ὁδοὺς τραπόμενοι κατὰ ὄρη, ὅσοι μὴ διεφθάρησαν ἢ αὐτίκα ἐν χερσὶν ἢ ὑπὸ τῆς Χαλ-
50 κιδικῆς ἵππου καὶ τῶν πελταστῶν, οἱ λοιποὶ ἀπεκομίσθησαν ἐς τὴν Ἠϊόνα. οἱ δὲ τὸν Βρασίδαν ἄραντες ἐκ τῆς 11 μάχης καὶ διασώσαντες ἐς τὴν πόλιν ἔτι ἔμπνουν ἐσεκόμισαν· καὶ ᾔσθετο μὲν ὅτι νικῶσιν οἱ μεθ᾽ αὑτοῦ, οὐ πολὺ δὲ διαλιπὼν ἐτελεύτησε. καὶ ἡ ἄλλη στρατιὰ ἀνα- 12
55 χωρήσασα μετὰ τοῦ Κλεαρίδου ἐκ τῆς διώξεως νεκροὺς
11 τε ἐσκύλευσε καὶ τροπαῖον ἔστησε.· μετὰ δὲ ταῦτα τὸν 1 Βρασίδαν οἱ ξύμμαχοι πάντες ξὺν ὅπλοις ἐπισπόμενοι δημοσίᾳ ἔθαψαν ἐν τῇ πόλει πρὸ τῆς νῦν ἀγορᾶς οὔσης· καὶ τὸ λοιπὸν οἱ Ἀμφιπολῖται, περιέρξαντες αὐτοῦ τὸ
5 μνημεῖον, ὡς ἥρῳ τε ἐντέμνουσι καὶ τιμὰς δεδώκασιν ἀγῶνας καὶ ἐτησίους θυσίας, καὶ τὴν ἀποικίαν ὡς οἰκιστῇ

δὶς ἢ τρίς: although he, etc. Cf. i. 82. 12, διελθόντων ἐτῶν καὶ δύο καὶ τριῶν and note. — 45. Μυρκινία: cf. c. 6. 18, where, however, only peltasts from Myrcinus are mentioned.
47. οὕτω δή: see App. — τὸ στράτευμα πᾶν φυγὸν ... τραπόμενοι ... ὅσοι μὴ διεφθάρησαν οἱ ... λοιποὶ ἀπεκομίσθησαν: the subj. is divided in the course of the period, and undergoes progressive modifications. Similarly ii. 4. 3 ff.; 65. 3 ff.; iv. 68. 3 ff. — 49. ἐν χερσίν: cf. c. 3. 12.
52. ἔτι ἔμπνουν: also in i. 134. 15. — 53. ᾔσθετο: i.e. he received the news while still in command of his faculties. Cf. c. 26. 5, where αἰσθανόμενος is used in a similar sense.
55. νεκρούς τε: the omission of the art. is occasioned by the close connexion with καὶ τρόπαιον.

11. *Brasidas receives a public funeral at Amphipolis, and is honoured by the Amphipolitans as a hero.*
The Athenians return home.
3. πρὸ τῆς νῦν ἀγορᾶς οὔσης: referring to later changes, as in c. 10. 26. Other cases in which the honour of burial within a city was conferred are mentioned in Xen. Hell. vii. 3. 12; Cic. ad Fam. iv. 12. 3. — 4. περιέρξαντες: see App. — 5. ἥρῳ: see App. — ἐντέμνουσι: of sacrifices made to the dead, διὰ τὸ ἐν τῇ γῇ τῶν σφαγίων ἀποτέμνεσθαι τὰς κεφαλάς· οὕτω γὰρ θύουσι τοῖς χθονίοις. Schol. The word does not occur again before Plutarch and Lucian. — δεδώκασιν: 'pf., as well as the pres. ἐντέμνουσι, is the expression of one who is present in the neighbourhood and sees the yearly repetition of this custom.

προσέθεσαν, καταβαλόντες τὰ Ἁγνώνεια οἰκοδομήματα καὶ ἀφανίσαντες εἴ τι μνημόσυνόν που ἔμελλεν αὐτοῦ τῆς οἰκίσεως περιέσεσθαι, νομίσαντες τὸν μὲν Βρασίδαν 10 σωτῆρά τε σφῶν γεγενῆσθαι καὶ ἐν τῷ παρόντι ἅμα τὴν τῶν Λακεδαιμονίων ξυμμαχίαν φόβῳ τῶν Ἀθηναίων θεραπεύοντες, τὸν δὲ Ἅγνωνα κατὰ τὸ πολέμιον τῶν Ἀθηναίων οὐκ ἂν ὁμοίως σφίσι ξυμφόρως οὐδ᾽ ἂν ἡδέως τὰς τιμὰς ἔχειν. καὶ τοὺς νεκροὺς τοῖς Ἀθηναίοις ἀπέδοσαν. 15 ἀπέθανον δὲ Ἀθηναίων μὲν περὶ ἑξακοσίους, τῶν δ᾽ ἐναν- 2 τίων ἑπτά, διὰ τὸ μὴ ἐκ παρατάξεως, ἀπὸ δὲ τοιαύτης

Thuc. writes while living on his Thracian estates' (Cl.). See Introd. to Book I. p. 15. Thuc. probably did write part of his history while in Thrace, but the tenses here employed might be used by any contemporaneous writer. — 7. προσέθεσαν: aor. is, on the other hand, merely the historical mention of the fact: "they attributed the town to him as founder." Arbitrary adoption and change of 'oecist' is mentioned in vi. 3. 13; 5. 10. — Ἁγνώνεια οἰκοδομήματα: the public buildings dating from the settlement of Hagnon (iv. 102. 13 ff.), especially the heroum, which was probably erected after Hagnon's death (Müller-Strübing, *Aristoph*. p. 718). That Hagnon was dead appears from 13. — 8. εἴ τι μνημόσυνον κτέ.: "whatever was likely to remind them of, *etc*." Such reminders would probably be continually met with in recurring festivals and in public proceedings and documents. — αὐτοῦ: refers to Hagnon implied in Ἁγνώνεια. — ἔμελλεν περιέσεσθαι: "was likely to remain in future as a reminder." A comprehensive expression. — 10. καὶ ἐν τῷ παρόντι ἅμα: connected in somewhat loose const.,

with σωτῆρά τε σφῶν γεγενῆσθαι: the services *already rendered* by Brasidas are placed in opposition to the *present* interest of the Amphipolitans in the alliance with Sparta, but both appear as the result of Brasidas's action; so the opposition of τὸν μὲν Βρασίδαν and τὸν δὲ Ἅγνωνα is preserved. — 12. κατὰ τὸ πολέμιον τῶν Ἀθηναίων: "in consequence of their hostile attitude towards Athens." *Cf*. iii. 56. 7, εἰ γὰρ τῷ αὐτίκα χρησίμῳ ὑμῶν τε καὶ ἐκείνων πολεμίῳ τὸ δίκαιον λήψεσθε. — 13. ὁμοίως: *sc*. as formerly, while their relation with Athens was a pleasant one. *Cf*. i. 99. 6; 124. 15 (not, "as Brasidas"). — οὐδ᾽ ἂν ἡδέως τὰς τιμὰς ἔχειν: not to be taken with the Schol. (and Jowett) as referring to σφίσι. "Hagnon himself would not receive honours paid him after the town had become an enemy of Athens, either with benefit to the citizens or with pleasure to himself." Such action and feeling after death was ascribed to the 'oecist' who was worshipped as a hero. See Hermann, *Gottesd. Alterthümer*, 16.

16. τοιαύτης ξυντυχίας: refers to the account in the preceding chapter, esp. to ξυνέβη τε . . . θορυβηθῆναι,

ξυντυχίας καὶ προεκφοβήσεως τὴν μάχην μᾶλλον γενέσθαι·
μετὰ δὲ τὴν ἀναίρεσιν οἱ μὲν ἐπ᾽ οἴκου ἀπέπλευσαν, οἱ
δὲ μετὰ τοῦ Κλεαρίδου τὰ περὶ τὴν Ἀμφίπολιν καθίσταντο.
12 Καὶ ὑπὸ τοὺς αὐτοὺς χρόνους τοῦ θέρους τελευτῶν- 1
τος Ῥαμφίας καὶ Αὐτοχαρίδας καὶ Ἐπικυδίδας Λακεδαιμόνιοι ἐς τὰ ἐπὶ Θρᾴκης χωρία βοήθειαν ἦγον ἐνα-
κοσίων ὁπλιτῶν, καὶ ἀφικόμενοι ἐς Ἡράκλειαν τὴν ἐν
5 Τραχῖνι καθίσταντο ὅ τι αὐτοῖς ἐδόκει μὴ καλῶς ἔχειν.
ἐνδιατριβόντων δὲ αὐτῶν ἔτυχεν ἡ μάχη αὕτη γενομένη, 2
13 καὶ τὸ θέρος ἐτελεύτα. τοῦ δ᾽ ἐπιγιγνομένου * χειμῶνος 1
εὐθὺς μέχρι μὲν Πιερίου τῆς Θεσσαλίας διῆλθον οἱ περὶ
τὸν Ῥαμφίαν, κωλυόντων δὲ τῶν Θεσσαλῶν καὶ ἅμα Βρασίδου τεθνεῶτος, ᾧπερ ἦγον τὴν στρατιάν, ἀπετράποντο
5 ἐπ᾽ οἴκου, νομίσαντες οὐδένα καιρὸν εἶναι ἔτι τῶν τε

33 f., of which the reader is here reminded by προεκφοβήσεως (the panic before the fight began). Even taking these things into account, the difference in the losses of the two sides is very great.
18. οἱ μέν: the Athenians. — 19. καθίσταντο: here and in c. 12. 5 the impf. esp. of political regulations intended to be permanent. *Cf.* ii. 6. 3; iii. 28. 17; 35. 7; v. 82. 3.
12. *A reinforcement under Rhamphias, sent by the Lacedaemonians to Thrace, is detained at Heraclea in Trachis.*
2. Ῥαμφίας: Rhamphias is the father of Clearchus, who is well known as a participator in the expedition of Cyrus. *Cf.* viii. 8. 14, Κλέαρχος ὁ Ῥαμφίου. — 3. βοήθειαν ἦγον: *were on the way with reinforcements.* A similar attempt had failed the year before. *Cf.* iv. 132. 5 ff. — 4. Ἡράκλειαν: Heraclea was founded by the Lacedaemonians in 426 B.C. *Cf.* iii. 92 f.

— 5. ὅ τι ... ἔχειν: Heraclea was not prosperous owing to the misconduct of the Lacedaemonian governors and the hostility of the Thessalians. See iii. 93. 12 ff.
13. *And, upon hearing of the battle at Amphipolis, returns home.*
2. Πιερίου: *Pierium*; its position is uncertain. Liv. xxxii. 15 has Pieria or Pierium. — 3. κωλυόντων τῶν Θεσσαλῶν: as they always tried to do. Brasidas alone succeeded in passing through by his tact and ingenuity, iv. 78 f. Ischagoras had been stopped, iv. 132. § 2, 3. — καὶ ἅμα: introduces, as usual, an important reason: *and besides since Brasidas was now dead*. Almost like ἄλλως τε καί. See on i. 2. 9. —
4. ᾧπερ ἦγον: dat. of the 'person for whom' coinciding with the limit of motion. *Cf.* iv. 37. 4, βουλόμενοι ἀγαγεῖν αὐτοὺς Ἀθηναίοις ζῶντας. —
5. οὐδένα καιρὸν εἶναι ἔτι: an abs. expression: "it was now no longer the time," "the favourable moment

Ἀθηναίων ἥσση ἀπεληλυθότων καὶ οὐκ ἀξιόχρεων αὐτῶν ὄντων δρᾶν τι ὧν κἀκεῖνος ἐπενόει· μάλιστα δὲ ἀπῆλθον 2 εἰδότες τοὺς Λακεδαιμονίους, ὅτε ἐξῇεσαν, πρὸς τὴν
14 εἰρήνην μᾶλλον τὴν γνώμην ἔχοντας. ξυνέβη τε εὐθὺς 1 μετὰ τὴν ἐν Ἀμφιπόλει μάχην καὶ τὴν Ῥαμφίου ἀναχώ-

was past." The connexion is made plain by the inf. δρᾶν τι ... ἐπενόει, which belongs to ἀξιόχρεων. Herbst, Philol. Anz. 1871, p. 51, connects δρᾶν τι with καιρὸν εἶναι, and takes ἀξιόχρεων as abs., as elsewhere in Thuc. But the position of the words and the emphasis upon αὐτῶν seems to demand the connexion of δρᾶν τι with ἀξιόχρεων. In the rel. clause ὧν κἀκεῖνος ἐπενόει, καί has its freq. observed proleptic force. Cf. i. 74. 25; 83. 7; 117. 16; ii. 86. 5. "Since the Athenians, in consequence of a defeat (ἥσση expresses the reason more distinctly than μεθ᾽ ἧσσαν) had gone away, and they themselves were not prepared to carry out on their own account any part of what he had had in mind."

7. μάλιστα δὲ ἀπῆλθον εἰδότες τοὺς Λακεδαιμονίους κτἑ.: Thuc. here lays peculiar stress upon the state of public feeling which prevailed at Sparta. This has been kept in the background throughout the narrative of Brasidas's successes, though plain reference was made to it in iv. 80 and 108. 35 ff., in contrast with Brasidas's eagerness for action. But now that Brasidas is dead, the weaker members of the war party feel the full force of the desire for peace which they well know prevails at home. With this accurate presentation of the reasons which induced the Lacedaemonian generals to return home without having accomplished anything, Thuc. closes his account of the actual events of the ten years' war, and prepares thereby a transition to a retrospective glance in the next three chapters at the general course of the war. In these chapters he also shows, as he proceeds, the inclination of both sides toward peace, and then, in c. 17, tells of its conclusion.

14. *The desire for peace gains ground both in Athens and in Sparta. The reasons for this.*

1. ξυνέβη τε: used to conclude and sum up what precedes, as in c. 10. 33. But the great importance attributed to the following presentation of the altered circumstances in the two hostile states, occasions first the use of the significant introductory particle ὥστε, and then the completely independent position of the second member of the sent., πρὸς δὲ τὴν εἰρήνην μᾶλλον τὴν γνώμην εἶχον κτἑ. This second member reaches with its subdivisions and explanations into the following chapters, and contains those observations which seemed to the author of most consequence in connexion with this important division between the two periods of the war. The first member of the result clause, πολέμου μὲν μηδὲν ἔτι ἅψασθαι μηδετέρους, is prefixed as a statement of fact (in the aor.) upon which depends the truth of the succeeding statements. This explains how the force of εὐθύς before μετὰ τὴν κτἑ. is felt only in connexion with the second consequence (πρὸς δὲ τὴν κτἑ.), and not with the first (μηδὲν ἔτι ἅψασθαι μηδετέρους), the neg. character of which

ρησιν ἐκ Θεσσαλίας ὥστε πολέμου μὲν μηδὲν ἔτι ἅψασθαι μηδετέρους, πρὸς δὲ τὴν εἰρήνην μᾶλλον τὴν γνώμην 5 εἶχον, οἱ μὲν Ἀθηναῖοι πληγέντες ἐπὶ τῷ Δηλίῳ καὶ δι' ὀλίγου αὖθις ἐν Ἀμφιπόλει, καὶ οὐκ ἔχοντες τὴν ἐλπίδα τῆς ῥώμης πιστὴν ἔτι, ᾗπερ οὐ προσεδέχοντο πρότερον τὰς σπονδάς, δοκοῦντες τῇ παρούσῃ εὐτυχίᾳ καθυπέρτεροι γενήσεσθαι· καὶ τοὺς ξυμμάχους ἅμα ἐδεδίεσαν σφῶν μὴ 2 10 διὰ τὰ σφάλματα ἐπαιρόμενοι ἐπὶ πλέον ἀποστῶσι, μετεμέλοντό τε ὅτι μετὰ τὰ ἐν Πύλῳ καλῶς παρασχὸν οὐ ξυνέβησαν· οἱ δ' αὖ Λακεδαιμόνιοι παρὰ γνώμην μὲν ἀπο- 3 βαίνοντος σφίσι τοῦ πολέμου, ἐν ᾧ ᾤοντο ὀλίγων ἐτῶν καθαιρήσειν τὴν τῶν Ἀθηναίων δύναμιν εἰ τὴν γῆν τέ-
15 μνοιεν, περιπεσόντες δὲ τῇ ἐν τῇ νήσῳ ξυμφορᾷ, οἷα οὔπω

is alone sufficient to preclude any relation to εὐθύς. — 3. ὥστε: an emphatic transition (though not after ξυμβαίνειν), also in i. 28. 18; 76. 17; 119. 7; iii. 75. 7; iv. 132. 17; Hdt. iii. 14. 24. — 4. πρὸς δὲ ... εἶχον: the repetition of the same words from the close of the preceding chap. is intentional. The state of mind there attributed to the Lacedaemonians is here expressly extended to both sides as the underlying reason for their subsequent conduct. — 5. οἱ μὲν Ἀθηναῖοι: the reasons are given as far as γενήσεσθαι in partics.; then in the finite verbs ἐδεδίεσαν and μετεμέλοντο. — ἐπὶ Δηλίῳ: cf. iv. 100 f. See Grote, VI. p. 173 f. — δι' ὀλίγου: after a short interval. Cf. i. 77. 22; v. 69. 19. — 7. πιστήν: in pred. position receives the chief emphasis of the sent., so that ᾗπερ refers to ἐλπὶς πιστή. — πρότερον: cf. iv. 21. 5 ff.; 41. 16 f. — 8. καθυπέρτεροι: also in vii. 56. 7.
9. τοὺς ξυμμάχους ... ἐδεδίεσαν ... μὴ ... ἀποστῶσι: proleptic as in ii. 67. 23. Not only was their confidence in their own strength diminished, but they feared more general (ἐπὶ πλέον) desertion by their allies, if they continued the war without success. See App. — 10. μετεμέλοντο: elsewhere const. with the partic. (iv. 27. 13; v. 35. 17; vii. 50. 21), is here used with ὅτι to avoid the awkwardness of two parties. side by side. — 11. παρασχόν: παρέσχεν and παρασχήσει (in Hdt. also παρέχει, iii. 73. 2; 142. 11) are used impers.: "the chance offers." Cf. iv. 85. 8; vi. 86. 22, most freq. the partic. abs. as in i. 120. 18; iv. 85. 8; v. 60. 25; 63. 3.
12. οἱ δὲ Λακεδαιμόνιοι: sc. πρὸς τὴν εἰρήνην μᾶλλον τὴν γνώμην εἶχον, the reasons for which are given partly in the gens. abs. ἀποβαίνοντος πολέμου, λῃστευομένης τῆς χώρας, αὐτομολούντων τῶν Εἱλώτων and προσδοκίας οὔσης, partly in the inserted clause with the nom. περιπεσόντες. — 13. ὀλίγων ἐτῶν: gen. of time as in i. 3. 11; vii. 3. 5. — 14. εἰ τὴν γῆν τέμνοιεν: by the system of ἐσβολαί adopted in the first years of the war. — 15. ἐν τῇ νήσῳ:

γεγένητο τῇ Σπάρτῃ, καὶ λῃστευομένης τῆς χώρας ἐκ τῆς Πύλου καὶ Κυθήρων, αὐτομολούντων τε τῶν Εἱλώτων καὶ ἀεὶ προσδοκίας οὔσης μή τι καὶ οἱ ὑπομένοντες τοῖς ἔξω πίσυνοι πρὸς τὰ παρόντα σφίσιν, ὥσπερ καὶ πρότερον, 20 νεωτερίσωσι· ξυνέβαινε δὲ καὶ πρὸς τοὺς Ἀργείους αὐτοῖς 4 τὰς τριακοντούτεις σπονδὰς ἐπ' ἐξόδῳ εἶναι καὶ ἄλλας οὐκ ἤθελον σπένδεσθαι οἱ Ἀργεῖοι, εἰ μή τις αὐτοῖς τὴν Κυνοσουρίαν γῆν ἀποδώσει· ὥστ' ἀδύνατα εἶναι ἐφαίνετο Ἀργείοις καὶ Ἀθηναίοις ἅμα πολεμεῖν. τῶν τε ἐν Πελο- 25 ποννήσῳ πόλεων ὑπώπτευόν τινας ἀποστήσεσθαι πρὸς 15 τοὺς Ἀργείους· ὅπερ καὶ ἐγένετο. ταῦτ' οὖν ἀμφοτέροις 1 αὐτοῖς λογιζομένοις ἐδόκει ποιητέα εἶναι ἡ ξύμβασις,

Sphacteria. *Cf.* iv. 29 to 39. — 17. ἐκ τῆς Πύλου: iv. 41. 5 ff. — καὶ Κυθήρων: iv. 54. 19. — 17. αὐτομολούντων τῶν Εἱλώτων: iv. 41. 11. — 18. προσδοκίας οὔσης μή: as in ii. 93. 14. — τοῖς ἔξω: those who were beyond the border. *Cf.* iv. 66. 8. — 19. ὥσπερ καὶ πρότερον: in the great revolt of the Helots, called the third Messenian war, mentioned in i. 101. 6.
20. ξυνέβαινε δὲ καὶ: "an additional consideration was," or, more literally, *it happened together with this also*. *Cf.* c. 10. 33 and note. — 21. τριακοντούτεις: after the analogy of i. 23. 19; 115. 3; ii. 2. 2; v. 27. 1 (the Mss. vary here between τριακονταέτεις and τριακονταετεῖς). The truce came to an end in the next year (*cf.* c. 28. 8) and had therefore been made in 451 B.C. — εἰ μή τις: a similar use occurs in ii. 37. 2; iii. 67. 33; iv. 68. 28, εἴ τε μὴ πείσεταί τις, αὐτοῦ τὴν μάχην ἔσεσθαι. — τὴν Κυνοσουρίαν: disputed territory on the borders of Laconia and Argolis. See on iv. 56. 12. *Cf.* c. 41. — 23. ὥστ' ἀδύνατα ... ἅμα πολεμεῖν: the emphasis rests upon ἅμα; "it was clearly impossible to carry on war against both at once." The neut. pl. as in i. 59. 4, where meaning and expression are very similar, except that instead of ἅμα as here, the same effect is there produced by τε ... καί. See App. — 24. τῶν τε ἐν Πελοποννήσῳ κτέ.: the general feeling against Sparta in the middle states of Peloponnesus, which came to a head after the conclusion of the peace (c. 27. 1 ff.; 29. 17 ff.), was gaining ground on account of the inclination to peace which had prevailed among them for some time. If the double war had arisen, Sparta would have been in the greatest danger. — 26. ὅπερ καὶ ἐγένετο: *cf.* c. 29.

15. *Especially strong was the desire of the Lacedaemonians to obtain the release of their citizens who had been captured at Sphacteria. They thought the Athenians, too, might now be ready for peace.*

1. ἀμφοτέροις αὐτοῖς: the reference of ταῦτα to both sides collectively is emphasized by the addition of αὐτοῖς, after which the subsequent separate mention of the Lacedaemonians is all

καὶ οὐχ ἧσσον τοῖς Λακεδαιμονίοις, ἐπιθυμίᾳ τῶν ἀνδρῶν
τῶν ἐκ τῆς νήσου κομίσασθαι· ἦσαν γὰρ οἱ Σπαρτιᾶται
αὐτῶν πρῶτοί τε καὶ * ὁμοίως σφίσι ξυγγενεῖς. ἤρξαντο 2
μὲν οὖν καὶ εὐθὺς μετὰ τὴν ἅλωσιν αὐτῶν πράσσειν,
ἀλλ' οἱ Ἀθηναῖοι οὔπως ἤθελον εὖ φερόμενοι ἐπὶ τῇ
ἴσῃ καταλύεσθαι. σφαλέντων δὲ αὐτῶν ἐπὶ τῷ Δηλίῳ
παραχρῆμα οἱ Λακεδαιμόνιοι γνόντες νῦν μᾶλλον ἂν ἐνδεξαμένους ποιοῦνται τὴν ἐνιαύσιον ἐκεχειρίαν, ἐν ᾗ ἔδει
ξυνιόντας καὶ περὶ τοῦ πλείονος χρόνου βουλεύεσθαι.
16 ἐπειδὴ δὲ καὶ ἡ ἐν Ἀμφιπόλει ἧσσα τοῖς Ἀθηναίοις 1
ἐγεγένητο καὶ ἐτεθνήκει Κλέων τε καὶ Βρασίδας, οἵπερ
ἀμφοτέρωθεν μάλιστα ἠναντιοῦντο τῇ εἰρήνῃ, ὁ μὲν
διὰ τὸ εὐτυχεῖν τε καὶ τιμᾶσθαι ἐκ τοῦ πολεμεῖν, ὁ δὲ

the more remarkable. *Cf.* iv. 20. 1, ἡμῖν ἀμφοτέροις. — 3. **καὶ οὐχ ἧσσον**: as often equiv. to καὶ μάλιστα. *Cf.* i. 82. 18; ii. 52. 3; iii. 45. 27; v. 26. 26. While, as has been shown above, the general state of things occasioned by the unexpected course of the war was discouraging to the Lacedaemonians, they were esp. influenced toward peace by the desire of obtaining the release of the prisoners. — 4. **κομίσασθαι**: added as an explanation of ἐπιθυμίᾳ τῶν ἀνδρῶν, as in Plat. *Crit.* 52 c, οὐδ' ἐπιθυμία σε ἄλλων νόμων ἔλαβεν εἰδέναι. *Cf.* iv. 108. 37, βουλόμενοι μᾶλλον τούς τε ἄνδρας τοὺς ἐκ τῆς νήσου κομίσασθαι. — **οἱ Σπαρτιᾶται αὐτῶν**: *the Spartiates among them*, about 120 in number. *Cf.* iv. 38. 29. — 5. **καὶ ὁμοίως σφίσι ξυγγενεῖς**: see App.

5. **ἤρξαντο . . . πράσσειν**: *they immediately began negotiations*, mentioned also in iv. 41. 14. — 6. **ἅλωσις**: not elsewhere used of the capture of persons; but here this is easily explained, since the capture of the men coincided with that of the island. — 7.

οὔπως: see App. — **εὖ φερόμενοι**: "as long as they got on well." *Cf.* c. 16. 9; ii. 60. 7, καλῶς μὲν γὰρ φερόμενος ἀνὴρ τὸ καθ' ἑαυτὸν διαφθειρομένης τῆς πατρίδος οὐδὲν ἧσσον ξυναπόλλυται. — **ἐπὶ τῇ ἴσῃ**: elliptical, though no particular subst. is to be supplied; *on equal conditions*. See on i. 27. 3. — 9. **παραχρῆμα**: belongs primarily with γνόντες. The Lacedaemonians perceived immediately that the defeat at Delium (iv. 89 ff.) would incline the Athenians to make concessions. The conclusion of the truce was brought about somewhat later. *Cf.* iv. 117. 1. — **ἐνδεξαμένους**: see App. — 10. **τὴν ἐνιαύσιον ἐκεχειρίαν**: *cf.* iv. 117. 15. — **ἐν ᾗ ἔδει . . . βουλεύεσθαι**: *cf.* iv. 118. 50 ff.; iv. 119. 11 f.

16. *Now that Cleon and Brasidas were dead, the disposition to peace was encouraged in Athens by Nicias, and in Sparta by King Pleistoanax, about whose return from exile evil stories were circulated.*

3. **ὁ μὲν . . . ὁ δέ**: chiastic order, as in 10 ff. — 4. **διὰ τὸ εὐτυχεῖν τε**

THUCYDIDES V. 16.

5 γενομένης ἡσυχίας καταφανέστερος νομίζων ἂν εἶναι κακουργῶν καὶ ἀπιστότερος διαβάλλων, τότε δὲ ἑκατέρᾳ τῇ πόλει σπεύδοντες τὰ μάλιστ' αὐτὴν Πλειστοάναξ τε ὁ Παυσανίου, βασιλεὺς Λακεδαιμονίων, καὶ Νικίας ὁ Νικηράτου, πλεῖστα τῶν τότε εὖ φερόμενος ἐν στρατη-
10 γίαις, πολλῷ δὲ μᾶλλον προεθυμοῦντο, Νικίας μὲν βουλόμενος, ἐν ᾧ ἀπαθὴς ἦν καὶ ἠξιοῦτο, διασώσασθαι τὴν εὐτυχίαν, καὶ ἔς τε τὸ αὐτίκα πόνων πεπαῦσθαι καὶ αὐτὸς καὶ τοὺς πολίτας παῦσαι, καὶ τῷ μέλλοντι χρόνῳ καταλιπεῖν ὄνομα ὡς οὐδὲν σφήλας τὴν πόλιν
15 διεγένετο, νομίζων ἐκ τοῦ ἀκινδύνου τοῦτο ξυμβαίνειν καὶ ὅστις ἐλάχιστα τύχῃ αὐτὸν παραδίδωσι, τὸ δὲ ἀκίνδυνον τὴν εἰρήνην παρέχειν· Πλειστοάναξ δὲ ὑπὸ τῶν ἐχθρῶν διαβαλλόμενος περὶ τῆς καθόδου καὶ ἐς ἐνθυ-

καὶ τιμᾶσθαι ἐκ τοῦ πολεμεῖν: "because he owed his great successes as well as his reputation (not at Sparta only, but among all the Greeks) to his previous activity as general," and could therefore only hope to retain his influence by a continuance of the war. — 5. κακουργῶν: with καταφανέστερος, as διαβάλλων with ἀπιστότερος: "with his rascalities, with his (continual) calumnies"; and therefore διαβάλλων is necessary instead of διαβαλών of good Mss. In these words a severe judgment of Cleon's general character and conduct, special traits of which have been mentioned before (cf. iii. 36. 26; iv. 21. 9; 27. 18 ff.; 28. 26 f.; 39. 11; v. 7. 3 ff.), is unequivocally expressed. — 6. τότε δέ: see App. — ἑκατέρᾳ τῇ πόλει σπεύδοντες τὰ μάλιστ' αὐτήν: urging it (sc. τὴν εἰρήνην) most rigorously for each of the two cities, i.e. trying to bring it about. See App. — 9. πλεῖστα: adv. — 11. ἠξιοῦτο: in other words, ἐν ἀξιώματι ἦν, as in

i. 130. 2 f.; not elsewhere found in this signification. — ἐν ᾧ κτέ: "now while his good fortune and influence were still at their height, he wished to take care that they should remain unimpaired." (διασώσασθαι, aor.) — 12. πεπαῦσθαι: pf., "to have attained his end," "to have come to rest." GMT. 18, 3 b, N. — 14. καταλιπεῖν ὄνομα: reputation; also in vi. 33. 29 f. — 15. διεγένετο: had reached his end. Like διεσώθη, iv. 96. 33. Closely connected with οὐδὲν σφήλας: without having injured the state. διαγίγνεσθαι in this sense does not occur again before Plutarch. — 16. καὶ ὅστις: i.e. καὶ τούτῳ ὅς. — ἐλάχιστα τύχῃ αὐτὸν παραδίδωσι: the same expression is employed by Nicias in vi. 23. 11 about himself. ἐλάχιστα like πλεῖστα, 9. — 18. περὶ τῆς καθόδου: his return from his exile after the unsuccessful campaign of 446 B.C. Cf. i. 114. 9 ff.; ii. 21. 8 f. — ἐς ἐνθυμίαν προβαλλόμενος: pers. const. The explanation follows in the

μίαν τοῖς Λακεδαιμονίοις ἀεὶ προβαλλόμενος ὑπ' αὐτῶν, ὁπότε τι πταίσειαν, ὡς διὰ τὴν ἐκείνου κάθοδον
παρανομηθεῖσαν ταῦτα ξυμβαίνοι. τὴν γὰρ πρόμαντιν 2
τὴν ἐν Δελφοῖς ἐπῃτιῶντο αὐτὸν πεῖσαι μετ' Ἀριστο-
κλέους τοῦ ἀδελφοῦ ὥστε χρῆσαι Λακεδαιμονίοις ἐπὶ
πολὺ τάδε θεωροῖς ἀφικνουμένοις, Διὸς υἱοῦ ἡμιθέου
τὸ σπέρμα ἐκ τῆς ἀλλοτρίας εἰς τὸν ἑαυτῶν ἀναφέρειν·
εἰ δὲ μή, ἀργυρέᾳ εὐλάκᾳ εὐλαξεῖν· χρόνῳ δὲ προ- 3
τρέψαι τοὺς Λακεδαιμονίους φεύγοντα αὐτὸν ἐς Λύκαιον
διὰ τὴν ἐκ τῆς Ἀττικῆς ποτε μετὰ δώρων δοκοῦσαν ἀναχώρησιν, καὶ ἥμισυ τῆς οἰκίας τοῦ ἱεροῦ τότε τοῦ Διὸς

words ὡς διὰ τὴν ἐκείνου κάθοδον παρανομηθεῖσαν ταῦτα ξυμβαίνοι. ἐς ἐνθυμίαν προβάλλειν is "to cast as a reproach," "to cause to weigh upon the conscience." Cf. προβαλλόμενα, i. 73. 13; τὸν προβαλλόμενον λόγον, vi. 92. 19. See App.—20. ὁπότε τι πταίσειαν: explanatory modification of ἀεί, 19.—21. παρανομηθεῖσαν: attrib. partic. placed after its subst. *On account of his illegally accomplished return.* Thuc. freq. places the attrib. partic. after its subst. when other modifiers are added. See on i. 11. 19.
23. ἀδελφοῖ: see App.— ὥστε: const. with πείθειν. Cf. ii. 2. 23; iii. 70. 21.— ἐπὶ πολύ: temporal, as in i. 7. 6; ii. 16. 1. Lit. *for a long time,* i.e. *repeatedly,* to which the pres. partic. ἀφικνουμένοις corresponds. "Every time messengers came (on other business) to Delphi." See on ἀφικνουμένων, i. 91. 3.— 24. Διὸς υἱοῦ: so here the Mss. For υἱοῦ see Foucart, Revue de philol. 1, p. 36. Ἡρακλέους, τὸ σπέρμα, τὸν ἀπόγονον, εὐλάκαν δὲ τὴν ὕνιν Λακεδαιμόνιοι λέγουσιν, εὐλαξεῖν (this form also in the text, with Schol. and Plut. de Pyth. oraculis 403 B, instead of εὐλα-κεῖν) δὲ ἀρόσειν, ἀργυρέᾳ εὐλάκᾳ εὐλαξεῖν τοῦτ' ἔστι λιμὸν ἔσεσθαι καὶ πολλοῦ σφόδρα τὸν σῖτον ὠνήσεσθαι ὥσπερ ἀργυροῖς ἐργαλείοις χρωμένους. Schol. On εὐλαξεῖν, Cobet, Mnem. 6, p. 155, justly observes that the Dor. form of the fut. must be written with the Dor. accent.
26. χρόνῳ δέ: referring to ἐπὶ πολύ, 23; and therefore the subj. of προτρέψαι is τὴν πρόμαντιν, not Πλειστοάνακτα. — 27. ἐς Λύκαιον: in the Arcadian mountains, with an ancient and celebrated sanctuary of Zeus. — 28. μετὰ δώρων δοκοῦσαν ἀναχώρησιν, δοκοῦσαν, as in i. 32. 15, of the belief which was, though not proved, generally received. This corresponds to the report in ii. 21. 8, ἡ φυγὴ αὐτῷ ἐγένετο ἐκ Σπάρτης δόξαντι χρήμασι πεισθῆναι τὴν ἀναχώρησιν. See App. —29. τότε: he occupied this dwelling at that time while in banishment.— ἥμισυ τῆς οἰκίας τοῦ ἱεροῦ: i.e. a house, half of which belonged to the temple of Zeus, so that he could, φόβῳ τῶν (with Vat. for τῷ, cf. c. 11. 11) Λακεδαιμονίων, retreat at any moment to the shelter of the sanctuary. ἱεροῦ is

30 οἰκοῦντα φόβῳ τῶν Λακεδαιμονίων, ἔτει ἑνὸς δέοντι εἰκοστῷ τοῖς ὁμοίοις χοροῖς καὶ θυσίαις καταγαγεῖν ὥσπερ
ὅτε τὸ πρῶτον Λακεδαίμονα κτίζοντες τοὺς βασιλέας καθ-
17 ίσταντο.   ἀχθόμενος οὖν τῇ διαβολῇ ταύτῃ καὶ νομίζων 1
ἐν εἰρήνῃ μὲν οὐδενὸς σφάλματος γιγνομένου καὶ ἅμα
τῶν Λακεδαιμονίων τοὺς ἄνδρας κομιζομένων κἂν αὐτὸς
τοῖς ἐχθροῖς ἀνεπίληπτος εἶναι, πολέμου δὲ καθεστῶ-
5 τος ἀεὶ ἀνάγκην εἶναι τοὺς προύχοντας ἀπὸ τῶν ξυμφορῶν διαβάλλεσθαι, προυθυμήθη τὴν ξύμβασιν. καὶ τόν
τε χειμῶνα τοῦτον ἦσαν ἐς λόγους, καὶ * πρὸς τὸ ἔαρ ἤδη 2
παρασκευή τε προεπανεσείσθη ἀπὸ τῶν Λακεδαιμονίων

pred. part. gen. H. 732 a. — 30. ἔτει ἑνὸς δέοντι εἰκοστῷ: i.e. 427 B.C., since he had left the country in 446 B.C. (i. 114. 9 ff.; cf. ii. 21. 6). — 32. τοὺς βασιλέας: the pl. refers doubtless to the two kings at Sparta; prob. without reference to the controversy mentioned by Hdt. vi. 52. 1 ff., as to whether Aristodemus himself originally occupied the throne. See O. Müller, *Dorier*, p. 90.

17. *On this account Pleistoanax was all the more active in furthering the reconciliation; and after long negotiations a peace was brought about toward the end of the winter between the Athenians on one side, and the Lacedaemonians, with most of their allies, on the other.*

1. ἀχθόμενος οὖν τῇ διαβολῇ ταύτῃ: resumes διαβαλλόμενος, in c. 16. 18, with its results, while νομίζων introduces the other considerations by which he was influenced, which led to the result προυθυμήθη (aor.), *he conceived the ardent wish;* with subst. obj. as in viii. 1. 5; 90. 9. — 3. κομιζομένων: i.e. εἰ κομίζοιντο. — 5. ἀπὸ τῶν ξυμφορῶν: " on occasion of," etc., as in ii. 25. 13, ἀπὸ τούτου τοῦ τολμήμα-

τος ἐπῃνέθη. — 7. ἐς λόγους, καὶ πρὸς τὸ ἔαρ ἤδη: the punctuation is that adopted by St. and Cl., who put a comma after λόγους, and, 10, a comma instead of a period after ἐσακούοιεν, and, 17, a third comma after Νίσαιαν. The τε in τόν τε χειμῶνα τοῦτον brings into close connexion with one another not the times τὸν χειμῶνα and πρὸς τὸ ἔαρ ἤδη, but the events ἦσαν ἐς λόγους and παρασκευὴ προεπανεσείσθη, κτέ., and the τε of παρασκευή τε corresponds further to καί, 10. This καί introduces the third member of the period, i.e. as far as 17, τότε δή. The temporal force of the long clause ἐπειδὴ . . . τὴν Νίσαιαν is repeated by τότε δή. See App. — ἦσαν: see App.

7. καὶ πρὸς τὸ ἔαρ ἤδη: in close connexion: "and when the spring was already near." See on i. 30. 20. — 8. παρασκευή τε: corresponding to τόν τε χειμῶνα ἦσαν ἐς λόγους: on the one hand, negotiations were conducted; *on the other hand*, warlike demonstrations were made. On the use of τε . . . τε to give equal importance to two ideas, see on i. 8. 14; also iii. 81. 5. — προεπανεσείσθη: ἡ πο-

περιαγγελλομένη κατὰ πόλεις ὡς ἐς ἐπιτειχισμόν, ὅπως οἱ
10 Ἀθηναῖοι μᾶλλον ἐσακούοιεν, καὶ ἐπειδὴ ἐκ τῶν ξυνόδων ἅμα πολλὰς δικαιώσεις προενεγκόντων ἀλλήλοις ξυνεχωρεῖτο ὥστε ἃ ἑκάτεροι πολέμῳ ἔσχον ἀποδόντας τὴν εἰρήνην ποιεῖσθαι, Νίσαιαν δ' ἔχειν Ἀθηναίους (ἀνταπαιτούντων γὰρ Πλάταιαν οἱ Θηβαῖοι ἔφασαν οὐ βίᾳ,
15 ἀλλ' ὁμολογίᾳ αὐτῶν προσχωρησάντων καὶ οὐ προδόντων ἔχειν τὸ χωρίον· καὶ οἱ Ἀθηναῖοι τῷ αὐτῷ τρόπῳ τὴν Νίσαιαν), τότε δὴ παρακαλέσαντες τοὺς ἑαυτῶν ξυμμάχους οἱ Λακεδαιμόνιοι καὶ ψηφισαμένων πλὴν Βοιωτῶν καὶ Κορινθίων καὶ Ἠλείων καὶ Μεγαρέων τῶν ἄλ-
20 λων ὥστε καταλύεσθαι (τούτοις δὲ οὐκ ἤρεσκε τὰ πρασσόμενα), ποιοῦνται τὴν ξύμβασιν καὶ ἐσπείσαντο πρὸς

λεμικὴ παρασκευὴ προηπειλήθη, Schol. The same figurative expression occurs in ἐπανάσεισις τῶν ὅπλων, iv. 126. 22. Cf. vi. 86. 2, προσείοντες φόβον. — ἀπὸ τῶν Λακεδαιμονίων: *from the Lacedaemonian side*, similarly i. 141. 6; iii. 36. 24, γνῶμαι ἀφ' ἑκάστων ἐλέγοντο. — 9. περιαγγελλομένη: closely connected with παρασκευή. The warlike demonstration of the Lacedaemonians consisted of proclamations calling for military service. — ὡς ἐς ἐπιτειχισμόν: see App. — 10. ἐσακούοιεν: *give heed, obey*. Cf. i. 82. 11; 126. 3; iii. 4. 3; iv. 110. 1; 'v. 45. 18; 50. 1; viii. 31. 10. — 11. δικαιώσεις: "demands made with an assumption of right." See on i. 141. 6. — προενεγκόντων: gen. abs. with no subj. expressed. Cf. i. 2. 8 and note; ii. 52. 9; iii. 82. 6; iv. 94. 10. For the force of προφέρειν, see on iii. 59. 11, προφερόμενοι ὅρκους; iii. 64. 7, μὴ προφέρετε τὴν τότε γενομένην ξυνωμοσίαν. — ξυνεχωρεῖτο: only here in neut. pass. The impf. denotes the hardly attained result. The agree-

ment reached is introduced by ὥστε. Cf. i. 28. 18, ἑτοῖμοι δὲ εἶναι καὶ ὥστε ἀμφοτέρους μένειν κατὰ χώραν. GMT. 98, 2, N. 2. See App. — 12. ἔσχον: *had acquired*. Inceptive aor. G. 200, N. 5 b; H. 841. — 13. ἔχειν: *retain, keep*. — ἀνταπαιτούντων: sc. τῶν Ἀθηναίων. — 14. ἔφασαν οὐ βίᾳ κτέ.: cf. iii. 52. 10, where the still more positive expression αὐτῶν ἑκόντων προσχωρησάντων is used. — 15. καὶ οὐ προδόντων: does not continue the idea of προσχωρησάντων with entire accuracy, since the subj. of προδόντων comprises only part of the subj. of προσχωρησάντων, but the sense is easily understood from the connexion, and the antithesis is a natural one. — 16. καὶ οἱ Ἀθηναῖοι . . . Νίσαιαν: sc. ἔχειν ἔφασαν. A remark of the author, not of the Thebans. — 17. παρακαλέσαντες: a word used esp. of the ξύμμαχοι. Cf. i. 67. 3; 68. 10; v. 30. 12. — 20. ὥστε: cf. 12. — τούτοις δέ: refers back to the words before τῶν ἄλλων. — οὐκ ἤρεσκε τὰ πρασσόμενα:

τοὺς Ἀθηναίους καὶ ὤμοσαν, ἐκεῖνοί τε πρὸς τοὺς Λακεδαιμονίους, τάδε·

18 "Σπονδὰς ἐποιήσαντο Ἀθηναῖοι καὶ Λακεδαιμό- 1
νιοι καὶ οἱ ξύμμαχοι κατὰ τάδε, καὶ ὤμοσαν κατὰ πόλεις· περὶ μὲν τῶν ἱερῶν τῶν κοινῶν, θύειν ἐξεῖναι 2
καὶ μαντεύεσθαι καὶ θεωρεῖν κατὰ τὰ πάτρια τὸν βου-
5 λόμενον καὶ κατὰ γῆν καὶ κατὰ θάλασσαν ἀδεῶς. τὸ
δ' ἱερὸν καὶ τὸν νεὼν τὸν ἐν Δελφοῖς τοῦ Ἀπόλλωνος καὶ
Δελφοὺς αὐτονόμους εἶναι καὶ αὐτοτελεῖς καὶ αὐτοδίκους
καὶ αὑτῶν καὶ τῆς γῆς τῆς ἑαυτῶν κατὰ τὰ πάτρια. ἔτη δὲ 3
εἶναι τὰς σπονδὰς πεντήκοντα Ἀθηναίοις καὶ τοῖς ξυμμά-
10 χοις τοῖς Ἀθηναίων καὶ Λακεδαιμονίοις καὶ τοῖς ξυμμάχοις
τοῖς Λακεδαιμονίων ἀδόλους καὶ ἀβλαβεῖς καὶ κατὰ γῆν
καὶ κατὰ θάλασσαν. ὅπλα δὲ μὴ ἐξέστω ἐπιφέρειν ἐπὶ πη- 4
μονῇ μήτε Λακεδαιμονίους καὶ τοὺς ξυμμάχους ἐπὶ Ἀθη-

the separate negotiations between the Lacedaemonians and Athenians, as in iv. 121. § 1. — 21. ποιοῦνται τὴν ξύμβασιν, κτέ.: the conclusion of the peace took place in Sparta, as appears also from παρακαλέσαντες, 17. See Ullrich, *Beitr.*, 1862, p. 4.

18. *The terms of the treaty between the Athenians on the one hand and the Lacedaemonians, with such of their allies as joined them, on the other.*
1. Σπονδὰς ἐποιήσαντο κτέ.: see App. — 2. καὶ οἱ ξύμμαχοι: refers esp. to the allies of Sparta. The allies of the Athenians rarely (but see 10) appear in independent action. *Cf.* c. 47. 1 f. The same relation exists below § 9; and therefore κατὰ πόλεις here and in 48 refers only to the allies of the Lacedaemonians.
3. περὶ μὲν τῶν ἱερῶν τῶν κοινῶν: standing at the beginning of the sent., is used almost abs. *as regards*

the national sanctuaries. The sanctuaries referred to are esp. those at Delphi and Olympia. *Cf.* iii. 57. 7, and see on iv. 118. 1 f. — ἐξεῖναι: see App. —
5. τὸ ἱερὸν καὶ τὸν νεών: νεώς is the temple proper, ἱερόν the consecrated enclosure about the temple. *Cf.* iv. 90.
7. — 7. αὐτονόμους κτέ.: i.e. free from external influence, esp. that of the Phocians, which had occasioned serious hostilities between Sparta and Athens. See i. 112. 13 ff. The unusual expression αὐτοτελεῖς καὶ αὐτοδίκους is used in order to exclude every kind of foreign interference. The temple and the inhabitants of Delphi are here joined in an indivisible community, and the following preds. apply to both in common.
11. ἀδόλους καὶ ἀβλαβεῖς καὶ κατὰ γῆν καὶ κατὰ θάλασσαν: this, like several other expressions in this chapter, is the regular formula. *Cf.* c. 47. § 1–4.

ναίους καὶ τοὺς ξυμμάχους μήτε Ἀθηναίους καὶ τοὺς
15 ξυμμάχους ἐπὶ Λακεδαιμονίους καὶ τοὺς ξυμμάχους, μήτε
τέχνῃ μήτε μηχανῇ μηδεμιᾷ. ἢν δέ τι διάφορον ᾖ πρὸς
ἀλλήλους, δικαίῳ χρήσθων καὶ ὅρκοις, καθ' ὅ τι ἂν ξυν-
θῶνται. ἀποδόντων δὲ Ἀθηναίοις Λακεδαιμόνιοι καὶ οἱ
ξύμμαχοι Ἀμφίπολιν· ὅσας δὲ πόλεις παρέδοσαν Λακε-
20 δαιμόνιοι Ἀθηναίοις, ἐξέστω ἀπιέναι ὅποι ἂν βούλωνται
αὐτοὺς καὶ τὰ ἑαυτῶν ἔχοντας· τὰς δὲ πόλεις φερούσας
τὸν φόρον τὸν ἐπ' Ἀριστείδου αὐτονόμους εἶναι. ὅπλα
δὲ μὴ ἐξίστω ἐπιφέρειν Ἀθηναίους μηδὲ τοὺς ξυμμάχους
ἐπὶ κακῷ, ἀποδιδόντων τὸν φόρον, ἐπειδὴ αἱ σπονδαὶ
25 ἐγένοντο· εἰσὶ δὲ Ἄργιλος, Στάγειρος, Ἄκανθος, Σκῶλος,
Ὄλυνθος, Σπάρτωλος. ξυμμάχους δ' εἶναι μηδετέρων,
μήτε Λακεδαιμονίων μήτε Ἀθηναίων· ἢν δὲ Ἀθηναῖοι
πείθωσι τὰς πόλεις βουλομένας ταύτας, ἐξέστω ξυμμά-

16. ἤν: see App.—διάφορον: adj. *disputed*, as in i. 56. 2.— 17. δικαίῳ: subst. *legal means, settlement by law*. Elsewhere with the art., as in iii. 39. 20.

18. ἀποδόντων δέ: this paragraph concerning the restoration of the places taken by the Lacedaemonians extends to 31. After the mention of the most important one among them, Amphipolis, the stipulations regarding their treatment are inserted (ὅσας δὲ πόλεις ... ἐγένοντο, 25); and then the smaller towns which had revolted from Athens in the course of the war, and are to be restored, are mentioned by name: εἰσὶ δέ (αἵδε, which the inferior Mss. insert here, interferes with the connexion) Ἄργιλος ... Σπάρτωλος. Then follows a number of special provisions. See App. — 19. παρέδοσαν: we should expect ἂν παραδῶσι, but in the language of the treaty the provision requiring the restoration of the towns is regarded as already fulfilled. *Cf.* ἐπειδὴ ἐγένοντο in 24. But see App. on 18.— 21. αὐτούς: the inhabitants (or, accepting Kirchhoff's reading, παρέλαβον for παρέδοσαν in 19, the Athenians who were in these cities) *themselves*. This emphasis upon the pronoun necessitates the use of the connective καί before ἔχοντες. — φερούσας τὸν φόρον: expresses the same condition as ἀποδόντων τὸν φόρον, 24, *if they* or *as long as they pay the tribute*. — 22. τὸν ἐπ' Ἀριστείδου: the first appointment of the tribute to be paid by members of the Delian confederacy was ascribed to Aristides (Plut. *Arist.* 24; Dem. XXIII. 209; Paus. viii. 52). See on i. 96. 5. — 24. ἐπειδὴ ... ἐγένοντο: *i.e.* after the ratification of the treaty. See on 19, above. Until then the Athenians could try to subject the cities by violence, and the above provisions of the treaty were not in force. — 25. Στάγειρος: see App. on c. 6. 2.— 28. βουλομένας: "with their own

χους ποιεῖσθαι αὐτοὺς Ἀθηναίοις. Μηκυβερναίους δὲ 6
30 καὶ Σαναίους καὶ Σιγγαίους οἰκεῖν τὰς πόλεις τὰς ἑαυτῶν, καθάπερ Ὀλύνθιοι καὶ Ἀκάνθιοι. ἀποδόντων δὲ 7
Ἀθηναίοις Λακεδαιμόνιοι καὶ οἱ ξύμμαχοι Πάνακτον.
ἀποδόντων δὲ καὶ Ἀθηναῖοι Λακεδαιμονίοις Κορυφάσιον
καὶ Κύθηρα καὶ Μεθώνην καὶ Πτελεὸν καὶ Ἀταλάντην,
35 καὶ τοὺς ἄνδρας ὅσοι εἰσὶ Λακεδαιμονίων ἐν τῷ δημοσίῳ
τῷ Ἀθηναίων ἢ ἄλλοθί που ὅσης Ἀθηναῖοι ἄρχουσιν ἐν
δημοσίῳ· καὶ τοὺς ἐν Σκιώνῃ πολιορκουμένους Πελο-
ποιννησίων ἀφεῖναι καὶ τοὺς ἄλλους ὅσοι Λακεδαιμονίων
ξύμμαχοι ἐν Σκιώνῃ εἰσὶ καὶ ὅσους Βρασίδας ἐσέπεμψε,
40 καὶ εἴ τις τῶν ξυμμάχων τῶν Λακεδαιμονίων ἐν Ἀθήναις ἐστὶν ἐν τῷ δημοσίῳ ἢ ἄλλοθί που ἧς Ἀθηναῖοι ἄρ-

free will and consent." See App.—
29. Ἀθηναίοις: const. with ἐξέστω.
Because this provision applies only
to the Athenians, they are mentioned
a second time at the end of the sent.
Μηκυβερναίους καὶ Σαναίους καὶ
Σιγγαίους: St. conjectures that these
places were among those mentioned
in i. 58. 11 ff., which had united in
the foundation of Olynthus. Steup,
Stud. Thuc. I. p. 40 ff., and Kirchhoff,
Sitzungsber. d. Berl. Akad. 1882, p.
924, assume that the Olynthians
claimed the rights of suzerainty over
Mecyberna, the Acanthians over Sane
and Singus. These claims are here
denied, and the three towns are, at
the instance of the Athenians, placed
upon an equal footing with Olynthus
and Acanthus.
32. Πάνακτον: this provision,
made without the consent of the
Boeotians (see c. 3. 24 and 17. 18),
was only imperfectly executed. See
c. 42. 2 ff. — 33. Κορυφάσιον: the
Lacedaemonian name for Pylos. It
was taken by the Athenians in 425
B.C. See iv. 3 ff. — 34. Κύθηρα: was
taken by the Athenians in 424 B.C.
See iv. 53 ff. — Μεθώνην: was seized
by the Athenians in 425 B.C. See iv.
45. 5 ff. See App. — Πτελεόν: has
not been mentioned elsewhere by
Thuc. Perhaps it is the place in
Boeotia mentioned in Pliny, iv. 7. 26.
— Ἀταλάντην: an island near the
Opuntian Locrians, was occupied by
the Athenians in 431 B.C. See ii. 32.—
35. ἐν τῷ δημοσίῳ: ἐν τῷ δεσμωτηρίῳ,
Schol. Cf. iv. 41. 1, οἱ Ἀθηναῖοι ἐβού-
λευσαν δεσμοῖς μὲν αὐτοὺς φυλάσσειν
μέχρι οὗ τι ξυμβῶσιν. — 36. ἄλλοθί που
ὅσης: like ἄλλοθί που ἧς, 41, with the
rare ellipsis of γῆς. Part. gen. G.
168, N. 3; H. 757. — 37. τοὺς ἐν
Σκιώνῃ πολιορκουμένους: see iv. 130.
34 and 131. 8. — 38. ἀφεῖναι: here,
as above, § 3 and 4, and below, § 9
and 10, the inf. and imv. interchange.
GMT. 103; H. 957 a; Kühn. 474 b, and
595, 5. — 39. ὅσους Βρασίδας ἐσέπεμψε: see iv. 123. 16,

χουσιν ἐν δημοσίῳ. ἀποδόντων δὲ καὶ Λακεδαιμόνιοι καὶ οἱ ξύμμαχοι οὕστινας ἔχουσιν Ἀθηναίων καὶ τῶν ξυμμάχων κατὰ ταυτά. Σκιωναίων δὲ καὶ Τορωναίων καὶ 8 Σερμυλιῶν καὶ εἴ τινα ἄλλην πόλιν ἔχουσιν Ἀθηναῖοι, Ἀθηναίους βουλεύεσθαι περὶ αὐτῶν καὶ τῶν ἄλλων πόλεων ὅ τι ἂν δοκῇ αὐτοῖς. ὅρκους δὲ ποιήσασθαι Ἀθη- 9 ναίους πρὸς Λακεδαιμονίους καὶ τοὺς ξυμμάχους κατὰ πόλεις. ὀμνύντων δὲ τὸν ἐπιχώριον ὅρκον ἑκάτεροι τὸν μέγιστον (ἑπτακαίδεκα ἐξ ἑκάστης πόλεως)· ὁ δ' ὅρκος ἔστω ὅδε· ' Ἐμμενῶ ταῖς ξυνθήκαις καὶ ταῖς σπονδαῖς ταῖσδε δικαίως καὶ ἀδόλως.' ἔστω δὲ Λακεδαιμονίοις καὶ τοῖς ξυμμάχοις κατὰ ταυτὰ ὅρκος πρὸς Ἀθηναίους, τὸν δὲ ὅρκον ἀνανεοῦσθαι κατ' ἐνιαυτὸν ἀμφοτέρους. στήλας δὲ στῆσαι 10 Ὀλυμπίασι καὶ Πυθοῖ καὶ Ἰσθμοῖ καὶ Ἀθήνησι ἐν πόλει καὶ ἐν Λακεδαίμονι ἐν Ἀμυκλαίῳ. εἰ δέ τι ἀμνημονοῦσιν 11 ὁποτεροιοῦν καὶ ὅτου πέρι, λόγοις δικαίοις χρωμένοις

45. **Σερμυλιῶν**: from inscriptions for Ms. Ἑρμυλίων. The gens., at first loosely joined with εἴ τινα ἄλλην πόλιν, are taken up again in the following περὶ αὐτῶν. See App.—49. **ὀμνύντων δέ**: this provision concerning the form of oath is, like the one above, 19 ff., concerning the treatment of the restored cities, inserted as a parenthesis between the corresponding members of the sent., ὅρκους δὲ . . . πόλεις and 52, ἔστω δὲ . . . ἀμφοτέρους. The Athenians are to make oath to the Lacedaemonians as well as to those of their allies who unite in the peace; hence the pl. ὅρκους, 47. The Lacedaemonians and their allies take an oath to the Athenians only; hence, 53, ὅρκος πρὸς Ἀθηναίους.—**ἑκάτεροι**: i.e. the Athenians on one side, the Lacedaemonians and their allies on the other. (Kirchhoff brackets ἑκάτεροι.) —**τὸν ἐπιχώριον ὅρκον τὸν μέγιστον**: Fränkel, Hermes, 13, p. 460, has shown that the oath by which the Athenians usually ratified treaties was sworn by Zeus, Demeter, and Apollo. Ullrich, Beitr. 1862, p. 7 ff., suggests for Sparta the Dioscuri, τὼ Σιώ.—50. **ἑπτακαίδεκα ἐξ ἑκάστης πόλεως**: see App.

55. **Ἀθήνησι**: see App.—**ἐν πόλει**: i.e. ἐν τῇ Ἀκροπόλει. Cf. ii. 15. 33 f. —**ἐν Ἀμυκλαίῳ**: i.e. in the temple of Apollo of Amyclae, which lay, acc. to Polyb. v. 19, twenty stadia from the city.

57. **ὅτου**: after ὁποτεροιοῦν is easily understood in place of ὁτουοῦν.—**λόγοις δικαίοις**: "negotiations about what is just," "the just or legal method," opp. to every sort of violence. So also in c. 98. 2.—58. **εὐορ**-

εὔορκον εἶναι ἀμφοτέροις ταύτῃ μεταθεῖναι ὅπῃ ἂν δοκῇ ἀμφοτέροις, Ἀθηναίοις καὶ Λακεδαιμονίοις."

19 "Ἄρχει δὲ τῶν σπονδῶν ἔφορος Πλειστόλας Ἀρτε- 1 μισίου μηνὸς τετάρτῃ φθίνοντος, ἐν δὲ Ἀθήναις ἄρχων Ἀλκαῖος Ἐλαφηβολιῶνος μηνὸς ἕκτῃ φθίνοντος. ὤμνυον δὲ οἴδε καὶ ἐσπένδοντο· Λακεδαιμονίων μὲν 2
5 (Πλειστοάναξ, Ἆγις,) Πλειστόλας, Δαμάγητος, Χίονις, Μεταγένης, Ἄκανθος, Δάϊθος, Ἰσχαγόρας, Φιλοχαρίδας, Ζευξίδας, Ἄντιππος, Τέλλις, Ἀλκινάδας, Ἐμπεδίας, Μηνᾶς, Λάφιλος· Ἀθηναίων δὲ οἴδε· Λάμπων, Ἰσθμιόνικος, Νικίας, Λάχης, Εὐθύδημος, Προκλῆς, Πυθόδωρος,

κον: consistent with their oath, i.e. with the sworn treaty.

19. *The day of the ratification of the treaty and the names of those on both sides who took the oath.*

This chapter is part of the official document recording the peace. It determines the day with which the peace shall begin for all parties, and gives the names of the men who are to take the oath. In c. 20 the narrative is resumed with the mention of the date of the ratification of the treaty. The indics. ἄρχει, ὤμνυον καὶ ἐσπένδοντο, are not unusual in treaties. See Steup, *Stud.* I. p. 68.

1. ἄρχει: the manner of dating differs from that of iv. 118. 49, inasmuch as here, not the day, but the year appears as subj.; for ἔφορος Πλειστόλας and ἄρχων Ἀλκαῖος are the usual expressions for the year, Ol. 89, 3. The dats. (τετάρτῃ and ἕκτῃ) denoting the day immediately follow the nouns denoting the year. Lit., *the year of the Ephor Pleistolas, etc., begins the peace on the fourth day from the end of Artemisios*; i.e. the peace begins on the fourth, etc. The 27th of Artemisios in Sparta or the 25th of Elephe-

bolion in Athens for the year 421 B.C. fell about the middle of April. See Curtius, *Hist. of Greece*, III. p. 207.

5. Πλειστοάναξ, Ἆγις: see App.—
8. Ἀθηναίων δέ: of the seventeen Athenians, eleven (since for Ἀριστοκρίτης of the Mss. we must certainly write Ἀριστοκράτης from c. 24; cf. viii. 89. 12) are known to us as generals in the course of the war. Among these Nicias, Laches, Hagnon, Lamachus, and Demosthenes are the most noted. Lampon was celebrated (Plut. *Per.* c. 6) and derided (Ar. *Av.* 521, 988) as an oracle-monger. Only Isthmionicus, Procles (for the general Procles of Ol. 88. 2 fell in the campaign against the Aetolians; see iii. 98. 23), Myrtilus, Iolcius, and Timocrates are not elsewhere mentioned. The reason for the number seventeen cannot be determined with any degree of certainty. Ullrich suggests on the Athenian side perhaps two priests, half of the generals of that year, and one citizen of each phyle. Perhaps the oath was taken on the Lacedaemonian side by a number of Lacedaemonians and one each from the allied cities which took part in the peace. Certainly the words καὶ

10 Ἄγνων, Μυρτίλος, Θρασυκλῆς, Θεαγένης, Ἀριστοκράτης, Ἰώλκιος, Τιμοκράτης, Λέων, Λάμαχος, Δημοσθένης."
20 Αὗται αἱ σπονδαὶ ἐγένοντο * τελευτῶντος τοῦ χει- 1
μῶνος ἅμα ἦρι ἐκ Διονυσίων εὐθὺς τῶν ἀστικῶν, αὐτόδεκα ἐτῶν διελθόντων καὶ ἡμερῶν ὀλίγων παρενεγκουσῶν ἢ ὡς τὸ πρῶτον ἡ ἐσβολὴ ἡ ἐς τὴν Ἀττικὴν καὶ ἡ
5 ἀρχὴ τοῦ πολέμου τοῦδε ἐγένετο. σκοπείτω δέ τις κατὰ 2
τοὺς χρόνους καὶ μὴ τὴν ἀπαρίθμησιν τῶν ὀνομάτων τῶν
ἑκασταχοῦ ἢ ἀρχόντων ἢ ἀπὸ τιμῆς τινος [ἐς] τὰ προ-

ὤμοσαν κατὰ πόλεις in c. 18. 2 seem to imply that the allies took part in the oath as prescribed in c. 18. 47 ff., though Ullrich, p. 19, believes that they did not. Perhaps the number of Athenian envoys at Sparta had gradually risen to seventeen, all of whom were then commissioned to take the oath, or perhaps Kirchhoff is right in deducing the number from the peculiar Spartan constitution, in which case the seventeen Athenians would be appointed to correspond to the seventeen Spartans. See App. on c. 18. 50.

20. *Previous duration of the war. Remarks on the best way of reckoning periods of time.*

1. **αὗται αἱ σπονδαὶ ἐγένοντο**: is a brief re-statement of the contents of the latter part of c. 17 (τότε δὴ παρακαλέσαντες, . . . τάδε).—2. **ἐκ Διονυσίων εὐθὺς τῶν ἀστικῶν**: the city or greater Dionysia began before the vernal equinox, and lasted several days, until about the end of March. ἐκ of immediate sequence, as in i. 120. 17, ἐκ μὲν εἰρήνης πολεμεῖν; ii. 49. 9, ἔπειτα ἐξ αὐτῶν πταρμὸς καὶ βράγχος ἐπεγίγνετο.—**αὐτόδεκα ἔτη**: *exactly ten years*, corresponding to Lat. decem ipsi dies. (Kr. compares αὐτοτραγικὸς πίθηκος, Dem. XVIII. 242.) — 3. **παρ-**

ενεγκουσῶν: παραφέρειν here and in c. 26. 8 intr. like διαφέρειν, προφέρειν (i. 93. 13), ὑπερφέρειν (i. 81. 2) *be in excess, vary*. With this ἢ ὡς stands in close connexion: *after exactly ten years had passed, and a few days were in excess since* (i.e. had passed along further than when), *etc.* In accordance with the date of the beginning of the war as given in ii. 2, the words ἡ ἐσβολὴ . . . τοῦ πολέμου τοῦδε must be closely connected, so that ἡ ἀρχὴ τοῦ πολέμου τοῦδε refers to the attack upon Plataea, i.e. to the beginning of April, 431 B.C. ἡ ἐσβολὴ ἡ ἐς τὴν Ἀττικὴν is mentioned first, as the more important event, but in the computation of the time it is made subordinate to the attack upon Plataea. The ὀλίγαι ἡμέραι παρενεγκοῦσαι are, then, in the early part of April. The day upon which the peace began is mentioned in c. 19. 1, and falls about the middle of April. Here the same day is referred to as a few days after the first of April. But ten days, or even two weeks, may well be called a few days when a ten years' war is under consideration. See App.

6. **καὶ μὴ τὴν ἀπαρίθμησιν**: this passage (to πιστεύσας μᾶλλον) is corrupt in all Mss. But the sense is evidently: *one must* (in order to understand

γεγενημένα σημαινόντων πιστεύσας μᾶλλον· οὐ γὰρ ἀκριβές ἐστιν· οἷς καὶ ἀρχομένοις καὶ μεσοῦσι καὶ ὅπως
10 ἔτυχέ τῳ ἐπεγένετό τι. κατὰ θέρη δὲ καὶ χειμῶνας ἀρι- 3
θμῶν, ὥσπερ γέγραπται, εὑρήσει, ἐξ ἡμισείας ἑκατέρου
τοῦ ἐνιαυτοῦ τὴν δύναμιν ἔχοντος, δέκα μὲν θέρη, ἴσους
δὲ χειμῶνας τῷ πρώτῳ πολέμῳ τῷδε γεγενημένους.

21 Λακεδαιμόνιοι δὲ (ἔλαχον γὰρ πρότεροι ἀποδιδόναι 1
ἃ εἶχον) τούς τε ἄνδρας εὐθὺς τοὺς παρὰ σφίσιν αἰχμαλώτους ἀφίεσαν καὶ πέμψαντες ἐς τὰ ἐπὶ Θρᾴκης πρέσβεις Ἰσχαγόραν καὶ Μηνᾶν καὶ Φιλοχαρίδαν ἐκέλευον

events properly) *date them according to the* (natural) *divisions of time, and not acc. to* (κατά is understood with ἀπαρίθμησιν; see on i. 6. 21; ii. 63. 4; iii. 21. 10) *the count of the names of the persons who serve in each place, either as highest magistrate or from any* (other, *e.g.* priestly) *office* (as in Argos; *cf.* ii. 2. 4), *to designate the year, because one considers that safer, for that is inexact* (*i.e.* to embrace a whole year in this way), *since something happened at the beginning as well as in the middle or at any other time of their tenure of office*. οἷς is used in the sense of ἐπεὶ τούτοις to explain ἀρχόντων ἢ ἀπὸ τιμῆς τινος. See App. — 9. καὶ ὅπως ἔτυχέ τῳ: *sc.* ἐπιγενόμενον. " In whatever other part of their time of office an event may have happened," whether at the end, or in the first or in the second half, etc. — 10. ἐπεγένετο: as in i. 16. 1 and vii. 87. 14.
11. ὥσπερ γέγραπται: "as has been done hitherto in my narrative." *Cf.* ii. 1. 4. — ἐξ ἡμισείας κτέ.: acc. to the explanation given in the Introd. to Book I. p. 40, equiv. to ἑκατέρου (τοῦ τε θέρους καὶ τοῦ χειμῶνος) τὴν δύναμιν ἔχοντος ἐξ ἡμισείας τοῦ ἐνιαυτοῦ, "inasmuch as each of the two divisions of the year is to be reckoned (on an average) as half a year," *i.e.* so that the two divisions, though not necessarily equal to one another, when taken together always make a year. — 13. τῷ πρώτῳ πολέμῳ: also in c. 24. 12 and c. 26. 15. This and ὁ πρότερος πόλεμος (vii. 18. 12) and ὁ δεκαετὴς πόλεμος (c. 25. 3 and 26. 15) are the words used by Thuc. to denote the first period of the Peloponnesian war, for which the designation Ἀρχιδάμειος πόλεμος came into use among the orators. See Ullrich, *Beitr.*, 1845, p. 13 ff.
21. *The execution of the terms of the treaty meets with opposition at Amphipolis and other places in Thrace.*
1. ἔλαχον γάρ: *i.e.* in the drawing of lots, which evidently took place immediately after the conclusion of the treaty. *Cf.* c. 35. 7. — 3. ἀφίεσαν: impf. after analogy of the use of πέμπειν. It expresses continuance of the action. *Cf.* iii. 111. 14, τοὺς μὲν Μαντινέας καὶ τοὺς Πελοποννησίους ἀφίεσαν, τοὺς δ' Ἀμπρακιώτας ἔκτεινον, and viii. 41. 13.
— 4. Ἰσχαγόραν: he took part (see iv. 132. 6 and 13) in the Thracian expedition. These three men all shared in the conclusion of the treaty. *Cf.* c.

5 τὸν Κλεαρίδαν τὴν Ἀμφίπολιν παραδιδόναι τοῖς Ἀθηναίοις καὶ τοὺς ἄλλους τὰς σπονδάς, ὡς εἴρητο ἑκάστοις, δέχεσθαι. οἱ δ᾽ οὐκ ἤθελον, νομίζοντες οὐκ ἐπιτηδείας 2 εἶναι· οὐδὲ ὁ Κλεαρίδας παρέδωκε τὴν πόλιν, χαριζόμενος τοῖς Χαλκιδεῦσι, λέγων ὡς οὐ δυνατὸς εἴη βίᾳ ἐκεί-
10 νων παραδιδόναι. ἐλθὼν δὲ αὐτὸς κατὰ τάχος μετὰ πρέσ- 3
βεων αὐτόθεν ἀπολογησόμενός τε ἐς τὴν Λακεδαίμονα,
ἤν κατηγορῶσιν οἱ περὶ τὸν Ἰσχαγόραν ὅτι οὐκ ἐπείθετο,
καὶ ἅμα βουλόμενος εἰδέναι εἰ ἔτι μετακινητὴ εἴη ἡ ὁμολογία, ἐπειδὴ ηὗρε κατειλημμένους, αὐτὸς μὲν πάλιν πεμ-
15 πόντων τῶν Λακεδαιμονίων καὶ κελευόντων μάλιστα μὲ
καὶ τὸ χωρίον παραδοῦναι, εἰ δὲ μή, ὁπόσοι Πελοποννησίων ἔνεισιν ἐξαγαγεῖν, κατὰ τάχος ἐπορεύετο.

22 Οἱ δὲ ξύμμαχοι ἐν τῇ Λακεδαίμονι αὐτοῦ ἔτυχον 1
ὄντες, καὶ αὐτῶν τοὺς μὴ δεξαμένους τὰς σπονδὰς ἐκέλευον οἱ Λακεδαιμόνιοι ποιεῖσθαι. οἱ δὲ τῇ αὐτῇ προφάσει, ᾗπερ καὶ τὸ πρῶτον ἀπεώσαντο, οὐκ ἔφασαν δέξα-

19. 6 f.—5. τὸν Κλεαρίδαν: cf. c. 11.
19.—6. τοὺς ἄλλους: i.e. the inhabitants of the towns mentioned in c. 18.
19 ff.—ὡς εἴρητο ἑκάστοις: i.e. acc. to the conditions mentioned in c. 18.
7. ἐπιτηδείας : this adj. is used with σπονδαί also in c. 112. 12 (where it is declined as an adj. of two terminations), proper, acceptable.—9. τοῖς Χαλκιδεῦσι: the inhabitants of Amphipolis of Chalcidic descent.—βίᾳ ἐκείνων: this use of βίᾳ with gen. occurs also in i. 43. 8; 68. 19; iv. 99. 6.
10. ἐλθών: sc. Clearidas. Const. ἐς τὴν Λακεδαίμονα with ἐλθών.—μετὰ πρέσβεων: not those mentioned in 4, but envoys of the Amphipolitans themselves, αὐτόθεν.—11. ἀπολογησόμενος: see App.—14. κατειλημμέ-
νους: see App.—αὐτός: opp. to the πρέσβεις (10) with whom he had come. He was now sent back; the envoys probably stayed to see if they might not still accomplish something.—16. καὶ τὸ χωρίον: καί is emphatic. He was to surrender the town itself if possible.

22. After vain attempts to induce the rest of their allies to join in the peace, the Lacedaemonians make a formal alliance with the Athenians.
1. οἱ δὲ ξύμμαχοι: the narrative recurs to the end of c. 17. See App.—3. προφάσει: the expressed reason, not a pretended one. Cf. i. 23. 23 and note.—4. τὸ πρῶτον: see c. 17. 18 ff., where a hint of their reasons is given in οὐκ ἤρεσκε τὰ πρασσόμενα.—δέξασθαι: on this rare use of the aor.

5 σθαι, ἢν μή τινας δικαιοτέρας τούτων ποιῶνται. ὡς δ' αὐτῶν οὐκ ἐσήκουον, ἐκείνους μὲν ἀπέπεμψαν, αὐτοὶ δὲ πρὸς τοὺς Ἀθηναίους ξυμμαχίαν ἐποιοῦντο, νομίζοντες ἥκιστα ἂν σφίσι τούς τε Ἀργείους, ἐπειδὴ οὐκ ἤθελον Ἀμπελίδου καὶ Λίχου ἐλθόντων ἐπισπένδεσθαι, νομί-
10 σαντες αὐτοὺς ἄνευ Ἀθηναίων οὐ δεινοὺς εἶναι καὶ τὴν ἄλλην Πελοπόννησον μάλιστ' ἂν ἡσυχάζειν· πρὸς γὰρ ἂν τοὺς Ἀθηναίους, εἰ ἐξῆν, χωρεῖν. παρόντων οὖν πρέσβεων ἀπὸ τῶν Ἀθηναίων καὶ γενομένων λόγων ξυνέβησαν, καὶ ἐγένοντο ὅρκοι καὶ ξυμμαχία ἥδε·

23 "Κατὰ τάδε ξύμμαχοι ἔσονται Λακεδαιμόνιοι (καὶ Ἀθηναῖοι) πεντήκοντα ἔτη· ἤν τινες ἴωσιν ἐς τὴν γῆν πολέμιοι τὴν Λακεδαιμονίων καὶ κακῶς ποιῶσι Λακεδαιμονίους,

inf. where the fut. inf. seems to be required, see GMT. 23, 2, N. 3. See App.
6. ἐκείνους: i.e. all the allies, both those who had and those who had not accepted the peace; hence αὐτοί, the Lacedaemonians alone. — αὐτοὶ δὲ πρὸς τοὺς Ἀθηναίους . . . εἰ ἐξῆν, χωρεῖν: this reading of the Mss. may be translated as follows: *They themselves were about to make an alliance with the Athenians, thinking that* (if they did this) *the Argives would by no means* (ἥκιστα, Lat. minime), *since they had not been willing to renew their treaty when Ampelidas and Lichas came to them for that purpose,—thinking, I say, that they without the Athenians would not be dangerous to them, and that the rest of Peloponnesus would be least likely to stir.* This is certainly very harsh, and is open to so many objections that an emendation seems necessary. For a full discussion of the passage, see App. — 7. ἐποιοῦντο: impf. expressing intended action: "they decided to form an alliance with Athens."— 8. τούς τε Ἀργείους: stands first, being the most important consideration (as in c. 14. 20, πρὸς τοὺς Ἀργείους). — 9. ἐπισπένδεσθαι: is equiv. to ἄλλας σπένδεσθαι of c. 14. 21. The names of the envoys are not given in c. 14. — νομίσαντες: repeats the meaning of νομίζοντες (7). It is difficult to see why the tense is changed to the aor., and the repetition is certainly unnecessary, or rather, as Kr. says, is inexcusable. — 11. πρὸς γὰρ ἂν κτέ.: "for they thought that the Peloponnesians would join the Athenians if it were possible," i.e. if the Spartans did not make an alliance with Athens, but in this case the Peloponnesians could no longer join with Athens to the detriment of Sparta.
12. παρόντων οὖν πρέσβεων: the same who had arranged the treaty of peace, and taken the oaths. See c. 24. § 1.
23. *The terms of the treaty of alliance between the Lacedaemonians and the Athenians.*
1. (καὶ Ἀθηναῖοι): see App. — 4.

ὠφελεῖν Ἀθηναίους Λακεδαιμονίους τρόπῳ ὁποίῳ ἂν δύνωνται ἰσχυροτάτῳ κατὰ τὸ δυνατόν· ἢν δὲ δηώσαντες
οἴχωνται, πολεμίαν εἶναι ταύτην τὴν πόλιν Λακεδαιμονίοις καὶ Ἀθηναίοις καὶ κακῶς πάσχειν ὑπὸ ἀμφοτέρων,
καταλύειν δὲ ἅμα ἄμφω τὼ πόλεε. ταῦτα δ᾽ εἶναι δικαίως 2
καὶ προθύμως καὶ ἀδόλως. καὶ ἤν τινες ἐς τὴν Ἀθηναίων
γῆν ἴωσι πολέμιοι καὶ κακῶς ποιῶσιν, Ἀθηναίους ὠφελεῖν Λακεδαιμονίους τρόπῳ ὅτῳ ἂν δύνωνται ἰσχυροτάτῳ κατὰ τὸ δυνατόν. ἢν δὲ δηώσαντες οἴχωνται, πολεμίαν εἶναι ταύτην τὴν πόλιν Λακεδαιμονίοις καὶ Ἀθηναίοις καὶ κακῶς πάσχειν ὑπ᾽ ἀμφοτέρων, καταλύειν δὲ
ἅμα ἄμφω τὼ πόλεε. ταῦτα δ᾽ εἶναι δικαίως καὶ προθύμως καὶ ἀδόλως. ἢν δὲ ἡ δουλεία ἐπανιστῆται, ἐπικου- 3
ρεῖν Ἀθηναίους Λακεδαιμονίοις παντὶ σθένει κατὰ τὸ
δυνατόν. ὀμοῦνται δὲ ταῦτα οἵπερ καὶ τὰς ἄλλας σπον- 4
δὰς ὤμνυον ἑκατέρων. ἀνανεοῦσθαι δὲ κατ᾽ ἐνιαυτὸν
Λακεδαιμονίους μὲν ἰόντας ἐς Ἀθήνας πρὸς τὰ Διονύσια,
Ἀθηναίους δὲ ἰόντας ἐς Λακεδαίμονα πρὸς τὰ Ὑακίνθια.
στήλην δὲ ἑκατέρους στῆσαι, τὴν μὲν ἐν Λακεδαίμονι 5
παρ᾽ Ἀπόλλωνι ἐν Ἀμυκλαίῳ, τὴν δὲ ἐν Ἀθήναις ἐν πόλει παρ᾽ Ἀθηνᾷ. ἢν δέ τι δοκῇ Λακεδαιμονίοις καὶ Ἀθη- 6
ναίοις προσθεῖναι καὶ ἀφελεῖν περὶ τῆς ξυμμαχίας, ὅ τι
ἂν δοκῇ, εὔορκον ἀμφοτέροις εἶναι."

τρόπῳ... δυνατόν: the formal and somewhat verbose language is characteristic of the style of documents. Cf. 11, and c. 47. 14 and 23. Kühn. 582, 2, N. 4.

8. καταλύειν: abs. without πόλεμον. So also in 14 and vii. 58. 8 f.

8. εἶναι : used like γίγνεσθαι with advs. is a somewhat antiquated usage. Cf. 15.

16. ἡ δουλεία: in collective sense occurs also in Plato, Legg. vi. 776 c.

and Arist. Pol. ii. 5. The danger here referred to was also mentioned in c. 14. 17 ff. as one of the reasons for concluding the peace. — 17. Ἀθηναίους: see App.

18. ὀμοῦνται: the same transition to a finite mood as in c. 18. 12. — 20. τὰ Διονύσια: the great or city Dionysia (cf. c. 20. 2) at which time many foreigners visited Athens. — 21. τὰ Ὑακίνθια: the festival of Apollo of Amyclae in the month Hyacinthios,

24   "Τὸν δὲ ὅρκον ὤμνυον Λακεδαιμονίων μὲν οἵδε· 1
Πλειστοάναξ, Ἆγις, Πλειστόλας, Δαμάγητος, Χίονις,
Μεταγένης, Ἄκανθος, Δάϊθος, Ἰσχαγόρας, Φιλοχαρίδας,
Ζευξίδας, Ἄντιππος, Ἀλκινάδας, Τέλλις, Ἐμπεδίας,
5 Μηνᾶς, Λάφιλος· Ἀθηναίων δὲ Λάμπων, Ἰσθμιόνικος,
Λάχης, Νικίας, Εὐθύδημος, Προκλῆς, Πυθόδωρος,
Ἅγνων, Μυρτίλος, Θρασυκλῆς, Θεαγένης, Ἀριστοκρά-
της, Ἰώλκιος, Τιμοκράτης, Λέων, Λάμαχος, Δημοσθένης."

   Αὕτη ἡ ξυμμαχία ἐγένετο μετὰ τὰς σπονδὰς οὐ πολ- 2
10 λῷ ὕστερον, καὶ τοὺς ἄνδρας τοὺς ἐκ τῆς νήσου ἀπέδοσαν οἱ Ἀθηναῖοι τοῖς Λακεδαιμονίοις, καὶ τὸ θέρος ἦρχε
* τοῦ ἑνδεκάτου ἔτους. ταῦτα δὲ τὰ δέκα ἔτη ὁ πρῶτος
25 πόλεμος ξυνεχῶς γενόμενος γέγραπται. μετὰ δὲ τὰς 1

corresponding to the Attic Hecatom-
baeon.
24. *The names of the Lacedaemonians and Athenians who took the oath.
Restoration of the prisoners taken at
Sphacteria.*
1. τὸν δὲ ὅρκον κτέ.: as Steup,
Stud. I. p. 84, observes, c. 24. § 1 belongs to the document recording the
treaty. The narrative begins again
in 9, αὕτη ἡ ξυμμαχία. The same relation exists between c. 19 and c. 20.
— **2.** Πλειστοάναξ κτέ.: with the
exception of some slight differences
in the order (Τέλλις, Ἀλκινάδας, and
Νικίας, Λάχης above) this list is identical with that of c. 19.
10. καὶ τοὺς ἄνδρας: καί denotes
immediate connexion: "and straight-
way." — τοὺς ἄνδρας τοὺς ἐκ τῆς
νήσου: cf. c. 15. 2 f. and iv. 108. 38.
— **12.** ταῦτα τὰ δέκα ἔτη: continues
the idea of τοῦ ἑνδεκάτου ἔτους (in
which the δέκα ἔτη are contained by
implication), and therefore stands
first, though these words belong grammatically, as acc. of duration of time,

with ξυνεχῶς γενόμενος. This attrib.
partic. is placed after its subst. in
accordance with the usage discussed
in the note on i. 11. 17. The more
usual order would be: ὁ πρῶτος ταῦτα
τὰ δέκα ἔτη ξυνεχῶς γενόμενος πόλεμος
γέγραπται, *i.e.* "the history of the first
(part of the) war which lasted without interruption for these ten years
is finished" (pf.). With this ξυνεχῶς
γενόμενος πόλεμος the period of uncertain and unquiet peace until the
renewal of the φανερὸς πόλεμος is contrasted in c. 25, and in c. 26 we
have a general retrospect of the whole
twenty-seven years' war with its three
divisions. This furnishes Thuc. an
occasion to speak of his own relation
to the war. The division introduced
by the peace occasions a break in the
continuous narrative of the war, and
the great importance of this division
calls forth these remarks from the
author.
25. *Character and duration of the
time of peace between the first and second
war.*

σπονδὰς καὶ τὴν ξυμμαχίαν τῶν Λακεδαιμονίων καὶ τῶν
Ἀθηναίων, αἳ ἐγένοντο μετὰ τὸν δεκαετῆ πόλεμον ἐπὶ
Πλειστόλα μὲν ἐν Λακεδαίμονι ἐφόρου, Ἀλκαίου δ' ἄρ-
χοντος Ἀθήνησι, τοῖς μὲν δεξαμένοις αὐτὰς εἰρήνη ἦν,
οἱ δὲ Κορίνθιοι καὶ τῶν ἐν Πελοποννήσῳ πόλεών τινες
διεκίνουν τὰ πεπραγμένα, καὶ εὐθὺς ἄλλη ταραχὴ καθίστατο τῶν ξυμμάχων πρὸς τὴν Λακεδαίμονα. καὶ ἅμα 2
καὶ τοῖς Ἀθηναίοις οἱ Λακεδαιμόνιοι προϊόντος τοῦ χρόνου ὕποπτοι ἐγένοντο, ἔστιν ἐν οἷς οὐ ποιοῦντες ἐκ τῶν
ξυγκειμένων ἃ εἴρητο. καὶ ἐπὶ ἓξ ἔτη μὲν καὶ δέκα μῆνας ἀπέσχοντο μὴ ἐπὶ τὴν ἑκατέρων γῆν στρατεῦσαι, ἔξωθεν δὲ μετ' ἀνοκωχῆς οὐ βεβαίου ἔβλαπτον ἀλλήλους τὰ
μάλιστα· ἔπειτα μέντοι καὶ ἀναγκασθέντες λῦσαι τὰς

3. **δεκαετῆ**: see App. — 5. **Ἀθήνησι**: *cf.* c. 18. 55. — 6. **Κορίνθιοι**: see c. 17. 19 and 27. 5 ff. — 7. **διεκίνουν**: hardly occurs elsewhere in Attic prose. *Cf.* Ar. *Nub.* 477, διακίνει τὸν νοῦν αὐτοῦ. It seems here to denote the attempt to break up and unsettle by intrigues the agreements (τὰ πεπραγμένα) which had been made. — **καὶ εὐθὺς ἄλλη ταραχή**: "and besides these intrigues of the Corinthians, other disturbances began immediately (after the end of the conflict between Athens and Sparta) between the Lacedaemonians and their (former) allies." ἄλλη refers to what precedes, not to the following καὶ ἅμα; hence St. is wrong in inserting τε after ἄλλη without Ms. authority. This is evident, for the Athenians, although they had just made an alliance with Sparta, are certainly not included among the ξύμμαχοι of 8. καὶ ἅμα introduces, as it freq. does (*e.g.* c. 14. 9), a new and important statement. For this was the most serious matter, that the friendly relations between Sparta and Athens were so soon disturbed.

11. **ἃ εἴρητο**: are the separate articles of the ξυγκείμενα. *Cf.* c. 35. 5 ff. — **καὶ ἐπὶ ἓξ ἔτη καὶ δέκα μῆνας**: neither beginning nor end of this period is accurately fixed. The beginning is not μετὰ τὰς σπονδάς, but μετὰ τὴν ξυμμαχίαν, which was formed οὐ πολλῷ ὕστερον (*cf.* c. 24. 9). (Grote, VI. p. 276 and note, thinks this interval between the two treaties was 'not more than a month or two.' Curtius, *Hist.* III. p. 285, thinks it was 'a few weeks.') The end is only loosely marked by the words ἀπέσχοντο μὴ ἐπὶ τὴν ἑκατέρων γῆν στρατεῦσαι. See App. — 12. **μή**: after the neg. ἀπέσχοντο. See on iii. 32. 14; iv. 40. 5. G. 263; H. 1029. — **ἔξωθεν**: *i.e.* without invading the territory of one another, but by taking part in hostile complications with others such as are mentioned in c. 26. § 2. Among these, the war in Sicily is most important. — 13. **μετ' ἀνοκωχῆς**: see App. — **μετά**: "during the continuance," "un-

15 μετὰ τὰ δέκα ἔτη σπονδὰς αὖθις ἐς πόλεμον φανερὸν
26 κατέστησαν. γέγραφε δὲ καὶ ταῦτα ὁ αὐτὸς Θουκυδίδης 1
Ἀθηναῖος ἑξῆς ὡς ἕκαστα ἐγίγνετο κατὰ θέρη καὶ χειμῶνας, μέχρι οὗ τήν τε ἀρχὴν κατέπαυσαν τῶν Ἀθηναίων Λακεδαιμόνιοι καὶ οἱ ξύμμαχοι, καὶ τὰ μακρὰ τείχη
5 καὶ τὸν Πειραιᾶ κατέλαβον. ἔτη δὲ ἐς τοῦτο τὰ ξύμπαντα ἐγένετο τῷ πολέμῳ ἑπτὰ καὶ εἴκοσι. καὶ τὴν διὰ μέσου ξύμβασιν εἴ τις μὴ ἀξιώσει πόλεμον νομίζειν, οὐκ ὀρθῶς δικαιώσει. τοῖς τε γὰρ ἔργοις ὡς διῄρηται ἀθρεί-

der the influence of." — 14. ἔπειτα μέντοι: i.e. when they no longer avoided direct attacks. — ἀναγκασθέντες... κατέστησαν: the subj. must be here as in 11, Λακεδαιμόνιοι καὶ Ἀθηναῖοι. Therefore the sent. cannot refer to any single act. First the Athenians with thirty triremes ravaged the coast of Laconia in the latter part of the summer of 414 B.C. (vi. 105. 13 f.); the Lacedaemonians entered Attica to fortify Decelea early in the spring of 413 B.C. (vii. 19. § 1). This last act is probably considered as the beginning of the πόλεμος φανερός, and strictly speaking ἀναγκασθέντες λῦσαι applies only to the Lacedaemonians whose condition is described in vii. 18. § 3, 4. But the various stages in the renewal of the war overlap one another chronologically, as do the events which mark its beginning. Cf. c. 20. § 1. — 15. ἐς πόλεμον φανερόν: the same words are used to designate the beginning of the first war in i. 23. 26.

26. Remarks concerning the duration and the division of the whole war, and the author's personal relations to it.

1. γέγραφε δὲ καὶ ταῦτα: with reference to the introductory words of the whole work, i. 1. 1. The pf. serves to establish the identity of the author, like the aor. in i. 1. 1 and i. 97. 7, and, like γέγραπται in ii. 1. 4, anticipates the completion of the work. "The same Thuc. has written (i.e. is the author of) this also" does not necessarily imply that the work was ever finished, but is the natural expression of one who expects his work to be finished before these words come before his readers. So when the actual narrative is to begin, we find the fut. ἐξηγήσομαι in 30. — 2. ἑξῆς ... χειμῶνας: identical with ii. 1. 4 f., and accordingly ἐγίγνετο, which better expresses the successive development of events (ἑξῆς), is preferred to Ms. ἐγένετο. — 4. τὰ μακρὰ τείχη καὶ τὸν Πειραιᾶ κατέλαβον: acc. to Plut. Lys. 15, ἕκτῃ καὶ δεκάτῃ Μουνυχιῶνος, i.e. the middle of April, 404 B.C. — 6. ἐγένετο: used in comprehensive statements of numbers. See on ii. 20. 11.

7. τὴν διὰ μέσου ξύμβασιν: i.e. the time of truce between the earlier and the later war. See on iv. 20. 2. — ἀξιώσει: in characteristic opposition to δικαιώσει. "If any one thinks the period of truce does not deserve (ἄξιον) the name of war, he will ignore the relation which is founded upon the nature of the case (δίκαιον)." — 8. ὡς διῄρηται: the only possible subj. appears to be ἡ διὰ μέσου ξύμβασις.

τω καὶ εὑρήσει οὐκ εἰκὸς ὂν εἰρήνην αὐτὴν κριθῆναι, ἐν
ᾗ οὔτε ἀπέδοσαν πάντα οὔτ' ἀπεδέξαντο ἃ ξυνέθεντο,
ἔξω τε τούτων πρὸς τὸν Μαντινικὸν καὶ Ἐπιδαύριον πόλεμον καὶ ἐς ἄλλα ἀμφοτέροις ἁμαρτήματα ἐγένοντο, καὶ
οἱ ἐπὶ Θράκης ξύμμαχοι οὐδὲν ἧσσον πολέμιοι ἦσαν,
Βοιωτοί τε ἐκεχειρίαν δεχήμερον ἦγον. ὥστε ξὺν τῷ πρώ- 3
τῳ πολέμῳ τῷ δεκαετεῖ καὶ τῇ μετ' αὐτὸν ὑπόπτῳ ἀνο-
κωχῇ καὶ τῷ ὕστερον ἐξ αὐτῆς πολέμῳ εὑρήσει τις τοσαῦτα ἔτη, λογιζόμενος κατὰ τοὺς χρόνους, καὶ ἡμέρας
οὐ πολλὰς παρενεγκούσας, καὶ τοῖς ἀπὸ χρησμῶν τι ἰσχυ-
ρισαμένοις μόνον δὴ τοῦτο ἐχυρῶς ξυμβάν. ἀεὶ γὰρ ἔγω- 4
γε μέμνημαι καὶ ἀρχομένου τοῦ πολέμου καὶ μέχρι οὗ
ἐτελεύτησε προφερόμενον ὑπὸ πολλῶν, ὅτι τρὶς ἐννέα ἔτη

The best rendering seems, then, to be: *how this* (so-called) *period of truce was really interrupted and torn asunder by the actual circumstances.* The usual meaning of διαιρεῖν, *rend asunder, break through* a fortification (cf. ii. 75. 24; 76. 2; iv. 48. 10; 110. 18; v. 2. 14; 3. 9), is transferred to the interruption of the state of peace; so that διαιρεῖν appears as the opposite of ξυμβαίνειν. See App. — 10. οὔτ' ἀπεδέξαντο: see App.—11. ἔξω τε τούτων: after the negative infringements of the treaty (10), the more positive breaches of its provisions are mentioned; esp. of that in c. 18. § 4, by supporting insurrections of allies. See App. — πρὸς τὸν Μαντινικόν: see c. 33 ff. — πρὸς τὸν Ἐπιδαύριον: see c. 53 ff. — 12. ἐς ἄλλα: refers particularly to the Sicilian expedition. — ἁμαρτήματα ἐγένοντο: the pl. of the verb on account of the previously expressed reference to a variety of cases. II. 604 b. ἀμφοτέροις ἐγένοντο is equiv. to ἀμφότεροι ἐποιήσαντο. — 13. πολέμιοι ἦσαν: sc. τοῖς Ἀθηναίοις. — 14. ἐκεχειρίαν δεχήμερον:

"a truce which was (or must be) renewed every ten days." Βοιωτοὶ πρὸς δέκα ἡμέρας ἐκεχειρίαν ἐσπένδοντο πρὸς Ἀθηναίους. Schol. Cf. c. 32. 17; vi. 7. 23; 10. 13. See App.

16. ἐξ αὐτῆς: see on c. 20. 2. — 17. κατὰ τοὺς χρόνους: see on c. 20. 6 and 10. — ἡμέρας οὐ πολλὰς παρενεγκούσας: see on c. 20. 2. The time is to be computed from the beginning of April, 431 B.C., to the middle of April, 404 B.C. See App. on ii. 2. 5. — 18. ἀπὸ χρησμῶν: *relying upon prophecies*. See on iv. 67. 1. — 19. μόνον δὴ τοῦτο: refers perhaps to the various interpretations of the oracle in ii. 54. § 2 and 3. — ἀεί: const. with προφερόμενον (cf. vii. 68. 6). It is explained by καὶ ἀρχομένου τοῦ πολέμου καὶ μέχρι οὗ ἐτελεύτησε. The whole is further explained by ἐπεβίων δέ, which serves to establish the credibility of μέμνημαι ἔγωγε, an essential element of the author's fitness for his task of writing the history of the Peloponnesian war.

21. τρὶς ἐννέα: a reminiscence of

δέοι γενέσθαι αὐτόν. ἐπεβίων δὲ διὰ παντὸς αὐτοῦ, αἰσθανόμενός τε τῇ ἡλικίᾳ καὶ προσέχων τὴν γνώμην, ὅπως ἀκριβές τι εἴσομαι· καὶ ξυνέβη μοι φεύγειν τὴν ἐμαυτοῦ ἔτη εἴκοσι μετὰ τὴν ἐς Ἀμφίπολιν στρατηγίαν, καὶ γενομένῳ παρ' ἀμφοτέροις τοῖς πράγμασι, καὶ οὐχ ἧσσον τοῖς Πελοποννησίων διὰ τὴν φυγήν, καθ' ἡσυχίαν τι αὐτῶν μᾶλλον αἰσθέσθαι. τὴν οὖν μετὰ τὰ δέκα ἔτη διαφοράν τε καὶ ξύγχυσιν τῶν σπονδῶν καὶ τὰ ἔπειτα ὡς ἐπολεμήθη ἐξηγήσομαι.

27 Ἐπειδὴ γὰρ αἱ πεντηκοντούτεις σπονδαὶ ἐγένοντο, καὶ ὕστερον ἡ ξυμμαχία, καὶ αἱ ἀπὸ τῆς Πελοποννήσου πρεσβεῖαι, αἵπερ παρεκλήθησαν ἐς αὐτά, ἀνεχώ-

the original metrical form of the oracle. Also in Plut. Nic. 9.
22. αἰσθανόμενος (cf. i. 71. 21) τῇ ἡλικίᾳ: "having the necessary degree of understanding in consequence of my age" (his age was probably from about forty years upwards). See Introd. to Book I. p. 4. Dat. of cause. G.188,1; II. 776.—25. μετὰ τὴν ἐς Ἀμφίπολιν στρατηγίαν: see iv. 104 15 ff.; 106. 16 ff.; and Introd. to Book I. p. 11. —γενομένῳ ... πράγμασι: since I became acquainted with the affairs of both sides. οὐχ ἧσσον, i.e. μάλιστα. Cf. c. 15. 3. The results of this accurate acquaintance with the circumstances of the various states of Peloponnesus are very evident in the subsequent narrative.—28. αἰσθέσθαι. see App. —διαφοράν τε καὶ ξύγχυσιν τῶν σπονδῶν: with these words Thuc. characterizes the period of uncertain peace, much as he calls the unstable condition before the breaking out of the war σπονδῶν ξύγχυσις (i. 146.4). The διαφορά, which is closely connected with the ξύγχυσις τῶν σπονδῶν by the common art. (cf. i. 120. 10; iii. 82.

8 f.), refers particularly, as in i. 81. 10; 102. 7; 146. 1; v. 43. 1; viii. 85. 2, to the disagreements which presently arose.— 29. τὰ ἔπειτα ὡς ἐπολεμήθη: i.e. the events of the second war.
27. Continuation of the narrative. The Corinthians are discontented, and make overtures to the Argives in order to bring about an alliance against Sparta.
1. γάρ: introduces the narrative announced in the previous chap.—
2. καὶ ὕστερον ἡ ξυμμαχία: is added to αἱ ... σπονδαί almost parenthetically to remind us that the alliance followed the peace, as mentioned in c. 24. 9. It has the effect of a rel. clause ("which was presently followed by the alliance"), and must not be understood as determining the time of the following clause. "After the fifty years' peace had been concluded, and then the alliance also, the ambassadors, too, went home." The treaty of alliance was concluded so soon after the peace, that it is referred to in the negotiations at Argos (8). See App. — 3. αὐτά: is the

ρουν ἐκ τῆς Λακεδαίμονος· καὶ οἱ μὲν ἄλλοι ἐπ' οἴκου 2
ἀπῆλθον, Κορίνθιοι δὲ ἐς Ἄργος τραπόμενοι πρῶτον λόγους ποιοῦνται πρός τινας τῶν ἐν τέλει ὄντων Ἀργείων ὡς χρή, ἐπειδὴ Λακεδαιμόνιοι οὐκ ἐπ' ἀγαθῷ ἀλλ' ἐπὶ καταδουλώσει τῆς Πελοποννήσου σπονδὰς καὶ ξυμμαχίαν πρὸς Ἀθηναίους τοὺς πρὶν ἐχθίστους πεποίηνται, ὁρᾶν τοὺς Ἀργείους ὅπως σωθήσεται ἡ Πελοπόννησος, καὶ ψηφίσασθαι τὴν βουλομένην πόλιν τῶν Ἑλλήνων, ἥτις αὐτόνομός τέ ἐστι καὶ δίκας ἴσας καὶ ὁμοίας δίδωσι, πρὸς Ἀργείους ξυμμαχίαν ποιεῖσθαι ὥστε τῇ ἀλλήλων ἐπιμαχεῖν, ἀποδεῖξαι δὲ ἄνδρας ὀλίγους ἀρχὴν αὐτοκράτορας καὶ μὴ πρὸς τὸν δῆμον τοὺς λόγους εἶναι, τοῦ μὴ καταφανεῖς γίγνεσθαι τοὺς μὴ πείσαντας τὸ πλῆθος. ἔφασαν

neut. pl. in a pregnant sense referring to the matter in hand. This Thuc. not infreq. uses. See on i. 1. 10. It refers very properly to the negotiations preceding the treaty as well as to the σπονδαί (*cf.* παρακαλέσαντες, c. 17. 17, where the purpose of the summons is left unexpressed) and is therefore not to be changed (with St.) to αὐτάς.

5. πρῶτον: refers to preliminary negotiations with prominent men at Argos. The further consequences appear in Argos (c. 28) and in Corinth (c. 30). — **7. ἐπ' ἀγαθῷ**: *cf.* i. 131. 7; ii. 17. 15; iv. 87. 10; and see on ἐπὶ κακῷ, iv. 86. 1, for further examples. — **ἐπὶ καταδουλώσει**: *cf.* iii. 10. 10. — **9. ὁρᾶν**: with ὅπως and fut. ind., as in iii. 46. 16; vi. 41. 6. So with ὅτῳ τρόπῳ in vi. 33. 13; viii. 63. 20. GMT. 45 Rem.; H. 1054, 3. — **12. αὐτόνομος**: denotes political independence; δίκας ἴσας καὶ ὁμοίας διδόναι denotes conduct which respects the independence of others. The first is intended to exclude the dependent allies of Athens and Sparta, the second more particularly Athens itself, which obliged the ὑπήκοοι ξύμμαχοι to come to Athens for the conduct of certain cases (see on i. 77. 1), and therefore could not be said δίκας ἴσας καὶ ὁμοίας διδόναι. — **13. ὥστε**: on condition that. See on i. 28. 18. GMT. 98, 2, and N. 2; H. 953 b. — **τῇ ἀλλήλων ἐπιμαχεῖν**: like ἐπιμαχίαν in c. 48. 8, a merely defensive alliance; in i. 44. 8 defined by τῇ ἀλλήλων βοηθεῖν. — **14. ἀρχήν**: to be taken with αὐτοκράτορας, but not in the sense of "power" or "authority" (Kr. "in regard to their authority"), but like τὴν ἀρχήν in ii. 74. 10; iv. 98. 4; 56. 5; here, however, as in Hdt. i. 193. 14; ii. 95. 13; iii. 16. 31, without the art. Originally *from the beginning*, and thence *absolutely, entirely*. See App. — **15. τοῦ μὴ καταφανεῖς γίγνεσθαι**: *sc.* τοῖς Λακεδαιμονίοις. On the gen. of the inf., see on i. 4. 7; GMT. 92, 1, N. 5; H. 960. The envoys from

δὲ πολλοὺς προσχωρήσεσθαι μίσει τῶν Λακεδαιμονίων. καὶ οἱ μὲν Κορίνθιοι διδάξαντες ταῦτα ἀνεχώρησαν ἐπ' 3 28 οἴκου. οἱ δὲ τῶν Ἀργείων ἄνδρες ἀκούσαντες ἐπειδὴ 1 ἀνήνεγκαν τοὺς λόγους ἔς τε τὰς ἀρχὰς καὶ τὸν δῆμον, ἐψηφίσαντο Ἀργεῖοι καὶ ἄνδρας εἵλοντο δώδεκα, πρὸς οὓς τὸν βουλόμενον τῶν Ἑλλήνων ξυμμαχίαν ποιεῖσθαι 5 πλὴν Ἀθηναίων καὶ Λακεδαιμονίων· τούτων δὲ μηδετέροις ἐξεῖναι ἄνευ τοῦ δήμου τοῦ Ἀργείων σπείσασθαι. ἐδέξαντό τε ταῦτα οἱ Ἀργεῖοι μᾶλλον, ὁρῶντες τόν τε τῶν 2 Λακεδαιμονίων σφίσι πόλεμον ἐσόμενον (ἐπ' ἐξόδῳ γὰρ πρὸς αὐτοὺς αἱ σπονδαὶ ἦσαν) καὶ ἅμα ἐλπίσαντες τῆς 10 Πελοποννήσου ἡγήσεσθαι. κατὰ γὰρ τὸν χρόνον τοῦτον

other states were to be relieved from the necessity of addressing the popular assembly concerning offers of alliance, in order that those who might wish to join the Argive alliance, but could not persuade the Argive popular assembly to accept them as allies (τοὺς μὴ πείσαντας τὸ πλῆθος), should not be exposed to danger from the Lacedaemonians. See App. — 17. προσχωρήσεσθαι: sc. to the new alliance to be formed under the leadership of Argos.
18. διδάξαντες: like διδασκάλους γενομένους in c. 30. 2, of plans and deliberations set forth with arguments, esp. of such as are undertaken with hostile intent. Cf. ii. 93. 4; iii. 71. 7; vii. 18. 6; viii. 45. 9.
28. *The Argives accept the proposals of the Corinthians, and declare themselves ready for the formation of the new alliance.*
1. οἱ δὲ τῶν Ἀργείων ἄνδρες κτέ.: on the order of words in the dependent clause, see on iii. 4. 1. — 2. ἀναφέρειν: like referre ad senatum, also in Hdt. iii. 71. 20, and 80. 30. —

τοὺς λόγους: i.e. the proposals of the Corinthians. — τὰς ἀρχάς: magistratus, also in c. 47. 52 and 55; 84. 20; i. 90. 27. — 4. ποιεῖσθαι: depends grammatically upon ἐψηφίσαντο, though we should expect ποιήσεται or ποιεῖσθαι ἐξείη. This use of the inf. in rel. clauses occurs most freq. in quotations from laws and decrees. GMT. 92, 2, N. 3 b. — 5. μηδετέροις: depends upon σπείσασθαι. — 6. ἄνευ τοῦ δήμου: "without express consent of the assembly." See on i. 91. 23.
- 7. ἐδέξαντό τε: by the particle τε Thuc. here introduces a sent. explanatory of what precedes. Cf. ii. 8. 16; 13. 22. Cl.'s change to δέ is unnecessary. — τόν τε: the const. is planned with reference to a second obj.; but the general ὁρῶντες is subsequently replaced by the more specific ἐλπίσαντες ("because they had come to hope"), in consequence of which the order of words seems perverted, since we should expect ὁρῶντές τε τόν κτέ. — 8. ἐπ' ἐξόδῳ... ἦσαν: this fact is mentioned in c. 14. 20 and 22. 9 as influencing the Lacedaemonians to

ἥ τε Λακεδαίμων μάλιστα δὴ κακῶς ἤκουσε καὶ ὑπερώφθη διὰ τὰς ξυμφοράς, οἵ τε Ἀργεῖοι ἄριστα ἔσχον τοῖς πᾶσιν, οὐ ξυναράμενοι τοῦ Ἀττικοῦ πολέμου, ἀμφοτέροις δὲ μᾶλλον ἔνσπονδοι ὄντες ἐκκαρπωσάμενοι. οἱ μὲν οὖν Ἀργεῖοι οὕτως ἐς τὴν ξυμμαχίαν προσεδέχοντο τοὺς ἐθέλοντας τῶν Ἑλλήνων. Μαντινῆς δ' αὐτοῖς καὶ οἱ ξύμμαχοι αὐτῶν πρῶτοι προσεχώρησαν, δεδιότες τοὺς Λακεδαιμονίους. τοῖς γὰρ Μαντινεῦσι μέρος τι τῆς Ἀρκαδίας κατέστραπτο ὑπήκοον, ἔτι τοῦ πρὸς Ἀθηναίους πολέμου ὄντος, καὶ ἐνόμιζον οὐ περιόψεσθαι σφᾶς τοὺς Λακεδαιμονίους ἄρχειν, ἐπειδὴ καὶ σχολὴν ἦγον· ὥστε ἄσμενοι πρὸς τοὺς Ἀργείους ἐτρά-

make peace. Here reference is made to it to explain the motives of the Argives (Steup, Rhein. Mus. 25, p. 285 note, suggests that it be omitted as a superfluous gloss).— 11. ἥ τε Λακεδαίμων, οἵ τε Ἀργεῖοι: the two equally prominent reasons are symmetrically opposed. See on i. 8. 14.— 11. μάλιστα δή: cf. i. 1. 8; 50. 10; 138. 10. — ἤκουσε: like ὑπερώφθη and, 12, ἄριστα ἔσχον, aor. with the signification: Lacedaemon had fallen into ill repute and had become an object of contempt, whereas the Argives had attained a desirable position. — 12. τοῖς πᾶσιν: in every respect. Cf. ii. 11. 25; 36. 10; 64. 20; vii. 50. 20.— 13. τοῦ Ἀττικοῦ πολέμου: so the Peloponnesian war is called here and in c. 31. 11 from the point of view of Peloponnesus, as in viii. 18. 10 and 37. 15, ὁ πρὸς Ἀθηναίους πόλεμος. See Ullrich, Hellen. Kriege, p. 3, note 6. — ξυναράμενοι: const. with gen. as a verb of sharing, also in iv. 10. 1. G. 170, 2; H. 737. — 14. μᾶλλον: rather. "Far from taking part in the war they stood rather (i.e. on the contrary) on terms of peace with both parties." — ἐκκαρπωσάμενοι: like καρποῦσθαι in ii. 38. 7; vii. 68. 16, (ἐκ- referring to the source): "they derived profit from it (the ἔνσπονδοι ὄντες)." τοὺς καρποὺς καὶ τὰς προσόδους λαβόντες ἀπὸ τῆς γῆς ἀκεραίους διὰ τὸ μὴ πολεμεῖν. Schol. — 15. προσεδέχοντο: impf. they were ready to receive.

29. The Mantineans are the first to join the league, and a sentiment favourable to it spreads throughout Peloponnesus.

3. τοῖς Μαντινεῦσι: with κατέστραπτο, equiv. to ὑπὸ τῶν Μαντινέων, a freq. use of the dat. with the plpf. pass. Cf. i. 46. 1; 48. 1; 118. 18. — μέρος τι τῆς Ἀρκαδίας: among others the Parrhasians. Cf. c. 33. 3. — κατέστραπτο ὑπήκοον: like i. 8. 16, προσεποιοῦντο ὑπηκόους, the pred. adj. expressing result. — 6. σφᾶς ... ἄρχειν: depends upon οὐ περιόψεσθαι Cf. i. 35. 14, δύναμιν προσλαβεῖν περιόψεσθε. GMT. 112, 2, N. 6; H. 986; Kühn. 484, 24. — ἐπειδὴ καὶ σχολὴν ἦγον: "since, inasmuch as the war with Athens

ποντο, πόλιν τε μεγάλην νομίζοντες καὶ Λακεδαιμονίοις ἀεὶ διάφορον, δημοκρατουμένην τε ὥσπερ καὶ
αὐτοί. ἀποστάντων δὲ τῶν Μαντινέων καὶ ἡ ἄλλη Πελοπόννησος ἐς θροῦν καθίστατο ὡς καὶ σφίσι ποιητέον
τοῦτο, νομίσαντες πλέον τέ τι εἰδότας μεταστῆναι αὐτοὺς καὶ τοὺς Λακεδαιμονίους ἅμα δι' ὀργῆς ἔχοντες, ἐπ'
ἄλλοις τε καὶ ὅτι ἐν ταῖς σπονδαῖς ταῖς Ἀττικαῖς ἐγέγραπτο εὔορκον εἶναι προσθεῖναι καὶ ἀφελεῖν ὅ τι ἂν ἀμφοῖν τοῖν πολέοιν δοκῇ, Λακεδαιμονίοις καὶ Ἀθηναίοις.
τοῦτο γὰρ τὸ γράμμα μάλιστα τὴν Πελοπόννησον διεθορύβει καὶ ἐς ὑποψίαν καθίστη μὴ μετὰ Ἀθηναίων σφᾶς
βούλωνται Λακεδαιμόνιοι δουλώσασθαι· δίκαιον γὰρ εἶναι πᾶσι τοῖς ξυμμάχοις γεγράφθαι τὴν μετάθεσιν· ὥστε
φοβούμενοι οἱ πολλοὶ ὥρμηντο πρὸς τοὺς Ἀργείους καὶ
αὐτοὶ ἕκαστοι ξυμμαχίαν ποιεῖσθαι.

was over, they now had leisure also (as well as inclination) to turn their attention to Mantinea." — 9. **δημοκρατουμένην τε**: the third member of a series of words or clauses is freq. connected by τε with the preceding. See on i. 2. 6; 76. 12. This is the first positive mention of a democracy at Argos. It may possibly have been introduced when Argos made an alliance with Athens in 460 B.C. See i. 102; Paus. i. 29. 9; Grote V. p. 175 ff. — **ὥσπερ καὶ αὐτοί**: sc. ἐδημοκρατοῦντο as in c. 44. 9. Cf. i. 32. 3. Kühn. 58, 3.
11. **ἐς θροῦν καθίστατο**: in act. signification: "they began to talk"; not "they began to be talked about." —
12. **νομίσαντες**: aor., their opinion concerning a particular case; νομίζοντες (8), concerning permanent conditions. — **πλέον τι εἰδότας**: rebus melius compertis (St.), and therefore their example would have more weight. Cf. vii. 49. 22. — **αὐτούς**: sc. τοὺς Μαντινέας. — 13. **δι' ὀργῆς ἔχοντες**. Cf. ii. 37. 12; 64. 2; v. 46. 32. See on ii. 8. 19. — **ἐπ' ἄλλοις**: on other grounds. Cobet, Mnem. 14, p. 9 for ἐν ἄλλοις. — 14. **ἐγέγραπτο**: cf. c. 18, § 11, and c. 23, § 6. This refers to both documents.
17. **τὸ γράμμα**: the single article of the treaty. A rare use of the word. — **διεθορύβει**: set in commotion far and wide. — 19. **δίκαιον γὰρ εἶναι**: would in dir. disc. have been δίκαιον γὰρ ἦν without ἄν, like καλὸν ἦν, i. 38. 10; εἰκὸς ἦν, iii. 40. 26. —
20. **πᾶσι τοῖς ξυμμάχοις**: for all the allies. — **τὴν μετάθεσιν**: the power to προσθεῖναι καὶ ἀφελεῖν or to μεταθεῖναι ὅπῃ ἂν δοκῇ ἀμφοτέροις, c. 18. 58.
21. **πρὸς τοὺς Ἀργείους**: as in c. 27. 12; 28. 3. — **καὶ αὐτοὶ ἕκαστοι**: pred. to οἱ πολλοί: "for their part also."

30 Λακεδαιμόνιοι δὲ αἰσθόμενοι τὸν θροῦν τοῦτον ἐν
τῇ Πελοποννήσῳ καθεστῶτα καὶ τοὺς Κορινθίους διδασκάλους τε γενομένους καὶ αὐτοὺς μέλλοντας στείλασθαι
πρὸς τὸ Ἄργος, πέμπουσι πρέσβεις ἐς τὴν Κόρινθον,
βουλόμενοι προκαταλαβεῖν τὸ μέλλον, καὶ ᾐτιῶντο τήν
τε ἐσήγησιν τοῦ παντός, καὶ εἰ Ἀργείοις σφῶν ἀποστάντες ξύμμαχοι ἔσονται παραβήσεσθαί τε ἔφασαν αὐτοὺς
τοὺς ὅρκους, καὶ ἤδη ἀδικεῖν ὅτι οὐ δέχονται τὰς Ἀθηναίων σπονδάς, εἰρημένον κύριον εἶναι ὅ τι ἂν τὸ πλῆθος τῶν ξυμμάχων ψηφίσηται, ἢν μή τι θεῶν ἢ ἡρώων
κώλυμα ᾖ. Κορίνθιοι δὲ παρόντων σφίσι τῶν ξυμμάχων,
ὅσοι οὐδ᾽ αὐτοὶ ἐδέξαντο τὰς σπονδάς (παρεκάλεσαν δὲ
αὐτοὺς αὐτοὶ πρότερον), ἀντέλεγον τοῖς Λακεδαιμονίοις,

30. *The Lacedaemonians protest in Corinth against the intended alliance with Argos, but meet with a rebuff; for the Corinthians declare that they cannot betray the Chalcidian cities.*

2. καθεστῶτα, γενομένους, μέλλοντας: are all pred. (supplementary) partics. dependent upon αἰσθόμενοι. *Cf.* c. 10. 38. GMT. 113; II. 982. — 2. διδασκάλους γενομένους: see on iii. 2. 11; v. 27. 18. — 5. προκαταλαβεῖν τὸ μέλλον: φθάσαι πρὶν μέλλειν τοὺς Κορινθίους προσχωρεῖν τοῖς Ἀργείοις, Schol. With obj. of the thing affected, as in i. 57. 16; with pers. obj. in i. 33. 20; 36. 18. — 6. τήν τε ἐσήγησιν τοῦ παντός: *the instigation of the whole movement*, corresponding to ἐσηγεῖσθαι in iii. 20. 7; iv. 76. 8; vi. 99. 7, and ἐσηγητής in viii. 48. 40. τε is the correlative of the following καί, which belongs with ἔφασαν. τε belongs with ᾐτιῶντο, but stands after τήν. τε is occasionally carelessly put between the art. and its noun even when it belongs with the word preceding the art. — καὶ εἰ ... ἔσονται: Cl. takes this with ᾐτιῶντο, or rather with an ἠγανάκτουν, δεινὸν ἐποιοῦντο, or δεινὸν αὐτοῖς ἐφαίνετο supplied from ᾐτιῶντο, and cites iv. 85. § 6; vii. 73. § 1; viii. 53. § 2. These passages do not offer any very close analogy. It is better, with Jowett, to take καὶ εἰ ... ἔσονται as prot. with παραβήσεσθαι, and to put the comma before καὶ εἰ, instead of after ἔσονται. — 9. εἰρημένον: acc. abs. See on i. 140. 13, and *cf.* c. 39. 12; vii. 18. 14. The provision to which the Lacedaemonians here refer must have been contained in the original treaty of alliance between the Peloponnesian states and Sparta, which is called by the Corinthians (20) οἱ τῶν ξυμμάχων ὅρκοι, and by Thuc. (24) οἱ παλαιοὶ ὅρκοι. — τὸ πλῆθος: *the majority*, as in i. 125. 4.

11. σφίσι: i.e. in Corinth. — 12. ὅσοι ... τὰς σπονδάς: those mentioned in c. 17. § 2. οὐδ᾽ αὐτοί corresponds to καὶ αὐτός (*cf.* i. 50. 18; 62. 21), "also not." — παρεκάλεσαν δέ: epexegetical δέ. See on c. 10. 21. Aor. in the sense of plpf. — 13. αὐτοί:

ἃ μὲν ἠδικοῦντο οὐ δηλοῦντες ἄντικρυς, ὅτι οὔτε Σόλλιον σφίσιν ἀπέλαβον παρ' Ἀθηναίων οὔτε Ἀνακτόριον,
εἴ τέ τι ἄλλο ἐνόμιζον ἐλασσοῦσθαι, πρόσχημα δὲ ποιούμενοι τοὺς ἐπὶ Θράκης μὴ προδώσειν· ὀμόσαι γὰρ αὐτοῖς ὅρκους ἰδίᾳ τε, ὅτε μετὰ Ποτιδαιατῶν τὸ πρῶτον
ἀφίσταντο, καὶ ἄλλους ὕστερον. οὐκ οὖν παραβαίνειν 3
τοὺς τῶν ξυμμάχων ὅρκους ἔφασαν οὐκ ἐσιόντες ἐς τὰς
τῶν Ἀθηναίων σπονδάς· θεῶν γὰρ πίστεις ὀμόσαντες
ἐκείνοις οὐκ ἂν εὐορκεῖν προδιδόντες αὐτούς. εἰρῆσθαι
δ' ὅτι " ἢν μὴ θεῶν ἢ ἡρώων κώλυμα ᾖ"· φαίνεσθαι οὖν
σφίσι κώλυμα θεῖον τοῦτο. καὶ περὶ μὲν τῶν παλαιῶν 4

on *their own responsibility*, paying no attention to the Lacedaemonians, whose opposition they naturally expected. — 14. ἃ μὲν ἠδικοῦντο: *in what respects* (acc. to their opinion) *they had been wronged*. — ἄντικρυς: *straightforwardly, openly,* also in viii. 92. 65. — Σόλλιον: Κορινθίων πόλισμα in Acarnania, was taken by the Athenians in the first year of the war (*cf.* ii. 30. 2), Anactorium in the seventh (*cf.* iv. 49). — 15. οὔτε ... σφίσιν ἀπέλαβον παρ' Ἀθηναίων: *that they* (the Lacedaemonians) *had not recovered these places from the Athenians for them* (the Corinthians), *i.e.* that in making the peace they had not forced the Athenians to restore them. — 16. εἴ τέ τι ἄλλο: parallel to ὅτι ... Ἀνακτόριον, is in appos. to the obj. of δηλοῦντες. τε is not a correlative of οὔτε in 15. — ἐλασσοῦσθαι: "they were getting less than their rights"; also in i. 77. 1. — 17. τοὺς ἐπὶ Θράκης μὴ προδώσειν: collectively the obj. of πρόσχημα (see on i. 96. 4). *That they* (the Corinthians) *would not give up the Greeks on the Thracian coast* (to the rule of Athens) was the chief reason they gave for their opposition to Sparta. — 18. ἰδίᾳ: the Corinthians alone, so that with ἄλλους ὕστερον (sc. ὅρκους) some word like κοινῇ (Kr.) is to be understood, although not expressed. — ὅτε ... ἀφίσταντο: *cf.* i. 58. § 1.
19. οὐκ οὖν: written (with Cl.) as two words. — 20. οὐκ ἐσιόντες: *by not joining*, as the Lacedaemonians had asserted in 8, ἀδικεῖν ὅτι οὐ δέχονται τὰς Ἀθηναίων σπονδάς (here τῶν Ἀθηναίων; the usual variation in the use of the art. with names of peoples). — 21. θεῶν ... ὀμόσαντες: θεῶν ὅρκους ἐπὶ πίστει, Schol. "Since they had bound themselves by oaths sworn by the gods." — 22. οὐκ ἂν εὐορκεῖν: in dir. disc. οὐκ ἂν εὐορκοῖμεν ("preserve the εὔορκον"; *cf.* c. 18. 58), εἰ προδιδοῖμεν. — εἰρῆσθαι: "that the words of the agreement were"; after which ὅτι has no effect upon the const., but serves as a mark of punctuation. GMT. 79; H. 928 b. — 23. φαίνεσθαι οὖν σφίσι κτέ.: "so it seemed *to them* that this, the solemn oath, was a hindrance interposed by the gods themselves."

25 ὅρκων τοσαῦτα εἶπον, περὶ δὲ τῆς Ἀργείας ξυμμαχίας, μετὰ τῶν φίλων βουλευσάμενοι ποιήσειν ὅ τι ἂν δίκαιον ᾖ. καὶ οἱ μὲν Λακεδαιμονίων πρέσβεις ἀνεχώρησαν ἐπ' οἴκου. ἔτυχον δὲ παρόντες ἐν Κορίνθῳ καὶ Ἀργείων πρέσβεις, οἳ ἐκέλευον τοὺς Κορινθίους ἰέναι ἐς τὴν ξυμμα-
30 χίαν καὶ μὴ μέλλειν· οἱ δὲ ἐς τὸν ὕστερον ξύλλογον αὐ-
31 τοῖς τὸν παρὰ σφίσι προεῖπον ἥκειν. ἦλθε δὲ καὶ 1 Ἠλείων πρεσβεία εὐθὺς καὶ ἐποιήσαντο πρὸς Κορινθίους ξυμμαχίαν πρῶτον, ἔπειτα ἐκεῖθεν ἐς Ἄργος ἐλθόντες, καθάπερ προείρητο, Ἀργείων ξύμμαχοι ἐγέ-
5 νοντο. διαφερόμενοι γὰρ ἐτύγχανον τοῖς Λακεδαιμονίοις περὶ Λεπρέου. πολέμου γὰρ γενομένου ποτὲ 2 πρὸς Ἀρκάδων τινὰς Λεπρεάταις καὶ Ἠλείων παρακληθέντων ὑπὸ Λεπρεατῶν ἐς ξυμμαχίαν ἐπὶ τῇ ἡμισείᾳ τῆς γῆς καὶ λυσάντων τὸν πόλεμον, Ἠλεῖοι τὴν
10 γῆν νεμομένοις αὐτοῖς τοῖς Λεπρεάταις τάλαντον ἔταξαν

25. **περὶ δὲ τῆς Ἀργείας ξυμμαχίας**: (so with the best Mss. for Ἀργείων; the less usual expression like αἱ Ἀττικαὶ σπονδαί in c. 29. 14 and 36. 13) const. with εἶπον. "In regard to the Argive alliance, they declared that they would," etc.
28. **ἔτυχον παρόντες**: they were already present in Corinth during these negotiations with the Lacedaemonian envoys. — 29. **ἰέναι ἐς**: equiv. to ἐσιέναι, 20. — 30. **αὐτοῖς προεῖπον**: equiv. to ἐκέλευον αὐτούς. Cf. i. 26. 20.
31. *The Eleans make an alliance with Corinth and Argos, because they have a quarrel with the Lacedaemonians about Lepreum. Thereupon the Corinthians join the Argive alliance, as do also the Thracian Chalcidians. The Boeotians and Megarians keep quiet.*
2. **ἐποιήσαντο**: see App. — 4. **καθάπερ προείρητο**: in the proclamation which the Argives made (c. 28. § 1), acting on the advice of the Corinthians (c. 27. § 2). — 6. **Λεπρέου**: Lepreum in Triphylia, not far from the boundaries of Elis and Laconia (c. 34. 7). Remains of its fortifications still exist. Curtius, Pelop. II. p. 84.
8. **ἐπὶ τῇ ἡμισείᾳ τῆς γῆς**: "on the condition that they should cede half of their land" to the Eleans. Kühn. 405, 5 c. — 9. **καὶ λυσάντων**: see App. The same subj. in the main clause and in the gen. abs. occurs freq. in Thuc. See on ii. 83. 15 and iii. 13. 30. — **τὴν γῆν νεμομένοις αὐτοῖς**: the Eleans allowed the Lepreans to remain in possession of the half of their land which they had relinquished, but obliged them to pay a rent of a talent to Olympian Zeus, whose temple was under the control of the Eleans. —
10. **ἔταξαν**: τάξαι is used of the im-

τῷ Διὶ τῷ Ὀλυμπίῳ ἀποφέρειν. καὶ μέχρι τοῦ Ἀττικοῦ 3 πολέμου ἀπέφερον, ἔπειτα παυσαμένων διὰ πρόφασιν τοῦ πολέμου οἱ Ἠλεῖοι ἐπηνάγκαζον, οἱ δ' ἐτράποντο πρὸς τοὺς Λακεδαιμονίους. καὶ δίκης Λακεδαιμονίοις ἐπιτραπείσης, ὑποτοπήσαντες οἱ Ἠλεῖοι μὴ ἴσον ἕξειν, ἀνέντες τὴν ἐπιτροπὴν Λεπρεατῶν τὴν γῆν ἔτεμον. οἱ δὲ Λακε- 4 δαιμόνιοι οὐδὲν ἧσσον ἐδίκασαν αὐτονόμους εἶναι Λεπρεάτας καὶ ἀδικεῖν Ἠλείους, καὶ ὡς οὐκ ἐμμεινάντων τῇ ἐπιτροπῇ φρουρὰν ὁπλιτῶν ἐσέπεμψαν ἐς Λέπρεον. οἱ 5 δὲ Ἠλεῖοι νομίζοντες πόλιν σφῶν ἀφεστηκυῖαν δέξασθαι τοὺς Λακεδαιμονίους καὶ τὴν ξυνθήκην προφέροντες ἐν ᾗ εἴρητο, ἃ ἔχοντες ἐς τὸν Ἀττικὸν πόλεμον καθίσταντό τινες, ταῦτα ἔχοντας καὶ ἐξελθεῖν, ὡς οὐκ ἴσον ἔχοντες ἀφίστανται πρὸς τοὺς Ἀργείους, καὶ τὴν ξυμμαχίαν, ὥσπερ προείρητο, καὶ οὗτοι ἐποιήσαντο. ἐγένοντο δὲ καὶ οἱ 6 Κορίνθιοι εὐθὺς μετ' ἐκείνους καὶ οἱ ἐπὶ Θρᾴκης Χαλ-

position of tribute in i. 19. 6; iii. 50. 6.
11. τοῦ Ἀττικοῦ πολέμου: see on c. 28. 13. — 12. παυσαμένων: sc. τοῦ φόρου. — 13. ἐπηνάγκαζον: "they prepared to force them," impf. ἐπαναγκάζειν also in Plat. Prot. p. 345 e. —
14. ἐπιτραπείσης: "having been referred to the Lacedaemonians for arbitration." Cf. i. 28. 9; iv. 83. 10; vii. 18. 24. — 15. μὴ ἴσον ἕξειν: that they would not receive fair treatment at the hands of the Lacedaemonians. — ἀνέντες: shows that they had originally agreed to accept the arbitration: παυσάμενοι τοῦ ἐπιτρέψαι τὴν δίκην τοῖς Λακεδαιμονίοις, Schol. Equiv. to οὐκ ἐμμεινάντων τῇ ἐπιτροπῇ, 18.
17. οὐδὲν ἧσσον ἐδίκασαν: they gave their decision notwithstanding the refusal of the Eleans to acknowledge their jurisdiction. — 18. ἀδικεῖν: were in the wrong. — ὡς οὐκ ἐμμεινάν-

των: "because they had, as they said, refused to submit to the judgment of those whom they had previously accepted as arbitrators."
20. δέξασθαι: had taken under protection. Cf. i. 34. 2; 40. 17, 22. — 21. τὴν ξυνθήκην: this agreement between the states hostile to Athens must have been made shortly before the outbreak of the Peloponnesian war. See Grote VI. p. 290. It is not mentioned elsewhere. See App. — προφέροντες: cf. c. 17. 11. — 22. ἃ ἔχοντες, ταῦτα ἔχοντας: a quotation from the treaty, the formality of the expression being part of the official style "what any (τινες) had when they entered upon the war, that shall they have when they leave it." — 23. ὡς οὐκ ἴσον ἔχοντες: "on the ground that they had not received what was their due." — 24. ὥσπερ προείρητο: cf. καθάπερ προείρητο, 3.

κιδῆς Ἀργείων ξύμμαχοι. Βοιωτοὶ δὲ καὶ Μεγαρῆς τὸ αὐτὸ λέγοντες ἡσύχαζον περιορώμενοι [ὑπὸ τῶν Λακεδαιμονίων] καὶ νομίζοντες σφίσι τὴν Ἀργείων δημοκρα-
30 τίαν αὐτοῖς ὀλιγαρχουμένοις ἧσσον ξύμφορον εἶναι τῆς Λακεδαιμονίων πολιτείας.

32 Περὶ δὲ τοὺς αὐτοὺς χρόνους τοῦ θέρους τούτου * Σκι- 1 ωναίους μὲν Ἀθηναῖοι ἐκπολιορκήσαντες ἀπέκτειναν τοὺς ἡβῶντας, παῖδας δὲ καὶ γυναῖκας ἠνδραπόδισαν καὶ τὴν γῆν Πλαταιεῦσιν ἔδοσαν νέμεσθαι· Δηλίους δὲ κατήγα-
5 γον πάλιν ἐς Δῆλον, ἐνθυμούμενοι τάς τε ἐν ταῖς μάχαις

26. οἱ ἐπὶ Θράκης Χαλκιδῆς: their independence was most endangered by the peace (see c. 18. § 5 and § 8).
— 27. Βοιωτοὶ δὲ καὶ Μεγαρῆς: their envoys were present in Corinth at the discussions, acc. to c. 30. 11 f. and 17. 18 f. — τὸ αὐτὸ λέγοντες: τὴν αὐτὴν γνώμην ἔχοντες, Schol., and so also in iv. 20. 17, i.e. "though they were of the same mind" as the Corinthians and Chalcidians. Böhme and Jowett explain "saying the same thing," i.e. "agreeing": "the Boeotians and Megarians agreed to refuse" (Jowett).
— 28. ἡσύχαζον: equiv. to οὐκ ἐνεωτέριζον, as in ii. 3. 5; v. 22. 12, they remained quiet. — περιορώμενοι: mid. as in vi. 93. 3, μέλλοντες δ᾽ ἔτι καὶ περιορώμενοι. See on iv. 71. 7, ἀμφοτέροις ἐδόκει ἡσυχάσασι τὸ μέλλον περιιδεῖν (the aor. mid. is not in use), where the two expressions are joined as here. The sense of the passage is: "they were of the same mind as the Corinthians, but remained quiet awaiting the event and thinking," etc. See App. — 30. αὐτοῖς: them themselves. Boeotians as well as Megarians, who in the summer of 424 B.C., ἐς ὀλιγαρχίαν τὰ μάλιστα κατέστησαν τὴν πολιτείαν. Cf. iv. 74. 16. — 31. πολιτείας:

political constitution, as in i. 18. 9; ii. 37. 1.
32. The Athenians take Scione and treat the inhabitants with great severity. They restore the Delians to their island. The Corinthians and Argives try without success to induce the Tegeans to leave the alliance with Sparta. The Boeotians and Corinthians enter into ineffectual negotiations with Athens.
1. Σκιωναίους: their fate had been decided at Athens two years before at the instigation of Cleon (see iv. 122. § 6), and they had been left at the mercy of the Athenians by the Lacedaemonians in making the peace. See c. 18. § 8. — 2. ἀπέκτειναν: τῷ φόβῳ βουλόμενοι καταπλήξασθαι τοὺς ἐν ὑποψίᾳ ἀποστάσεως ὄντας παράδειγμα πᾶσιν ἀνέδειξαν τὴν ἐκ τῶν Σκιωναίων τιμωρίαν, acc. to Diod. xii. 76. But this severe measure did not have the desired effect. — 3. παῖδας ... ἠνδραπόδισαν: see App. — 4. Πλαταιεῦσιν: those who had been received in Athens before the siege of Plataea (cf. ii. 78. 10), and those who had made their escape thither by a successful sally (cf. iii. 24. § 3). — κατήγαγον πάλιν: cf. c. 1. — 5. ἐνθυμούμενοι: here equiv. to ἐνθύμιον ποιούμενοι. Cf.

ξυμφορὰς καὶ τοῦ ἐν Δελφοῖς θεοῦ χρήσαντος. καὶ Φωκῆς 2
καὶ Λοκροὶ ἤρξαντο πολεμεῖν. καὶ Κορίνθιοι καὶ Ἀρ- 3
γεῖοι ἤδη ξύμμαχοι ὄντες ἔρχονται ἐς Τεγέαν, ἀποστή-
σοντες Λακεδαιμονίων, ὁρῶντες μέγα μέρος ὄν, καὶ εἰ
σφίσι προσγένοιτο, νομίζοντες ἅπασαν ἂν ἔχειν Πελοπόννησον. ὡς δὲ οὐδὲν ἂν ἔφασαν ἐναντιωθῆναι οἱ Τεγεᾶται 4
Λακεδαιμονίοις, οἱ Κορίνθιοι μέχρι τούτου προθύμως
πράσσοντες ἀνεῖσαν τῆς φιλονικίας καὶ ὠρρώδησαν μὴ
οὐδεὶς σφίσιν ἔτι τῶν ἄλλων προσχωρῇ. ὅμως δὲ ἐλ- 5
θόντες ἐς τοὺς Βοιωτοὺς ἐδέοντο σφῶν τε καὶ Ἀργείων
γίγνεσθαι ξυμμάχους καὶ τἆλλα κοινῇ πράσσειν· τάς τε
δεχημέρους ἐπισπονδάς, αἳ ἦσαν Ἀθηναίοις καὶ Βοιωτοῖς
πρὸς ἀλλήλους οὐ πολλῷ ὕστερον γενόμεναι [τούτων] τῶν

vii. 50. 29; c. 16. 18. "Since they took their mishaps (at Delium and Amphipolis) to heart," seeing in them a proof of the divine wrath. — τάς τε: much as in c. 28. 7 after ὁρῶντες, we should here after τάς τε ... ξυμφοράς expect a second obj. of ἐνθυμούμενοι, instead of which we find the gen. abs. καὶ τοῦ ... χρήσαντος. Kühn. 417, 5, N. 9. Still a change of the reading in either passage is unadvisable (Cobet, Mnem. 14, p. 9, proposes τε τάς).
— 6. χρήσαντος: the restoration of the Delians was, then, commanded by the god.
καὶ Φωκῆς κτέ.: this isolated statement is all the notice that is taken of this war. See Introd. p. 2.
8. Τεγέαν: Bekker and others accent Τέγεαν wrongly, as the Ion. form is Τεγέη. Göttling, Doctr. Accent., p. 128. This town and its territory on the border of Laconia always maintained an independent position in Arcadia as well against Spartan plans of conquest as in this instance against

the anti-Spartan alliance of the Corinthians and Argives. Curtius, Pelopon. I. p. 152. — 9. μέγα μέρος: (as in ii. 20. 10 of Acharnae) "a place of importance"; perhaps implying that its adherence would throw the balance of power upon one side or the other. — 10. ἅπασαν ἂν ἔχειν Πελοπόννησον: equiv. to c. 28. 9 f., τῆς Πελοποννήσου ἡγήσεσθαι.
12. προθύμως πράσσοντες: "who had hitherto been zealous" in carrying out the plan of c. 27. § 2. — 13. ἀνεῖσαν: with gen. as in vii. 43. 45, ἀνέντων τῆς ἐφόδου. G. 174; II. 748.—
14. μὴ οὐδείς ... προσχωρῇ: they relinquished their hopes as quickly as they had (c. 27. § 2) accepted and expressed them.
17. ἐπισπονδάς: this word, which does not occur elsewhere, is formed like ἐπισπένδεσθαι (renew a treaty, c. 22. 9), and is adapted to express the nature of these constantly renewed truces. See on c. 26. 14. — 18. [τούτων] τῶν πεντηκοντουτίδων: see App.

πεντηκοντουτίδων σπονδῶν, ἐκέλευον οἱ Κορίνθιοι τοὺς
Βοιωτοὺς ἀκολουθήσαντας Ἀθήναζε καὶ σφίσι ποιῆσαι,
ὥσπερ Βοιωτοὶ εἶχον, μὴ δεχομένων δὲ Ἀθηναίων ἀπειπεῖν
τὴν ἐκεχειρίαν καὶ τὸ λοιπὸν μὴ σπένδεσθαι ἄνευ
αὐτῶν. Βοιωτοὶ δὲ δεομένων τῶν Κορινθίων περὶ μὲν 6
τῆς Ἀργείων ξυμμαχίας ἐπισχεῖν αὐτοὺς ἐκέλευον, ἐλθόντες
δὲ Ἀθήναζε μετὰ Κορινθίων οὐχ ηὕροντο τὰς δεχημέρους
σπονδάς, ἀλλ' ἀπεκρίναντο οἱ Ἀθηναῖοι Κορινθίοις
εἶναι σπονδάς, εἴπερ Λακεδαιμονίων εἰσὶ ξύμμαχοι.
Βοιωτοὶ μὲν οὖν οὐδὲν μᾶλλον ἀπεῖπον τὰς δεχημέρους, 7
ἀξιούντων καὶ αἰτιωμένων Κορινθίων ξυνθέσθαι σφίσι·
Κορινθίοις δὲ ἀνοκωχὴ ἄσπονδος ἦν πρὸς Ἀθηναίους.

33 Λακεδαιμόνιοι δὲ τοῦ αὐτοῦ θέρους πανδημεὶ ἐστράτευσαν, 1
Πλειστοάνακτος τοῦ Παυσανίου Λακεδαιμονίων
βασιλέως ἡγουμένου, τῆς Ἀρκαδίας ἐς Παρρασίους,
Μαντινέων ὑπηκόους ὄντας, κατὰ στάσιν ἐπικαλεσαμένων
σφᾶς, ἅμα δὲ καὶ τὸ ἐν Κυψέλοις τεῖχος ἀναιρήσοντες,

— 20. καὶ σφίσι ποιῆσαι: *procure for them also* from the Athenians. — 21. ὥσπερ Βοιωτοὶ εἶχον: see App. — 22. μὴ σπένδεσθαι: sc. τοῖς Ἀθηναίοις. 24. ἐπισχεῖν: *wait a while, have patience*. Cf. viii. 5. 11. — 25. οὐχ ηὕροντο: *did not succeed in obtaining*. Cf. i. 31. 10, ὠφελίαν τινὰ πειρᾶσθαι ἀπ' αὐτῶν εὑρίσκεσθαι, and i. 58. 6. Lat. non impetraverunt.
29. ἀξιούντων: sc. ἀπειπεῖν. ξυνθέσθαι σφίσι depends upon αἰτιωμένων (not, as Kr. thinks, upon ἀξιούντων): "although the Corinthians demanded that they give up their agreement with Athens, and accused them (the Boeotians) of having agreed with them (the Corinthians) to do so if the Athenians did not accede to their request." The Corinthians had asked the Boeotians to do this (22), and believed, apparently, that they had agreed. — 30. ἀνοκωχὴ ἄσπονδος: opp. to the δεχήμεροι σπονδαί; an actual *cessation of hostilities*, but *without any guarantee*.

33. The first hostile acts of the Lacedaemonians against the Mantineans in consequence of their alliance with the Argives.

3. τῆς Ἀρκαδίας: stands first as in iii. 19. 6, τῆς Καρίας, and freq. — Παρρασίους: an old Pelasgic tribe the capital of which, Parrhasia, is mentioned in Il. B 608. They dwelt at the base of Mt. Lycaeum toward the southeast. See Curtius, *Pelop.* I. p. 279; Bursian, II. p. 225 and 235. — 4. ἐπικαλεσαμένων: τῶν Παρρασίων, Schol. On the gen., see GMT. 110, 1. N. 5; II. 972 d. — 5. σφᾶς: τοὺς Λακεδαιμονίους, Schol. — τὸ ἐν Κυψέλοις

ἢν δύνωνται, ὃ ἐτείχισαν Μαντινῆς καὶ αὐτοὶ ἐφρούρουν, ἐν τῇ Παρρασικῇ κείμενον ἐπὶ τῇ Σκιρίτιδι τῆς Λακωνικῆς. καὶ οἱ μὲν Λακεδαιμόνιοι τὴν γῆν τῶν Παρρασίων ἐδῄουν, οἱ δὲ Μαντινῆς τὴν πόλιν Ἀργείοις φύλαξι παραδόντες αὐτοὶ τὴν ξυμμαχίαν ἐφρούρουν· ἀδύνατοι δ' ὄντες διασῶσαι τό τε ἐν Κυψέλοις τεῖχος καὶ τὰς ἐν Παρρασίοις πόλεις ἀπῆλθον. Λακεδαιμόνιοι δὲ τούς τε Παρρασίους αὐτονόμους ποιήσαντες καὶ τὸ τεῖχος καθελόντες ἀνεχώρησαν ἐπ' οἴκου.

34 * Καὶ τοῦ αὐτοῦ θέρους, ἤδη ἡκόντων αὐτοῖς τῶν ἀπὸ Θρᾴκης μετὰ Βρασίδου ἐξελθόντων στρατιωτῶν, οὓς ὁ Κλεαρίδας μετὰ τὰς σπονδὰς ἐκόμισεν, οἱ Λακεδαιμόνιοι ἐψηφίσαντο τοὺς μὲν μετὰ Βρασίδου Εἵλωτας μαχεσαμένους ἐλευθέρους εἶναι καὶ οἰκεῖν ὅπου ἂν βούλωνται· καὶ

τεῖχος: its exact position is now unknown. Curtius, *Pelop.* I. p. 340; Bursian, II. p. 243. — ἀναιρήσοντες: *cf.* c. 77. 5, καὶ τὸ τεῖχος ἀναιροῦντας; viii. 24. 7. Therefore not to be changed (with Meineke) to καθαιρήσοντες. — 7. τῇ Σκιρίτιδι: the mountainous region between the upper Eurotas and the valley of the Oenus, one of the most important districts inhabited by Laconian periocci. See Curtius, *Pelop.* II. p. 263. ἐπὶ τῇ Σκιρίτιδι, i.e. threatening the border. *Cf.* c. 51. 4; iii. 16. 4, τὸ ἐπὶ Λέσβῳ ναυτικόν; iv. 14. 20, ἔμενον ἐπὶ τῇ Πύλῳ. 9. τὴν πόλιν: i.e. their own city, Mantinea. — 10. τὴν ξυμμαχίαν: the region under their supremacy and protection. *Cf.* iv. 118. 17 and 27; viii. 44. 5; ἣν ὑπήκοον κατεστρέψαντο, c. 29. 4. — 11. τὰς ἐν Παρρασίοις πόλεις: the names of none of these can be given with certainty. Curtius, *Pelop.* I. p. 340; Bursian, II. p. 241.

34. *Measures adopted by the Lace-*daemonians to confer honours upon the troops which had taken part in Brasidas's expedition to Thrace, and to render those citizens who had returned from captivity incapable of causing trouble to the state.

1. τῶν ἀπὸ Θρᾴκης: the use of ἀπό is occasioned by ἡκόντων. It is here ambiguous on account of ἐξελθόντων. τῶν ἀπὸ Θρᾴκης μετὰ Βρασίδου ἐξελθόντων seems to imply that Brasidas returned from Thrace, so that Kr.'s suggestion to read τῶν μετὰ Βρασίδου is not without reason. — 2. ἐξελθόντων: *cf.* iv. 78. § 1, and 80. § 5. — 3. ἐκόμισεν: *brought home*, in accordance with the command received in c. 21. 15 ff. κομίζειν is used in the same sense in iv. 16. 19, ἀποστεῖλαι δὲ αὐτοὺς τριήρει Ἀθηναίους καὶ πάλιν κομίσαι, but with πάλιν. — 4. μαχεσαμένους: placed after its subst. acc. to the usage discussed on i. 11. 18. — 5. οἰκεῖν ὅπου ἂν βούλωνται: i.e. no longer as serfs glebae ad-

ὕστερον οὐ πολλῷ αὐτοὺς μετὰ τῶν νεοδαμώδων ἐς Λέπρεον κατέστησαν, κείμενον ἐπὶ τῆς Λακωνικῆς καὶ τῆς 2 Ἠλείας, ὄντες ἤδη διάφοροι Ἠλείοις· τοὺς δ' ἐκ τῆς νήσου ληφθέντας σφῶν καὶ τὰ ὅπλα παραδόντας, δεί10 σαντες μή τι διὰ τὴν ξυμφορὰν νομίσαντες ἐλασσωθήσεσθαι καὶ ὄντες ἐπίτιμοι νεωτερίσωσιν, ἤδη καὶ ἀρχάς τινας ἔχοντας ἀτίμους ἐποίησαν, ἀτιμίαν δὲ τοιάνδε ὥστε μήτε ἄρχειν μήτε πριαμένους τι ἢ πωλοῦντας κυρίους εἶναι. ὕστερον δὲ αὖθις χρόνῳ ἐπίτιμοι ἐγένοντο.
35 Τοῦ δ' αὐτοῦ θέρους καὶ Θυσσὸν τὴν ἐν τῇ Ἄθῳ 1 Ἀκτῇ Διῆς εἷλον, Ἀθηναίων οὖσαν ξύμμαχον.

scripti. This is one of the first requisites of ἐλευθερία. — **6. τῶν νεοδαμώδων**: a class of new citizens composed of liberated Helots, though they seem to be distinct from the Helots who have just received their freedom. They are mentioned here for the first time, then freq. in Thuc. (vii. 19. 16; 58. 12; viii. 5. 7) and Xen., but not afterwards. See Schömann, *Antiq. of Greece*, I. p. 198 ff.; Gilbert, *Griech. Staatsalt.* I. p. 35 f. The accent acc. to Hdn. i. p. 428, 13. See v. Bamberg, Ztschr. f. d. Gymn.-Wesen, 28, p. 7. — **6. ἐς Λέπρεον**: see c. 31. § 1 and § 2.
8. ὄντες ἤδη διάφοροι: with reference to c. 3:. 5, διαφερόμενοι γὰρ ἐτύγχανον. — **9. ληφθέντας, καὶ τὰ ὅπλα παραδόντας**: the ultimate result stands first. *Cf.* iv. 38. § 3 f. — **10. διὰ τὴν ξυνφορὰν νομίσαντες**: the Spartans were afraid that these men who had returned from captivity would fear lest their misfortune might be regarded as their fault and cause them to be less respected (ἐλασσωθήσεσθαι here in the form of the fut. pass. as in Dem. xxiv. 66, while in c. 104. 4 and 105. 12, the mid. form ἐλασσώσεσθαι is used), and that they would therefore endeavour to change the constitution of the state (νεωτερίσωσι) if they remained in the exercise of all their rights as citizens (καὶ ὄντες ἔντιμοι). To prevent this, ἀτίμους ἐποίησαν, they took from them for a time the most important rights of citizenship, making them incapable of holding office and of conducting business transactions. — **11. ἤδη καὶ ἀρχάς τινας ἔχοντας**: this adds to the whole obj. τοὺς ... παραδόντας a special part as appos. in the same case. See on c. 3. 23; ii. 95. 4; iii. 13. 17. It is not remarkable that they already held offices, ἦσαν γὰρ οἱ Σπαρτιᾶται αὐτῶν πρῶτοι κτέ. *Cf.* c. 15. 4. On ἀτιμία and its degrees, esp. in Athens, but also in other Greek states, see Hermann, *Griech. Staatsalt.* § 124, 6; Schömann *Antiq. of Greece*, 1. p. 360 f.
35. *The summer passed while the Athenians and the Lacedaemonians were vainly endeavouring to obtain from one another the fulfilment of the conditions of the treaty.*
1. Θυσσόν: for the accent, see on iv. 109. 9. — ἐν τῇ Ἄθῳ Ἀκτῇ Διῆς: see App. — **2. Ἀθηναιων οὖσαν ξύμμα-**

Καὶ τὸ θέρος τοῦτο πᾶν ἐπιμιξίαι μὲν ἦσαν τοῖς Ἀθη- 2
ναίοις καὶ Πελοποννησίοις, ὑπώπτευον δὲ ἀλλήλους εὐθὺς
μετὰ τὰς σπονδὰς οἵ τε Ἀθηναῖοι καὶ οἱ Λακεδαιμόνιοι κατὰ
τὴν τῶν χωρίων ἀλλήλοις οὐκ ἀπόδοσιν. τὴν γὰρ Ἀμφίπολιν 3
πρότεροι λαχόντες οἱ Λακεδαιμόνιοι ἀποδιδόναι καὶ τὰ
ἄλλα οὐκ ἀποδεδώκεσαν, οὐδὲ τοὺς ἐπὶ Θρᾴκης παρεῖχον
ξυμμάχους τὰς σπονδὰς δεχομένους οὐδὲ Βοιωτοὺς οὐδὲ
Κορινθίους, λέγοντες ἀεὶ ὡς μετ' Ἀθηναίων τούτους, ἢν
μὴ θέλωσι, κοινῇ ἀναγκάσουσι, χρόνους τε προύθεντο
ἄνευ ξυγγραφῆς ἐν οἷς χρῆν τοὺς μὴ ἐσιόντας ἀμφοτέροις
πολεμίους εἶναι. τούτων οὖν ὁρῶντες οἱ Ἀθηναῖοι οὐδὲν 4
ἔργῳ γιγνόμενον, ὑπώπτευον τοὺς Λακεδαιμονίους μηδὲν
δίκαιον διανοεῖσθαι, ὥστε οὔτε Πύλον ἀπαιτούντων αὐτῶν ἀπεδίδοσαν, ἀλλὰ καὶ τοὺς ἐκ τῆς νήσου δεσμώτας
μετεμέλοντο ἀποδεδωκότες, τά τε ἄλλα χωρία εἶχον, μέ-
νοντες ἕως σφίσι κἀκεῖνοι ποιήσειαν τὰ εἰρημένα. Λακε- 5

χον: since the Dians also, acc. to c. 82. 1, belonged to the Athenian alliance, their attack upon an allied town is incomprehensible. Steup. *Stud.* I. p. 34, therefore regards these words as an interpolation. But in several places in this book where events are briefly mentioned, the connexion is not made clear. See Introd. p. 2.

3. ἐπιμιξίαι: used of friendly intercourse, like the related verbal forms ἐπιμιγνύναι and ἐπιμίγνυσθαι. See on i. 2. 5. — 6. τὴν οὐκ ἀπόδοσιν: see on i. 137. 29. ἀλλήλοις depends upon the verbal force of ἀπόδοσιν. See on i. 63. 9; 73. 1; iii. 66. 17. G. 185; H. 765 a.

7. πρότεροι λαχόντες: cf. c. 21. 1.—8. ἀποδεδώκεσαν: so the Mss. St. writes the plpf. everywhere with syllabic aug. See Stahl, *Quaest. Graec.* p. 17.—οὐδὲ παρεῖχον δεχομένους: the partic.

const. with παρέχειν after the analogy of adjs. *Cf.* ii. 84. 20, ἀπειθεστέρας (τὰς ναῦς); iii. 12. 6, ἐχυρόν; iv. 67. 31, βεβαίους (τὰς πύλας). — 10. λέγοντες ἀεί: *although they constantly assured them*. — 11. προύθεντο: the composition is the same as that of προθεσμία, *fore-appointed time*. — 12. ξυγγραφῆς: *written agreement;* συμφωνία γεγραμμένη, Schol. — τοὺς μὴ ἐσιόντας: with this ἐς τὰς σπονδάς (*cf.* c. 30. 20) is to be supplied from the preceding τὰς σπονδὰς δεχομένους (but not, with Meineke, to be received into the text).

13. οὐδὲν ἔργῳ γιγνόμενον: in spite of the ἀεὶ λέγειν. — 14. ὑπώπτευον: here and in viii. 76. 6 for Mss. ὑπετόπευον. See on i. 20. 9. — 15. ἀπαιτούντων: this (pres.) and ἀπεδίδοσαν (impf.) imply repeated negotiations. — 17. μετεμέλοντο ἀποδεδωκότες: see

δαιμόνιοι δὲ τὰ μὲν δυνατὰ ἔφασαν πεποιηκέναι· τοὺς
20 γὰρ παρὰ σφίσι δεσμώτας ὄντας Ἀθηναίων ἀποδοῦναι
καὶ τοὺς ἐπὶ Θρᾴκης στρατιώτας ἀπαγαγεῖν καὶ εἴ του
ἄλλου ἐγκρατεῖς ἦσαν· Ἀμφιπόλεως δὲ οὐκ ἔφασαν κρατεῖν ὥστε παραδοῦναι, Βοιωτοὺς δὲ πειράσεσθαι καὶ Κορινθίους ἐς τὰς σπονδὰς ἐσαγαγεῖν καὶ Πάνακτον ἀπο-
25 λαβεῖν, καὶ Ἀθηναίων ὅσοι ἦσαν ἐν Βοιωτοῖς αἰχμάλωτοι
κομιεῖν. Πύλον μέντοι ἠξίουν σφίσιν ἀποδοῦναι· εἰ δὲ 6
μή, Μεσσηνίους τε καὶ τοὺς Εἵλωτας ἐξαγαγεῖν, ὥσπερ
καὶ αὐτοὶ ἀπὸ Θρᾴκης, Ἀθηναίους δὲ φρουρεῖν τὸ χωρίον
αὐτούς, εἰ βούλονται. πολλάκις δὲ καὶ πολλῶν λόγων 7
30 γενομένων ἐν τῷ θέρει τούτῳ ἔπεισαν τοὺς Ἀθηναίους
ὥστε ἐξαγαγεῖν ἐκ Πύλου Μεσσηνίους καὶ τοὺς ἄλλους
[Εἵλωτάς τε καὶ] ὅσοι ηὐτομολήκεσαν ἐκ τῆς Λακωνι-
κῆς· καὶ κατῴκισαν αὐτοὺς ἐν Κρανίοις τῆς Κεφαλλη-
νίας. τὸ μὲν οὖν θέρος τοῦτο ἡσυχία ἦν καὶ ἔφοδοι παρ' 8
35 ἀλλήλους.

on c. 14. 10.—18. ποιήσειαν: for the form, see on iii. 49. 10. Stahl, *Quaest. Graec.* p. 18. On the mood, see GMT. 77, 1 d; H. 937 a.
21. τοὺς ἐπὶ Θρᾴκης στρατιώτας: as in c. 67. 4.—καὶ εἴ του ἄλλου (neut. not masc.) ἐκρατεῖς ἦσαν: in a perfectly general sense: *and whatever else they had been able;* and accordingly a general expression like ποιῆσαι, not ἀποδοῦναι or ἀπαγαγεῖν is to be supplied. *Cf.* 19, τὰ μὲν δυνατὰ ἔφασαν πεποιηκέναι.—23. ὥστε: see on c. 14. 1.—24. ἀπολαβεῖν: *cf.* c. 30. 15.—26. κομιεῖν: depends upon ἔφασαν, not upon πειράσεσθαι: *they said they would attend to the restoration of the captives.*
27. Μεσσηνίους τε καὶ τοὺς Εἵλωτας: several editt. following Reiske have adopted γε for τε. But since, acc. to iv. 41. § 2, the Messenians had been expressly transferred to Pylos from Naupactus, whereas the Helots had simply run away thither, the separation by means of τε, καί seems very appropriate.
30. ἔπεισαν ὥστε: *cf.* c. 16. 23.—31. καὶ τοὺς ἄλλους [Εἵλωτάς τε καὶ] ὅσοι: see App.—33. κατῴκισαν: elsewhere const. with ἐς. See on i. 103. 9.—ἐν Κρανίοις: from nom. Κράνιοι acc. to Steph. Byz. *s.v.* Κράνιοι πόλις ἐν Κεφαλληνίᾳ, τὸ ἐθνικὸν Κρανιεῖς. (Bursian, *Geogr. v. Griech.* II. p. 373, calls the town Krane; Jowett, Cranii.) The Athenians had been in possession of Cephallenia since the first year of the war. See ii. 30. § 2 (where Κράνιοι seems to be used as ἐθνικόν).
34. ἔφοδοι: equiv. to ἐπιμιξίαι, 3. *Cf.* i. 6. 2, διὰ τὰς οὐκ ἀσφαλεῖς παρ' ἀλλήλους ἐφόδους.

36 * Τοῦ δ' ἐπιγιγνομένου χειμῶνος (ἔτυχον γὰρ ἔφοροι 1
ἕτεροι, καὶ οὐκ ἐφ' ὧν αἱ σπονδαὶ ἐγένοντο, ἄρχοντες ἤδη,
καί τινες αὐτῶν καὶ ἐναντίοι σπονδαῖς) ἐλθουσῶν
πρεσβειῶν ἀπὸ τῆς ξυμμαχίδος καὶ παρόντων Ἀθηναίων
5 καὶ Βοιωτῶν καὶ Κορινθίων καὶ πολλὰ ἐν ἀλλήλοις εἰπόντων καὶ οὐδὲν ξυμβάντων, ὡς ἀπῇσαν ἐπ' οἴκου,
τοῖς Βοιωτοῖς καὶ Κορινθίοις Κλεόβουλος καὶ Ξενάρης,
οὗτοι οἵπερ τῶν ἐφόρων ἐβούλοντο μάλιστα διαλῦσαι τὰς
σπονδάς, λόγους ποιοῦνται ἰδίους, παραινοῦντες ὅτι μά-
10 λιστα ταὐτά γε γιγνώσκειν καὶ πειρᾶσθαι Βοιωτούς, Ἀργείων γενομένους πρῶτον αὐτοὺς ξυμμάχους, αὖθις μετὰ
Βοιωτῶν Ἀργείους Λακεδαιμονίοις ποιῆσαι ξυμμάχους·

36. *Endeavours of the Lacedaemonian war party to induce the Boeotians to join the Argive alliance, in order that through their instrumentality an alliance between Argos and Sparta may be brought about.*

1. ἔφοροι ἕτεροι: the annual change of the five ephors took place at the autumnal equinox, the beginning of the Lacedaemonian year. See Hermann, *Griech. Staatsalt.* § 45, 3. — **2.** ἄρχοντες ἤδη: const. with ἔτυχον. — **3.** σπονδαῖς: see App. — **4.** τῆς ξυμμαχίδος: i.e. the allied states, as in i. 110. 10, ἐκ δὲ τῶν Ἀθηνῶν καὶ τῆς ἄλλης ξυμμαχίδος. Of the whole body of allies the three most important are esp. mentioned; the Athenians as new allies, the Boeotians and Corinthians as members of the old alliance, though not participators in the peace with Athens. — **6.** ὡς ἀπῇσαν: *as they were on the point of departing.* — **7.** Ξενάρης: see App. — **9.** ἰδίους: is not as common as ἰδίᾳ, but is not (with v. Herwerden) to be emended. *Cf.* c. 39. 10; viii. 9. 5. — **10.** ταὐτά: adopted by Poppo and subsequent editt. for ταῦτα of the Mss. — ταὐτὰ γιγνώσκειν: *agree, adopt the same policy.* — These negotiations with the Boeotians and Corinthians, have for their first object to induce the Boeotians to accept the proposal made them in c. 32. § 5, 6 (*i.e.* to join the Argive alliance as the Corinthians had done), in regard to which they had asked for time to consider (ἐπισχεῖν). Taking it for granted that the Boeotians will now agree to the proposal of the Corinthians, the two ephors address the second part of their proposition (τε καί shows this division into two heads) to the Boeotians alone, πειρᾶσθαι Βοιωτούς κτέ. The great importance of the part the Boeotians have to play occasions the unusual repetition of the subst. μετὰ Βοιωτῶν, instead of the pron. μεθ' ἑαυτῶν. We must connect Βοιωτῶν closely in thought with ξυμμάχους. If the Boeotians were once allies of the Argives, then it would be possible to bring about an alliance between Sparta and Argos. The repetition of ξυμμάχους increases the emphasis laid upon this

οὕτω γὰρ ἥκιστ᾽ ἂν ἀναγκασθῆναι Βοιωτοὺς ἐς τὰς Ἀττικὰς σπονδὰς ἐσελθεῖν· ἑλέσθαι γὰρ Λακεδαιμονίους πρὸ τῆς Ἀθηναίων ἔχθρας καὶ διαλύσεως τῶν σπονδῶν Ἀργείους σφίσι φίλους καὶ ξυμμάχους γενέσθαι. τὸ γὰρ Ἄργος ἀεὶ ἠπίσταντο ἐπιθυμοῦντας τοὺς Λακεδαιμονίους καλῶς σφίσι φίλιον γενέσθαι, ἡγουμένους τὸν ἔξω Πελοποννήσου πόλεμον ῥᾴω ἂν εἶναι. τὸ μέντοι Πάνακτον 2 ἐδέοντο Βοιωτοὺς ὅπως παραδώσουσι Λακεδαιμονίοις, ἵνα ἀντ᾽ αὐτοῦ Πύλον, ἢν δύνωνται, ἀπολαβόντες ῥᾷον καθιστῶνται Ἀθηναίοις ἐς πόλεμον. καὶ οἱ μὲν Βοιω- 1 τοὶ καὶ Κορίνθιοι ταῦτα ἐπεσταλμένοι ἀπό τε τοῦ Ξενάρους καὶ Κλεοβούλου καὶ ὅσοι φίλοι ἦσαν αὐτοῖς τῶν

idea. See App. — 11. αὖθις: after πρῶτον as in c. 76. 9. — 13. οὕτω γὰρ ἥκιστ᾽ ἂν ἀναγκασθῆναι κτέ.: the argument likely to persuade the Boeotians is stated first, viz. that the possibility (referred to in c. 35. 11) that the Lacedaemonians and Athenians together would force the Boeotians to accept the peace, would disappear. Then in 14, in the words ἑλέσθαι γὰρ (ἂν) Λακεδαιμονίους κτέ. the interest which the Lacedaemonians would have in an alliance with Argos is set forth. See App. — 14. ἑλέσθαι: choose, be glad. Here πρό is not equiv. to ἀντί (cf. iv. 20. 6) but temporal (as may be the case in iii. 59. 21, ἑλοίμεθα ἂν πρό γε τούτου λιμῷ τελευτῆσαι, "before we do that we would starve to death"): "the Lacedaemonians would prefer that the Argives (Ἀργείους first for emphasis) should join them in friendship and alliance before they declared their hostility to the Athenians and put an end to the peace," which they would probably do before long, since their friendly relations had been disturbed

εὐθὺς μετὰ τὰς σπονδάς, c. 35. 2. This is then further explained in 16, τὸ γὰρ Ἄργος ... ῥᾴω ἂν εἶναι, "the Boeotians knew that the Lacedaemonians wished all along to be on good terms with Argos, because then their rear would not be exposed in case of a war outside of Peloponnesus," i.e. with Athens. See App. — 18. καλῶς: rightly explained by St.: opportune; "under favourable circumstances," "if they had a good opportunity." Cf. i. 124. 1; v. 65. 24. — ἡγουμένους: the statement is evidently to be made of the Lacedaemonians. See App.
20. ἐδέοντο κτέ.: see App. — 21. ῥᾷον: in the same sense as in 19, with greater safity.
37. Similar proposals are made by influential Argives. Negotiations are begun between the Boeotians and the Argives.
2. ταῦτα ἐπεσταλμένοι: ἐπιστέλλειν in pass., const. like ἐπιτρέπειν in i. 126. 33. G. 197, N. 2; H. 819 b. With this, ἀπό, not ὑπό, acc. to the usage established by Herbst, gegen Cobet, p. 50 f. Cf. i. 141. 6; iii. 36. 24; 82. 41.

Λακεδαιμονίων ὥστε ἀπαγγεῖλαι ἐπὶ τὰ κοινά, ἑκάτεροι ἀνεχώρουν. Ἀργείων δὲ δύο ἄνδρες τῆς ἀρχῆς τῆς μεγίστης ἐπετήρουν ἀπιόντας αὐτοὺς καθ' ὁδὸν καὶ ξυγγενόμενοι ἐς λόγους ἦλθον, εἴ πως οἱ Βοιωτοὶ σφίσι ξύμμαχοι γένοιντο, ὥσπερ Κορίνθιοι καὶ Ἠλεῖοι καὶ Μαντινῆς· νομίζειν γὰρ ἂν τούτου προχωρήσαντος ῥᾳδίως ἤδη καὶ πολεμεῖν καὶ σπένδεσθαι, καὶ πρὸς Λακεδαιμονίους, εἰ βούλοιντο, κοινῷ λόγῳ χρωμένους, καὶ εἴ τινα πρὸς ἄλλον δέοι. τοῖς δὲ τῶν Βοιωτῶν πρέσβεσιν ἀκούουσιν ἤρεσκε· κατὰ τύχην γὰρ ἐδέοντο τούτων ὧνπερ καὶ οἱ ἐκ τῆς Λακεδαίμονος αὐτοῖς φίλοι ἐπεστάλκεσαν. καὶ οἱ τῶν Ἀργείων ἄνδρες ὡς ᾔσθοντο αὐτοὺς δεχομένους τὸν λόγον, εἰπόντες ὅτι πρέσβεις πέμψουσιν ἐς Βοιωτοὺς ἀπῆλθον. ἀφικόμενοι δὲ οἱ Βοιωτοὶ ἀπήγγειλαν τοῖς

— **4.** ὥστε: with ἐπιστέλλειν, as in c. 16. 23 with πείθειν. — ἐπὶ τὰ κοινά: pl. of κοινόν. *Cf.* i. 89. 14; 90. 29; ii. 12. 6. The most important legislative body is meant. Here pl. because both Thebes and Corinth are referred to.
5. τῆς ἀρχῆς τῆς μεγίστης: prob. the ἀρτῦναι mentioned in c. 47. 53, though it may be that the strategi are intended. See Gilbert, *Griech. Staatsalt.* II. p. 79, note 2. — **6.** ἀπιόντας: *sc.* ἐπ' οἴκου. *Cf.* c. 36. 6. — καθ' ὁδόν: *i.e.* on the way home through Argive territory. — **8.** γένοιντο: the opt. depends upon the notion of indir. disc. implied in ἐς λόγους ἦλθον. GMT. 77, 1 c; 53, N. 2; H. 937. — ὥσπερ Κορίνθιοι: *cf.* c. 31. 26. — Ἠλεῖοι: *cf.* c. 31. 20. — Μαντινῆς: *cf.* c. 29. 1. — **10.** καὶ πολεμεῖν καὶ σπένδεσθαι, καὶ πρὸς Λακεδαιμονίους καὶ εἴ τινα πρὸς ἄλλον δέοι: two pairs of alternatives. The first concerns the fact (peace or war), the second the persons (Lacedaemonians or anybody else). εἴ τις is equiv. to ὅστισοῦν (*cf.* i. 14. 11; iv. 26. 16), and cannot be separated, which accounts for the peculiar position of the prep. πρός. — **11.** κοινῷ λόγῳ χρωμένους: is the consequence arising from τούτου προχωρήσαντος: "if the Argives, Boeotians, Corinthians, Eleans, and Mantineans pursued a joint policy." The subj. of νομίζειν is still the two Argives, but when we come to the dependent infs. πολεμεῖν καὶ σπένδεσθαι (with ἂν) introduced by τούτου προχωρήσαντος the subj. embraces the whole body of allies. — εἰ δέοι: *if circumstances demanded it.*
13. ἐδέοντο: *sc.* the two Argives. — ὧνπερ: const. with ἐπεστάλκεσαν. Gen. by assimilation for ἅπερ. See on i. 1. 12; iv. 20. 4. G. 153; H. 994. For τούτων, Schütz and Naber, Mnem. 14, p. 319, prefer τῶν αὐτῶν. — οἱ ... φίλοι: οἱ περὶ τὸν Κλεόβουλον δηλονότι, Schol. — **15.** δεχομένους τὸν λόγον: almost like an adj., *inclined to accept the proposal. Cf.* c. 35. 9.
17. ἀφικόμενοι: *sc.* at Thebes. — τοῖς Βοιωτάρχαις: see on iv. 91. 4.

βοιωτάρχαις τά τε ἐκ τῆς Λακεδαίμονος καὶ τὰ ἀπὸ τῶν ξυγγενομένων Ἀργείων· καὶ οἱ βοιωτάρχαι ἠρέσκοντό τε
20 καὶ πολλῷ προθυμότεροι ἦσαν, ὅτι ἀμφοτέρωθεν ξυνεβεβήκει αὐτοῖς τούς τε φίλους τῶν Λακεδαιμονίων τῶν αὐτῶν δεῖσθαι καὶ τοὺς Ἀργείους ἐς τὰ ὁμοῖα σπεύδειν. καὶ οὐ πολλῷ ὕστερον πρέσβεις παρῆσαν Ἀργείων τὰ εἰρη- 5 μένα προκαλούμενοι· καὶ αὐτοὺς ἀπέπεμψαν ἐπαινέσαντες
25 τοὺς λόγους οἱ βοιωτάρχαι καὶ πρέσβεις ὑποσχόμενοι ἀποστελεῖν περὶ τῆς ξυμμαχίας ἐς Ἄργος.

38 Ἐν δὲ τούτῳ ἐδόκει πρῶτον τοῖς βοιωτάρχαις καὶ 1 Κορινθίοις καὶ Μεγαρεῦσιν καὶ τοῖς ἀπὸ Θρᾴκης πρέσβεσιν ὀμόσαι ὅρκους ἀλλήλοις ἦ μὴν ἔν τε τῷ παρατυχόντι ἀμυνεῖν τῷ δεομένῳ καὶ μὴ πολεμήσειν τῳ μηδὲ ξυμβή-
5 σεσθαι ἄνευ κοινῆς γνώμης, καὶ οὕτως ἤδη τοὺς Βοιωτοὺς καὶ Μεγαρέας (τὸ γὰρ αὐτὸ ἐποίουν) πρὸς τοὺς Ἀρ-

The Boeotarchs were the chief magistrates of the Boeotian confederacy. At this time they seem to have been eleven in number. Later they were only seven. See Boeckh, *Corp. Insc. Gr.* I. 729. Hermann, *Griech. Staatsalt.* § 179, 10. Gilbert, *Griech. Staatsalt.* II. p. 54 f. — **19. ἠρέσκοντο**: see on c. 4. 11. — **20. ξυνεβεβήκει**: see on c. 10. 33. — **21. τῶν Λακεδαιμονίων**: part. gen. as in 3. — **τῶν αὐτῶν**: depends upon δεῖσθαι, *wanted the same things*, i.e. had the same needs and desires as themselves. G. 172, 1; H. 743. — **22. ἐς τὰ ὁμοῖα**: Thuc. elsewhere uses σπεύδειν without a prep. (cf. c. 16. 7; vi. 10. 15), but Xen. *Cyr.* i. 4. 4 has ἐς τὸ αὐτὸ ἡμῖν σπεύδετε. Cf. Aesch. *Prom.* 192; Eur. *Ion.* 599 (Kr. proposes to omit ἐς).

23. παρῆσαν: sc. ἐν Θήβαις. — **τὰ εἰρημένα**: here refers only to the proposals of 6 ff., not "that which had been agreed upon," as in c. 35. 18. — **24. προκαλούμενοι**: with acc. as in ii. 74. 15, προκαλεσάμενοι γὰρ πολλὰ καὶ εἰκότα οὐ τυγχάνομεν. Cf. c. III. 19.

38. *But owing to the resistance of an opposing party in Boeotia, nothing is accomplished.*

1. ἐδόκει: not ἔδοξε. As presently appears, it was only a proposition, not a decision. — **2. Κορινθίοις κτέ.**: that the envoys of these states had come to Thebes has not been stated, but is evident from the context. See 20 f. — **τοῖς ἀπὸ Θρᾴκης**: cf. c. 31. 26. — **3. ἐν τῷ παρατυχόντι**: "under the circumstances that might at any time arise." παρα- has the force of ἀεί, and hence the sing. See on i. 122. 6; iii. 82. 47. — **4. τῷ δεομένῳ**: general, like τὸν βουλόμενον, i. 26. 3, and freq. — **5. οὕτως ἤδη**: *thereupon*, "then and not till then." οὕτως denotes the fulfilment of certain conditions. Cf. i. 37. 4; iii. 96. 8; iv. 88. 8; v. 55. 8. — **6. τὸ γὰρ αὐτὸ ἐποίουν**: like c. 31. 27, τὸ αὐτὸ

γείους σπένδεσθαι. πρὶν δὲ τοὺς ὅρκους γενέσθαι οἱ βοι- 2
ωτάρχαι ἐκοίνωσαν ταῖς τέσσαρσι βουλαῖς τῶν Βοιωτῶν
ταῦτα, αἵπερ ἅπαν τὸ κῦρος ἔχουσι, καὶ παρῄνουν γενέσθαι ὅρκους ταῖς πόλεσιν, ὅσαι βούλονται ἐπ' ὠφελίᾳ
σφίσι ξυνομνύναι. οἱ δ' ἐν ταῖς βουλαῖς τῶν Βοιωτῶν 3
ὄντες οὐ προσδέχονται τὸν λόγον, δεδιότες μὴ ἐναντία
Λακεδαιμονίοις ποιήσωσι, τοῖς ἐκείνων ἀφεστῶσι Κορινθίοις ξυνομνύντες· οὐ γὰρ εἶπον αὐτοῖς οἱ βοιωτάρχαι
τὰ ἐκ τῆς Λακεδαίμονος, ὅτι τῶν τε ἐφόρων Κλεόβουλος
καὶ Ξενάρης καὶ οἱ φίλοι παραινοῦσιν Ἀργείων πρῶτον
καὶ Κορινθίων γενομένους ξυμμάχους ὕστερον μετ' αὐτῶν
Λακεδαιμονίων γίγνεσθαι, οἰόμενοι τὴν βουλήν, κἂν μὴ

λέγοντες, and c. 36. 10, ταυτὰ γιγνώ-σκειν, denotes, esp. in the impf., general agreement in act and word.
8. **ταῖς τέσσαρσι βουλαῖς**: they are not mentioned elsewhere, and the organization of the Boeotian confederacy is altogether but imperfectly known. See Hermann, *Griech. Staatsalt.* § 179, 11. Gilbert, *Griech. Staatsalt.* II. p. 57. — 10. **ἐπ' ὠφελίᾳ**: cf. i. 3. 9. ἐπαγομένων αὐτοὺς ἐπ' ὠφελίᾳ ἐς τὰς ἄλλας πόλεις.
13. **τοῖς ἐκείνων ἀφεστῶσι**: cf. c. 27. § 2; 30. § 2 ff. — 14. **οὐ γὰρ εἶπον**: they had not informed them. — 15. **τῶν τε ἐφόρων**: part. gen. opp. to **καὶ οἱ φίλοι**. Cf. c. 37. 2. — 16. **παραινοῦσιν**: sc. τοῖς Βοιωτοῖς, as in c. 36. 9 f. — 17. **μετ' αὐτῶν**: rightly restored by St. for μετὰ τῶν (on this error of the Mss. see App. on c. 16. 6); for upon this the whole plan of the ephors and their party depended. They wished first to induce the Boeotians to form an alliance with Argos (and Corinth, which was already in the Argive confederacy), and then to bring about an alliance between these and Sparta,

so that Athens should be entirely isolated. Where the reconciliation of Argos and Sparta is the main point, we read in c. 36. 11 f., μετὰ Βοιωτῶν Ἀργείους Λακεδαιμονίοις ποιῆσαι ξυμμάχους; here where the restoration of the somewhat loosened alliance between Thebes and Sparta is most prominent, the same idea is expressed somewhat differently: (τοὺς Βοιωτούς, for this is the obj. of παραινοῦσιν and subj. of γίγνεσθαι) μετ' αὐτῶν (sc. τῶν Ἀργείων καὶ Κορινθίων) Λακεδαιμονίων (sc. ξυμμάχους) γίγνεσθαι. The way to the goal is in both cases the same: Ἀργείων πρῶτον (καὶ Κορινθίων, which is omitted as superfluous in c. 36) γενομένους ξυμμάχους. Only the difference between ποιῆσαι and γίγνεσθαι occasions that between μετὰ Βοιωτῶν and μετ' αὐτῶν, i.e. μετὰ τῶν Ἀργείων καὶ Κορινθίων. — 19. **σφίσι**: refers to the subj. of ψηφιεῖσθαι: "they would adopt no other measures than those which they (the Boeotarchs) recommend to them after previous deliberation." The indir. refl. pron. often refers in Thuc. to the subj. of a de-

εἴπωσιν, οὐκ ἄλλα ψηφιεῖσθαι ἢ ἃ σφίσι προδιαγνόντες
παραινοῦσιν. ὡς δὲ ἀντέστη τὸ πρᾶγμα, οἱ μὲν Κορίν- 4
θιοι καὶ οἱ ἀπὸ Θρᾴκης πρέσβεις ἄπρακτοι ἀπῆλθον, οἱ
δὲ βοιωτάρχαι, μέλλοντες πρότερον, εἰ ταῦτα ἔπεισαν,
καὶ τὴν ξυμμαχίαν πειράσεσθαι πρὸς Ἀργείους ποιεῖν,
οὐκέτι ἐσήνεγκαν περὶ Ἀργείων ἐς τὰς βουλάς, οὐδὲ ἐς
τὸ Ἄργος τοὺς πρέσβεις οὓς ὑπέσχοντο ἔπεμπον, ἀμέλεια
δέ τις ἐνῆν καὶ διατριβὴ τῶν πάντων.

39 Καὶ ἐν τῷ αὐτῷ χειμῶνι τούτῳ Μηκύβερναν Ὀλύν- 1
θιοι Ἀθηναίων φρουρούντων ἐπιδραμόντες εἷλον.

Μετὰ δὲ ταῦτα (ἐγίγνοντο γὰρ ἀεὶ λόγοι τοῖς τε 2
Ἀθηναίοις καὶ Λακεδαιμονίοις περὶ ὧν εἶχον ἀλλήλων)
ἐλπίζοντες οἱ Λακεδαιμόνιοι, εἰ Πάνακτον Ἀθηναῖοι παρὰ Βοιωτῶν ἀπολάβοιεν, κομίσασθαι ἂν αὐτοὶ Πύλον,
ἦλθον ἐς τοὺς Βοιωτοὺς πρεσβευόμενοι καὶ ἐδέοντο σφίσι
Πάνακτόν τε καὶ τοὺς Ἀθηναίων δεσμώτας παραδοῦναι,

pendent verb. *Cf.* i. 20. 10; 30. 14; 58. 7; iii. 3. 19; iv. 113. 11. Kühn. 555, N. 9. The change to σφεῖς or ἐν σφίσι, which has been proposed, is therefore unnecessary.
20. ἀντέστη: see on c. 4. 22. — 22. εἰ ταῦτα ἔπεισαν: the aor. indic. is chosen under the influence of the failure of their attempt ("if they had succeeded, which they did not"); μέλλοντες πειράσεσθαι would otherwise lead us to expect here a fut. prot., ἐὰν πείσωσι or εἰ πείσειαν. GMT. 49, 2, N. 3 c. — 23. καὶ τὴν ξυμμαχίαν: the alliance with the Argives, which has been previously mentioned, is the important one; hence the art. — 24. ἐσήνεγκαν: ἐσφέρειν, *propose for deliberation*, occurs also in viii. 67. 5 and 9. — 25. οὓς ὑπέσχοντο: *cf.* c. 37. 25.

39. *The Lacedaemonians make a separate alliance with the Boeotians.*

1. Μηκύβερναν: mentioned by Strabo, vii. frg. 29, as ἐπίνειον of Olynthus on the Toronaic Gulf. It now loses its independence, which Athens had tried to secure (c. 18. 29) in the treaty of peace.
3. ἐγίγνοντο λόγοι τοῖς τε Ἀθηναίοις κτέ.: *i.e.* οἱ Ἀθηναῖοι κτέ. λόγους ἐποιοῦντο. τε intimates that sometimes one party and sometimes the other took the initiative. — 4. περὶ ὧν ἀλλήλων εἶχον: *i.e.* by conquest during the war. These places were to be restored acc. to the treaty. *Cf.* c. 35. 5, κατὰ τὴν τῶν χωρίων ἀλλήλοις οὐκ ἀπόδοσιν. — 6. ἀπολάβοιεν: ἀπολαβεῖν, *get back*, either directly or by the mediation of others. *Cf.* c. 30. 15; 35. 24; 36. 21; iv. 99. 9. — κομίσασθαι: *cf.* c. 15. 4; 17.3; iv. 41. 15. — 7. πρεσβευόμενοι: *cf.* i. 31. 13, where the fut. partic. πρεσβευσόμενοι is used in the same way.

ἵνα ἀντ' αὐτῶν Πύλον κομίσωνται. οἱ δὲ Βοιωτοὶ οὐκ 3
10 ἔφασαν ἀποδώσειν, ἢν μὴ σφίσι ξυμμαχίαν ἰδίαν ποιήσωνται ὥσπερ Ἀθηναίοις. Λακεδαιμόνιοι δὲ εἰδότες μὲν
ὅτι ἀδικήσουσιν Ἀθηναίους, εἰρημένον ἄνευ ἀλλήλων
μήτε σπένδεσθαί τῳ μήτε πολεμεῖν, βουλόμενοι δὲ τὸ
Πάνακτον παραλαβεῖν ὡς τὴν Πύλον ἀντ' αὐτοῦ κομιού-
15 μενοι, καὶ ἅμα τῶν ξυγχέαι σπευδόντων τὰς σπονδὰς
προθυμουμένων τὰ ἐς Βοιωτούς, ἐποιήσαντο τὴν ξυμμαχίαν, τοῦ χειμῶνος τελευτῶντος * ἤδη καὶ πρὸς ἔαρ, καὶ
τὸ Πάνακτον εὐθὺς καθῃρεῖτο. καὶ ἑνδέκατον ἔτος τῷ
πολέμῳ ἐτελεύτα.
40 ** Ἅμα δὲ τῷ ἦρι εὐθὺς τοῦ ἐπιγιγνομένου θέρους οἱ 1
Ἀργεῖοι, ὡς οἵ τε πρέσβεις τῶν Βοιωτῶν οὓς ἔφασαν
πέμψειν οὐχ ἧκον, τό τε Πάνακτον ᾔσθοντο καθαιρούμενον καὶ ξυμμαχίαν ἰδίαν γεγενημένην τοῖς Βοιωτοῖς
5 πρὸς τοὺς Λακεδαιμονίους, ἔδεισαν μὴ μονωθῶσι καὶ ἐς

12. **εἰρημένον κτέ.**: either this provision is regarded as contained in c. 23. § 1, or it was subsequently added to the treaty. See App. *Cf.* c. 46. 15. — 14. **παραλαβεῖν**: denotes the acquisition of Panactum preparatory to exchanging it with the Athenians. — 15. **τῶν ξυγχέαι σπευδόντων τὰς σπονδάς**: *i.e.* the party of the two ephors. See c. 36. 7. The verb ξυγχεῖν occurs only here in Thuc.; but σπονδῶν ξύγχυσις in i. 146. 5 and c. 26. 29. *Cf.* confundere foedus, Verg. *Aen.* v. 496. — 16. **προθυμουμένων**: with acc. See on c. 17. 6. — **τὰ ἐς Βοιωτούς**: a general expression: *the connexion with the Boeotians. Cf.* c. 46. 5, ἐπισχόντας τὰ πρὸς Ἀργείους. — 17. **ἤδη**: const. with τοῦ χειμῶνος τελευτῶντος (not as in iv. 135. 2 with ἔαρ), intimates that the winter had been frittered away in the repeated negoti-

ations. — **καί**: connects the following words closely with ἐποιήσαντο τὴν ξυμμαχίαν, and makes the destruction of Panactum appear as a consequence of the alliance.— 18. **καθῃρεῖτο**: ὑπὸ τῶν Βοιωτῶν, Schol. The impf. denotes the beginning of the work which is still uncompleted in c. 40. 3 (καθαιρούμενον), and is not finished (καθῃρημένον) until c. 42. 6. The reasons for it are given in c. 42. 7 f. The words of Plut. *Alc.* 14, Λακεδαιμόνιοι ... Πάνακτον οὐχ ἑστῶσαν, ὥσπερ ἔδει, τοῖς Ἀθηναίοις παρέδωκαν, ἀλλὰ καταλύσαντες show that the Lacedaemonians were regarded as morally responsible for this breach of the spirit of the provision (see c. 18. 31 f.) of the treaty.

40. *Thereupon the Argives, fearful of being isolated, begin to negotiate with Sparta.*

3. **ἧκον**: see App. — 6. **χωρήσῃ**:

Λακεδαιμονίους πᾶσα ἡ ξυμμαχία χωρήσῃ· τοὺς γὰρ Βοι- 2
ωτοὺς ᾤοντο πεπεῖσθαι ὑπὸ Λακεδαιμονίων τό τε Πάνακτον καθελεῖν καὶ ἐς τὰς Ἀθηναίων σπονδὰς ἐσιέναι,
τούς τε Ἀθηναίους εἰδέναι ταῦτα, ὥστε οὐδὲ πρὸς Ἀθη-
10 ναίους ἔτι σφίσιν εἶναι ξυμμαχίαν ποιήσασθαι, πρότερον
ἐλπίζοντες ἐκ τῶν διαφορῶν, εἰ μὴ μείνειαν αὐτοῖς αἱ
πρὸς Λακεδαιμονίους σπονδαί, τοῖς γοῦν Ἀθηναίοις ξύμμαχοι ἔσεσθαι. ἀποροῦντες οὖν ταῦτα οἱ Ἀργεῖοι καὶ φο- 3
βούμενοι μὴ Λακεδαιμονίοις καὶ Τεγεάταις, Βοιωτοῖς
15 καὶ Ἀθηναίοις ἅμα πολεμῶσι, πρότερον οὐ δεχόμενοι τὰς
Λακεδαιμονίων σπονδάς, ἀλλ᾽ ἐν φρονήματι ὄντες τῆς
Πελοποννήσου ἡγήσεσθαι, ἔπεμπον ὡς ἐδύναντο τάχιστα
ἐς τὴν Λακεδαίμονα πρέσβεις Εὔστροφον καὶ Αἴσωνα,
οἳ ἐδόκουν προσφιλέστατοι αὐτοῖς εἶναι, ἡγούμενοι ἐκ τῶν
20 παρόντων κράτιστα πρὸς Λακεδαιμονίους σπονδὰς ποιη-

χωρεῖν ἔς τινα seems to differ from the more usual χωρεῖν πρός τινα (cf. i. 18. 28; v. 22. 10; 43. 6) as accedere ad aliquem differs from se convertere ad aliquem, and thus lays more stress upon the central position of Sparta.

9. τούς τε Ἀθηναίους εἰδέναι ταῦτα: the Argives were in error, believing that the Athenians had agreed to the destruction of Panactum preparatory to admitting the Boeotians into the alliance headed by Sparta and Athens. — ὥστε οὐδέ ... ποιήσασθαι: a consequence of this erroneous opinion. The inf. εἶναι still depends upon ᾤοντο. The neg. οὐδέ (not μηδέ) is retained. Their thought was ὥστε οὐδέ ... ἔστι. — 10. εἶναι: equiv. to παρεῖναι, as in ii. 97. 4, οὐ γὰρ ἦν πρᾶξαι οὐδὲν μὴ διδόντα δῶρα. — 11. ἐκ τῶν διαφορῶν: in consequence of the differences existing between the Lacedae-

monians and Athenians, which the Argives falsely believed were now removed. — αἱ πρὸς Λακεδαιμονίους σπονδαί: the expiration of this truce was at hand (see c. 14. 21; 22. 8 f.; 28. 8). Cleobulus and Xenares had tried to renew it (see c. 36. § 1). εἰ μὴ μείνειαν then means: "if the thirty years' truce should not be renewed." See App.

13. ἀποροῦντες οὖν ταῦτα: the adv. acc. of the neut. pron. (as with other similar verbs) occurs also in vii. 48. 36, τὰ μὲν ἀπορεῖν, and 55. 11, τά τε πρὸ αὐτῶν ἠπόρουν. Cf. Xen. Hell. vi. 1. 4. — 15. πρότερον οὐ δεχόμενοι: cf. c. 22. 8 f. — 16. ἐν φρονήματι ὄντες: "proudly hoping"; a stronger expression for ἐλπίσαντες of c. 28. 9. — 19. αὑτοῖς: i.e. τοῖς Λακεδαιμονίοις. — 20. κράτιστα: const. with ἡγούμενοι as pred. adj. modifying ἡσυχίαν ἔχειν. Cf. i. 85. 11, ταῦτα γὰρ κράτιστα βου-

41 σάμενοι, ὅπῃ ἂν ξυγχωρῇ, ἡσυχίαν ἔχειν. καὶ οἱ πρέ- 1
σβεις ἀφικόμενοι αὐτῶν λόγους ἐποιοῦντο πρὸς τοὺς Λακεδαιμονίους ἐφ' ᾧ ἂν σφίσιν αἱ σπονδαὶ γίγνοιντο. καὶ 2
τὸ μὲν πρῶτον οἱ Ἀργεῖοι ἠξίουν δίκης ἐπιτροπὴν σφίσι
5 γενέσθαι ἢ ἐς πόλιν τινὰ ἢ ἰδιώτην περὶ τῆς Κυνοσου-
ρίας γῆς, ἧς ἀεὶ πέρι διαφέρονται μεθορίας οὔσης (ἔχει
δὲ ἐν αὐτῇ Θυρέαν καὶ Ἀνθήνην πόλιν, νέμονται δ'
αὐτὴν Λακεδαιμόνιοι)· ἔπειτα δ' οὐκ ἐώντων Λακεδαιμονίων μεμνῆσθαι περὶ αὐτῆς, ἀλλ' εἰ βούλονται σπέν-
10 δεσθαι ὥσπερ πρότερον, ἑτοῖμοι εἶναι, οἱ Ἀργεῖοι πρέσβεις τάδε ὅμως ἐπηγάγοντο τοὺς Λακεδαιμονίους ξυγχωρῆσαι, ἐν μὲν τῷ παρόντι σπονδὰς ποιήσασθαι ἔτη πεν-

λεύσεσθε. — 21. ξυγχωρῇ: impers. liceat, it should be feasible; a usage found only in Xen. Eq. 9. 11, but assured by the analogy of ἐγχωρεῖ in Plat. Phaedo, 116 c; Sophist. 246 c; Gorg. 520 d: "they thought it was, under the circumstances, best to make peace with the Lacedaemonians in whatever way (i.e. on whatever terms) was possible, and to keep quiet," i.e. give up their pretensions to the hegemony. — ἡσυχίαν ἔχειν: like ἡσυχάζειν in c. 22. 12; 31. 28.

41. The Argive envoys arrive at Sparta, and after making a foolish stipulation about Cynuria, prepare to conclude a treaty of peace with the Lacedaemonians for fifty years.

2. αὐτῶν: sc. τῶν Ἀργείων. — 3. αἱ σπονδαί: the treaty of peace which was now ardently desired. σφίσιν also here and in 4 (where Kr. and v. Herwerden would omit it) points to the lively interest of the Argives in the matter.

5. ἐς πόλιν: with the subst. ἐπιτροπή, whereas with the verb ἐπιτρέπειν the dat. is used. Cf. i. 28. 9; iv. 83. 10; v. 31. 14. — 6. ἧς ἀεὶ πέρι: ἀεί is freq. inserted between closely connected words. See on i. 18. 29. — 7. νέμονται δ' αὐτὴν Λακεδαιμόνιοι: the Lacedaemonians had established there the Aeginetans who had been expelled from their home. See iv. 56. 13 f. On the situation of the towns, see Curtius, Pelopon. II. p. 376; Bursian, Geogr. v. Griech. II. p. 71. — 9. μεμνῆσθαι: mentionem facere: elsewhere used by Thuc. only in the aor. μνησθῆναι (i. 10. 26; 37. 4; ii. 45. 7; iii. 90. 6; vi. 15. 6; viii. 47. 10); nor is the pf. found in other Att. writers, nor in Hdt. (hence v. Herwerden writes μνησθῆναι). — 10. ὥσπερ πρότερον: i.e. on the same conditions as in the thirty years' peace concluded in 451 B.C. See on c. 14. 21. — ἑτοῖμοι εἶναι: anacoluthon after ἐώντων, but no change in the text should be made, for οὐκ ἐώντων suggests the idea of indir. disc., as if we had λεγόντων after ἀλλά, 9. Cf. viii. 48. § 6; 104. 13 ff., ἐπειγομένων δὲ τῶν Πελοποννησίων πρότερόν τε ξυμμῖξαι, καὶ . . . ὑπερσχόντες αὐτοί. Kühn. 593, N. 1. — 11. τάδε: const. with ξυγχωρῆσαι. — 14. διαμάχεσθαι:

τήκοντα, ἐξεῖναι δ' ὁποτεροισοῦν προκαλεσαμένοις, μήτε νόσου οὔσης μήτε πολέμου Λακεδαίμονι καὶ Ἄργει, δια-
15 μάχεσθαι περὶ τῆς γῆς ταύτης, ὥσπερ καὶ πρότερόν ποτε, ὅτε αὐτοὶ ἑκάτεροι ἠξίωσαν νικᾶν. διώκειν δὲ μὴ ἐξεῖναι περαιτέρω τῶν πρὸς Ἄργος καὶ Λακεδαίμονα ὅρων. τοῖς 3 δὲ Λακεδαιμονίοις τὸ μὲν πρῶτον ἐδόκει μωρία εἶναι ταῦτα, ἔπειτα (ἐπεθύμουν γὰρ τὸ Ἄργος πάντως φίλιον
20 ἔχειν) ξυνεχώρησαν ἐφ' οἷς ἠξίουν καὶ ξυνεγράψαντο. ἐκέλευον δ' οἱ Λακεδαιμόνιοι, πρὶν τέλος τι αὐτῶν ἔχειν, ἐς τὸ Ἄργος πρῶτον ἐπαναχωρήσαντας αὐτοὺς δεῖξαι τῷ πλήθει, καὶ ἢν ἀρέσκοντα ᾖ, ἥκειν ἐς τὰ Ὑακίνθια τοὺς 42 ὅρκους ποιησομένους. καὶ οἱ μὲν ἀνεχώρησαν, ἐν δὲ τῷ 1 χρόνῳ τούτῳ ᾧ οἱ Ἀργεῖοι ταῦτα ἔπρασσον οἱ πρέσβεις τῶν Λακεδαιμονίων Ἀνδρομένης καὶ Φαίδιμος καὶ Ἀντιμενίδας, οὓς ἔδει τὸ Πάνακτον καὶ τοὺς ἄνδρας τοὺς

decertare, "fight it out." *Cf.* i. 143. 25. — 15. ὥσπερ καὶ πρότερον: this battle is described in detail in Hdt. i. 82. The conditions of the struggle were to be agreed upon now as in the old days (about 550 B.C.). Fair warning was to be given (προκαλεσαμένοις), the enemy was not to be taken at a disadvantage (μήτε νόσου μήτε πολέμου κτέ.), nor was the defeated party to be pursued beyond the boundary of Cynuria (16. διώκειν δὲ μὴ ἐξεῖναι κτέ.). — 16. αὐτοὶ ἑκάτεροι ἠξίωσαν (claimed) νικᾶν: so in Hdt. i. 82. 27, αὐτοὶ ἑκάτεροι ἔφασαν νικᾶν. *Cf.* i. 105. 23, καὶ ἐνόμισαν αὐτοὶ ἑκάτεροι οὐκ ἔλασσον ἔχειν.
19. ἐπεθύμουν γάρ: *cf.* c. 36. 17, where καλῶς is quite as justifiable as here πάντως, under all circumstances, in any case. — φίλιον: for Mss. φίλον. *Cf.* c. 36. 18. — 20. ξυνεγράψοντο: συνθήκην ἔγγραφον δεδώκασι, Schol.

They drew up the treaty in writing, but withheld the ratification for the present, and ἐκέλευον δεῖξαι (to present it, *cf.* i. 133. 1) τῷ πλήθει. — 21. τέλος ἔχειν: *go into effect*. The subj. is τι αὐτῶν. — 23. ἀρέσκοντα: adj.; *cf.* i. 38. 8. εἰ τοῖς πλέοσιν ἀρέσκοντές ἐσμεν. — τὰ Ὑακίνθια: about midsummer. See on c. 23. 21.

42. *Meanwhile the Athenians are greatly incensed against the Lacedaemonians on account of the destruction of Panactum and the conclusion of the alliance between Sparta and the Boeotians.*
1. ἐν δὲ τῷ...ἔπρασσον: the events recorded in c. 42 and 43 are contemporaneous with those of c. 40 and 41. — 2. ᾧ: the dat. is to be explained rather by the continuation of the force of ἐν than by assimilation. *Cf.* i. 41. 10, καὶ ἐν καιροῖς τοιούτοις ἐγένετο, οἷς μάλιστα ἄνθρωποι ἀπερίοπτοί εἰσι. — 3. Ἀνδρομένης: see App. — 5. πα-

5 παρὰ Βοιωτῶν παραλαβόντας Ἀθηναίοις ἀποδοῦναι, τὸ μὲν Πάνακτον ὑπὸ τῶν Βοιωτῶν αὐτῶν καθῃρημένον ηὗρον ἐπὶ προφάσει ὡς ἦσάν ποτε Ἀθηναίοις καὶ Βοιωτοῖς ἐκ διαφορᾶς περὶ αὐτοῦ ὅρκοι παλαιοὶ μηδετέρους οἰκεῖν τὸ χωρίον ἀλλὰ κοινῇ νέμειν, τοὺς δ' ἄνδρας οὓς
10 εἶχον αἰχμαλώτους Βοιωτοὶ Ἀθηναίων, παραλαβόντες οἱ περὶ τὸν Ἀνδρομένη ἐκόμισαν τοῖς Ἀθηναίοις καὶ ἀπέδοσαν, τοῦ τε Πανάκτου τὴν καθαίρεσιν ἔλεγον αὐτοῖς, νομίζοντες καὶ τοῦτο ἀποδιδόναι· πολέμιον γὰρ οὐκέτι ἐν αὐτῷ Ἀθηναίοις οἰκήσειν οὐδένα. λεγομένων δὲ τού- 2
15 των οἱ Ἀθηναῖοι δεινὰ ἐποίουν, νομίζοντες ἀδικεῖσθαι ὑπὸ Λακεδαιμονίων τοῦ τε Πανάκτου τῇ καθαιρέσει, ὃ ἔδει ὀρθὸν παραδοῦναι, καὶ πυνθανόμενοι ὅτι καὶ Βοιωτοῖς ἰδίᾳ ξυμμαχίαν πεποίηνται, φάσκοντες πρότερον κοινῇ τοὺς μὴ δεχομένους τὰς σπονδὰς προσαναγκάσειν.
20 τά τε ἄλλα ἐσκόπουν ὅσα ἐξελελοίπεσαν τῆς ξυνθήκης καὶ

ραλαβόντας: see on c. 39. 14. — 6. τῶν Βοιωτῶν: the genuineness of these words is wrongly doubted by v. Herwerden, *Stud. Thuc.* p. 74. But the suspicion expressed in c. 40. 7, πεπεῖσθαι ὑπὸ Λακεδαιμονίων, is meant to be met by saying that "the Boeotians themselves," *etc*. — καθῃρημένον: see on c. 39. 18. ἐπὶ προφάσει is to be const. with καθῃρημένον. "They had destroyed the fort, giving as their reason that," *etc*. — 9. κοινῇ νέμειν: κοινὴν νομὴν ἔχειν ἐν αὐτῷ, Schol. Only the use of the land, not its permanent occupation, was to be permitted. — 11. ἐκόμισαν: *cf.* c. 35. 26. — 13. νομίζοντες καὶ τοῦτο ἀποδιδόναι: sc. εἶναι. "They thought that this, too, was restoring it," *i.e.* that in this way also they were fulfilling the conditions of the treaty. *Cf.* c. 18. 31 f., ἀποδόντων ... Πάνακτον. (Cobet, Mnem. 14, p. 10,

proposes to insert εἶναι after ἀποδιδόναι; Naber, *ibid.* p. 319, would read οὕτως for τοῦτο.)
14. λεγομένων τούτων: (pres. partic.) "the moment this was said," "as soon as they heard this." — 15. δεινὰ ἐποίουν: only here in Thuc., who uses the mid. δεινὸν ποιεῖσθαί τι in i. 102. 17 and vi. 60. 21. The two expressions arise from different points of view. The latter means, strictly speaking, "to regard something as terrible or intolerable"; the former, "to do terrible things," "to act so as to inspire terror." — 17. ὀρθὸν παραδοῦναι: though this was not expressly stipulated, it was naturally their duty, ἔδει. — καὶ πυνθανόμενοι: continues τοῦ τε Πανάκτου τῇ καθαιρέσει with a different const. — 18. ἰδίᾳ: ἄνευ τῶν Ἀθηναίων, Schol. — φάσκοντες πρότερον: *cf.* c. 35. 10 f. — 20. τά τε ἄλλα:

ἐνόμιζον ἐξηπατῆσθαι, ὥστε χαλεπῶς πρὸς τοὺς πρέσβεις ἀποκρινάμενοι ἀπέπεμψαν.

43 Κατὰ τοιαύτην δὴ διαφορὰν ὄντων τῶν Λακεδαι- 1 μονίων πρὸς τοὺς Ἀθηναίους οἱ ἐν ταῖς Ἀθήναις αὖ βουλόμενοι λῦσαι τὰς σπονδὰς εὐθὺς ἐνέκειντο. ἦσαν δὲ 2 ἄλλοι τε καὶ Ἀλκιβιάδης ὁ Κλεινίου, ἀνὴρ ἡλικίᾳ μὲν ἔτι 5 τότε ὢν νέος ὡς ἐν ἄλλῃ πόλει, ἀξιώματι δὲ προγόνων τιμώμενος· ᾧ ἐδόκει μὲν καὶ ἄμεινον εἶναι πρὸς τοὺς Ἀργείους μᾶλλον χωρεῖν, οὐ μέντοι ἀλλὰ καὶ φρονήματι φιλονικῶν ἠναντιοῦτο, ὅτι Λακεδαιμόνιοι διὰ Νικίου

τε connects with what precedes, and is not the correlative of the following καί. The reference is to the complaints of c. 35. § 2 and 3. — ἐσκόπουν: *they took into consideration.* A clearer expression would be ἀνεσκόπουν, as in i. 132. 8; vii. 42. 24. — τῆς ξυνθήκης: part. gen. with ὅσα, which belongs not only with ἐξελελοίπεσαν, but also with ἐξηπατῆσθαι: *and the things in which they thought they had been deceived.* — 21. πρὸς τοὺς πρέσβεις: unusual for τοῖς πρέσβεσιν. *Cf.* i. 144. 6, τούτοις ἀποκρινάμενοι.

43. *This increases the influence of the war party at Athens, and Alcibiades in particular exerts himself to attract Argos and her allies to the Athenian alliance.*

2. αὖ: with reference to the party in Sparta which was working for the same end (*cf.* c. 36. § 1): *likewise.* αὖ belongs with ἐνέκειντο. *Cf.* c. 14. 12; ii. 45. 1. — 3. ἐνέκειντο: abs. *exerted themselves eagerly.* See on iv. 22. 5, where (as also in viii. 85. 18) it is used in much the same sense. Elsewhere it refers to hostile attacks.

4. Ἀλκιβιάδης: this is the first mention of him by Thuc. He was born about 450 B.C., since he is said to have been in his fifth year when his father was killed in the battle of Coronea in 446 B.C. He must therefore have been at this time about thirty years of age. See Grote, VI. c. 55, p. 301. — 5. ὡς ἐν ἄλλῃ πόλει: ut in alia civitate; *according to the view held in other cities,* implying that at Athens younger men were influential in politics than elsewhere. ὡς us in iii. 113. 25, ὡς πρὸς τὸ μέγεθος τῆς πόλεως; iv. 84. 9; vi. 20. 8, and like ut in Lat., as in magno ut populo, Hor. Sat. i. 6. 79. — προγόνων: the founder of his family was said to be Eurysaces, the son of Ajax. His father Clinias fought in his own trireme in the battle of Artemisium in 480 B.C. His mother Deinomache was the daughter of the Alcmaeonid Megacles. — 6. ἐδόκει μέν: "it was *to be sure* his sincere opinion, but his chief motive (οὐ μέντοι ἀλλά with increasing emphasis, see App.; also note on i. 3. 17) was ambition." — 7. φρονήματι: *pride,* as in ii. 43. 28, ἀλγεινοτέρα γὰρ ἀνδρί γε φρόνημα ἔχοντι ἡ ... κάκωσις ἢ ὁ ... θάνατος. — 8. φιλονικῶν: (not φιλονεικῶν, see Stahl, *Qu. Gr.* p.

καὶ Λάχητος ἔπραξαν τὰς σπονδάς, ἑαυτὸν κατά τε τὴν
10 νεότητα ὑπεριδόντες καὶ κατὰ τὴν παλαιὰν προξενίαν
ποτὲ οὖσαν οὐ τιμήσαντες, ἣν τοῦ πάππου ἀπειπόντος
αὐτὸς τοὺς ἐκ τῆς νήσου αὐτῶν αἰχμαλώτους θεραπεύων
διενοεῖτο ἀνανεώσασθαι. πανταχόθεν τε νομίζων ἐλασ- 3
σοῦσθαι τό τε πρῶτον ἀντεῖπεν, οὐ βεβαίους φάσκων
15 εἶναι Λακεδαιμονίους, ἀλλ' ἵνα Ἀργείους σφίσι σπεισά-
μενοι ἐξέλωσι καὶ αὖθις ἐπ' Ἀθηναίους μόνους ἴωσι,
τούτου ἕνεκα σπένδεσθαι αὐτούς, καὶ τότε, ἐπειδὴ ἡ δια-
φορὰ ἐγεγένητο, πέμπει εὐθὺς ἐς Ἄργος ἰδίᾳ, κελεύων
ὡς τάχιστα ἐπὶ τὴν ξυμμαχίαν προκαλουμένους ἥκειν με-
20 τὰ Μαντινέων καὶ Ἠλείων, ὡς καιροῦ ὄντος καὶ αὐτὸς
44 ξυμπράξων τὰ μάλιστα. οἱ δὲ Ἀργεῖοι ἀκούσαντες 1
τῆς τε ἀγγελίας καὶ ἐπειδὴ ἔγνωσαν οὐ μετ' Ἀθηναίων πραχθεῖσαν τὴν τῶν Βοιωτῶν ξυμμαχίαν, ἀλλ'

13) is used of jealous striving for advancement, as in iv. 64. 5. — 9. Λάχητος: Laches appears also in c. 19 and c. 24, with Nicias, among the seventeen who took the oaths at the conclusion of the two treaties. — ἑαυτόν: see App. — 10. τὴν παλαιὰν προξενίαν ποτὲ οὖσαν: cf. vi. 89. § 2, τῶν δ' ἐμῶν προγόνων τὴν προξενίαν ὑμῶν κατά τι ἔγκλημα ἀπειπόντων αὐτὸς ἐγὼ πάλιν ἀναλαμβάνων ἐθεράπευον ὑμᾶς ἄλλα τε καὶ περὶ τὴν ἐκ Πύλου ξυμφοράν, and Plut. Alc. 14. — 11. οὐ τιμήσαντες: they did not treat him with the respect he had anticipated. — τοῦ πάππου: i.e. his paternal grandfather, Alcibiades the elder. — 12. θεραπεύων: also in vi. 89. 5. See on 10.
13. πανταχόθεν: in general. Const. with ἀντεῖπεν. Cf. i. 17. 7, οὕτω πανταχόθεν ἡ Ἑλλὰς κατείχετο μήτε . . . κατεργάζεσθαι. — 14. τό τε πρῶτον: opp. to καὶ τότε, 17. — οὐ βεβαίους: untrustworthy. Cf. ii. 102. 8,

ἄνδρας οὐ δοκοῦντας βεβαίους εἶναι ἐξήλασαν, and note. — 15. σφίσι: τοῖς Ἀθηναίοις, Schol. — 16. ἐξέλωσι: overthrow, conquer utterly. See on iii. 113. 27. In this sense used only in aor. — αὖθις: as in c. 36. 11; 76. 9, thereupon, afterwards. — 19. ἥκειν: he told them to "come (in the persons of ambassadors) to Athens as quickly as possible in order to invite (προκαλουμένους, fut.) the Athenians to form an alliance." — 20. ὡς: with the gen. abs. and also with the nom. partic. ξυμπράξων, so that the two are very closely connected. Cf. iv. 5. 2 f.
44. The Argives, Eleans, and Mantineans immediately send envoys to Athens. Envoys from Sparta also arrive.
2. τῆς τε ἀγγελίας: the connective particle belongs in strictness with ἀκούσαντες, but is joined instead with the obj., because ἀγγελίας really contains the idea opp. to ἔγνωσαν: "on

ἐς διαφορὰν μεγάλην καθεστῶτας αὐτοὺς πρὸς τοὺς
Λακεδαιμονίους, τῶν μὲν ἐν Λακεδαίμονι πρέσβεων,
οἳ σφίσι περὶ τῶν σπονδῶν ἔτυχον ἀπόντες, ἠμέλουν,
πρὸς δὲ τοὺς Ἀθηναίους μᾶλλον τὴν γνώμην εἶχον,
νομίζοντες πόλιν τε σφίσι φιλίαν ἀπὸ παλαιοῦ καὶ
δημοκρατουμένην ὥσπερ καὶ αὐτοὶ καὶ δύναμιν μεγάλην ἔχουσαν τὴν κατὰ θάλασσαν ξυμπολεμήσειν σφίσιν, ἢν καθιστῶνται ἐς πόλεμον. ἔπεμπον οὖν εὐθὺς 2
πρέσβεις ὡς τοὺς Ἀθηναίους περὶ τῆς ξυμμαχίας·
ξυνεπρεσβεύοντο δὲ καὶ οἱ Ἠλεῖοι καὶ Μαντινῆς. ἀφ- 3
ίκοντο δὲ καὶ Λακεδαιμονίων πρέσβεις κατὰ τάχος δοκοῦντες ἐπιτήδειοι εἶναι τοῖς Ἀθηναίοις, Φιλοχαρίδας καὶ
Λέων καὶ Ἔνδιος, δείσαντες μὴ τήν τε ξυμμαχίαν ὀργι-

the one hand the message of Alcibiades reached them; on the other hand they had obtained information from other sources" that their suspicion in regard to Athens (c. 40. § 2) had been unfounded, οὐ μετ' Ἀθηναίων (i.e. ἄνευ Ἀθηναίων, Atheniensibus invitis) πραχθεῖσαν τὴν τῶν Βοιωτῶν ξυμμαχίαν. — 6. οἳ σφίσι περὶ τῶν σπονδῶν ἔτυχον ἀπόντες: i.e. those who were carrying on the negotiations of c. 41. But the Argives had as yet received no news of the result of these negotiations or of the departure of their envoys (c. 42. 1), nor did they wait for such news (ἠμέλουν) before acting upon the suggestion of Alcibiades. Consequently the recommendations of the Lacedaemonians (see c. 41. 21 ff.) were never carried out. — σφίσι: a free use of the dat. (ethical dat.), as in c. 3. 21, αὐτοῖς. G. 184, 3, N. 6; H. 770. — 7. πρὸς δὲ τοὺς ... τὴν γνώμην εἶχον: see on iii. 25. 10. Used with a common noun in c. 13. 8; 14. 4. — 8. νομίζοντες κτἑ.: reflecting that it was a city which had been friendly to them of old, and that since it was, like themselves, governed by a democracy, it would aid them with its great naval power if they were involved in war. — ἀπὸ παλαιοῦ: an alliance had been formed between Athens and Argos in 460 B.C. Cf. i. 102. 19 f. — 9. δημοκρατουμένην κτἑ.: the same words are used in c. 29. 9, in explaining the feelings of the Mantineans toward the Argives. — 10. τὴν κατὰ θάλασσαν: see App.
13. Ἠλεῖοι καὶ Μαντινῆς: the Mantineans (see c. 29. 1) and Eleans (see c. 31. 1 ff.) were the first to join the Argive league.
14. δοκοῦντες κτἑ.: attrib. with πρέσβεις: "such as were thought to be acceptable to the Athenians." Philocharidas is one of those who took the oaths in concluding the treaties (c. 19 and 24); Endius appears in viii. 6. 17 as a friend of the family of Alcibiades. —
16. δείσαντες: refers not merely to the envoys, but to the Lacedaemonians

ζόμενοι πρὸς τοὺς Ἀργείους ποιήσωνται, καὶ ἅμα Πύλον ἀπαιτήσοντες ἀντὶ Πανάκτου, καὶ περὶ τῆς Βοιωτῶν ξυμμαχίας ἀπολογησόμενοι ὡς οὐκ ἐπὶ κακῷ τῶν Ἀθηναίων
45 ἐποιήσαντο. καὶ λέγοντες ἐν τῇ βουλῇ περί τε τούτων καὶ 1 ὡς αὐτοκράτορές ἤκουσι περὶ πάντων ξυμβῆναι τῶν διαφόρων, τὸν Ἀλκιβιάδην ἐφόβουν μή, ἢν καὶ ἐς τὸν δῆμον ταῦτα λέγωσιν, ἐπαγάγωνται τὸ πλῆθος καὶ ἀπωσθῇ ἡ
5 Ἀργείων ξυμμαχία· μηχανᾶται δὲ πρὸς αὐτοὺς τοιόνδε τι 2 ὁ Ἀλκιβιάδης· τοὺς Λακεδαιμονίους πείθει, πίστιν αὐτοῖς δούς, ἢν μὴ ὁμολογήσωσιν ἐν τῷ δήμῳ αὐτοκράτορές ἤκειν, Πύλον τε αὐτοῖς ἀποδώσειν (πείσειν γὰρ αὐτὸς Ἀθηναίους, ὥσπερ καὶ νῦν ἀντιλέγειν) καὶ τἆλλα
10 ξυναλλάξειν. βουλόμενος δὲ αὐτοὺς Νικίου τε ἀποστῆ- 3 σαι ταῦτα ἔπρασσε καὶ ὅπως ἐν τῷ δήμῳ διαβαλὼν αὐτοὺς ὡς οὐδὲν ἀληθὲς ἐν νῷ ἔχουσιν οὐδὲ λέγουσιν οὐ-

in general, as freq. in such cases.—
17. καὶ ἅμα Πύλον κτέ.: this second reason for their haste in reaching Athens is no longer dependent upon δείσαντες, as we should expect after τήν τε ξυμμαχίαν. The inexact use of the particles does not, however, justify a change in the text.— 19. ἐπὶ κακῷ: as in iv. 86. 1, and like ἐπ' ἀγαθῷ in c. 27. 7.— ἀπολογησόμενοι: although we read in c. 39. 11, Λακεδαιμόνιοι εἰδότες ὅτι ἀδικήσουσιν Ἀθηναίους.
45. *Alcibiades by a trick frustrates the endeavours of the Lacedaemonian envoys, and inclines the Athenians to accept the advances of the Argives and their allies. Further proceedings are, however, interrupted by an earthquake.*
2. ξυμβῆναι: aor. "come to a *final* agreement."— τῶν διαφόρων: *points of difference*, as in i. 56. 2; 78. 13.—
3. ἐς τὸν δῆμον: cf. i. 72. 14; iv. 58. 9; vi. 41.13; 89. 1.— ἢν καί: see App.

— 4. ταῦτά: see App.— ἀπωσθῇ: used of rejecting the ξυμμαχία, as in c. 22. 4, the σπονδαί.
5. μηχανᾶται δέ: see App.— 6. πίστιν... δούς: *assuring them with an oath*. Cf. i. 133. 14; viii. 73. 13. — 7. μὴ ὁμολογήσωσιν: μὴ φανερῶς εἴπωσι, Schol.— 9. καί: after ὥσπερ is proleptic in the rel. clause, for καί really belongs with πείσειν. See on i. 74. 25. For the inf. (ἀντιλέγειν) in a rel. clause in indir. disc., see on i. 91. 23. GMT. 92, 2, N. 3; H. 947; Kr. Spr. 55, 4, 9; 53, 2, 9; Kühn. 594, 5.
11. καὶ ὅπως... ποιήσῃ: parallel to βουλόμενος αὐτοὺς Νικίου τε ἀποστῆσαι. But τε, which would naturally stand after βουλόμενος, is forced out of its place by the connective δέ and so comes to stand after Νικίου.— 12. ὡς οὐδὲν ἀληθὲς ἐν νῷ ἔχουσιν: corresponds to οὐ βεβαίους φάσκων εἶναι in 43. 14 (Plut. says ὑγιές, which Kr.

δέποτε ταυτά, τοὺς Ἀργείους καὶ Ἠλείους καὶ Μαντινέας ξυμμάχους ποιήσῃ. καὶ ἐγένετο οὕτως. ἐπειδὴ γὰρ ἐς τὸν 4
15 δῆμον παρελθόντες καὶ ἐπερωτώμενοι οὐκ ἔφασαν ὥσπερ ἐν τῇ βουλῇ αὐτοκράτορες ἥκειν, οἱ Ἀθηναῖοι οὐκέτι ἠνείχοντο, ἀλλὰ τοῦ Ἀλκιβιάδου πολλῷ μᾶλλον ἢ πρότερον καταβοῶντος τῶν Λακεδαιμονίων ἐσήκουόν τε καὶ ἕτοιμοι ἦσαν εὐθὺς παραγαγόντες τοὺς Ἀργείους καὶ
20 τοὺς μετ' αὐτῶν ξυμμάχους ποιεῖσθαι· σεισμοῦ δὲ γενομένου πρίν τι ἐπικυρωθῆναι, ἡ ἐκκλησία αὕτη ἀνεβλήθη.
46 τῇ δ' ὑστεραίᾳ ἐκκλησίᾳ ὁ Νικίας, καίπερ τῶν Λα- 1 κεδαιμονίων αὐτῶν ἠπατημένων καὶ αὐτὸς ἐξηπατημένος περὶ τοῦ μὴ αὐτοκράτορας ὁμολογῆσαι ἥκειν, ὅμως τοῖς Λακεδαιμονίοις ἔφη χρῆναι φίλους μᾶλλον γίγνε-
5 σθαι, καὶ ἐπισχόντας τὰ πρὸς Ἀργείους πέμψαι ἔτι ὡς αὐτοὺς καὶ εἰδέναι ὅ τι διανοοῦνται, λέγων ἐν μὲν τῷ

prefers with no sufficient reason).: "that they were not to be trusted." — 14. **ποιήσῃ**: act., used of the statesman who influences the people; in 20 ποιεῖσθαι is mid. of the sovereign people. — **ἐς τὸν δῆμον**: i.e. after the preliminary discussion had been held ἐν τῇ βουλῇ (1).
15. **παρελθόντες**: παριέναι and παρελθεῖν are the regular expressions for coming before a deliberative assembly. See on i. 67. 10. To this corresponds παραγάγοντες in 19, and c. 46. 34. — 18. **καταβοῶντος**: inveighing against, as in i. 67. 4 and 115. 3. — 20. **σεισμοῦ δὲ γενομένου**: earthquakes were regarded as divine signs, and sufficed to put an end to all public business. Cf. c. 50. 26; viii. 6. 29; Plut. Nic. 10, σεισμός τις διὰ μέσου γενόμενος καὶ διαλύσας τὴν ἐκκλησίαν. On γίγνεσθαι used of natural phenomena, see on i. 54. 6.

46. *Next day Nicias persuades the Athenians to send ambassadors, of which he himself is one, to Sparta. The Spartans refuse to give up their alliance with the Boeotians; consequently the Athenians conclude the alliance with Argos.*
1. **ὑστεραίᾳ**: Thuc. uses this word most freq. to denote the following day (though ἡμέρᾳ is never expressed), but sometimes, as here, with other substs. to denote what happened on the following day. See on i. 44. 4. — **τῶν Λακεδαιμονίων αὐτῶν ἠπατημένων**: see App. — 3. **περὶ τοῦ μὴ ... ὁμολογῆσαι ἥκειν**: *in regard to the announcement that they had not come with full powers.* Const. with both ἠπατημένων and ἐξηπατημένος. — 5. **ἐπισχόντας**: in meaning as in c. 32. 24 (*delay, wait*); but here, as in c. 63. 13 and ii. 76. 4, const. with the acc. — **τὰ πρὸς Ἀργείους**: as in c. 39. 10, τὰ ἐς Βοιωτούς. τὴν ξυμμαχίαν τῶν Ἀργείων,

σφετέρῳ καλῷ, ἐν δὲ τῷ ἐκείνων ἀπρεπεῖ τὸν πόλεμον ἀναβάλλεσθαι· σφίσι μὲν γὰρ εὖ ἑστώτων τῶν πραγμάτων ὡς ἐπὶ πλεῖστον ἄριστον εἶναι διασώσασθαι τὴν εὐ-
10 πραγίαν, ἐκείνοις δὲ δυστυχοῦσιν ὅτι τάχιστα εὕρημα εἶναι διακινδυνεῦσαι. ἔπεισέ τε πέμψαι πρέσβεις, ὧν καὶ 2 αὐτὸς ἦν, κελεύσοντας Λακεδαιμονίους, εἴ τι δίκαιον διανοοῦνται, Πάνακτόν τε ὀρθὸν ἀποδιδόναι καὶ Ἀμφίπολιν, καὶ τὴν Βοιωτῶν ξυμμαχίαν ἀνεῖναι, ἢν μὴ ἐς τὰς
15 σπονδὰς ἐσίωσι, καθάπερ εἴρητο ἄνευ ἀλλήλων μηδενὶ ξυμβαίνειν. εἰπεῖν τε ἐκέλευον ὅτι καὶ σφεῖς, εἰ ἐβούλον- 3 το ἀδικεῖν, ἤδη ἂν Ἀργείους ξυμμάχους πεποιῆσθαι, ὡς παρεῖναί γ' αὐτοὺς αὐτοῦ τούτου ἕνεκα. εἴ τέ τι ἄλλο ἐνεκάλουν, πάντα ἐπιστείλαντες ἀπέπεμψαν τοὺς περὶ
20 τὸν Νικίαν πρέσβεις. καὶ ἀφικομένων αὐτῶν καὶ ἀπαγ- 4

Schol.— 6. ἐν ... καλῷ : ἐν (as in the conj. ἐν ᾧ, see on ii. 1. 2) denotes the circumstances, the state of things. "He urged them to put off the war, under circumstances (*i.e.* since the circumstances were) favourable for them, but humiliating for the Lacedaemonians." The words καλόν and ἀπρεπές are justified by the fact that Athens could very well remain in her present condition, whereas Sparta must try to improve hers by means of war. ἐν καλῷ as in c. 59. 17 ; 60. 11. *Cf.* i. 33. 1.— 9. ὡς ἐπὶ πλεῖστον : *as long as possible.* See on i. 82. 20.— διασώσασθαι τὴν εὐπραγίαν : as in iii. 39. 26, τὴν εὐδαιμονίαν, and c. 16. 11, τὴν εὐτυχίαν; mid., *preserve their own good fortune.* — 10. ὅτι τάχιστα : const. with διακινδυνεῦσαι. — εὕρημα : *a piece of good luck.* So in Hdt. vii. 155. 8; Xen. *Anab.* ii. 3. 18; vii. 3. 13 ; and ἕρμαιον, Plat. *Phaedo,* 107 c ; *Sympos.* 217 a.
11. ἔπεισέ τε : expresses the result :

"and he succeeded in persuading them."— 13. ὀρθόν : as in c. 42. 17. Const. with Πάνακτον only. — 14. ἀνεῖναι : *give up,* as in c. 31. 15, τὴν ἐπιτροπήν; i. 75. 13, τὴν ἀρχήν.— ἢν μὴ ... ἐσίωσι : *cf.* c. 42. § 2.— 15. καθάπερ εἴρητο : on the lack of agreement between this passage and c. 23. § 1, see App. on c. 39. 12.
16. ὅτι καὶ σφεῖς ... ἄν ... πεποιῆσθαι : instead of ἐπεποίηντο, as we should expect. Kr. *Spr.* 55, 4, N. 10, gives examples of a similar confusion of two consts. in Xen. All these cases seem to be the result of carelessness in the author. — 17. ὡς παρεῖναι αὐτούς : *sc.* τοὺς Ἀργείους. Here the inf. of the indir. disc. is retained in the dependent clause. *Cf.* c. 45. 9. GMT. 92, 2, N. 3 a ; II. 947. ὡς corresponds to the causal cum : "for this was just the purpose for which they had come."
— 19. πάντα : repeats εἴ τι ἄλλο. — τοὺς περὶ τὸν Νικίαν πρέσβεις : *i.e.* Νικίαν καὶ τοὺς ἄλλους πρέσβεις. So

γειλάντων τά τε ἄλλα καὶ τέλος εἰπόντων ὅτι, εἰ μὴ τὴν ξυμμαχίαν ἀνήσουσι Βοιωτοῖς μὴ ἐσιοῦσιν ἐς τὰς σπονδάς, ποιήσονται καὶ αὐτοὶ Ἀργείους καὶ τοὺς μετ' αὐτῶν ξυμμάχους, τὴν μὲν ξυμμαχίαν οἱ Λακεδαιμόνιοι Βοιω-
25 τοῖς οὐκ ἔφασαν ἀνήσειν, ἐπικρατούντων τῶν περὶ τὸν Ξενάρη τὸν ἔφορον ταῦτα γίγνεσθαι, καὶ ὅσοι ἄλλοι τῆς αὐτῆς γνώμης ἦσαν, τοὺς δὲ ὅρκους δεομένου Νικίου ἀνενεώσαντο· ἐφοβεῖτο γὰρ μὴ πάντα ἀτελῆ ἔχων ἀπέλθῃ καὶ διαβληθῇ, ὅπερ καὶ ἐγένετο, αἴτιος δοκῶν εἶναι
30 τῶν πρὸς Λακεδαιμονίους σπονδῶν. ἀναχωρήσαντός τε 5 αὐτοῦ ὡς ἤκουσαν οἱ Ἀθηναῖοι οὐδὲν ἐκ τῆς Λακεδαίμονος πεπραγμένον, εὐθὺς δι' ὀργῆς εἶχον, καὶ νομίζοντες ἀδικεῖσθαι (ἔτυχον γὰρ παρόντες οἱ Ἀργεῖοι καὶ οἱ ξύμμαχοι), παραγαγόντος Ἀλκιβιάδου, ἐποιήσαντο σπονδὰς
35 καὶ ξυμμαχίαν πρὸς αὐτοὺς τήνδε·

also in 25 and vi. 96. 14. G. 141, N. 3; H. 666 c.
22. Βοιωτοῖς μὴ ἐσιοῦσιν: 'dat. of interest,' loosely connected with the verb (ἀνήσουσι); not unlike the gen. abs. in meaning. See on iv. 56. 1, and App. on iv. 10. 11. II. 771 a. ἐσιοῦσιν is the cond. partic., and so μή, not οὐ. Cf. 14.
— 25. ἐπικρατούντων: with inf. of result, as in vi. 74. 8, ἐπεκράτουν μὴ δέχεσθαι. — 26. τὸν ἔφορον: cf. c. 36. 7. The art. is repeated with the explanatory designation, as in ii. 67. 14, τὸν Σάδοκον τὸν γεγενημένον Ἀθηναῖον. — τῆς αὐτῆς γνώμης ἦσαν: "were of the same political party." Cf. i. 113. 10.
— 28. ἀνενεώσαντο: this was to be done annually, acc. to the provision of the treaty. Cf. c. 18. 54. Since the conclusion of the treaty in the spring of 421 B.C. a year had passed. See on c. 40. 1. — ἐφοβεῖτο γάρ: gives a reason for δεομένου Νικίου. By the renewal of the oaths Nicias hoped at least to prove that the peace which he had been so prominent in arranging was still effective. — μή ... ἀπέλθῃ καὶ διαβληθῇ: "that his mission would be absolutely unsuccessful (which would be painful enough for him), and he would be exposed to the attacks of his enemies in addition." The sense would be more exactly expressed by μή, ἣν πάντα ἀτελῆ ἔχων ἀπέλθῃ, καὶ διαβληθῇ, taking καί in a pregnant sense.
32. δι' ὀργῆς εἶχον: abs. Cf. διὰ φυλακῆς (ii. 81. 16), ἐν φυλακῇ (iv. 14. 26), and ἐν ὀρρωδίᾳ (ii. 89. 3) with ἔχειν: "were in a state of angry excitement." — 33. παρόντες: refers to the presence of the envoys in Athens (see c. 44. 11 ff.), παραγαγόντος, 34, to their introduction into the assembly (see on c. 45. 15) where the treaty was concluded. The parenthe-

47 "Σπονδὰς ἐποιήσαντο ἑκατὸν Ἀθηναῖοι ἔτη καὶ 1
Ἀργεῖοι καὶ Μαντινῆς καὶ Ἠλεῖοι, ὑπὲρ σφῶν αὐτῶν καὶ
τῶν ξυμμάχων ὧν ἄρχουσιν ἑκάτεροι, ἀδόλους καὶ ἀβλαβεῖς καὶ κατὰ γῆν καὶ κατὰ θάλασσαν. ὅπλα δὲ μὴ ἐξέστω 2
5 ἐπιφέρειν ἐπὶ πημονῇ μήτε Ἀργείους καὶ Ἠλείους καὶ
Μαντινέας καὶ τοὺς ξυμμάχους ἐπὶ Ἀθηναίους καὶ τοὺς
ξυμμάχους ὧν ἄρχουσιν Ἀθηναῖοι μήτε Ἀθηναίους καὶ
τοὺς ξυμμάχους ἐπὶ Ἀργείους καὶ Ἠλείους καὶ Μαντινέας καὶ τοὺς ξυμμάχους, τέχνῃ μηδὲ μηχανῇ μηδεμιᾷ.
10 κατὰ τάδε ξυμμάχους εἶναι Ἀθηναίους καὶ Ἀργείους καὶ 3
Ἠλείους καὶ Μαντινέας ἑκατὸν ἔτη· ἢν πολέμιοι ἴωσιν
ἐς τὴν γῆν τὴν Ἀθηναίων, βοηθεῖν Ἀργείους καὶ Ἠλείους καὶ Μαντινέας Ἀθήναζε, καθ' ὅ τι ἂν ἐπαγγέλλωσιν
Ἀθηναῖοι, τρόπῳ ὁποίῳ ἂν δύνωνται ἰσχυροτάτῳ κατὰ τὸ
15 δυνατόν· ἢν δὲ δῃώσαντες οἴχωνται, πολεμίαν εἶναι
ταύτην τὴν πόλιν Ἀργείοις καὶ Μαντινεῦσι καὶ Ἠλείοις
καὶ Ἀθηναίοις καὶ κακῶς πάσχειν ὑπὸ πασῶν τῶν πόλεων τούτων· καταλύειν δὲ μὴ ἐξεῖναι τὸν πόλεμον πρὸς
ταύτην τὴν πόλιν μηδεμιᾷ τῶν πόλεων, ἢν μὴ ἁπάσαις
20 δοκῇ. βοηθεῖν δὲ καὶ Ἀθηναίους ἐς Ἄργος καὶ Μαντί- 4
νειαν καὶ Ἦλιν, ἢν πολέμιοι ἴωσιν ἐπὶ τὴν γῆν τὴν
Ἠλείων ἢ τὴν Μαντινέων ἢ τὴν Ἀργείων, καθ' ὅ τι ἂν

sis includes therefore only ἔτυχον . . . ξύμμαχοι, not παραγαγόντος Ἀλκιβιάδου, as Bekker and others have thought.
47. *Terms of the alliance between the Athenians on one side, and the Argives, Mantineans, and Eleans on the other.*
1. σπονδὰς ἐποιήσαντο κτέ.: see App. — 3. ἀδόλους καὶ ἀβλαβεῖς: the same formula as in c. 18. 11. Several other expressions of c. 18 and 23 are repeated here. — 4. ὅπλα δέ:

also occurs in c. 18. 12 preceded by the same words as here. It stands very properly opp. to the declaration of peace, so that δέ should not (with Kr.) be omitted.
9. τέχνῃ μηδὲ μηχανῇ: a slight variation from c. 18. 15, but there is no change in meaning.
11. ἢν πολέμιοι ἴωσιν κτέ.: cf. c. 23. 2-15 and below 21 and 36. — 13. ἐπαγγέλλωσιν: *demand, call for*; also in vi. 56. 5.

ἐπαγγέλλωσιν αἱ πόλεις αὗται, τρόπῳ ὁποίῳ ἂν δύνωνται ἰσχυροτάτῳ κατὰ τὸ δυνατόν· ἢν δὲ δῃώσαντες οἴχωνται, πολεμίαν εἶναι ταύτην τὴν πόλιν Ἀθηναίοις καὶ
Ἀργείοις καὶ Μαντινεῦσι καὶ Ἠλείοις καὶ κακῶς πάσχειν
ὑπὸ πασῶν τούτων τῶν πόλεων· καταλύειν δὲ μὴ ἐξεῖναι τὸν πόλεμον πρὸς ταύτην τὴν πόλιν, ἢν μὴ ἁπάσαις
δοκῇ ταῖς πόλεσιν. ὅπλα δὲ μὴ ἐᾶν ἔχοντας διιέναι ἐπὶ 5
πολέμῳ διὰ τῆς γῆς τῆς σφετέρας αὐτῶν καὶ τῶν ξυμμάχων ὧν ἂν ἄρχωσιν ἕκαστοι μηδὲ κατὰ θάλασσαν, ἢν
μὴ ψηφισαμένων τῶν πόλεων ἁπασῶν τὴν δίοδον εἶναι,
Ἀθηναίων καὶ Ἀργείων καὶ Μαντινέων καὶ Ἠλείων. τοῖς 6
δὲ βοηθοῦσιν ἡ πόλις ἡ πέμπουσα παρεχέτω μέχρι μὲν
τριάκοντα ἡμερῶν σῖτον, ἐπὴν ἔλθῃ ἐς τὴν πόλιν τὴν
ἐπαγγείλασαν βοηθεῖν, καὶ ἀπιοῦσι κατὰ ταὐτά· ἢν δὲ
πλέονα βούλωνται χρόνον τῇ στρατιᾷ χρῆσθαι, ἡ πόλις
ἡ μεταπεμψαμένη διδότω σῖτον, τῷ μὲν ὁπλίτῃ καὶ ψιλῷ

31. **μηδὲ κατὰ θάλασσαν**: Kr. considered these words an interpolation, as they disagree with c. 56. 6; it appears, however, from the count of the letters and spaces in the inscription discussed in the App., that they were contained in the original document (see App.). This provision evidently affects the Athenians only, as the other members of the alliance were powerless at sea, and seems to prove that the sea was regarded as part of the domain of Athens, through which she binds herself to allow no one διιέναι ἐπὶ πολέμῳ. (Pericles, in ii. 62. 10 ff., says: δύο μερῶν ἐς χρῆσιν φανερῶν, γῆς καὶ θαλάσσης, τοῦ ἑτέρου ὑμᾶς παντὸς κυριωτάτους ὄντας.) The expression διὰ τῆς γῆς is, therefore, not to be taken too literally; and indeed γῆς is omitted in c. 56. 5. — **ἢν μή**: elliptical, as elsewhere εἰ μή. Cf. Dem. XXIV. 46, οὐκ ἐῶν λέγειν οὐδὲ χρηματίζειν ἂν μὴ τῆς ἀδείας δοθείσης. In Thuc. supply διῶσι with ἢν μή, in Dem. λέγωσι καὶ χρηματίζωσι. GMT. 42, 3, N. 2; H. 905 a.

35. **ἐπὴν ἔλθῃ**: the sing. may be explained by supposing that the city herself is supposed to go in the persons of her soldiers or by supplying a sing. from βοηθοῦσιν, such as βοήθεια or ὁ βοηθῶν. St. and v. Herwerden (following Kirchhoff) read ἔλθωσιν, which is obtained by calculating the space on this line of the inscription, and is certainly easier and simpler. These words are closely connected with μέχρι τριάκοντα ἡμερῶν, "from the day on which," etc. Cf. viii. 58. 19 and 24, ἐπὴν αἱ βασιλέως νῆες ἀφίκωνται, and Ar. Av. 1355. — 37. **βούλωνται**: this, which is the reading of the Mss., is a rather awkward con-

καὶ τοξότῃ τρεῖς ὀβολοὺς Αἰγιναίους τῆς ἡμέρας ἑκάστης,
40 τῷ δ᾽ ἱππεῖ δραχμὴν Αἰγιναίαν. ἡ δὲ πόλις ἡ μετα- 7
πεμψαμένη τὴν ἡγεμονίαν ἐχέτω, ὅταν ἐν τῇ αὑτῆς ὁ
πόλεμος ᾖ. ἢν δέ ποι δόξῃ ταῖς πόλεσι κοινῇ στρατεύ-
εσθαι, τὸ ἴσον τῆς ἡγεμονίας μετεῖναι πάσαις ταῖς πόλεσιν. ὀμόσαι δὲ τὰς σπονδὰς Ἀθηναίους μὲν ὑπέρ τε 8
45 σφῶν αὐτῶν καὶ τῶν ξυμμάχων, Ἀργεῖοι δὲ καὶ Μαντινῆς καὶ Ἠλεῖοι καὶ οἱ ξύμμαχοι τούτων κατὰ πόλεις
ὀμνύντων. ὀμνύντων δὲ τὸν ἐπιχώριον ὅρκον ἕκαστοι τὸν 9
μέγιστον κατὰ ἱερῶν τελείων. ὁ δὲ ὅρκος ἔστω ὅδε·
' Ἐμμενῶ τῇ ξυμμαχίᾳ κατὰ τὰ ξυγκείμενα δικαίως καὶ
50 ἀβλαβῶς καὶ ἀδόλως, καὶ οὐ παραβήσομαι τέχνῃ οὐδὲ
μηχανῇ οὐδεμιᾷ.' ὀμνύντων δὲ Ἀθήνησι μὲν ἡ βουλὴ καὶ
αἱ ἔνδημοι ἀρχαί, ἐξορκούντων δὲ οἱ πρυτάνεις· ἐν Ἄργει
δὲ ἡ βουλὴ καὶ οἱ ὀγδοήκοντα καὶ αἱ ἀρτῦναι, ἐξορκούντων δὲ οἱ ὀγδοήκοντα· ἐν δὲ Μαντινείᾳ οἱ δημιουργοὶ
55 καὶ ἡ βουλὴ καὶ αἱ ἄλλαι ἀρχαί, ἐξορκούντων δὲ οἱ θεω-
ροὶ καὶ οἱ πολέμαρχοι· ἐν δὲ Ἤλιδι οἱ δημιουργοὶ καὶ

structio ad sensum with πόλις. Kirchhoff, St., and v. Herwerden read βούληται. — 39. Αἰγιναίους: the Aeginetan system of coinage was the one most in vogue throughout Greece, and therefore best adapted for use in international transactions. The Aeginetan drachma, also called παχεῖα, was heavier than the Attic, containing, as Hultsch, *Metrol.* p. 192 ff., shows from the weight of coins which have been preserved, 8.3 Attic obols, while the Attic drachma contained six. Poll. ix. 76 and 86 says wrongly that the Aeginetan drachma contained ten Attic obols.
41. τῇ αὑτῆς: Duker for Mss. τῇ αὐτῇ.
46. κατὰ πόλεις: cf. c. 18. 48.
47. ὀμνύντων ... κατὰ ἱερῶν: cf. Ar.

Ran. 101, ὀμόσαι καθ᾽ ἱερῶν. The ἱερὰ τέλεια are probably the hostiae maiores, full-grown victims, which Hdt. i. 183. 8 opposes to τὰ γαληθινά. — 52. αἱ ἔνδημοι ἀρχαί: magistrates whose official functions were confined to the city, and did not, like those of the generals, extend beyond its limits; opp. to ὑπερόριοι ἀρχαί. — ἐξορκούντων: used of the magistrates who preside over the ceremony and administer the oath; also in Hdt. iii. 133. 7; iv. 154. 13. — 53. αἱ ἀρτῦναι: probably as in αἱ ἀρχαί above the office stands for the officials; therefore the reading of the Mss. is not to be changed to οἱ ἀρ-τῦναι. But little is known of these and the following magistrates. See on c. 37. 5.

οἱ τὰ τέλη ἔχοντες καὶ οἱ ἑξακόσιοι, ἐξορκούντων δὲ οἱ δημιουργοὶ καὶ οἱ θεσμοφύλακες. ἀνανεοῦσθαι δὲ τοὺς 10 ὅρκους Ἀθηναίους μὲν ἰόντας ἐς Ἦλιν καὶ ἐς Μαντίνειαν καὶ ἐς Ἄργος τριάκοντα ἡμέραις πρὸ Ὀλυμπίων, Ἀργείους δὲ καὶ Ἠλείους καὶ Μαντινέας ἰόντας Ἀθήναζε δέκα ἡμέραις πρὸ Παναθηναίων τῶν μεγάλων. τὰς δὲ ξυν- 11 θήκας τὰς περὶ τῶν σπονδῶν καὶ τῶν ὅρκων καὶ τῆς ξυμμαχίας ἀναγράψαι ἐν στήλῃ λιθίνῃ Ἀθηναίους μὲν ἐν πόλει, Ἀργείους δὲ ἐν ἀγορᾷ ἐν τοῦ Ἀπόλλωνος τῷ ἱερῷ, Μαντινέας δὲ ἐν τοῦ Διὸς τῷ ἱερῷ ἐν τῇ ἀγορᾷ· καταθέντων δὲ καὶ Ὀλυμπίασι στήλην χαλκῆν κοινῇ Ὀλυμπίοις τοῖς νυνί. ἐὰν δέ τι δοκῇ ἄμεινον εἶναι ταῖς πόλεσι ταύ- 12 ταις προσθεῖναι πρὸς τοῖς ξυγκειμένοις, ὅ τι ἂν δόξῃ ταῖς πόλεσιν ἁπάσαις κοινῇ βουλευομέναις, τοῦτο κύριον εἶναι."

48 Αἱ μὲν σπονδαὶ καὶ ἡ ξυμμαχία οὕτως ἐγένοντο· καὶ 1

60. τριάκοντα ἡμέραις: the difference between the thirty days here and the ten days in 61 arises from the fact that the Athenian envoys were to take the oaths in three cities, the others only in Athens. ἡμέραις is ' dat. of degree of difference' before πρὸ Ὀλυμπίων. — Παναθηναίων: in the third year of each olympiad. The two festivals were therefore two years apart.

64. ἐν πόλει: see on c. 18. 55. — 66. καταθέντων δὲ καὶ Ὀλυμπίασι: to be executed by the Eleans as sovereigns and directors of the temple of Zeus and the Olympic festival, but in the name of all the members of the league, κοινῇ. — 67. Ὀλυμπίοις τοῖς νυνί: "at the Olympic games of this year." Cf. c. 49. 1.

68. ἐάν ... εἶναι: see App.

48. The treaty between Athens and Sparta (c. 18) is, however, not renounced. The Corinthians refuse to join the Argives in the Athenian alliance, but turn their thoughts again toward the Lacedaemonians.

1. ἡ ξυμμαχία: to correspond to c. 46. 35 (see on c. 27. 2), for αἱ ξυμμαχίαι of the Mss. ἐγένοντο (not ἐγένετο, as in c. 80. 1 and l. 102. 22, κατέστη) has for its subj. αἱ σπονδαὶ καὶ ἡ ξυμμαχία regarded as a compound subst. of which the pl. αἱ σπονδαί is the most important part; accordingly the following αἱ τῶν Λακεδαιμονίων καὶ Ἀθηναίων refers grammatically only to σπονδαί. Indeed the ξυμμαχία (c. 23) of the Lacedaemonians and Athenians was practically if not formally at an end, since both parties had entered into obligations which conflicted with

αἱ τῶν Λακεδαιμονίων καὶ Ἀθηναίων οὐκ ἀπείρηντο τούτου ἕνεκα οὐδ' ὑφ' ἑτέρων. Κορίνθιοι δὲ Ἀργείων 2 ὄντες ξύμμαχοι οὐκ ἐσῆλθον ἐς αὐτάς, (ἀλλὰ καὶ γενομένης πρὸ τούτου Ἠλείοις καὶ Ἀργείοις καὶ Μαντινεῦσι ξυμμαχίας, τοῖς αὐτοῖς πολεμεῖν καὶ εἰρήνην ἄγειν, οὐ ξυνώμοσαν,) ἀρκεῖν δ' ἔφασαν σφίσι τὴν πρώτην γενομένην ἐπιμαχίαν, ἀλλήλοις βοηθεῖν, ξυνεπιστρατεύειν δὲ μηδενί. οἱ μὲν Κορίνθιοι οὕτως ἀπέστησαν τῶν ξυμ- 3

it.—2. οὐκ ἀπείρηντο: the treaty was not renounced, i.e. was not regarded as void. — 3. οὐδ' ὑφ' ἑτέρων: not by either party. Equiv. to ὑπ' οὐδετέρων. Cf. ii. 67. 3.4, τοὺς μηδὲ μεθ' ἑτέρων.
3. Κορίνθιοι δὲ Ἀργείων ὄντες ξύμμαχοι κτέ.: the conduct of the Corinthians is represented as equivocal from the beginning: "although they were allies of the Argives (see c. 31. 25 ff.), they did not join the alliance with the Athenians." To this is added the parenthetical sent., ἀλλὰ καὶ . . . οὐ ξυνώμοσαν (see a similar parenthesis in c. 72. 3 f.). This refers, as explanation and confirmation, to the events recorded in c. 29-31: "for that matter, when the Eleans, Mantineans, and Argives had (at their instigation) made an alliance (see c. 29. 1 f. and 31. 2.4) the year before (πρὸ τούτου), they had not joined it." (ξυνώμοσαν, aor. in parenthetical clause with the force of plpf.; see on ii. 2. 12. GMT. 19. N. 4; H. 837.) We now learn for the first time that the Eleans and Mantineans had bound themselves to the Argives τοῖς αὐτοῖς πολεμεῖν καὶ εἰρήνην ἄγειν (either when they first became allies of Argos, or by some subsequent agreement of which no mention is made), whereas the Corinthians, who in c. 31. 25 εὐθὺς μετ' ἐκείνους Ἀργείων ξύμμαχοι ἐγένοντο, had confined themselves, in accordance with their invitation to the Argives (c. 27. 13), to an ἐπιμαχία, ἀλλήλοις βοηθεῖν, ξυνεπιστρατεύειν δὲ μηδενί, i.e. to a defensive alliance. Now they declare themselves contented with this treaty (ἀρκεῖν σφίσι τὴν πρώτην γενομένην ἐπιμαχίαν, which is no other than that mentioned in c. 31. 25 f.), and refuse to join in the new alliance with Athens. This Thuc. regards as a departure from their previous connexions (οὕτως ἀπέστησαν τῶν ξυμμάχων) and a return to their old relations with the Lacedaemonians, πάλιν pointing to a renewal of earlier relations (cf. c. 32. 5). — 4. ἀλλὰ καὶ . . . οὐ ξυνώμοσαν: is properly a parenthesis, for ἀρκεῖν δ' ἔφασαν κτέ. must explain οὐκ ἐσῆλθον ἐς αὐτάς, and the fact that they had not joined the Eleans, Argives, and Mantineans in their offensive and defensive alliance is merely introduced as an illustration of the half-heartedness of the Corinthians, but is not of sufficient importance to warrant the further explanation ἀρ' κεῖν δ' ἔφασαν κτέ. (St. and Schütz think ἀρκεῖν δ' ἔφασαν κτέ. explains ξυνώμοσαν, and that there is therefore no parenthesis.)

10 μάχων καὶ πρὸς τοὺς Λακεδαιμονίους πάλιν τὴν γνώμην εἶχον.

49 * Ὀλύμπια δ' ἐγένετο τοῦ θέρους τούτου, οἷς Ἀνδρο- 1 σθένης Ἀρκὰς παγκράτιον τὸ πρῶτον ἐνίκα· καὶ Λακεδαιμόνιοι τοῦ ἱεροῦ ὑπὸ Ἠλείων εἴρχθησαν ὥστε μὴ θύειν μηδ' ἀγωνίζεσθαι, οὐκ ἐκτίνοντες τὴν δίκην αὐ-
5 τοῖς ἦν ἐν τῷ Ὀλυμπιακῷ νόμῳ Ἠλεῖοι κατεδικάσαντο αὐτῶν, φάσκοντες σφᾶς ἐπὶ Φύρκον τε τεῖχος ὅπλα ἐπενεγκεῖν καὶ ἐς Λέπρεον αὐτῶν ὁπλίτας ἐν ταῖς Ὀλυμπιακαῖς σπονδαῖς ἐσπέμψαι. ἡ δὲ καταδίκη δισχίλιαι μναῖ ἦσαν, κατὰ τὸν ὁπλίτην ἕκαστον δύο μναῖ,
10 ὥσπερ ὁ νόμος ἔχει. Λακεδαιμόνιοι δὲ πρέσβεις πέμ- 2 ψαντες ἀντέλεγον μὴ δικαίως σφῶν καταδεδικάσθαι, λέγοντες μὴ ἐπηγγέλθαι πω ἐς Λακεδαίμονα τὰς σπονδάς, ὅτ' ἐσέπεμψαν τοὺς ὁπλίτας. Ἠλεῖοι δὲ τὴν παρ' αὐ- 3 τοῖς ἐκεχειρίαν ἤδη ἔφασαν εἶναι (πρώτοις γὰρ σφίσιν
15 αὐτοῖς ἐπαγγέλλουσι), καὶ ἡσυχαζόντων σφῶν καὶ οὐ

10. πρὸς τούς... γνώμην εἶχον: see on c. 44. 7 and iii. 25. 10.

49. *The Eleans exclude the Lacedaemonians from the Olympic games, on the ground that they had broken the Olympic truce and refused to pay the fine imposed upon them.*

2. παγκράτιον: in later times the name of the victor in the stadium is usually the one given. In iii. 8. 5 the kind of contest is not specified. — τὸ πρῶτον: points to subsequent victories of the same man. — 4. δίκην: fine or punishment imposed by judicial sentence. *Cf.* vi. 29. 5. — 5. ἐν τῷ νόμῳ: see App. — κατεδικάσαντο: mid. because they gave sentence in their own case. — 6. σφᾶς: see App. — Φύρκον: Phyrcus was a fort near Lepreum not far from the southern border of Triphylia. Paus., iii. 8. 3, gives some details of this attack under King Agis. — 7. αὐτῶν ὁπλίτας: see App. — ἐν ταῖς σπονδαῖς: temporal, as in 16 below; i. 55. 14; ii. 2. 19; iii. 52. 20. — 9. ἦσαν: agrees with the pred. *Cf.* i. 10. 30, ὅτι μὲν Μυκῆναι μικρὸν ἦν.

11. καταδεδικάσθαι: mid. with subj. αὐτούς understood, not pass. — 12. μὴ ἐπηγγέλθαι πω: "that the sacred truce had not yet been proclaimed."

13. τήν... ἐκεχειρίαν: the truce occasioned by the festival. See App. on c. 1. 1. — παρ' αὐτοῖς: const. with εἶναι ("it had been already in force in their country"; εἶναι as preterite), stands proleptically with the subst. — 14. πρώτοις γὰρ σφίσιν αὐτοῖς: refers to the Eleans, not (as E. Curtius, Hermes 14, p. 131, thinks) to the

THUCYDIDES V. 49, 50.

προσδεχομένων ὡς ἐν σπονδαῖς, αὐτοὺς λαθεῖν ἀδικήσαντας. οἱ δὲ Λακεδαιμόνιοι ὑπελάμβανον οὐ χρεὼν 4 εἶναι αὐτοὺς ἐπαγγεῖλαι ἔτι ἐς Λακεδαίμονα, εἰ ἀδικεῖν γε ἤδη ἐνόμιζον αὐτούς, ἀλλ' οὐχ ὡς νομίζοντας τοῦτο 20 δρᾶσαι, καὶ ὅπλα οὐδαμόσε ἔτι αὐτοῖς ἐπενεγκεῖν. Ἠλεῖοι 5 δὲ τοῦ αὐτοῦ λόγου εἴχοντο, ὡς μὲν οὐκ ἀδικοῦσι μὴ ἂν πεισθῆναι, εἰ δὲ βούλονται σφίσι Λέπρεον ἀποδοῦναι, τό τε αὐτῶν μέρος ἀφιέναι τοῦ ἀργυρίου καὶ ὃ τῷ θεῷ 50 γίγνεται αὐτοὶ ὑπὲρ ἐκείνων ἐκτίσειν. ὡς δ' οὐκ ἐσ- 1 ήκουον, αὖθις τάδε ἠξίουν, Λέπρεον μὲν μὴ ἀποδοῦναι, εἰ μὴ βούλονται, ἀναβάντας δὲ ἐπὶ τὸν βωμὸν τοῦ Διὸς τοῦ Ὀλυμπίου, ἐπειδὴ προθυμοῦνται χρῆσθαι τῷ ἱερῷ, 5 ἐπομόσαι ἐναντίον τῶν Ἑλλήνων ἦ μὴν ἀποδώσειν ὕστερον τὴν καταδίκην. ὡς δὲ οὐδὲ ταῦτα ἤθελον, Λακεδαι- 2 μόνιοι μὲν εἴργοντο τοῦ ἱεροῦ, θυσίας καὶ ἀγώνων, καὶ

Lacedaemonians. — 16. λαθεῖν: *i.e.* before they (the Eleans) knew anything about it.

17. ὑπελάμβανον: *replied* (took speech against them) as in ὑπολαβὼν εἶπε, ii. 72. 1; iii. 113. 11. — οὐ χρεών εἶναι κτέ.: *they need not have announced* (GMT. 49, 2, N. 3 a) *the truce in Sparta if they had been of the opinion that the Lacedaemonians had already transgressed it* (by beginning hostilities); *but they had not done it* (i.e. proclaimed the truce) *in this belief at all.* For τοῦτο δρᾶσαι, see on i. 5. 11; ii. 49. 22; iii. 40. 21; iv. 59. 6). — 19. οὐχ ὡς νομίζοντες: *not as if they thought so,* but as if they didn't think so. (Naber, Mnem. 14, p. 320, suggests οὐχ οὕτω νομίζοντες.) — 20. καὶ ὅπλα οὐδαμόσε ἔτι αὐτοῖς ἐπενεγκεῖν: *they* (the Lacedaemonians) *had not continued hostilities against them* after the truce had been announced at Sparta.

21. μὴ ἂν πεισθῆναι: 'the Eleans were still positive that the Lacedaemonians were in the wrong, and said that they *would never be persuaded* of the contrary' (Jowett). — 23. τό τε αὐτῶν μέρος: the fine of 2000 minae would, if paid, have been divided between the state of Elis and the temple. — γίγνεται: ὀφείλεται, Schol.

50. *Still the fear of a disturbance at the games turns out to be unfounded. Fruitless negotiations at Corinth.*

3. ἀναβάντας: a necessary correction for ἀναβάντες of most Mss. — 4. ἐπειδὴ προθυμοῦνται: *since they eagerly desired.* — 5. ἐπομόσαι: see App.

7. θυσίας καὶ ἀγώνων: in appos. with τοῦ ἱεροῦ, answering the same purpose as ὥστε with the corresponding infs. in c. 49. 3. These words are not necessary, but are not out of place here (Kr. and St. bracket them

οἴκοι ἔθυον, οἱ δὲ ἄλλοι Ἕλληνες ἐθεώρουν πλὴν Λεπρεατῶν. ὅμως δὲ οἱ Ἠλεῖοι δεδιότες μὴ βίᾳ θύσωσι, ξὺν 3 ὅπλοις τῶν νεωτέρων φυλακὴν εἶχον· ἦλθον δὲ αὐτοῖς καὶ Ἀργεῖοι καὶ Μαντινῆς, χίλιοι ἑκατέρων, καὶ Ἀθηναίων ἱππῆς, οἳ ἐν Ἁρπίνῃ ὑπέμενον τὴν ἑορτήν. δέος 4 δ᾽ ἐγένετο τῇ πανηγύρει μέγα μὴ ξὺν ὅπλοις ἔλθωσιν οἱ Λακεδαιμόνιοι, ἄλλως τε καὶ ἐπειδὴ καὶ Λίχας ὁ Ἀρκεσιλάου, Λακεδαιμόνιος, ἐν τῷ ἀγῶνι ὑπὸ τῶν ῥαβδούχων πληγὰς ἔλαβεν, ὅτι νικῶντος τοῦ ἑαυτοῦ ζεύγους καὶ ἀνακηρυχθέντος Βοιωτῶν δημοσίου κατὰ τὴν οὐκ ἐξουσίαν τῆς ἀγωνίσεως, προελθὼν ἐς τὸν ἀγῶνα ἀνέδησε

as an interpolation derived from c. 49. 3). — 8. **οἴκοι ἔθυον**: for 'participation in the sacrifice at the festival of the Olympian Zeus belonged to the state religion of the Spartans' (Curtius, Hermes 14, p. 131). — **ἐθεώρουν**: "were on the spot and took part in the festival." Cf. c. 18. 4; viii. 10. 2.

9. **μὴ βίᾳ θύσωσι**: "that they would force their way to the sacrifice by arms," aor. — **ξὺν ὅπλοις τῶν νεωτέρων**: an unusual expression: cum iuuentute armata, *with the young men under arms*. The simple ξὺν ὅπλοις or ξὺν τοῖς ὅπλοις (cf. 13; ii. 2. 11; 90. 28; iv. 14. 13; vi. 105. 10) freq. denotes arms in actual use, and is practically equiv. to ξὺν ὁπλίταις. Cf. Scott, *Marmion*, i. 20.

The sight of plundering Border spears
Might justify suspicious fears.

Here the ὅπλα are limited to the νεώτεροι because the rest of the population was just then busy with the festival. — 12. **Ἁρπίνῃ**: for Ἀργει of the Mss. is an emendation of Michaelis (Philol. 24, p. 166) adopted by Cl. and St. Harpina, one of the eight towns of the Pisatid (Strab. viii. 32), was situated in the valley of the Alpheus, twenty stadia above Olympia (Curtius, *Peloponn.* II. p. 50; Bursian, II. p. 287 f.), near enough for protection, and far enough away to avoid disturbing the festival by the sight of arms.

14. **Λίχας**: the same who appears freq. in the course of the war as a man of some influence. Cf. c. 76. 11; viii. 39. 8, etc. — 15. **ῥαβδούχων**: prob. the subordinates of the agonothetae or hellanodicae, whose duty was to keep order and correct offenders. Hermann, *Griech. Alt.* II. § 50, note 20. — 17. **Βοιωτῶν δημοσίου**: τοῦ δημοσίου τῶν Βοιωτῶν, Schol. Apparently Lichas had the community or state of the Boeotians proclaimed victor. Others take δημοσίου with ζεύγους. — **κατὰ τὴν οὐκ ἐξουσίαν**: διὰ τὸ μὴ ἐξεῖναι Λακεδαιμονίοις ἀγωνίζεσθαι, Schol. Cf. i. 137. 28, τὴν τῶν γεφυρῶν οὐ διάλυσιν, and c. 35. 6. Lichas had the Boeotians proclaimed victor because he, as a Lacedaemonian, could not take part in the games. He was struck by the beadles because he went upon the course and crowned his charioteer. — 18. **ἀγωνίσεως**: this word occurs only here in Thuc. and prob. nowhere else in Att. Greek. — **ἐς τὸν ἀγῶνα**:

τὸν ἡνίοχον, βουλόμενος δηλῶσαι ὅτι ἑαυτοῦ ἦν τὸ ἅρμα·
ὥστε πολλῷ δὴ μᾶλλον ἐπεφόβηντο πάντες καὶ ἐδόκει τι
νέον ἔσεσθαι. οἱ μέντοι Λακεδαιμόνιοι ἡσύχασάν τε καὶ
ἡ ἑορτὴ αὐτοῖς οὕτω διῆλθεν. ἐς δὲ Κόρινθον μετὰ τὰ
Ὀλύμπια Ἀργεῖοί τε καὶ οἱ ξύμμαχοι ἀφίκοντο δεησό-
μενοι αὐτῶν παρὰ σφᾶς ἐλθεῖν. καὶ Λακεδαιμονίων
πρέσβεις ἔτυχον παρόντες· καὶ πολλῶν λόγων γενομένων
τέλος οὐδὲν ἐπράχθη, ἀλλὰ σεισμοῦ γενομένου διελύθησαν
ἕκαστοι ἐπ' οἴκου. καὶ * τὸ θέρος ἐτελεύτα.

51   Τοῦ δ' ἐπιγιγνομένου χειμῶνος ** Ἡρακλεώταις τοῖς
ἐν Τραχῖνι μάχη ἐγένετο πρὸς Αἰνιᾶνας καὶ Δόλοπας
καὶ Μηλιᾶς καὶ Θεσσαλῶν τινας· προσοικοῦντα γὰρ τὰ
ἔθνη ταῦτα τῇ πόλει πολέμια ἦν· οὐ γὰρ ἐπ' ἄλλῃ
τινὶ γῇ ἢ τῇ τούτων τὸ χωρίον ἐτειχίσθη. καὶ εὐθύς τε
καθισταμένῃ τῇ πόλει ἠναντιοῦντο, ἐς ὅσον ἐδύναντο
φθείροντες, καὶ τότε τῇ μάχῃ ἐνίκησαν τοὺς Ἡρακλεώ-
τας, καὶ Ξενάρης ὁ Κνίδιος, Λακεδαιμόνιος, ἄρχων αὐτῶν ἀπέθανε, διεφθάρησαν δὲ καὶ ἄλλοι τῶν Ἡρακλεω-

---

upon the course. — ἀνέδησε: ἐστεφά-
νωσε, Schol. — 20. τι νέον: in the
sense of the more usual comp. νεώτε-
ρόν τι, as in i. 132. 25; vii. 86. 22. —
22. οὕτω διῆλθεν: i.e. without any
further disturbance. αὐτοῖς refers not
to the Lacedaemonians but the Greeks
(πάντες, 20) present at Olympia.
26. τέλος: adv. *finally.* — σεισμοῦ
γενομένου: cf. c. 45. 20.
51. *The Heracleans of Trachis are
defeated by the neighbouring tribes.*
1. Ἡρακλεώταις: Heraclea in Trachis was founded in 426 B.C. See iii.
92. — 3. Μηλιᾶς: see App.
3. προσοικοῦντα: in pred. position,
gives the reason for πολέμια ἦν. Being neighbours of the Heracleans they

felt that the town was dangerous to
them. The same idea is expressed by
ὧν ἐπὶ τῇ γῇ ἐκτίζετο, iii. 93. 7, where
the foundation of Heraclea is described. — 5. ἐτειχίσθη: τειχίζειν of
the fortified settlement, as in iii. 92.
24. — 6. καθισταμένῃ: pass. like καθίστασθαι, iii. 92. 14. — 7. φθείροντες:
denotes continued destructive action.
Cf. ἔφθειρον, iii. 93. 8. — ἐνίκησαν:
aor., expressing the momentary result without regard to further consequences. See on i. 29. 19. — 8. Κνίδιος: gen. of Κνῖδις. Cf. iv. 107. 11,
Γοάξιος. Meineke (Hermes 3, p. 363)
suggests Κνιδίου. The name is uncertain. Xenares is doubtless the
ephor of c. 36. 7.

10 τῶν. καὶ ὁ χειμὼν ἐτελεύτα, καὶ δωδέκατον ἔτος τῷ πολέμῳ ἐτελεύτα.

52 Τοῦ δ' * ἐπιγιγνομένου θέρους εὐθὺς ἀρχομένου τὴν 1
Ἡράκλειαν, ὡς μετὰ τὴν μάχην κακῶς ἐφθείρετο, Βοιωτοὶ παρέλαβον, καὶ Ἡγησιππίδαν τὸν Λακεδαιμόνιον ὡς οὐ καλῶς ἄρχοντα ἐξέπεμψαν. δείσαντες δὲ παρέλα-
5 βον τὸ χωρίον μὴ Λακεδαιμονίων τὰ κατὰ Πελοπόννησον θορυβουμένων Ἀθηναῖοι λάβωσι· Λακεδαιμόνιοι μέντοι ὠργίζοντο αὐτοῖς.

Καὶ τοῦ αὐτοῦ θέρους Ἀλκιβιάδης ὁ Κλεινίου, στρα- 2
τηγὸς ὢν Ἀθηναίων, Ἀργείων καὶ τῶν ξυμμάχων ξυμ-
10 πρασσόντων ἐλθὼν ἐς Πελοπόννησον μετ' ὀλίγων Ἀθηναίων ὁπλιτῶν καὶ τοξοτῶν, καὶ τῶν αὐτόθεν ξυμμάχων παραλαβὼν τά τε ἄλλα ξυγκαθίστη περὶ τὴν ξυμμαχίαν διαπορευόμενος Πελοπόννησον τῇ στρατιᾷ, καὶ Πατρέας τε τείχη καθεῖναι ἔπεισεν ἐς θάλασσαν καὶ αὐτὸς ἕτερον

52. *The Boeotians take possession of Heraclea to protect it against the Athenians. Alcibiades, acting in concert with the Argives and their allies, tries to increase the power of the confederacy in Peloponnesus.*
2. ἐφθείρετο: i.e. by its hostile neighbours. *Cf.* c. 51. 7. — 3. παρέλαβον: i.e. in a friendly way, for protection (not κατέλαβον); but the Lacedaemonians regarded it differently. — 4. ὡς οὐ καλῶς ἄρχοντα: about the misconduct of the Lacedaemonian governors in Heraclea complaints were made as early as iii. 93. 15, χαλεπῶς τε καὶ ἔστιν ἃ οὐ καλῶς ἐξηγούμενοι (sc. τῶν Λακεδαιμονίων οἱ ἀφικνούμενοι). — 5. Λακεδαιμονίων τὰ κατὰ Πελοπόννησον θορυβουμένων: " since the Lacedaemonians had their hands full with Peloponnesian affairs just then" (pres.).

8. Ἀλκιβιάδης: on his position and conduct at this time, see Müller-Strübing, *Aristoph. und die hist. Krit.* p. 398 f. — 11. τῶν αὐτόθεν (ἀπὸ Πελοποννήσου, Schol.) ξυμμάχων: part. gen. with παραλαβών, as in iv. 80. 7 with ἐκπέμψαι. — 12. περὶ τὴν ξυμμαχίαν: he made the arrangements required by the treaty of c. 47. — 13. Πατρέας: Patrae, now Patras. On the importance of its position at the entrance of the Gulf of Corinth, see Curtius, *Peloponnes.* I. p. 434 ff. Hertzberg, *Alkibiades*, p. 101, shows the importance of this expedition. — 14. τὰ τείχη καθεῖναι . . . ἐς θάλασσαν: i.e. μακρὰ τείχη ἐς θάλασσαν οἰκοδομεῖν acc. to a regular principle of Athenian policy, to make the town accessible from the sea. See on i. 103. 14. — ἕτερον (sc. τεῖχος) τειχίσαι: *cf.* i. 90. 7; 91. 3. — 15. τῷ Ῥίῳ τῷ Ἀχαϊκῷ:

15 διενοεῖτο τειχίσαι ἐπὶ τῷ 'Ρίῳ τῷ Ἀχαϊκῷ. Κορίνθιοι δὲ καὶ Σικυώνιοι καὶ οἷς ἦν ἐν βλάβῃ τειχισθὲν βοηθήσαντες διεκώλυσαν.

53 Τοῦ δ' αὐτοῦ θέρους Ἐπιδαυρίοις καὶ Ἀργείοις 1 πόλεμος ἐγένετο, προφάσει μὲν περὶ τοῦ θύματος τοῦ Ἀπόλλωνος τοῦ Πυθαέως, ὃ δέον ἀπαγαγεῖν οὐκ ἀπέπεμπον ὑπὲρ βοταμίων Ἐπιδαύριοι· κυριώτατοι δὲ τοῦ 5 ἱεροῦ ἦσαν Ἀργεῖοι· ἐδόκει δὲ καὶ ἄνευ τῆς αἰτίας τὴν Ἐπίδαυρον τῷ τε Ἀλκιβιάδῃ καὶ τοῖς Ἀργείοις προσλαβεῖν, ἢν δύνωνται, τῆς τε Κορίνθου ἕνεκα ἡσυχίας καὶ

a low point of land on the coast of Achaea. On the opposite side of the gulf is a similar cape called τὸ 'Ρίον τὸ Μολυκρινόν. Cf. ii. 84. 29; 86. 6 and 11.— 16. οἷς ἦν ἐν βλάβῃ τειχισθέν: (sc. τὸ 'Ρίον) "those to whom the fortification of Rhium by the Athenians was injurious" (because they would then have entire control of the entrance to the Gulf of Corinth). The const. is like i. 100. 16 f., οἷς πολέμιον ἦν τὸ χωρίον κτιζόμενον. ἐν βλάβῃ is a periphrasis for the adj. Cf. ἐν ἡδονῇ, Hdt. iv. 139. 8; vii. 15. 11.

53. *The Argives acting under the advice of Alcibiades make war against the Epidaurians.*

2. προφάσει: the dat. (here and in vi. 76. 5) and the acc. (in c. 80. 17; iii. 111. 2; vi. 33. 9) are used by Thuc. with the same signification. — θύματος: a rare word, corresponding to the Dor. σύματος in c. 77. 11. — 3. τοῦ Πυθαέως: from nom. Πυθαεύς, used by Paus. ii. 24. 1, who says of the inhabitants of Hermione, ii. 35. 2, τὸ τοῦ Πυθαέως ὄνομα μεμαθήκασι παρὰ Ἀργείων (the uncontracted form is retained after the analogy of Μηλιέως, iv. 100. 2). Prob. the temple of Apollo Pythaeus is meant, which was the only building left standing by the Argives when they destroyed Asine, acc. to Paus. ii. 36. 5. Perhaps the Epidaurians, even though the Argives were κυριώτατοι τοῦ ἱεροῦ, claimed a share in the use of the lands of the temple for pasturage or similar purposes, and the expression ὑπὲρ βοταμίων, which does not occur elsewhere, may refer to this. (St. writes ὑπὲρ βοτανῶν and cites Plat. *Rep.* 401 b, pro pascuis. παραποταμίων, which Poppo took from inferior Mss., is still more difficult to explain.) — δέον: acc. abs., equiv. to ἔδει. *When they ought to have* (but did not). — ἀπαγαγεῖν: *pay.* Cf. Ar. *Vesp.* 707, τὸν φόρον ἀπάγουσιν; Xen. *Cyr.* ii. 4. 12. — 5. ἐδόκει: "it was their opinion," "they favoured the plan." Cf. iii. 30. 2; iv. 71. 6. — καὶ ἄνευ τῆς αἰτίας: "even apart from the above-mentioned ground of complaint." — 6. προσλαβεῖν: *i.e.* to force them to join the Argive alliance. Cf. i. 35. 14; iii. 13. 31. — 7. τῆς τε Κορίνθου ἕνεκα ἡσυχίας καὶ ... βραχυτέραν ἔσεσθαι τὴν βοήθειαν: the first reason is expressed by ἕνεκα ἡσυχίας: "in order to keep Corinth quiet" (which was now in a position of doubtful

ἐκ τῆς Αἰγίνης βραχυτέραν ἔσεσθαι τὴν βοήθειαν ἢ Σκύλλαιον περιπλεῖν τοῖς Ἀθηναίοις. παρεσκευάζοντο οὖν οἱ Ἀργεῖοι ὡς αὐτοὶ ἐς τὴν Ἐπίδαυρον διὰ τοῦ θύματος τὴν ἔσπραξιν ἐσβαλοῦντες. ἐξεστράτευσαν δὲ καὶ οἱ Λακεδαιμόνιοι κατὰ τοὺς αὐτοὺς χρόνους πανδημεὶ ἐς Λεῦκτρα τῆς ἑαυτῶν μεθορίας πρὸς τὸ Λύκαιον, Ἄγιδος τοῦ Ἀρχιδάμου βασιλέως ἡγουμένου· ᾔδει δὲ οὐδεὶς ὅποι στρατεύουσιν, οὐδὲ αἱ πόλεις ἐξ ὧν ἐπέμφθησαν. ὡς δ᾽ αὐτοῖς τὰ διαβατήρια θυομένοις οὐ προυχώρει, αὐτοί τε ἀπῆλθον ἐπ᾽ οἴκου * καὶ τοῖς ξυμμάχοις περιήγγειλαν μετὰ τὸν μέλλοντα (Καρνεῖος δ᾽

friendship toward Argos; cf. c. 48. § 2); the second by the acc. and fut. inf. which is still under the influence of ἐδόκει: "and the Athenians (they thought) would be able to bring aid to Argos more quickly by way of Aegina (if they could march through the Epidaurian territory) than if they were obliged to sail around Scyllaeum."— 8. ἡ περιπλεῖν: a loose const. caused by attraction of the preceding inf. περιπλεῖν stands as the subj. of ἔσεσθαι which is to be supplied from the preceding line: "than (it would be) to sail round," etc. We should naturally expect a cond. clause after ἤ. Cf. iv. 66. 15, καὶ νομίζοντες ἐλάσσω σφίσι τὸν κίνδυνον ἢ τοὺς ἐκπεσόντας ὑπὸ σφῶν κατελθεῖν. — 9. Σκύλλαιον: Scyllaeum, a promontory between Hermione and Troezene. — 10. αὐτοί: sponte. They did not wish the influence of Alcibiades to be observed; and therefore they mentioned only one reason for hostilities, that they must collect the arrears of sacrifice. — διὰ τοῦ θύματος τὴν ἔσπραξιν: on the position of the words, see on i. 32. 8; iii. 46. 19.

54. *A demonstration of the Lacedae-*monians against Argos and for the assistance of Epidaurus is without result.

3. Λεῦκτρα: can be only the Arcadian Leuctra, since it is described as πρὸς τὸ Λύκαιον (another Leuctra was in Laconia, near the mouth of the Pamisus). At this time the Lacedaemonians counted it among their possessions, although it was situated in the μεθορία, and they wished to cross the border from this point. It afterwards belonged to the territory of Megalopolis. See Curtius, *Peloponn.* I. p. 293 and p. 336, note 9. — 5. αἱ πόλεις: αἱ Λακωνικαί, Schol., doubtless correctly. At first only the perioeci were called out (πανδημεί, 2). καὶ τοῖς ξυμμάχοις περιήγγειλαν, 7, applies only to the later campaign.

6. τὰ διαβατήρια: sc. ἱερά. Cf. c. 116. 3. The sacrifice offered to Zeus by the Spartan kings before crossing the border; freq. in Xen. *Hell.* (iii. 4. 3; iv. 7. 2; v. 3. 14; 4. 37 and 47), who describes it, *de Rep. Lac.* 13. 2 ff. —7. προυχώρει: cf. Xen. *Hell.* iii. 4. 3, ἐξῆλθε. Elsewhere in Thuc., c. 55. 15 and c. 116. 3, and Xen. ll.cc., ἐγένετο. — 8. μετὰ τὸν μέλλοντα: sc. μῆνα. The Laconian month Καρνεῖος corre-

ἦν μήν, ἱερομηνία Δωριεῦσι) παρασκευάζεσθαι ὡς στρατευσομένους. Ἀργεῖοι δ' ἀναχωρησάντων αὐτῶν τοῦ πρὸ τοῦ Καρνείου μηνὸς ἐξελθόντες τετράδι φθίνοντος, καὶ ἄγοντες τὴν ἡμέραν ταύτην πάντα τὸν χρόνον, ἐσέβαλον ἐς τὴν Ἐπιδαυρίαν καὶ ἐδῄουν. Ἐπιδαύριοι δὲ τοὺς ξυμμάχους ἐπεκαλοῦντο· ὧν τινες οἱ μὲν τὸν μῆνα προυφασίσαντο, οἱ δὲ καὶ ἐς μεθορίαν τῆς Ἐπιδαυρίας ἐλθόντες ἡσύχαζον. καὶ καθ' ὃν χρόνον ἐν τῇ Ἐπιδαύρῳ οἱ Ἀργεῖοι ἦσαν, ἐς Μαντίνειαν πρεσβεῖαι ἀπὸ τῶν πόλεων ξυνῆλθον, Ἀθηναίων παρακαλεσάντων. καὶ γιγνομένων λόγων Εὐφαμίδας ὁ Κορίνθιος οὐκ ἔφη τοὺς λόγους τοῖς ἔργοις ὁμολογεῖν· σφεῖς μὲν γὰρ περὶ εἰρήνης ξυγκαθῆ-

sponds to the Att. Μεταγειτνιών as the second month of summer, nearly our August. — 9. ἱερομηνία: see App.
11. τετράδι φθίνοντος: *i.e.* on the 27th of the month. — 12. ἄγοντες τὴν ἡμέραν ταύτην πάντα τὸν χρόνον: with this punctuation (comma after πάντα τὸν χρόνον, not before), which is that adopted by Bekker, Grote, VI. p. 336, explains: '*keeping that day during the whole time*': *i.e.* they called every day the 27th as long as they were in Epidaurian territory, and in that way postponed the following month as long as they pleased. Madvig (*Adv. Crit.* I. p. 324) gives the same explanation: Argivi fraude minime sane subtili utentes, ne mense Carneo, ut adversarii, quiescere cogerentur, per totum tempus unum diem se agere finxerunt eodemque omnes numero nomineque signarunt, τριακάδα [rather τετράδα] φθίνοντος mensis qui Carneum praecedebat appellantes. He compares with this a similar trick told of Alexander by Plut. *Alex.* 16.

Grote reminds us that the Argives once tried a similar trick against the Lacedaemonians. *Cf.* Xen. *Hell.* iv. 7. 1 f. (Schütz, Ztschr. für d. Gymn. Wesen 1, 31, p. 258, thinks it means "marching this day all the time," *i.e.* 'they employed the whole day in marching.')
14. τινες οἱ μέν: Kr. explains this by saying that τινες shows that οἱ μέν ... οἱ δέ do not include all the allies, some of whom may actually have come. This seems prob. from c. 55. 6, τοὺς δ' Ἐπιδαυρίους καὶ τοὺς ξυμμάχους. (Cl. explains τινες οἱ μέν as equiv to οἱ μέν τινες, but suggests that οἱ μέν may be a copyist's addition.)
55. *A conference held at Mantinea. The war between Argos and Epidaurus is intermitted at the suggestion of the Corinthians, but is presently renewed.*
2. ἀπὸ τῶν πόλεων: primarily from the allied cities (c. 47); but the narrative shows that envoys from other places, or at any rate from Corinth, were present. — 3. παρακαλεσάντων: used esp. of invitations to allies. *Cf.* i. 67. 3; v. 17. 17; 27. 3. — 5. ὁμολο-

σθαι, τοὺς δ' Ἐπιδαυρίους καὶ τοὺς ξυμμάχους καὶ τοὺς Ἀργείους μεθ' ὅπλων ἀντιτετάχθαι· διαλῦσαι οὖν πρῶτον χρῆναι ἐφ' ἑκατέρων ἐλθόντας τὰ στρατόπεδα, καὶ οὕτω πάλιν λέγειν περὶ τῆς εἰρήνης. καὶ πεισθέντες ᾤχοντο 2 καὶ τοὺς Ἀργείους ἀπήγαγον ἐκ τῆς Ἐπιδαυρίας. ὕστερον δὲ ἐς τὸ αὐτὸ ξυνελθόντες οὐδ' ὡς ἐδυνήθησαν ξυμβῆναι, ἀλλ' οἱ Ἀργεῖοι πάλιν ἐς τὴν Ἐπιδαυρίαν ἐσέβαλον καὶ ἐδῄουν. ἐξεστράτευσαν δὲ καὶ οἱ Λακεδαιμόνιοι ἐς 3 Καρύας· καὶ ὡς οὐδ' ἐνταῦθα τὰ διαβατήρια αὐτοῖς ἐγένετο, ἐπανεχώρησαν. Ἀργεῖοι δὲ τεμόντες τῆς Ἐπι- 4 δαυρίας ὡς τὸ τρίτον μέρος ἀπῆλθον ἐπ' οἴκου. καὶ Ἀθηναίων αὐτοῖς χίλιοι ἐβοήθησαν ὁπλῖται καὶ Ἀλκιβιάδης στρατηγός, πυθόμενοι [δὲ] τοὺς Λακεδαιμονίους ἐξεστρατεῦσθαι, καὶ ὡς οὐδὲν ἔτι αὐτῶν ἔδει, ἀπῆλθον. καὶ τὸ θέρος οὕτω διῆλθεν.

γείν: only here in figurative sense, *agree, correspond;* elsewhere used of persons, *come to an agreement.* — 8. ἐφ' ἑκατέρων ἐλθόντας: St. (followed by Cl. and v. Herwerden) for ἀφ' ἑκατέρων of Mss. Euphamidas calls upon the envoys present to go to the camps of the two hostile parties and bring about a cessation of hostilities (διαλῦσαι). — καὶ οὕτω: "and when that had been accomplished." See on c. 38. 5. — 9. πάλιν λέγειν: "they might renew their conference."
9. πεισθέντες: *sc.* the envoys. (Cl. says: 'the envoys of both parties, who had agreed to this.' Perhaps rather the envoys present at Mantinea, whose influence would certainly suffice to effect a truce.) — 10. ἀπήγαγον: *they induced them to depart.* Cf. iii. 36. 3; v. 35. 21. — 11. οὐδ' ὡς ἐδυνήθησαν ξυμβῆναι: refers esp. to those engaged in the war, *i.e.* the Argives and Epidaurians.

14. Καρύας: Caryae, on the road from Sparta to Tegea. In early times it was a canton of the Tegeans, later a town of the Perioeci. It lay near the present Arachova. Curtius, *Peloponn.* I. p. 261. — 15. ἐγένετο: see on c. 54. 7.
16. ὡς τὸ τρίτον μέρος: ὡς with numerals denotes that they are only to be taken approximately, as in iv. 31. 8, ὡς τριάκοντα. — 17. ἐβοήθησαν: aor., corresponds to our plpf., as in c. 48. 7, ξυνώμοσαν. Opp. to this and completing the account, stand the words καὶ ὡς ... ἀπῆλθον: "as soon as they heard that the Lacedaemonians had marched out, they hastened to take the field, and now that they were no longer needed, they went home." — 18. πυθόμενοι [δὲ] τοὺς Λακεδαιμονίους: see App. — 19. ὡς οὐδὲν ἔτι αὐτῶν ἔδει: intimates briefly that they had also heard of the departure of the Lacedaemonians. —

56 * Τοῦ δ' ἐπιγιγνομένου χειμῶνος Λακεδαιμόνιοι λα- 1
θόντες Ἀθηναίους φρουρούς τε τριακοσίους καὶ Ἀγη
σιππίδαν ἄρχοντα κατὰ θάλασσαν ἐς Ἐπίδαυρον ἐσέπεμ
ψαν. Ἀργεῖοι δ' ἐλθόντες παρ' Ἀθηναίους ἐπεκάλουν 2
ὅτι, γεγραμμένον ἐν ταῖς σπονδαῖς διὰ τῆς ἑαυτῶν ἑκά
στους μὴ ἐᾶν πολεμίους διιέναι, ἐάσειαν κατὰ θάλασσαν
παραπλεῦσαι· καὶ εἰ μὴ κἀκεῖνοι ἐς Πύλον κομιοῦσιν ἐπὶ
Λακεδαιμονίους τοὺς Μεσσηνίους καὶ Εἵλωτας, ἀδική
σεσθαι αὐτοί. Ἀθηναῖοι δὲ Ἀλκιβιάδου πείσαντος τῇ μὲν 3
Λακωνικῇ στήλῃ ὑπέγραψαν ὅτι οὐκ ἐνέμειναν οἱ Λακε
δαιμόνιοι τοῖς ὅρκοις, ἐς δὲ Πύλον ἐκόμισαν τοὺς ἐκ
Κρανίων Εἵλωτας λῄζεσθαι, τὰ δ' ἄλλα ἡσύχαζον. τὸν 4
δὲ χειμῶνα τοῦτον πολεμούντων Ἀργείων καὶ Ἐπιδαυ-

20. **οὕτω διῆλθεν**: Müller-Strübing, *Aristoph. und die hist. Krit.* p. 400, note, thinks this expression intimates that the summer had been uneventful. But διελθεῖν is so freq. used by Thuc. to denote the passage of time (*cf.* i. 82. 12; iv. 115. 1; v. 20. 3; 50. 22), that no special signification should be attached to it here.

56. *The Lacedaemonians send a garrison to Epidaurus. The Athenians bring Helots to Pylos to plunder Laconia. The Argives make an unsuccessful attack upon Epidaurus.*

1. **λαθόντες Ἀθηναίους**: their ships were doubtless on guard in the Gulf of Argos. These words express the opinion referred to in c. 47. 31, that the sea was under the rule of Athens. — 2. **Ἀγησιππίδαν**: prob. the same whose name is given in Att. form, Ἡγησιππίδαν, in c. 52. 3.

5. **γεγραμμένον**: acc. abs. of the impers. verb like εἰρημένον in c. 30. 9; 39. 12. G. 278, 2; H. 973. — **διὰ τῆς ἑαυτῶν**: with intentional omission of γῆς of c. 47. 30. See on c. 47. 31 and Grote VI. c. 56, p. 340. — **ἐν ταῖς σπονδαῖς**: const. with γεγραμμένον. σπονδαί, *treaty*, is here used to mean the written document. — **ἑκάστους**: corresponding to ὧν ἂν ἄρχωσιν ἕκαστοι, c. 47. 31. — 7. **κομιοῦσιν**: *transfer*, see to the transportation of. *Cf.* c. 35. 26. — 8. **τοὺς Μεσσηνίους καὶ Εἵλωτας**: *cf.* c. 35. 27. — **ἀδικήσεσθαι**: in pass. signification occurs also in vi. 87. 17.

10. **τῇ ... Λακωνικῇ στήλῃ**: ἣν ἔστησαν οἱ Ἀθηναῖοι ἔχουσαν τὰς Λακωνικὰς σπονδάς, Schol. On the Acropolis. See c. 23. 23. — **ὑπέγραψαν**: this did not officially put an end to the peace with Sparta, but prepared the way for war by showing that the Athenians no longer considered themselves bound by the treaty. — 12. **ἐκ Κρανίων**: on the island of Cephallenia, where they had given them a home. See c. 35. § 7. — **λῄζεσθαι**: for the simple inf. expressing purpose, *cf.* c. 2. 11, περιπλεῖν; ii. 84. 25, κατέστησαν τρέπεσθαι; vi. 16. 33. GMT. 97; H. 951.

ρίων μάχη μὲν οὐδεμία ἐγένετο ἐκ παρασκευῆς, ἐνέδραι
15 δὲ καὶ καταδρομαί, ἐν αἷς ὡς τύχοιεν ἑκατέρων τινὲς
διεφθείροντο. καὶ τελευτῶντος τοῦ χειμῶνος πρὸς ἔαρ
ἤδη κλίμακας ἔχοντες οἱ Ἀργεῖοι ἦλθον ἐπὶ τὴν Ἐπίδαυρον ὡς ἐρήμου οὔσης διὰ τὸν πόλεμον βίᾳ αἱρήσοντες·
καὶ ἄπρακτοι ἀπῆλθον. καὶ ὁ χειμὼν ἐτελεύτα, * καὶ
20 τρίτον καὶ δέκατον ἔτος τῷ πολέμῳ ἐτελεύτα.

57 Τοῦ δ' ἐπιγιγνομένου θέρους ** μεσοῦντος Λακε- 1
δαιμόνιοι, ὡς αὐτοῖς οἵ τε Ἐπιδαύριοι ξύμμαχοι ὄντες ἐτα-
λαιπώρουν καὶ τἆλλα ἐν τῇ Πελοποννήσῳ τὰ μὲν ἀφει-
στήκει, τὰ δ' οὐ καλῶς εἶχε, νομίσαντες, εἰ μὴ προκατα-
5 λήψονται ἐν τάχει, ἐπὶ πλέον χωρήσεσθαι αὐτά, ἐστράτευον αὐτοὶ καὶ οἱ Εἵλωτες πανδημεὶ ἐπ᾽ Ἄργος· ἡγεῖτο
δὲ Ἆγις ὁ Ἀρχιδάμου, Λακεδαιμονίων βασιλεύς. ξυν- 2
εστράτευον δ' αὐτοῖς Τεγεᾶται καὶ ὅσοι ἄλλοι Ἀρκάδων

14. ἐκ παρασκευῆς: ἐκ φανερᾶς παρατάξεως, Schol. Cf. iv. 94. 4. — 15. ὡς τύχοιεν, διεφθείροντο: impf. after the opt. of the cond. rel. sent. in general supposition. So ii. 4. 3, τὰς προσβολὰς ᾗ προσπίπτοιεν ἀπεωθοῦντο. GMT. 62; H. 914, B, (2).
16. πρὸς ἔαρ ἤδη: see on c. 17. 7; i. 30. 20. — 18. ὡς ἐρήμου οὔσης κτέ.: *in the belief that since the place was stripped of its defenders by the war they would take it by storm.* On the use of the gen. abs., see GMT. 110, 1, N. 5; H. 972 d. ὡς belongs with αἱρήσοντες, but also affects ἐρήμου οὔσης.
57. *The next summer* (418 B.C.) *the Lacedaemonians and their allies take the field with a great armament against Argos.*
2. αὐτοῖς: dat. as in c. 3. 21. — 3. τἆλλα: *the other states.* τὰ μέν and τὰ δέ distribute the preceding τἆλλα (part. appos. G. 137, N. 2; H. 624 d),

so that οὐ καλῶς εἶχε must be taken as referring to their disaffection. On the other hand, αὐτά, 5, refers, not to the separate states, but to the general condition of things, acc. to the usage of i. 1. 10. See on c. 27. 3. — 4. προκαταλήψονται: abs. here, as in iii. 2. 15; 3. 9. and 46. 25: "take measures of precaution" (Jowett). On the various uses of προκαταλαμβάνειν, see on i. 57. 15. (Herbst, Philol. 24, p. 626, defends the reading of inferior Mss. καταλήψονται.) — 5. ἐπὶ πλέον χωρήσεσθαι: *would go further,* as in vii. 50. 19, ἐπὶ τὸ βέλτιον. — ἐστράτευον ἐπ᾽ Ἄργος: in a general way, *they took the field against Argos.* Since the Boeotians and Corinthians chose Phlius as the place in which their contingents were to unite (10, ἐς Φλιοῦντα ξυνελέγοντο), Agis also marched in that direction.
8. ὅσοι ἄλλοι: i.e. the Heraeans

Λακεδαιμονίοις ξύμμαχοι ἦσαν. οἱ δ' ἐκ τῆς ἄλλης Πε-
10 λοποννήσου ξύμμαχοι καὶ οἱ ἔξωθεν ἐς Φλιοῦντα ξυνελέγοντο, Βοιωτοὶ μὲν πεντακισχίλιοι ὁπλῖται καὶ τοσοῦ-
τοι ψιλοὶ καὶ ἱππῆς πεντακόσιοι καὶ ἄμιπποι ἴσοι, Κορίνθιοι δὲ δισχίλιοι ὁπλῖται, οἱ δ' ἄλλοι ὡς ἕκαστοι, Φλιάσιοι δὲ πανστρατιᾷ, ὅτι ἐν τῇ ἐκείνων ἦν τὸ στράτευμα.
58 Ἀργεῖοι δὲ προαισθόμενοι τό τε πρῶτον τὴν παρασκευὴν 1
τῶν Λακεδαιμονίων, καὶ ἐπειδὴ ἐς τὸν Φλιοῦντα βουλόμενοι τοῖς ἄλλοις προσμῖξαι ἐχώρουν, τότε δὴ ἐξεστράτευσαν καὶ αὐτοί· ἐβοήθησαν δ' αὐτοῖς καὶ Μαντινῆς
5 ἔχοντες τοὺς σφετέρους ξυμμάχους καὶ Ἠλείων τρισχίλιοι
ὁπλῖται· καὶ προϊόντες ἀπαντῶσι τοῖς Λακεδαιμονίοις 2
ἐν Μεθυδρίῳ τῆς Ἀρκαδίας. καὶ καταλαμβάνουσιν ἑκάτεροι λόφον· καὶ οἱ μὲν Ἀργεῖοι ὡς μεμονωμένοις τοῖς
Λακεδαιμονίοις παρεσκευάζοντο μάχεσθαι, ὁ δὲ Ἆγις

and Maenalians. *Cf.* c. 67. 7. — 10. Φλιοῦντα: see Bursian, II. p. 35, note 5.
See App. — 12. ἄμιπποι: (*cf.* Xen.
Hell. vii. 5. 24, ἀμίππους πεζούς) 'foot-
soldiers, who being attached each to
a horseman (which is to be inferred
from ἴσοι), accompanied him on foot
or, as occasion demanded, sprang
upon his horse' (Kr.); 'foot-soldiers
who ran alongside with the horsemen'
(Grote). In Thuc. and Xen. a Boeotian custom. Caes., *Bell. Gall.* i. 48.
5, ascribes the same custom to the
Germans of Ariovistus; there we find
totidem, as here ἴσοι.
58. *The Argives march out to meet
them. The Lacedaemonians effect a
union with their allies at Phlius, after
which they advance in three divisions by
three roads into the plain of Argos.*
1. Ἀργεῖοι δὲ προαισθόμενοι ... ἐχώρουν, τότε δή κτἑ.: Ἀργεῖοι προαισθόμενοι τήν τε πρώτην τῶν Λακεδαιμονίων

παρασκευὴν καὶ αὖθις προσχωροῦντας
τοὺς Λακεδαιμονίους ἐπὶ Φλιοῦντος ὑπὲρ
τοῦ τοῖς ἰδίοις συμμίξαι συμμάχοις, Schol.
Two members of a period are connected, of which one is expressed by
a partic., while the other begins with
ἐπειδή and ends with a finite verb. *Cf.*
c. 44. § 1. See App. — 3. προσμῖξαι:
see App. — 4. ἐβοήθησαν δ' αὐτοῖς ...
τρισχίλιοι ὁπλῖται: inserted parenthetically, so that the story begins
again with καὶ προϊόντες. ἐβοήθησαν
has therefore the force of the plpf.,
had joined them. See on c. 48. 3 and
ii. 2. 12.
7. Μεθυδρίῳ: Methydrium in the
highlands of Arcadia, at the junction
of the brooks which form the Ladon.
Curtius, *Pelopon.* I. p. 306 ff. Hence
the name. The Lacedaemonians had
turned considerably toward the west
in order to avoid Mantinea. ἐν Μεθυδρίῳ as in c. 55. 1, ἐν τῇ Ἐπιδαύρῳ.

10 τῆς νυκτὸς ἀναστήσας τὸν στρατὸν καὶ λαθὼν ἐπορεύετο ἐς Φλιοῦντα παρὰ τοὺς ἄλλους ξυμμάχους. καὶ οἱ Ἀργεῖοι αἰσθόμενοι ἅμα ἔῳ ἐχώρουν, πρῶτον μὲν ἐς Ἄργος, ἔπειτα ᾗ προσεδέχοντο τοὺς Λακεδαιμονίους μετὰ τῶν ξυμμάχων καταβήσεσθαι, τὴν κατὰ Νεμέαν ὁδόν.
15 Ἆγις δὲ ταύτην μὲν ἣν προσεδέχοντο οὐκ ἐτράπετο, παραλλείλας δὲ τοῖς Λακεδαιμονίοις καὶ Ἀρκάσι καὶ Ἐπιδαυρίοις ἄλλην ἐχώρησε χαλεπὴν καὶ κατέβη ἐς τὸ Ἀργείων πεδίον· καὶ Κορίνθιοι καὶ Πελληνῆς καὶ Φλιάσιοι ὄρθιον ἑτέραν ἐπορεύοντο· τοῖς δὲ Βοιωτοῖς καὶ
20 Μεγαρεῦσι καὶ Σικυωνίοις εἴρητο τὴν ἐπὶ Νεμέας ὁδὸν καταβαίνειν, ᾗ οἱ Ἀργεῖοι ἐκάθηντο, ὅπως εἰ οἱ Ἀργεῖοι ἐπὶ σφᾶς ἰόντες ἐς τὸ πεδίον βοηθοῖεν, ἐφεπόμενοι τοῖς ἵπποις χρῷντο. καὶ ὁ μὲν οὕτω διατάξας καὶ ἐσβαλὼν ἐς

— 10. ἐπορεύετο: impf. *he set out* in a northerly direction through Orchomenus and Alea. — 12. ἐχώρουν: also impf.; therefore ἐς Ἄργος: "on the road to Argos." From this road they then turned more to the north toward Nemea, which lies between Argos and Phlius, but near Phlius.
13. ἔπειτα: without δέ. *Cf.* c. 7. 1.
15. ταύτην οὐκ ἐτράπετο: the acc. as in iii. 24. 1, ἐχώρουν τὴν ἐς Θήβας φέρουσαν ὁδόν, νομίζοντες ἥκιστα σφᾶς ταύτην αὐτοὺς ὑποτοπῆσαι τραπέσθαι. This is continued by the same case in the rel. clause (Cobet, Mnem. 14, p. 11, rejects ἢν προσεδέχοντο). — 16. τοῖς Λακεδαιμονίοις καὶ Ἀρκάσι καὶ Ἐπιδαυρίοις: *i.e.* those troops with which he had set out (see c. 57. 8), with the addition of the Epidaurians. παραγγείλας intimates that Agis commanded this division of the army in person. The allies, who had met in the territory of Phlius (see c. 57. 10) and had been joined by the Pellenaeans of Achaea (see ii. 9. 6), the Megarians and the Sicyonians, pressed forward by two different roads into the plain of Argos. — 19. ὄρθιον (less usual ending of the fem.) ἑτέραν: a road, which, like the one called χαλεπή just before, was also (that is the meaning of ἑτέραν, like ἑτέραν τοσαύτην, vi. 37. 13) steep. To the Boeotians, *etc.*, on the other hand, since they had cavalry with them (see c. 57. 12), the more level road by Nemea had been allotted (εἴρητο, *cf.* iv. 77. 8; v. 10. 4; vi. 30. 4; viii. 11. 15). On the various roads from Phlius into the plain of Argos, see Curtius, *Pelopon.* II. p. 582, note 56. His explanation of ὄρθιον ἑτέραν as the *straight* road is, however, very doubtful. — 21. ἐκάθηντο: see App. — 22. ἐπὶ σφᾶς: *i.e.* against the main force under Agis. — ἐφεπόμενοι τοῖς ἵπποις χρῷντο: that they might *following them use their horses*, *i.e.* attack the Argives in the rear with their cavalry. — 23. διατάξας: *cf.* iv. 31. 7.

59 τὸ πεδίον ἐδῄου Σάμινθόν τε καὶ ἄλλα. οἱ δὲ Ἀργεῖοι 1
γνόντες ἐβοήθουν ἡμέρας ἤδη ἐκ τῆς Νεμέας, καὶ περιτυχόντες τῷ Φλιασίων καὶ Κορινθίων στρατοπέδῳ τῶν
μὲν Φλιασίων ὀλίγους ἀπέκτειναν, ὑπὸ δὲ τῶν Κορινθίων
5 αὐτοὶ οὐ πολλῷ πλείους διεφθάρησαν. καὶ οἱ Βοιωτοὶ 2
καὶ οἱ Μεγαρῆς καὶ οἱ Σικυώνιοι ἐχώρουν, ὥσπερ εἴρητο
αὐτοῖς, ἐπὶ τῆς Νεμέας καὶ τοὺς Ἀργείους οὐκέτι κατέλαβον· ἀλλὰ καταβάντες, ὡς ἑώρων τὰ ἑαυτῶν δῃούμενα,
ἐς μάχην παρετάσσοντο, ἀντιπαρεσκευάζοντο δὲ καὶ οἱ
10 Λακεδαιμόνιοι. ἐν μέσῳ δὲ ἀπειλημμένοι ἦσαν οἱ Ἀρ- 3
γεῖοι· ἐκ μὲν γὰρ τοῦ πεδίου οἱ Λακεδαιμόνιοι εἶργον
τῆς πόλεως καὶ οἱ μετ' αὐτῶν, καθύπερθεν δὲ Κορίνθιοι
καὶ Φλιάσιοι καὶ Πελληνῆς, τὸ δὲ πρὸς Νεμέας Βοιωτοὶ
καὶ Σικυώνιοι καὶ Μεγαρῆς. ἵπποι δὲ αὐτοῖς οὐ παρ-

24. **Σάμινθον**: its position is very uncertain; 'it seems to be the name of a mountain,' Curtius, *Pelopon*. II. p. 582. See Bursian, II. p. 49.
59. *When the Argives are already surrounded by the three divisions of the enemy, two prominent citizens enter into negotiations with Agis.*
2. **ἡμέρας ἤδη**: equiv. to ἐπεὶ (ἤδη) ἡμέρα ἐγένετο (*cf.* iii. 24. 18), not long after the ἅμα ἔῳ of c. 58. 12. The gen. followed by ἤδη, as in i. 30. 20, χειμῶνος ἤδη. *Cf.* c. 17. 7, πρὸς τὸ ἔαρ ἤδη. — 5. **αὐτοί**: *on their side*.
6. **ὥσπερ εἴρητο αὐτοῖς**: *cf.* c. 58. 20. — 7. **οὐκέτι κατέλαβον**: *sc. κατὰ χώραν ὄντας. Cf.* ii. 56. 20, οὐκέτι κατέλαβον ἐν τῇ Ἀττικῇ ὄντας, ἀλλ' ἀνακεχωρηκότας. Everywhere else καταλαμβάνειν in the sense of *find, come upon* is used with a partic. or an expression denoting place. *Cf.* i. 59. 2; 61. 6; ii. 18. 17; 56. 20; 94. 19; iii. 69. 5; 115. 6; iv. 70. 7 (ἀνάλωτον as

pf. partic.); 92. 3; 129. 2; vi. 53. 1; 94. 17; vii. 2. 5; 33. 24; viii. 55. 3. —
8. **καταβάντες**: *sc. οἱ Ἀργεῖοι*. Change of subj. after ἀλλά, as in i. 26. 17. — **τὰ ἑαυτῶν δῃούμενα**: *cf.* c. 58. 24.
11. **ἐκ τοῦ πεδίου**: into this plain Agis himself with his Lacedaemonians ἐσέβαλε, c. 58. 23. They were drawn up between the Argive army and Argos, which is about fifteen miles south of Nemea. This position the Argives thought would be for their own advantage (18, ἀπειληφέναι ἐν τῇ αὐτῶν τε καὶ πρὸς τῇ πόλει), for the Lacedaemonians would be harassed from the city, to which special reference is made in c. 60. 26. The expression ἀπειληφέναι (18) is intentionally repeated from 10, not without irony. Each party thought it had caught the other in a trap. — 12. **καθύπερθεν**: for they had followed the ὄρθιος ὁδός of c. 58. 19. — 13. **τὸ πρὸς Νεμέας**: from the direction of Ne-

ἦσαν· οὐ γάρ πω οἱ Ἀθηναῖοι μόνοι τῶν ξυμμάχων
ἦκον. τὸ μὲν οὖν πλῆθος τῶν Ἀργείων καὶ τῶν ξυμμάχων οὐχ οὕτω δεινὸν τὸ παρὸν ἐνόμιζον, ἀλλ' ἐν καλῷ
ἐδόκει ἡ μάχη ἔσεσθαι, καὶ τοὺς Λακεδαιμονίους ἀπειληφέναι ἐν τῇ αὑτῶν τε καὶ πρὸς τῇ πόλει. τῶν δὲ
Ἀργείων δύο ἄνδρες, Θράσυλλός τε τῶν πέντε στρατηγῶν εἷς ὢν καὶ Ἀλκίφρων, πρόξενος Λακεδαιμονίων,
ἤδη τῶν στρατοπέδων ὅσον οὐ ξυνιόντων προσελθόντε
Ἄγιδι διελεγέσθην μὴ ποιεῖν μάχην· ἑτοίμους γὰρ εἶναι
Ἀργείους δίκας δοῦναι καὶ δέξασθαι ἴσας καὶ ὁμοίας, εἴ
τι ἐπικαλοῦσιν Ἀργείοις Λακεδαιμόνιοι, καὶ τὸ λοιπὸν
εἰρήνην ἄγειν σπονδὰς ποιησαμένους. καὶ οἱ μὲν ταῦτα
εἰπόντες [τῶν Ἀργείων] ἀφ' ἑαυτῶν καὶ οὐ τοῦ πλήθους
κελεύσαντος εἶπον, καὶ ὁ Ἆγις δεξάμενος τοὺς λόγους
αὐτὸς καὶ οὐ μετὰ τῶν πλειόνων, οὐδὲ αὐτὸς βουλευσά-

men, after they had marched ἐπὶ Νεμέας. — 15. οἱ Ἀθηναῖοι: upon their
cavalry the Argives had relied; but
they did not come until c. 61. 2.
17. οὐχ οὕτω δεινόν: not so very
dangerous. See on ii. 11. 24 and c.
104. 8. — ἐν καλῷ: under favourable
circumstances here and in c. 60. 11.
Similarly καλῶς, c. 36. 18. — 18. τοὺς
Λακεδαιμονίους ἀπειληφέναι: acc. and
inf. with ἐδόκει in spite of the nom. ἡ
μάχη, ἐδόκει being equiv. to ἐνόμιζον.
19. τῶν δὲ Ἀργείων δύο ἄνδρες:
opp. to τὸ μὲν πλῆθος, 16. — 20. τῶν
πέντε στρατηγῶν: there were in Argos five generals, as in Athens ten;
possibly the number at Argos has
some such connexion with the πέντε
λόχοι of c. 72. 21, as that at Athens
has with the ten tribes. — 21. πρόξενος: diplomatic representative. This
title was an honour bestowed upon
foreigners, who then represented the
state in their own cities. See on ii.

29. 4, and Schömann, Griech. Alt. II.
p. 25. — 22. ὅσον οὐ: cf. i. 36. 8, and
ὅσον οὔπω, iv. 125. 9. — ξυνιόντων:
confligere, also iv. 94. 11; v. 69.
2. — προσελθόντε: see App. — 23.
ποιεῖν μάχην: bring on a battle, or
"allow it to take place." See on ii.
86. 22. — 24. Ἀργείους: the two men
evidently claim to be representatives
of the state. — ἴσας καὶ ὁμοίας: as in
c. 27. 12.
60. Agis and the two Argives, without consulting the proper authorities of
either state, make a truce for four months,
which causes great displeasure in both
armies.
2. εἰπόντες [τῶν Ἀργείων]: see
App. — 4. αὐτός: for himself alone.
See on iv. 49. 5. — οὐδὲ αὐτὸς βουλευ-
σάμενος κτέ.: and without any deliberation on his own part, further than to
communicate the matter to one man. ἀλλ'
ἤ, nisi. Cf. c. 80. 6. See on iii. 71.
4. — 5. τῶν ἐν τέλει: probably one

5 μένος ἀλλ' ἢ ἑνὶ ἀνδρὶ κοινώσας τῶν ἐν τέλει ξυστρατευομένων, σπένδεται τέσσαρας μῆνας ἐν οἷς ἔδει ἐπιτελέσαι αὐτοὺς τὰ ῥηθέντα. καὶ ἀπήγαγε τὸν στρατὸν εὐθύς, οὐδενὶ φράσας τῶν ἄλλων ξυμμάχων. οἱ δὲ Λα- 2 κεδαιμόνιοι καὶ οἱ ξύμμαχοι εἵποντο μὲν ὡς ἡγεῖτο διὰ 10 τὸν νόμον, ἐν αἰτίᾳ δ' εἶχον κατ' ἀλλήλους πολλῇ τὸν Ἆγιν, νομίζοντες ἐν καλῷ παρατυχὸν σφίσι ξυμβαλεῖν καὶ πανταχόθεν αὐτῶν ἀποκεκλημένων καὶ ὑπὸ ἱππέων καὶ πεζῶν, οὐδὲν δράσαντες ἄξιον τῆς παρασκευῆς ἀπιέναι. στρατόπεδον γὰρ δὴ τοῦτο κάλλιστον Ἑλληνικὸν τῶν μέ- 3 15 χρι τοῦδε ξυνῆλθεν. ὤφθη δὲ μάλιστα ἕως ἔτι ἦν ἀθρόον ἐν Νεμέᾳ, ἐν ᾧ Λακεδαιμόνιοί τε πανστρατιᾷ ἦσαν καὶ

of the two ephors who accompanied the king upon military expeditions, as did also, acc. to Arnold, the polemarchs, ὅμοιοι, and two Pythii. See Gilbert, Griech. Staatsalt, I. p. 60, 64, 80. — ξυστρατευομένων: Cl. suggests ξυστρατευομένῳ. — 7. τὰ ῥηθέντα: i.e. what they had offered to do in c. 59. 23 ff. — 8. τῶν ἄλλων ξυμμάχων: as in i. 128. 21, in contradistinction to the Lacedaemonians. That he said nothing to his own countrymen has already been stated; but he was silent toward the allies as well. ἄλλων does not imply that the Lacedaemonians are put upon an equal footing with the allies, and should therefore be omitted in English. See on i. 128. 21. (St. and v. Herwerden follow Kr. in rejecting ξυμμάχων.)
9. εἵποντο μὲν ὡς ἡγεῖτο διὰ τὸν νόμον: "they followed his guidance (i.e. obeyed the order to march away, ἀπήγαγε τὸν στρατόν) because of their discipline, because the rules of military subordination compelled them; but," etc. — 10. ἐν αἰτίᾳ εἶχον πολλῇ: cf. i. 35. 10, ἐν πλείονι αἰτίᾳ ἡμεῖς . . .

ὑμᾶς ἕξομεν, and 21 below. — κατ' ἀλλήλους: as in iv. 84. 4. — 11. παρατυχόν: cf. i. 76. 14. — 12. αὐτῶν: i.e. τῶν Ἀργείων. See c. 59. § 3.
14. στρατόπεδον κτέ.: on the mode of expression and the order of words, see on i. 1. 8. — κάλλιστον: is esp. explained by the following λογάδες ἀφ' ἑκάστων. — 15. ὤφθη μάλιστα: this (the excellence of the army) was especially noticeable. — 16. ἐν Νεμέᾳ: Cl., St., and others take this as referring to c. 59. § 3. But the Argives had at that time descended into the plain of Argos (ἀλλὰ καταβάντες, c. 59. 8), and there they were surrounded by the Lacedaemonians and their allies (c. 59. 11 ff.). The valley of Nemea is completely separated from the plain of Argos, the only connexions being by passes neither broad nor low. It is therefore impossible to believe that ἐν Νεμέᾳ refers to any part of the plain of Argos. ζητεῖται πῶς, τριχῇ διαιρεθέντος τοῦ τῶν Πελοποννησίων στρατεύματος εἰς Φλιοῦντα, καὶ ἑνὸς μόνου μέρους τὴν ἐπὶ Νεμεαν ἰόντος, τῶν δὲ ἄλλων ἄλλαις χρησαμένων

Ἀρκάδες καὶ Βοιωτοὶ καὶ Κορίνθιοι καὶ Σικυώνιοι καὶ Πελληνῆς καὶ Φλιάσιοι καὶ Μεγαρῆς, καὶ οὗτοι πάντες λογάδες ἀφ' ἑκάστων, ἀξιόμαχοι δοκοῦντες εἶναι οὐ τῇ Ἀργείων μόνον ξυμμαχίᾳ, ἀλλὰ καὶ ἄλλῃ ἔτι προσγενομένῃ. τὸ μὲν οὖν στρατόπεδον οὕτως ἐν αἰτίᾳ ἔχοντες 4 τὸν Ἆγιν ἀνεχώρουν τε καὶ διελύθησαν ἐπ' οἴκου ἕκαστοι. Ἀργεῖοι δὲ καὶ αὐτοὶ ἔτι ἐν πολλῷ πλείονι αἰτίᾳ 5 εἶχον τοὺς σπεισαμένους ἄνευ τοῦ πλήθους, νομίζοντες κἀκεῖνοι μὴ ἂν σφίσι ποτὲ κάλλιον παρασχὸν Λακεδαιμονίους διαπεφευγέναι· πρός τε γὰρ τῇ σφετέρᾳ πόλει καὶ μετὰ πολλῶν καὶ ἀγαθῶν ξυμμάχων τὸν ἀγῶνα ἂν γίγνεσθαι. τόν τε Θράσυλλον ἀναχωρήσαντες ἐν τῷ Χα- 6

ὁδοῖς καὶ οὐδαμοῦ συμμιξάντων, ἔφη ἀθρόους αὐτοὺς ὦφθαι περὶ Νεμέαν, Schol., who is evidently puzzled. Philippi, Rhein. Mus. 36, p. 256, says ἐν Νεμέᾳ is a gloss. If it really belongs in the text, it must refer to something not made plain in the preceding narrative, prob. something connected with the movements of c. 58. — πανστρατιᾷ ἦσαν: Jowett takes this with Λακεδαιμόνιοι only, but the Phliasians were certainly present πανστρατιᾷ (cf. c. 57. 13). The Epidaurians are mentioned in c. 58. 16, but are omitted here, perhaps, as St. suggests, because only part of their force was present. We must take πανστρατιᾷ with all the subjs. This St. reconciles with λογάδες ἀφ' ἑκάστων by the assumption that πανστρατιᾷ means cum universis quas tum instructas habebant copiis, not πανδημεί. There seem to be considerable corruptions in the passage. — 20. καὶ ἄλλῃ κτέ.: *for another force, too, if it were added.* GMT. 52, 1 and Rem.; 74. 1; 77; II. 932, 2; 934; 937. See App.

22. ἀνεχώρουν: *they set out upon their way home*, impf. Pl. after τὸ στράτευμα, as in i. 89. 14 with τὸ κοινόν, and iii. 80. 1 with δῆμος.

24. ἄνευ: cf. i. 128. 11; iv. 25. 54. See on i. 91. 23. — 25. κἀκεῖνοι: is a repetition of καὶ αὐτοί with marked emphasis. — μὴ ἂν σφίσι ποτὲ κάλλιον παρασχόν: these words are in close connexion, so that the force of the neg. μή does not pass beyond παρασχόν. Cf. c. 63. 3. They thought it was the Lacedaemonians who had escaped, *since circumstances could never be more favourable for them* (the Argives). μή is used because it is in the inf. clause, although οὐ would be more regular after νομίζοντες. Kr. Spr. 67, 8. ἂν παρασχόν is here equiv. to παράσχοι ἄν. On the acc. abs., cf. παρατυχόν, 11. G. 278, 2; II. 973. — 26. πρὸς τῇ σφετέρᾳ πόλει: near Argos. Cf. c. 59. 11 and 19. — 27. μετὰ ... ξυμμάχων: the Mantineans and Eleans. See c. 58. 4 f. — ἂν γίγνεσθαι: the pres. inf., corresponding to the impf. ind. of dir. disc. (ὁ ἀγὼν ἂν ἐγίγνετο), represents the Argives as thinking, "we should have fought under these favourable circumstances."

28. ἐν τῷ Χαράδρῳ: 'about the

ῥάδρῳ, οὗπερ τὰς ἀπὸ στρατείας δίκας πρὶν ἐσιέναι κρί-
νουσιν, ἤρξαντο λεύειν, ὁ δὲ καταφυγὼν ἐπὶ τὸν βωμὸν
περιγίγνεται· τὰ μέντοι χρήματα ἐδήμευσαν αὐτοῦ.

61 Μετὰ δὲ τοῦτο Ἀθηναίων βοηθησάντων χιλίων
ὁπλιτῶν καὶ τριακοσίων ἱππέων, ὧν ἐστρατήγουν Λάχης
καὶ Νικόστρατος, οἱ Ἀργεῖοι (ὅμως γὰρ τὰς σπονδὰς
ὤκνουν λῦσαι πρὸς τοὺς Λακεδαιμονίους) ἀπιέναι ἐκέλευον αὐτοὺς καὶ πρὸς τὸν δῆμον οὐ προσῆγον βουλο-
μένους χρηματίσαι, πρὶν ἢ Μαντινῆς καὶ Ἠλεῖοι (ἔτι
γὰρ παρῆσαν) κατηνάγκασαν δεόμενοι. καὶ ἔλεγον οἱ
Ἀθηναῖοι Ἀλκιβιάδου πρεσβευτοῦ παρόντος ἔν τε τοῖς
Ἀργείοις καὶ ξυμμάχοις ταῦτα, ὅτι οὐκ ὀρθῶς αἱ σπονδαὶ
ἄνευ τῶν ἄλλων ξυμμάχων καὶ γένοιντο, καὶ νῦν (ἐν
καιρῷ γὰρ παρεῖναι σφεῖς) ἅπτεσθαι χρῆναι τοῦ πολέμου. καὶ πείσαντες ἐκ τῶν λόγων τοὺς ξυμμάχους εὐθὺς

northeast part of the city wall extended, like a natural moat, the gorge of the Charadrus, in the wide bed of which generals returning from the field were tried before they entered the city.' Curtius, *Pelopon*. II. p. 363. — 29. στρατείας: a necessary correction of the reading of most Mss. στρατιᾶς.

61. *After the arrival of troops from Athens, the Argives are persuaded by their allies to break the truce. Accordingly their united forces besiege Orchomenus, in Arcadia, which surrenders to them.*

2. τριακοσίων: Diod., xii. 79. 1, says two hundred. — Λάχης καὶ Νικόστρατος: are both freq. mentioned in the earlier course of the war (iii. 75. 15; 86. 2; 115. 7; iv. 53. 5; 119. 10). — 3. ὅμως: is to be explained by assuming that a concessive sent., "although they were dissatisfied with the truce," is understood. *Cf*. iii. 28. 13; 80. 4. — 6. χρηματίσαι: *cf*. c. 5. 2; i.

87. 17. — πρὶν ἤ: as elsewhere in Thuc. πρὶν δή (iii. 29. 5; vii. 71. 26; Haase, followed by St., writes πρὶν δή here) or the simple πρίν (see on i. 51. 5) with the aor. indic. (Perhaps Thuc. wrote πρὶν οἱ Μαντινῆς.)

8. παρόντος: see App. — 9. ταῦτα: see App. — 10. καὶ γένοιντο, καὶ νῦν ἅπτεσθαι χρῆναι: καί is used before γένοιντο, as if some similar const. (as καὶ νῦν ἔτι μένοιεν) were to follow (see on iii. 67. 24), instead of the inf. The present duty of the Argives is emphasized by νῦν as opp. to the past time expressed by γένοιντο. — 11. σφεῖς: is nom. referring to the subj. of the main verb. G. 138, N. 8; H. 940 b.

12. πείσαντες . . . ἐχώρουν πάντες: the subj. is at first only the Athenians (πείσαντες can refer only to them), but is enlarged until it includes πάντες πλὴν Ἀργείων. On similar changes of subj. (though usually contracting rather than expanding its content),

ἐχώρουν ἐπὶ Ὀρχομενὸν τὸν Ἀρκαδικὸν πάντες πλὴν Ἀργείων· οὗτοι δὲ ὅμως καὶ πεισθέντες ὑπελείποντο πρῶτον, ἔπειτα δ' ὕστερον καὶ οὗτοι ἦλθον. καὶ προσ- 4 καθεζόμενοι τὸν Ὀρχομενὸν πάντες ἐπολιόρκουν καὶ προσβολὰς ἐποιοῦντο, βουλόμενοι ἄλλως τε προσγενέσθαι σφίσι καὶ ὅμηροι ἐκ τῆς Ἀρκαδίας ἦσαν αὐτόθι ὑπὸ Λακεδαιμονίων κείμενοι. οἱ δὲ Ὀρχομένιοι δείσαντες τήν 5 τε τοῦ τείχους ἀσθένειαν καὶ τοῦ στρατοῦ τὸ πλῆθος, καί, ὡς οὐδεὶς αὐτοῖς ἐβοήθει, μὴ προαπόλωνται, ξυνέβησαν ὥστε ξύμμαχοί τε εἶναι καὶ ὁμήρους σφῶν τε αὐτῶν δοῦναι Μαντινεῦσι καὶ οὓς κατέθεντο Λακεδαιμόνιοι παραδοῦναι. μετὰ δὲ τοῦτο ἔχοντες ἤδη τὸν Ὀρχομε- 1 νὸν ἐβουλεύοντο οἱ ξύμμαχοι ἐφ' ὅ τι χρὴ πρῶτον ἰέναι τῶν λοιπῶν. καὶ Ἠλεῖοι μὲν ἐπὶ Λέπρεον ἐκέλευον, Μαντινῆς δὲ ἐπὶ Τεγέαν· καὶ προσέθεντο οἱ Ἀργεῖοι καὶ Ἀθηναῖοι τοῖς Μαντινεῦσι. καὶ οἱ μὲν Ἠλεῖοι ὀργισθέντες 2

see on i. 18. 21; 49. 14, and c. 64. 12. — ἐκ τῶν λόγων: cf. vii. 48. 23, ἐκ τούτων αὐτοὺς πείσεσθαι, and viii. 47. 5, πεῖσαι δ' ἂν ἐνόμιζε μάλιστα ἐκ τοῦ τοιούτου. — 13. τὸν Ἀρκαδικόν: to distinguish it from the Βοιώτιος of iii. 87. 11. — 14. ὅμως: const. with ὑπελείποντο. — καὶ πεισθέντες: "although the speech of the Athenians (i.e. of Alcibiades) had not failed to convince them."
15. προσκαθεζόμενοι: const. with acc. also in i. 26. 19; 61. 8. — 16. πάντες: here the Argives also are included. — 17. προσγενέσθαι σφίσι: cf. c. 32. 10. — 18. καὶ ὅμηροι αὐτόθι: the inorganic connexion of these words with the preceding βουλόμενοι ἄλλως τε προσγενέσθαι σφίσι makes them only more prominent: "and besides, there were," etc. — 19. κείμενοι: i.e. κατακείμενοι, as of pass. par-

tic. of κατέθεντο, 23. Cf. vi. 61. 16, ὁμήρους τοὺς ἐν ταῖς νήσοις κειμένους.
21. καὶ ... μὴ προαπόλωνται: is, like τήν τε τοῦ τείχους ἀσθένειαν καὶ τοῦ στρατοῦ τὸ πλῆθος, obj. of δείσαντες. καί introduces μὴ ἀπόλωνται; the explanatory ὡς οὐδεὶς αὐτοῖς ἐβοήθει is, then, a parenthesis. — ξυνέβησαν ὥστε: cf. iv. 46. 8. — 23. Μαντινεῦσι: the Mantineans, as the most powerful of the Arcadian allies, are given the charge of these Arcadian hostages.
62. *The allies decide to attack Tegea, whereupon the Eleans return home in anger because their proposal to attack Lepreum had been rejected.*
2. ἐφ' ὅ τι χρὴ ἰέναι: is the regular periphrasis for the deliberative subj. in dependent clauses. Cf. i. 40. 20; 91. 4; ii. 4. 10; iii. 11. 18; 53. 9; iv. 34. 25; 125. 5. — 3. ἐκέλευον: sc. ἰέναι. So also in 6, with ἐψηφίσαντο.

ὅτι οὐκ ἐπὶ Λέπρεον ἐψηφίσαντο, ἀνεχώρησαν ἐπ' οἴκου· οἱ δὲ ἄλλοι ξύμμαχοι παρεσκευάζοντο ἐν τῇ Μαντινείᾳ ὡς ἐπὶ Τεγέαν ἰόντες. καί τινες αὐτοῖς καὶ αὐτῶν [Τεγεα]τῶν ἐν τῇ πόλει ἐνεδίδοσαν τὰ πράγματα.

63 Λακεδαιμόνιοι δέ, ἐπειδὴ ἀνεχώρησαν ἐξ Ἄργους 1 τὰς τετραμήνους σπονδὰς ποιησάμενοι, Ἆγιν ἐν μεγάλῃ αἰτίᾳ εἶχον οὐ χειρωσάμενον σφίσιν Ἄργος, παρασχὸν καλῶς ὡς οὔπω πρότερον αὐτοὶ ἐνόμιζον. ἀθρόους γὰρ
5 τοσούτους ξυμμάχους καὶ τοιούτους οὐ ῥᾴδιον εἶναι λαβεῖν. ἐπειδὴ δὲ καὶ περὶ Ὀρχομενοῦ ἠγγέλλετο ἑαλωκέναι, 2 πολλῷ δὴ μᾶλλον ἐχαλέπαινον καὶ ἐβούλευον εὐθὺς ὑπ' ὀργῆς παρὰ τὸν τρόπον τὸν ἑαυτῶν, ὡς χρὴ τήν τε οἰκίαν αὐτοῦ κατασκάψαι καὶ δέκα μυριάσι δραχμῶν ζημιῶσαι.
10 ὁ δὲ παρῃτεῖτο μηδὲν τούτων δρᾶν· ἔργῳ γὰρ ἀγαθῷ 3

8. [Τεγεα]τῶν: see App. — 9. ἐνεδίδοσαν: impf. expressing attempted action. So also in iv. 76. 13. — τὰ πράγματα: cf. ii. 65. 43, τὰ πράγματα ἐνδιδόναι.
63. *The Lacedaemonians are very angry with Agis, and appoint ten Spartans to be his advisers.*
1. Λακεδαιμόνιοι δέ κτέ.: the narrative of c. 60. § 4 is resumed. The indignation which had already been expressed on the march (c. 60. 21) broke out with more violence ἐπειδὴ ἀνεχώρησαν. — 2. ἐν μεγάλῃ αἰτίᾳ εἶχον: is repeated from c. 60. 10 and 21. —
4. ὡς οὔπω πρότερον αὐτοὶ ἐνόμιζον: sc. παρασχεῖν. "When such an opportunity was offered as they, for their part, thought had never been offered before." Cf. c. 60. 25. οὔπω πρότερον occurs again in 13 and c. 64. 6. This repetition may be due to a lack of careful revision by the author. See App. —
5. λαβεῖν: ἀντὶ τοῦ συλλαβεῖν, ἀθροίζειν,

Schol. Cf. c. 102. 2, κοινοτέρας τὰς τύχας λαμβάνοντα; vi. 86. 13, ὅταν καιρὸν λάβωσιν.
6. περὶ Ὀρχομενοῦ ἠγγέλλετο ἑαλωκέναι: a loose const. for Ὀρχόμενος ἠγγέλλετο ἑαλωκώς. See Kühn. 600, 3 β. — 8. παρὰ τὸν τρόπον τὸν ἑαυτῶν: their usual mode of conduct is described in i. 132. 27, μὴ ταχεῖς εἶναι περὶ ἀνδρὸς Σπαρτιάτου κτέ. — 9. δέκα μυριάσι δραχμῶν: if these are Aeginetan drachmae, as is likely (see c. 47. 39), the sum amounts to about 824,840.
10. παρῃτεῖτο: deprecabatur. Cf. Plat. Rep. iii. 387 b; Dem. xxi. 58, παραιτήσομαι ὑμᾶς μηδὲν ἀχθεσθῆναί μοι. — 11. ῥύεσθαι: ἀπολύσειν, Schol. The word is seldom found elsewhere in this sense (but cf. Soph. O. T. 313), at least in Attic prose; but St.'s remark that this is prob. an expression of Agis, not of Thuc., makes any emendation unnecessary. In c. 75. 11 Thuc. uses ἀπολύεσθαι in the same

ῥύσεσθαι τὰς αἰτίας στρατευσάμενος· ἢ τότε ποιεῖν αὐτοὺς ὅ τι βούλονται. οἱ δὲ τὴν μὲν ζημίαν καὶ τὴν κατα- 4
σκαφὴν ἐπέσχον, νόμον δὲ ἔθεντο ἐν τῷ παρόντι, ὃς οὔπω πρότερον ἐγένετο αὐτοῖς· δέκα γὰρ ἄνδρας Σπαρτιατῶν προσείλοντο αὐτῷ ξυμβούλους, ἄνευ ὧν μὴ κύριον εἶναι ἀπάγειν στρατιὰν ἐκ τῆς πόλεως.

64 Ἐν τούτῳ δ' ἀφικνεῖται αὐτοῖς ἀγγελία παρὰ τῶν 1 ἐπιτηδείων ἐκ Τεγέας ὅτι, εἰ μὴ παρέσονται ἐν τάχει, ἀποστήσεται αὐτῶν Τεγέα πρὸς Ἀργείους καὶ τοὺς ξυμμάχους καὶ ὅσον οὐκ ἀφέστηκεν· ἐνταῦθα δὴ βοήθεια 2

sense. — **στρατευσάμενος**: see App. — ἤ: *i.e.* εἰ δὲ μή. *Cf.* i. 78. 13; 140. 8, βοηθεῖν, ἢ μηδὲ κατορθοῦντας τῆς ξυνέσεως μεταποιεῖσθαι. See Kr. *Spr.* § 69, 29, 1. — **τότε**: then, after he had tried to make good his fault. *Cf.* Dem. iv. 1, εἰ δὲ μή, τότ' ἂν αὐτὸς ἐπειρώμην. 13. **ἐπέσχον**: see on c. 46. 5; ii. 76. 4. — **νόμον δὲ ἔθεντο κτέ.**: the wording of the new law is not given, but merely the application of it to King Agis. ἐν τῷ παρόντι, *for the present*, may imply that the law was passed for this special case, and was intended to apply only to Agis. But if Arist., *Pol.* ii. 9. 30, ἐξέπεμπον συμπρεσβευτάς, refers to this law, it must have been a general one. — 14. **δέκα γὰρ ξυμβούλους**: a council of ten men was assigned to him, without whose consent or company he could not lead an army from the city. In this way his actions as general were under constant supervision. Advisers had accompanied Spartan admirals before (see ii. 85. 1; iii. 69. 7; 76. 6), but had never been forced upon an adult king in command of the army. Pleistoanax was accompanied by one or more on account of his youth. See Plut. *Per.* 22. See on ii. 85. 1, and Herbst,

Jahrbb. 1858, p. 682 ff. — 16. **εἶναι**: the inf. in rel. clauses occurs occasionally, as here, without a preceding inf. when provisions of a law are quoted. GMT. 92, 2, N. 3 (*b*); H. 957 a. — **ἀπάγειν**: is ordinarily used of the withdrawal of troops from foreign territory. Here it seems to show the strict nature of the new law. He was not allowed to lead troops away from the city. In other words, his power as general was entirely under the control of his advisers, whose authority did not cease with the ἐξάγειν but extended to the ἀπάγειν (and all subsequent action) after the army had left the city. It is then not necessary to follow Haase, *Lucubr. Thuc.* p. 88 ff., and read ἐκ τῆς πολεμίας for ἐκ τῆς πόλεως. Besides, as St. observes, if Thuc. had written ἐκ τῆς πολεμίας, we should expect τὴν στρατιάν with the art.

64. *The Lacedaemonians lead out their whole force to the support of Tegea. They invade the territory of Mantinea after having summoned their allies to meet them there.*

1. **παρὰ τῶν ἐπιτηδείων**: opp. to the hostile faction mentioned in c. 62. 8. — 4. **ὅσον οὐκ**: with pf. or plpf. *already almost*; so in iv. 69. 15; vii. 6. 4.

5 τῶν Λακεδαιμονίων γίγνεται αὐτῶν τε καὶ τῶν Εἱλώτων πανδημεὶ ὀξεῖα καὶ οἷα οὔπω πρότερον. ἐχώρουν δὲ ἐς Ὀρέσθειον τῆς Μαιναλίας· καὶ τοῖς μὲν Ἀρκάδων σφε- 3 τέροις οὖσι ξυμμάχοις προεῖπον ἀθροισθεῖσιν ἰέναι κατὰ πόδας αὐτῶν ἐς Τεγέαν, αὐτοὶ δὲ μέχρι μὲν τοῦ Ὀρε-
10 σθείου πάντες ἐλθόντες, ἐκεῖθεν δὲ τὸ ἕκτον μέρος σφῶν αὐτῶν ἀποπέμψαντες ἐπ' οἴκου, ἐν ᾧ τὸ πρεσβύτερόν τε καὶ τὸ νεώτερον ἦν, ὥστε τὰ οἴκοι φρουρεῖν, τῷ λοιπῷ στρατεύματι ἀφικνοῦνται ἐς Τεγέαν. καὶ οὐ πολλῷ ὕστερον οἱ ξύμμαχοι ἀπ' Ἀρκάδων παρῆσαν· πέμπουσι δὲ 4
15 καὶ ἐς τὴν Κόρινθον καὶ Βοιωτοὺς καὶ Φωκέας καὶ Λοκρούς, βοηθεῖν κελεύοντες κατὰ τάχος ἐς Μαντίνειαν. ἀλλὰ τοῖς μὲν ἐξ ὀλίγου τε ἐγίγνετο καὶ οὐ ῥᾴδιον ἦν μὴ ἁθρόοις καὶ ἀλλήλους περιμείνασι διελθεῖν τὴν πολεμίαν·

The pf. ind. (like the preceding fut. inds.) is of course retained in the indir. disc. after the pres. ἀφικνεῖται ἀγγελία. GMT. 70, 1; II. 932. 1.— βοήθεια τῶν Λακεδαιμονίων γίγνεται: equiv. to οἱ Λακεδαιμόνιοι ποιοῦνται βοήθειαν. — 6. οἷα οὔπω πρότερον: sc. ἐγένετο. They exerted themselves to the utmost, for the question whether Sparta or Argos should be leader in Peloponnesus was to be decided. — 7. Ὀρέσθειον: also called Ὀρεσθάσιον by Paus. viii. 27. 3. Thuc. calls the territory belonging to it Ὀρεσθίς in iv. 134.4.— Μαιναλίας: the whole mountainous district around the Maenalus range. See Curtius, Pelopon. I. p. 311 f.

8. προεῖπον: cf. c. 30. 31. — κατὰ πόδας αὐτῶν: close upon their heels. See on iii. 98. 11; iv. 126. 38; viii. 17. 15. — 9. αὐτοὶ πάντες, τῷ λοιπῷ στρατεύματι ἀφικνοῦνται: a change in the content of the subj. the reverse of that in c. 61. § 3. — 14. ἀπ' Ἀρκάδων: shows

that the summons of 8 had been obeyed. The Arcadian allies came at the proper time; on the other hand πέμπουσι καὶ . . . Λοκρούς, with whom the old alliance of ii. 9. 8 still existed.

17. τοῖς μέν: the more distant allies just mentioned. — ἐξ ὀλίγου ἐγίγνετο: it (with an indefinite subj. supplied from what precedes) came upon them suddenly. ἐξ ὀλίγου is similarly used in ii. 11. 17; 61. 11; iv. 108. 32. — μὴ ἁθρόοις κτἑ.: unless in a body, and after having waited for one another (Arnold). μή shows that the expression is hypothetical. G. 283, 4; H. 1025. — 18. τὴν πολεμίαν: as in i. 142. 7; ii. 11. 20; iii. 58. 24. This refers not only to Argolis, but also to the territory of Orchomenus, which was in the possession of the Argive alliance since the events of c. 61. § 5. This whole region ξυνέκλῃε διὰ μέσου, i.e. it closed up the communication (for those wishing to reach Mantinea from the north) by lying just in the

ξυνέκλῃε γὰρ διὰ μέσου· ὅμως δὲ ἠπείγοντο. Λακεδαι- 5
20 μόνιοι δὲ ἀναλαβόντες τοὺς παρόντας Ἀρκάδων ξυμμάχους ἐσέβαλον ἐς τὴν Μαντινικήν, καὶ στρατοπεδευσάμενοι πρὸς τῷ Ἡρακλείῳ ἐδῄουν τὴν γῆν.
65 Οἱ δὲ Ἀργεῖοι καὶ οἱ ξύμμαχοι, ὡς εἶδον αὐτούς, 1
καταλαβόντες χωρίον ἐρυμνὸν καὶ δυσπρόσοδον παρετάξαντο ὡς ἐς μάχην. καὶ οἱ Λακεδαιμόνιοι εὐθὺς αὐτοῖς 2
ἐπῇσαν· καὶ μέχρι μὲν λίθου καὶ ἀκοντίου βολῆς ἐχώ-
5 ρησαν· ἔπειτα τῶν πρεσβυτέρων τις Ἄγιδι ἐπεβόησεν,
ὁρῶν πρὸς χωρίον καρτερὸν ἰόντας σφᾶς, ὅτι διανοεῖται
κακὸν κακῷ ἰᾶσθαι, δηλῶν τῆς ἐξ Ἄργους ἐπαιτίου ἀναχωρήσεως τὴν παροῦσαν ἄκαιρον προθυμίαν ἀνάληψιν
βουλομένην εἶναι. ὁ δὲ εἴτε καὶ διὰ τὸ ἐπιβόημα εἴτε καὶ 3
10 αὐτῷ ἄλλο τι ἢ κατὰ τὸ αὐτὸ δόξαν, ἐξαίφνης πάλιν τὸ

way of it. ξυγκλῄειν is similarly used in c. 72. 14, κατὰ τὸ διάκενον καὶ οὐ ξυγκλησθέν. — 19. ἠπείγοντο : sc. διελθεῖν.
21. ἐσέβαλον: from the south, the side toward Tegea, where the site of the temple of Hercules must be sought (acc. to Curtius, *Pelopon.* I. p. 243, ' not far from the plain of Alcimedon by the heights of Capsa ').
65. *The hostile armies approach one another, but the Lacedaemonians suddenly retreat. After some delay the Argives follow them.*
2. χωρίον ἐρυμνὸν καὶ δυσπρόσοδον: apparently the southern part of the hill called Alesium, which was a point of considerable strategic importance for Mantinea. See Curtius, *Pelopon.* I. p. 241. It is therefore called (6) χωρίον καρτερόν.
5. τῶν πρεσβυτέρων τις: perhaps one of the ten ξύμβουλοι of c. 63. 15.
— 7. κακὸν κακῷ ἰᾶσθαι: proverbial. So Hdt. iii. 53. 15, μὴ τῷ κακῷ τὸ κακὸν ἰῶ. *Cf.* Soph. *Aj.* 362; Plat. *Prot.*

340 d. It refers to Agis's words in c. 63. 10 f. — ἐπαιτίου: *which had caused him to be blamed. Cf.* c. 60. 10; 63. 2. But in vi. 61. 4 we find the pers. use of ἐπαίτιος. — 9. βουλομένην: the partic. with δηλοῦν is used also in i. 21. 12; ii. 50. 4; with δηλοῦσθαι in i. 11. 17. The man called to Agis, pointing out (δηλῶν) *that his eagerness wished, etc.* See App.
εἴτε καί, εἴτε καί: the adv. καί adds liveliness and force to the expression, as in vi. 60. 11 f. Kühn. 541, 2, N. 2.
— τὸ ἐπιβόημα: (*cf.* ἐπεβόησεν, 5) occurs nowhere else in Thuc. Poll. vi. 208, objects to it as σκληρόν, but Dio C. uses it freq. — 10. ἢ κατὰ τὸ αὐτό: Kr. explains: "than in accordance with the line of action he had begun." See App. — δόξαν: acc. abs. (aor. partic.), as in viii. 79. 2; 93. 7. The partic. is used in a causal sense, and the whole expression αὐτῷ ... δόξαν is parallel to διὰ τὸ ἐπιβόημα, giving a second reason for his sudden

στράτευμα κατὰ τάχος πρὶν ξυμμῖξαι ἀπῆγε. καὶ ἀφικό- 4
μενος πρὸς τὴν Τεγεᾶτιν τὸ ὕδωρ ἐξέτρεπεν ἐς τὴν Μαντινικήν, περὶ οὗπερ ὡς τὰ πολλὰ βλάπτοντος ὁποτέρωσε
ἂν ἐσπίπτῃ Μαντινῆς καὶ Τεγεᾶται πολεμοῦσιν. ἐβούλετο δὲ τοὺς ἀπὸ τοῦ λόφου βοηθοῦντας ἐπὶ τὴν τοῦ
ὕδατος ἐκτροπήν, ἐπειδὰν πύθωνται, καταβιβάσαι [τοὺς
Ἀργείους καὶ τοὺς ξυμμάχους] καὶ ἐν τῷ ὁμαλῷ τὴν
μάχην ποιεῖσθαι· καὶ ὁ μὲν τὴν ἡμέραν ταύτην μείνας 5
αὐτοῦ περὶ τὸ ὕδωρ ἐξέτρεπεν· οἱ δ' Ἀργεῖοι καὶ οἱ ξύμμαχοι τὸ μὲν πρῶτον καταπλαγέντες τῇ ἐξ ὀλίγου αἰφνιδίῳ αὐτῶν ἀναχωρήσει οὐκ εἶχον ὅ τι εἰκάσωσιν· εἶτα·
ἐπειδὴ ἀναχωροῦντες ἐκεῖνοί τε ἀπέκρυψαν καὶ σφεῖς

retreat. — ἐξαίφνης: to be const. with what follows, and therefore separated by a comma (with Cl.) from what precedes. Not that his decision was sudden, but that he executed it suddenly is important. Hence below, 20, the astonishment of the enemy at the αἰφνίδιος ἀναχώρησις. Moreover κατὰ τάχος indicates the rapidity of the march.
12. πρὸς τὴν Τεγεᾶτιν: to the border of the territory of Tegea. — τὸ ὕδωρ: not the brook Ophis, but a stream which flows northward from the Tegean territory. See Curtius, Pelopon. I. p. 235; Baedeker, Griechenland, p. 274. — ἐξέτρεπεν: impf., he set about turning, etc. This task naturally required some time. See 18 f. — 13. ὁποτέρωσε ἂν ἐσπίπτῃ: since it had no sufficient outlet, and tended to flood the neighbouring land. — 15. τοὺς ἀπὸ τοῦ λόφου: acc. to the wellknown proleptic use for τοὺς ἐπὶ τοῦ λόφου (i.e. the χωρίον ἐρυμνὸν καὶ δυσπρόσοδον of 2). G. 191, N. 6; H. 788. Const. as obj. with the inf. καταβιβάσαι, with which βοηθοῦντας κτέ. is to be connected as a pred. adj.: "he wished to make the troops on the hill come down and try to stop the turning aside of the water (βοηθοῦντας ἐπὶ τὴν τοῦ ὕδατος ἐκτροπήν), as soon as they heard of it, and fight on the plain." τοὺς Ἀργείους καὶ τοὺς ξυμμάχους is rightly struck out by St., v. Herwerden, and Cl. as a useless gloss.
20. ἐξ ὀλίγου: this refers apparently to the near approach μέχρι λίθου καὶ ἀκοντίου βολῆς (4), i.e. it is to be taken in a local sense. αἰφνιδίῳ refers to the unexpectedness of the withdrawal. Cf. ἐξαίφνης, 10. See App. — 21. οὐκ εἶχον κτέ.: on the use of οὐκ ἔχειν with deliberative subjv., see on ii. 52. 11. — 22. ἀπέκρυψαν: ἑαυτοὺς δηλονότι. ἀφανεῖς ἐγένοντο. ἰδίως δὲ ἐπὶ τῶν πλοϊζομένων καὶ οὐκέτι ὁρωμένων λέγεται ὅτι ἀπέκρυψαν, Schol. Of this rare use only two examples are cited; one from Plat. Prot. p. 338 a, φεύγειν εἰς τὸ πέλαγος τῶν λόγων ἀποκρύψαντα γῆν, and one from Luc. Ver. Hist. ii. 38, ἐφεύγομεν . . . ἐπεὶ δ' ἀπέκρυψαν (got out of sight of) αὐτούς. Acc. to these examples, we should supply αὐτούς

ἡσύχαζον καὶ οὐκ ἐπηκολούθουν, ἐνταῦθα τοὺς ἑαυτῶν
στρατηγοὺς αὖθις ἐν αἰτίᾳ εἶχον τό τε πρότερον καλῶς
25 ληφθέντας πρὸς Ἄργει Λακεδαιμονίους ἀφεθῆναι καὶ
νῦν ὅτι ἀποδιδράσκοντας οὐδεὶς ἐπιδιώκει, ἀλλὰ καθ᾽
ἡσυχίαν οἱ μὲν σῴζονται, σφεῖς δὲ προδίδονται. οἱ δὲ 5
στρατηγοὶ ἐθορυβήθησαν μὲν τὸ παραυτίκα, ὕστερον
δὲ ἀπάγουσιν αὐτοὺς ἀπὸ τοῦ λόφου καὶ προελθόντες ἐς
30 τὸ ὁμαλὸν ἐστρατοπεδεύσαντο ὡς ἰόντες ἐπὶ τοὺς πολεμίους.

66 Τῇ δ᾽ ὑστεραίᾳ οἵ τε Ἀργεῖοι καὶ οἱ ξύμμαχοι ξυν- 1

rather than with the Schol. ἑαυτούς. — σφεῖς: is here opp. to ἐκεῖνοι and οἱ μέν, and is equiv. to an emphatic αὐτοί. This is rare in dir. disc. — 24. αὖθις ἐν αἰτίᾳ εἶχον: cf. c. 60. 23. — καλῶς ληφθέντας: "when they had caught them so finely." Used of the favourable opportunity, as in c. 36. 18, καλῶς σφίσι φίλιον γενέσθαι. — τό τε πρότερον ἀφεθῆναι: see c. 59. § 4; 60. § 5. The inf. depends upon the idea of speaking implied in ἐν αἰτίᾳ εἶχον (i.e. it is the inf. of indir. disc.), and refers to past time. They preferred the charge that the Lacedaemonians had been let off. Cf. vii. 81. 3, ἐν αἰτίᾳ τὸν Γύλιππον εἶχον ἑκόντα ἀφεῖναι τοὺς Ἀθηναίους. — 25. καὶ νῦν ὅτι: here introduces the continuation of the indir. disc., but the change from the inf. to ὅτι (which is far less usual than the change from ὅτι to the inf.) gives the following words somewhat the effect of dir. disc. Kr. says 'ὅτι here means *because*.' If Kr. were right, we should have here an example of a causal sent. after a secondary tense and implying that the cause is assigned by other persons than the writer in which the pres. ind. is retained. It would be difficult to find

other examples of this const. See GMT. 81, 2, Rem. — 26. καθ᾽ ἡσυχίαν: *at their leisure;* very ironical, esp. with προδίδονται. — 28. ἐθορυβήθησαν μὲν τὸ παραυτίκα: a higher degree of ἀπορεῖν. For a moment they lost their self-control (or, as we say, lost their heads) on account of the violence of the reproaches.

66. *Next day the two armies are drawn up opposite one another in the plain. The organization of the Lacedaemonian army appears in all its excellence.*

1. οἵ τε Ἀργεῖοι καὶ οἱ ξύμμαχοι: the copula τε does not connect the two substs., but stands opp. to τε in οἵ τε Λακεδαιμόνιοι. Thus a paratactical opposition of the two members of the sent. is brought about; *on the one hand ... on the other hand* (cf. i. 8. 14 f.; 26. 8 f.; 57. 3 f.; ii. 22. 3 ff.; 64. 28 f., etc.). If ὡς were inserted before ὁρῶσι (Kr. and Meineke), it would interfere with the peculiarly Thucydidean structure of the sent.: "on the one hand, the Argives drew themselves up for battle; on the other, the Lacedaemonians, as they are returning to their former position,

ἐτάξαντο, ὡς ἔμελλον μαχεῖσθαι ἢν περιτύχωσιν· οἵ τε Λακεδαιμόνιοι ἀπὸ τοῦ ὕδατος πρὸς τὸ Ἡράκλειον πάλιν ἐς τὸ αὐτὸ στρατόπεδον ἰόντες ὁρῶσι δι' ὀλίγου τοὺς ἐναντίους ἐν τάξει τε ἤδη πάντας καὶ ἀπὸ τοῦ λόφου προεληλυθότας. * μάλιστα δὴ Λακεδαιμόνιοι ἐς ὃ ἐμέμνηντο ἐν τούτῳ τῷ καιρῷ ἐξεπλάγησαν. διὰ βραχείας γὰρ μελλήσεως ἡ παρασκευὴ αὐτοῖς ἐγίγνετο· καὶ εὐθὺς ὑπὸ σπουδῆς καθίσταντο ἐς κόσμον τὸν ἑαυτῶν, Ἄγιδος τοῦ βασιλέως ἕκαστα ἐξηγουμένου κατὰ τὸν νόμον. βασιλέως γὰρ ἄγοντος ὑπ' ἐκείνου πάντα ἄρχεται, καὶ τοῖς μὲν πολεμάρχοις αὐτὸς φράζει τὸ δέον, οἱ δὲ τοῖς λοχαγοῖς, ἐκεῖνοι δὲ τοῖς πεντηκοντῆρσιν, αὖθις δ' οὗτοι τοῖς ἐνωμοτάρχαις, καὶ οὗτοι τῇ ἐνωμοτίᾳ. καὶ αἱ παραγγέλ-

---

see the enemy already drawn up in battle array and brought down from the hill." The order of these last words is the reverse of the order of the events. See on i. 90. 4. Cl. suggests that ὄντας may have been lost before πάντας. Since the Lacedaemonians had now attained their object of drawing the enemy down into the plain as expressed in c. 65. 14 ff., it seems strange that they should be surprised at finding them there, except in so far as they may have expected them to wait a little longer. What follows is evidently told by Thuc. as a peculiarly good example of their excellent military organization, and this idea must be contained in the next sent., μάλιστα δὴ κτἑ., since the continuation with the words διὰ βραχείας γάρ evidently gives a reason for what immediately precedes. Yet this necessary connexion is certainly not clearly expressed in the text. For the various emendations proposed, see App. — 2. ἢν περιτύχωσιν:

τοῖς Λακεδαιμονίοις, Schol. — 3. πρὸς τὸ Ἡράκλειον: cf. c. 64. 22. — 4. δι' ὀλίγου: at a short distance. διά, which is here used in a local sense, is used in a temporal sense in 7, διὰ βραχείας μελλήσεως, after a short hesitatation, i.e. after the interval of a short delay.

6. ἐς ὃ ἐμέμνηντο: as far back as they remembered: μετὰ τὴν τῶν ἀνθρώπων μνήμην, Schol. — 8. ἡ παρασκευὴ αὐτοῖς ἐγίγνετο: i.e. τὴν παρασκευὴν ἐποιοῦντο. — 9. ὑπὸ σπουδῆς: used also in iii. 33. 12; viii. 107. 1. Elsewhere κατὰ σπουδήν and διὰ σπουδῆς.

11. ἄρχεται: pass. as in ii. 41. 11; iii. 46. 21. — 12. πολεμάρχοις κτἑ.: on the Spartan military organization, see Hermann, Griech. Staatsalt. § 29; Schoemann, Antiq. of Greece, I. p. 279 ff.; Gilbert, Griech. Staatsalt. I. p. 75 f.; 49 f.

14. παραγγέλσεις: the special orders for the execution of δέον of 12. παράγγελσις is an order not given by the trumpet but passed along the

15 σεις, ἤν τι βούλωνται, κατὰ τὰ αὐτὰ χωροῦσι καὶ ταχεῖαι ἐπέρχονται· σχεδὸν γάρ τι πᾶν πλὴν ὀλίγου τὸ στρατόπεδον τῶν Λακεδαιμονίων ἄρχοντες ἀρχόντων εἰσί, καὶ 67 τὸ ἐπιμελὲς τοῦ δρωμένου πολλοῖς προσήκει. τότε δὲ 1 κέρας μὲν εὐώνυμον Σκιρῖται αὐτοῖς καθίσταντο, ἀεὶ ταύτην τὴν τάξιν μόνοι Λακεδαιμονίων ἐπὶ σφῶν αὐτῶν ἔχοντες· παρὰ δ' αὐτοῖς οἱ ἐπὶ Θρᾴκης Βρασίδειοι 5 στρατιῶται καὶ νεοδαμώδεις μετ' αὐτῶν· ἔπειτ' ἤδη Λακεδαιμόνιοι αὐτοὶ ἑξῆς καθίστασαν τοὺς λόχους καὶ παρ' αὐτοὺς Ἀρκάδων Ἡραιῆς, μετὰ δὲ τούτους Μαινάλιοι,

ranks in such a way as not to attract the attention of the enemy. See Kr. on Xen. *Anab.* iv. 1. 5. — 15. **ταχεῖαι ἐπέρχονται**: *they reach their destination quickly*. Cf. iii. 29. 4, σχολαῖοι κομισθέντες. Cobet's proposal, περιέρχονται, is less appropriate with ταχεῖαι used adv. — 16. **πᾶν ... τὸ στρατόπεδον ... ἄρχοντες ἀρχόντων εἰσί**: "nearly the whole army consists of officers who in turn have officers under them." (εἰσί is pl. agreeing with the pred. subst.) Further details are given in c. 68. § 3, from which it appears that πλὴν ὀλίγου, referring to those who have no one under them, is not to be taken too literally. — 18. **τὸ ἐπιμελὲς τοῦ δρωμένου**: the use of the neut. adj. or partic. for the corresponding abstract subst. is very common in Thuc. See on i. 36. 4.

67. *The disposition of the troops on both sides.*

1. **τότε δέ**: the narrative is resumed after the digression of c. 66. § 3 f. — 2. **κέρας εὐώνυμον**: stands as pred. with καθίσταντο: *as the left wing*. The dat. αὐτοῖς is acc. to the usage of c. 44. 6; 57. 2. — **Σκιρῖται**: λόχος Λακωνικὸς οὕτω λεγόμενος, Schol. The Sciritae inhabited the rough hilly country toward the borders of the Tegean territory (Curtius, *Pelopon.* II. p. 217). On their precedence in the Lacedaemonian army, cf. Xen. *Cyr.* iv. 2. 1; *Rep. Lac.* 12.3; 13.6. This is the only passage which records that the position on the left wing was their special privilege (ἐπὶ σφῶν αὐτῶν *for themselves alone*; see on ii. 63. 10). — 4. **οἱ ἐπὶ Θρᾴκης Βρασίδειοι**: cf. c. 35. 21. This had apparently become the usual designation for the soldiers who had served in Thrace with Brasidas, though the expression in c. 34. 1, τῶν ἀπὸ Θρᾴκης μετὰ Βρασίδου ἐξελθόντων στρατιωτῶν was at this time more accurate, for ἐπί cannot properly be used of them after their return to Greece. Still, it seems that this prep. had become part of their designation, so that a change to ἀπό (Haase followed by v. Herwerden and St.) or ἐκ (Cobet, Mnem. 14, p. 11) is not advisable. — 5. **νεοδαμώδεις**: see on c. 34. 6. — 6. **παρ' αὐτούς**: no less admissible than παρ' αὐτοῖς, as in 4. Cf. ii. 2. 28; τίθεσθαι παρ' αὐτοὺς τὰ ὅπλα; vi. 67. 17. But it is not necessary to change αὐτοῖς above to αὐτούς (St. and Badham). — 7. **Ἀρκάδων Ἡραιῆς**:

καὶ ἐπὶ τῷ δεξιῷ κέρᾳ Τεγεᾶται καὶ Λακεδαιμονίων ὀλίγοι, τὸ ἔσχατον ἔχοντες, καὶ οἱ ἱππῆς αὐτῶν ἐφ' ἑκατέρῳ τῷ κέρᾳ. Λακεδαιμόνιοι μὲν οὕτως ἐτάξαντο· οἱ δ' ἐναντίοι αὐτοῖς δεξιὸν μὲν κέρας Μαντινῆς εἶχον ὅτι ἐν τῇ ἐκείνων τὸ ἔργον ἐγίγνετο, παρὰ δ' αὐτοὺς οἱ ξύμμαχοι Ἀρκάδων ἦσαν, ἔπειτα Ἀργείων οἱ χίλιοι λογάδες, οἷς ἡ πόλις ἐκ πολλοῦ ἄσκησιν τῶν ἐς τὸν πόλεμον δημοσίᾳ παρεῖχε, καὶ ἐχόμενοι αὐτῶν οἱ ἄλλοι Ἀργεῖοι, καὶ μετ' αὐτοὺς οἱ ξύμμαχοι αὐτῶν, Κλεωναῖοι καὶ Ὀρνεᾶται, ἔπειτα Ἀθηναῖοι ἔσχατοι τὸ εὐώνυμον κέρας ἔχοντες καὶ ἱππῆς μετ' αὐτῶν οἱ οἰκεῖοι.

68   Τάξις μὲν ἥδε καὶ παρασκευὴ ἀμφοτέρων ἦν, τὸ δὲ στρατόπεδον τῶν Λακεδαιμονίων μεῖζον ἐφάνη. ἀριθμὸν δὲ γράψαι, ἢ καθ' ἑκάστους ἑκατέρων ἢ ξύμπαντας οὐκ ἂν ἐδυνάμην ἀκριβῶς· τὸ μὲν γὰρ Λακεδαιμο-

part. gen. as in i. 27. 11, Παλῆς Κεφαλλήνων. The men of Heraea, which was situated in the valley of the Alpheus between the confined mountain territory of Arcadia and the open country of the Elean coast. Curtius, *Pelopon.* I. p. 363 f. It had attained importance through the union of nine communities at the instance of King Cleombrotus (Strab. viii. 3. 2); hence, probably, the honourable position of the Heraeans beside the Lacedaemonians. — Μαινάλιοι: from the Arcadian district Maenalia. *Cf.* c. 64. 7.

10. οἱ δ' ἐναντίοι: the nom. of the whole with the parts in the same case. *Cf.* i. 89. 18; ii. 65. 3; iii. 32. 2. G. 137. N. 2; II. 624 d. — 12. τὸ ἔργον: *the action.* *Cf.* i. 105. 24; ii. 89. 42; iv. 25. 9. — 13. Ἀρκάδων: *from Arcadia,* as in c. 64. 7. — Ἀργείων οἱ χίλιοι λογάδες κτἑ.: this institution is further described by Diod. Sic. xii. 75. 77: ἀπολύσαντες αὐτοὺς καὶ τῆς ἄλλης λειτουργίας καὶ τροφὰς δημοσίας χορηγοῦντες προσέταξαν γυμνάζεσθαι συνεχεῖς μελέτας. Arist. *Pol.* v. 4. p. 1304 tells of its political results. — 14. ἐκ πολλοῦ: to be explained with the help of Diod.'s συνεχεῖς μελέται: *for a long time, i.e.* from their youth up. *Cf.* c. 69. 19. — 16. Κλεωναῖοι καὶ Ὀρνεᾶται: Cleonae and Orneae were on the northern border of Argolis, toward Phlius and Corinth. As allies of Argos they were among the ξύμμαχοι ὧν ἄρχουσι. *Cf.* c. 47. 3.

68. *The difficulty of ascertaining with accuracy the numbers of either army.*

1. τάξις: this refers to the arrangement, παρασκευή to the armament (*cf.* c. 67. 13 and 18) of the troops. — ἥδε: the more usual word to refer to what precedes is αὕτη, as in ii. 9. 22. — 2. μεῖζον ἐφάνη: *was evidently larger.* — 4. οὐκ ἂν ἐδυνάμην: *I could not* (even if I were trying to do so)

5 νέων πλῆθος διὰ τῆς πολιτείας τὸ κρυπτὸν ἠγνοεῖτο,
τῶν δ' αὖ διὰ τὸ ἀνθρώπειον κομπῶδες ἐς τὰ οἰκεῖα
[πλήθη] ἠπιστεῖτο. ἐκ μέντοι τοιοῦδε λογισμοῦ ἔξεστί
τῳ σκοπεῖν τὸ Λακεδαιμονίων τότε παραγενόμενον πλῆ-
θος· λόχοι μὲν γὰρ ἐμάχοντο ἑπτὰ ἄνευ Σκιριτῶν ὄντων
10 ἑξακοσίων, ἐν δὲ ἑκάστῳ λόχῳ πεντηκοστύες ἦσαν τέσσαρες, καὶ ἐν τῇ πεντηκοστύι ἐνωμοτίαι τέσσαρες. τῆς τε
ἐνωμοτίας ἐμάχοντο ἐν τῷ πρώτῳ ζυγῷ τέσσαρες· ἐπὶ
δὲ βάθος ἐτάξαντο μὲν οὐ πάντες ὁμοίως, ἀλλ' ὡς λοχαγὸς ἕκαστος ἐβούλετο, ἐπὶ πᾶν δὲ κατέστησαν ἐπὶ ὀκτώ.
15 παρὰ δὲ ἅπαν πλὴν Σκιριτῶν τετρακόσιοι καὶ δυοῖν

write the number accurately. Kr. supplies εἰ ἐπεχείρουν, Poppo and Böhme εἰ ἐβουλόμην. Either answers the purpose of introducing a prot. for ἂν ἐδυνάμην. See App.
5. διὰ τῆς πολιτείας τὸ κρυπτόν: διὰ τὸ ἔθος εἶναι Λακεδαιμονίοις πάντα κρύφα πράττειν, Schol. The order of words as in i. 32. 8, μετὰ τῆς ξυμμαχίας τῆς αἰτήσεως. — 7. [πλήθη]: see App.
9. λόχοι μὲν γὰρ κτέ.: the computation of Thuc., which is undoubtedly correct as applied to the army engaged in the battle of Mantinea, though Xen. Rep. Lac. 11. 4 makes a different statement, is correctly summed up by the Schol.: ἔχει ἕκαστος λόχος πεντηκοστύας τέσσαρας, καὶ γίνονται τῶν ἑπτὰ λόχων εἴκοσι ὀκτώ, ἔχει ἑκάστη πεντηκοστὺς ἐνωμοτίας τέσσαρας, καὶ γίνονται τῶν εἴκοσι ὀκτὼ πεντηκοστύων ἐνωμοτίαι ἑκατὸν δώδεκα. ἔχει ἑκάστη ἐνωμοτία ἄνδρας τριάκοντα δύο (i.e. 4×8, because four men stood in the first rank of each enomoty, and they were drawn up as a rule, ἐπὶ πᾶν, eight deep), ὥστε γίνεσθαι τὸν πάντα στρατὸν τρισχιλίους πεντακοσίους ὀγδοήκοντα τέσσαρας (7 × 4 × 4 × 4 × 8 = 3584). Thuc. himself gives only the sum of the front rank of the army when drawn up: 7 (λόχοι) × 4 (πεντηκοστύες) × 4 (ἐνωμοτίαι) × 4 (ἄνδρες ἐν τῷ πρώτῳ ζυγῷ) = 448. This multiplied by 8 for the depth of the array gives likewise 3584, and with the 600 Sciritae, makes the whole army of the Lacedaemonians 4184. See Rüstow and Koechly, Gesch. d. gr. Kriegswesens, p. 90 ff.; Gilbert, Griechische Staatsalt. I. p. 73 ff. — 12. ἐπὶ δὲ βάθος ... κατέστησαν ἐπὶ ὀκτώ: because it seemed strange that the depth of the lochi should be left to the discretion of the lochagi, Dobree struck out the words ἀλλ' ὡς λοχαγὸς ἕκαστος ἐβούλετο, and went so far as to propose the omission of the whole passage, τῆς τε ἐνωμοτίας ... ἐβούλετο. Others also, and esp. Grote, find the passage troublesome. If we take the enomoty at 32 men (with the Schol.) and assume (with Thuc.) that four men stood in the front rank, then the arrangement of the remaining 28 men may have varied somewhat, so as to cause a variation in the depth of the column. Still complete certainty is hardly to be obtained in this matter. — 16. ἡ πρώτη τάξις: the

69 δέοντες πεντήκοντα ἄνδρες ἡ πρώτη τάξις ἦν. ἐπεὶ δὲ 1
ξυνιέναι ἔμελλον ἤδη, ἐνταῦθα καὶ παραινέσεις καθ'
ἑκάστους ὑπὸ τῶν οἰκείων στρατηγῶν τοιαίδε ἐγίγνοντο·
Μαντινεῦσι μὲν ὅτι ὑπέρ τε πατρίδος ἡ μάχη ἔσται καὶ
5 ὑπὲρ ἀρχῆς ἅμα καὶ δουλείας, τὴν μὲν μὴ πειρασαμένοις
ἀφαιρεθῆναι, τῆς δὲ μὴ αὖθις πειρᾶσθαι· Ἀργείοις δὲ
ὑπὲρ τῆς τε παλαιᾶς ἡγεμονίας καὶ τῆς ἐν Πελοποννήσῳ
ποτὲ ἰσομοιρίας, μὴ διὰ παντὸς στερισκομένους ἀνέχεσθαι,
καὶ ἄνδρας ἅμα ἐχθροὺς καὶ ἀστυγείτονας ὑπὲρ πολλῶν
10 ἀδικημάτων ἀμύνασθαι· τοῖς δὲ Ἀθηναίοις, καλὸν εἶναι
μετὰ πολλῶν καὶ ἀγαθῶν ξυμμάχων ἀγωνιζομένους μη-
δενὸς λείπεσθαι, καὶ ὅτι ἐν Πελοποννήσῳ Λακεδαιμο-

front rank, the meaning being here further determined by παρὰ ἅπαν, *all along the line*.
69. *The leaders encourage their troops by suitable addresses*.
2. ξυνιέναι ἔμελλον: *cf*. c. 59. 22; iv. 94. 10. — 4. καὶ ἅμα: *and besides*, stands opp. to and in close connexion with the preceding τε, adding emphasis to the second clause. ἅμα is not to be const. with ἀρχῆς καὶ δουλείας. — 5. τὴν μέν: τουτέστι τὴν ἀρχήν, Schol. — μη: const. with ἀφαιρεθῆναι: *not to lose*. πειρασαμένοις is affirmative: *after they had made a trial of it*. (This relation is reversed in ii. 44. 9, ὧν ἄντις μὴ πειρασάμενος ἀγαθῶν στερίσκηται.) For the truth of the statement, see c. 29. 3 ff. — 6. ἀφαιρεθῆναι, πειρᾶσθαι: the infs. denote the end or purpose of ἡ μάχη ἔσται, as in ii. 89. 45, ὁ δὲ ἀγὼν μέγας ὑμῖν, ἢ καταλῦσαι τὴν ἐλπίδα ἢ καταστῆσαι τὸν φόβον, the infs. express the purpose of ὁ ἀγών. GMT. 97; H. 951. — τῆς δέ: *sc*. τῆς δουλείας, their former subjection to the supremacy of Sparta, for this is the meaning of δουλεία. —'Ἀργείοις δέ:

sc. παραινέσεις ἐγίγνοντο. The object of the struggle is introduced as above by the prep. ὑπέρ, and the end to be attained is expressed by the infs. μὴ ἀνέχεσθαι and καὶ ἅμα ἀμύνασθαι. — 7. τῆς τε παλαιᾶς ἡγεμονίας: this refers to the earliest times and the rule of Atridae, while τῆς ἐν Πελοποννήσῳ ἰσομορίας refers to the later relation to Sparta (in the times before the Persian war; see c. 41. 15), which is thus expressed by Hdt. vii. 149. 17, οἱ Ἀργεῖοί φασι οὐκ ἀνασχέσθαι τῶν Σπαρτιητέων τὴν πλεονεξίην. The opposition of these two relations is expressed by τε, καί. — 8. διὰ παντός: *for ever*. See on i. 38. 2. — στερισκομένους: supplementary partic. with ἀνέχεσθαι. GMT. 112, 1; H. 983. *Cf*. i. 77. 6, δεινότερα τούτων πάσχοντες ἠνείχοντο; ii. 74. 2, ἠνείχοντο καὶ γῆν τεμνομένην; vi. 16. 20. — 9. καὶ ἅμα: as in 4. — 10. ἀμύνασθαι: aor., refers to the particular battle before them. — εἶναι: the inf. depends, as does also the clause ὅτι ... ἕξουσι, upon the idea of indir. disc. introduced by παραινέσεις ἐγίγνοντο. — 12. ἐν Πελοποννήσῳ: is em-

νίους νικήσαντες τήν τε ἀρχὴν βεβαιοτέραν καὶ μείζω
ἕξουσι, καὶ οὐ μή ποτέ τις αὐτοῖς ἄλλος ἐς τὴν γῆν
15 ἔλθῃ. τοῖς μὲν Ἀργείοις καὶ ξυμμάχοις τοιαῦτα παρῃνέθη· 2
Λακεδαιμόνιοι δὲ καθ' ἑκάστους τε καὶ μετὰ τῶν πολεμικῶν νόμων ἐν σφίσιν αὐτοῖς ὧν ἠπίσταντο τὴν παρακέλευσιν τῆς μνήμης * ἀγαθοῖς οὖσιν ἐποιοῦντο, εἰδότες ἔργων ἐκ πολλοῦ μελέτην πλείω σῴζουσαν ἢ λόγων δι' ὀλί-
20 γου καλῶς ῥηθεῖσαν παραίνεσιν.
70 Καὶ μετὰ ταῦτα ἡ ξύνοδος ἦν, Ἀργεῖοι μὲν καὶ οἱ 1
ξύμμαχοι ἐντόνως καὶ ὀργῇ χωροῦντες, Λακεδαιμόνιοι

phatic: "on their own ground." If the Lacedaemonians could be defeated there, the Athenians need never fear an attack from them in Attica, either by ἐσβολαί or ἐπιτειχισμός. This confident expectation is expressed here, as in iv. 95. 6, by the strongest form of the neg. fut. οὐ μή ποτε with the aor. subjv. GMT. 89, 1; H. 1032. This clause is dependent upon ὅτι in 12.

16. καθ' ἑκάστους: refers to the various parts of the Lacedaemonian army as Herbst, Jahrbb. 1858, p. 712, has shown, who says, 'for the Spartans regarded an army composed of Peloponnesian contingents as their own, as Lacedaemonian.' Cf. ii. 39. 11. Opp. to the various contingents (καθ' ἑκάστους) stand the Lacedaemonians themselves (ἐν σφίσιν αὐτοῖς). τὴν παρακέλευσιν ἐποιοῦντο belongs with both. But with καθ' ἑκάστους this conveys only the general notion of exhortation, while for the Lacedaemonians proper the characteristic manner of the exhortation is described. Among themselves with (the aid of) war-songs they made their exhortation of the memory (i.e. by awakening the memory) of those things which they knew. μετὰ τῶν πολεμικῶν νόμων· νόμους πολεμικοὺς λέγει τὰ ᾄσμα-

τα ἅπερ ᾖδον οἱ Λακεδαιμόνιοι μέλλοντες μάχεσθαι, Schol. They sang the war-songs which arouse the courage. Cf. the fragments of Tyrt., Bergk, Poet. Lyr. Gr. II. p. 8 ff. νόμος is used in this sense by Plat. Legg. iii. 700 b. See App. — 17. ἐν σφίσιν αὐτοῖς ὧν ἠπίσταντο τὴν παρακέλευσιν τῆς μνήμης ἐποιοῦντο, κτέ.: παρεκελεύοντο ἀλλήλοις μεμνῆσθαι ὧν μεμαθήκεσαν καὶ ἠπίσταντο, Schol. This consciousness, which they were to renew in their memory, is expressed in εἰδότες ... παραίνεσιν. — 18. ἀγαθοῖς οὖσιν: see App.

70. Both armies march into battle, the Lacedaemonians advancing to the music of flutes.

A. Gellius, Noct. Att. i. 11. 5 quotes this chap. with the remark: auctor historiae graecae grauissimus Thucydides Lacedaemonios summos bellatores non cornuum tubarumue signis, sed tibiarum modulis in proeliis esse usos refert.

1. ἡ ξύνοδος ἦν, Ἀργεῖοι μὲν χωροῦντες Λακεδαιμόνιοι δέ: a decided anacoluthon, ἡ ξύνοδος ἦν being treated as if it were ξυνῆλθον. See on ii. 53. 13. —2. ὀργῇ: summa alacritate

δὲ βραδέως καὶ ὑπὸ αὐλητῶν πολλῶν νόμῳ ἐγκαθεστώτων, οὐ τοῦ θείου χάριν, ἀλλ' ἵνα ὁμαλῶς μετὰ ῥυθμοῦ βαίνοντες προέλθοιεν καὶ μὴ διασπασθείη αὐτοῖς ἡ τάξις, ὅπερ φιλεῖ τὰ μεγάλα στρατόπεδα ἐν ταῖς προσόδοις ποιεῖν.

71 Ξυνιόντων δ' ἔτι Ἆγις ὁ βασιλεὺς τοιόνδε ἐβουλεύ- 1
σατο δρᾶσαι· τὰ στρατόπεδα ποιεῖ μὲν καὶ ἅπαντα
τοῦτο· ἐπὶ τὰ δεξιὰ κέρατα αὐτῶν ἐν ταῖς ξυνόδοις μᾶλ
λον ἐξωθεῖται, καὶ περιίσχουσι κατὰ τὸ τῶν ἐναντίων
5 εὐώνυμον ἀμφότεροι τῷ δεξιῷ, διὰ τὸ φοβουμένους προσ
στέλλειν τὰ γυμνὰ ἕκαστον ὡς μάλιστα τῇ τοῦ ἐν δεξιᾷ
παρατεταγμένου ἀσπίδι καὶ νομίζειν τὴν πυκνότητα τῆς
ξυγκλῄσεως εὐσκεπαστότατον εἶναι· καὶ ἡγεῖται μὲν τῆς

(Cl.). *Cf.* ii. 85. 9; vii. 68. 2. — 3. **ὑπὸ αὐλητῶν πολλῶν νόμῳ ἐγκαθεστώτων**: to the sound of many flute-players placed among them according to custom. This custom is freq. mentioned. *Cf.* Hdt. i. 17. 5 f., ὑπὸ συρίγγων; Cic. *Tusc.* ii. 16. 37, Spartiatarum, quorum procedit mora ad tibiam; Plut. *Lyc.* 22, ῥυθμῷ πρὸς τὸν αὐλὸν ἐμβαινόντων. See also Milton, *Paradise Lost*, i. 549 ff. See App. — **ἐγκαθεστώτων**: *i.e.* καθεστώτων ἐν αὐτοῖς, referring to their position in the ranks: inter exercitum positi, Gellius. — 4. **οὐ τοῦ θείου χάριν**: non prorsus ex aliquo ritu religionum neque rei diuinae gratia, Gellius. — 5. **προέλθοιεν**: see App. — 6. **φιλεῖ**: solent. See on i. 78. 5. — 7. **ποιεῖν**: almost in the sense of πάσχειν. So also in c. 71. 2.

71. *Agis tries to extend his left wing and strengthen it by a detachment from his right.*

1. **ξυνιόντων**: gen. abs. without a subst. *Cf.* c. 17. 11; i. 2. 9. — 2. **τὰ στρατόπεδα ποιεῖ μέν κτέ.**: the explanation of τοιόνδε, which begins with δείσας δὲ Ἆγις, 14, is preceded by some observations on the disposition of all armies (const. καὶ ἅπαντα with τὰ στρατόπεδα) before a battle. The application of these remarks to this particular battle explains the purpose of the movement undertaken by Agis. ποιεῖ is used like ποιεῖν in c. 70. 7. **τοῦτο**, explaining what follows, is elsewhere in Thuc. followed by γάρ. See App. — 3. **ἐν ταῖς ξυνόδοις**: *i.e.* ἐν τῷ ξυνιέναι: not in the battle itself, but in the advance to attack. — **μᾶλλον ἐξωθεῖται**: *i.e.* beyond their original position, more toward the right. ἐξωθεῖται, ἐκτείνεται, Schol. — 4. **περιίσχουσι**: like περιέσχον, 12; outflank, extend further. *Cf.* iii. 107. 16. μεῖζον γὰρ ἐγένετο καὶ περιέσχε τὸ τῶν Πελοποννησίων στρατόπεδον. — **κατὰ τὸ ... εὐώνυμον**: opposite their opponents' left wing. See on i. 33. 22, κατ' αὐτούς; 48. 12. — 5. **προσστέλλειν**: see App. — 8. **εὐσκεπαστότατον**: prob. neut., acc. to the usage of Thuc. *Cf.* i. 10. 1; 138. 27; iii. 37. 2; iv. 62. 3; 76. 15; vi. 39. 1. So far as the form is

αἰτίας ταύτης ὁ πρωτοστάτης τοῦ δεξιοῦ κέρως, προθυ-
μούμενος ἐξαλλάσσειν ἀεὶ τῶν ἐναντίων τὴν ἑαυτοῦ γύμνωσιν, ἕπονται δὲ διὰ τὸν αὐτὸν φόβον καὶ οἱ ἄλλοι.
καὶ τότε περιέσχον μὲν οἱ Μαντινῆς πολὺ τῷ κέρᾳ τῶν 2
Σκιριτῶν, ἔτι δὲ πλέον οἱ Λακεδαιμόνιοι καὶ Τεγεᾶται
τῶν Ἀθηναίων, ὅσῳ μεῖζον τὸ στράτευμα εἶχον. δείσας 3
δὲ Ἆγις μὴ σφῶν κυκλωθῇ τὸ εὐώνυμον, καὶ νομίσας
ἄγαν περιέχειν τοὺς Μαντινέας, τοῖς μὲν Σκιρίταις καὶ
Βρασιδείοις ἐσήμηνεν ἐπεξαγαγόντας ἀπὸ σφῶν ἐξισῶσαι
τοῖς Μαντινεῦσιν, ἐς δὲ τὸ διάκενον τοῦτο παρήγγελλεν
ἀπὸ τοῦ δεξιοῦ κέρως δύο λόχους τῶν πολεμάρχων Ἱπ-
πονοΐδᾳ καὶ Ἀριστοκλεῖ ἔχουσι παρελθεῖν καὶ ἐσβαλόντας
πληρῶσαι, νομίζων τῷ θ' ἑαυτῶν δεξιῷ ἔτι περιουσίαν

concerned, it might also be fem. See on iii. 89. 21; 101. 9. — ἡγεῖται τῆς αἰτίας: "is originally responsible" (Jowett). — 9. ὁ πρωτοστάτης: the man at the extreme right of the front rank. Cf. Poll. i. 127. — 10. ἐξαλλάσσε ... γύμνωσιν: μὴ κατὰ δόρυ τοῦ ἐναντίου ἔχειν τὰ γυμνὰ τοῦ σώματος, τουτέστι τὰ δεξιά, Schol. ἐξαλλάσσειν with gen., as here, means *withdraw from*. 12. καὶ τότε: *and in this case*. The special case illustrates the preceding general statements. One would expect here τότε δὲ καὶ οἱ Μαντινῆς to correspond to τὰ στρατόπεδα ποιεῖ μὲν καὶ ἅπαντα ταῦτα in 2, but the clause with δέ corresponding to μέν of 2 has been so long deferred that it is at last omitted entirely, and a new sent. is begun. — οἱ Μαντινῆς . . . τῶν Ἀθηναίων: cf. c. 67. 17. ἐσήμηνεν: σημαίνειν (cf. c. 10. 13; ii. 84. 5; vii. 50. 20) and παραγγέλλειν (cf. c. 10. 14; 73. 11) are used esp. of military orders. — ἐπεξαγαγόν-

τας: *advancing their line*. — ἀπὸ σφῶν: *from themselves*, i.e. from their main body. Agis said "from us" (ἀφ' ἡμῶν), which becomes in indir. disc. ἀπὸ σφῶν. — ἐξισῶσαι: is intrans. Cf. vi. 87. 23. They were to move to the left, that they might become equal to the Mantineans who form the enemy's right wing, i.e. in order to avoid being outflanked. — 18. τὸ διάκενον τοῦτο: the gap formed by advancing the Sciritae and the Brasidean contingent toward the left. — 19. τῶν πολεμάρχων: is part. gen., depending immediately upon the proper names. Cf. i. 24. 5; 126. 7. — 20. Ἀριστοκλεῖ: perhaps the brother of King Pleistoanax, mentioned in c. 16. 23, if the reading ἀδελφοῦ is correct. — ἐσβαλόντας: i.e. throwing themselves into the space made vacant by the movement of the Sciritae and Brasideans toward the left. — 21. πληρῶσαι: sc. τὸ διάκενον. — περιουσίαν: cf. 14, ὅσῳ μεῖζον τὸ στράτευμα εἶχον. — 22. τὸ κατὰ τοὺς Μαντινέας: *the part opposed*

ἔσεσθαι καὶ τὸ κατὰ τοὺς Μαντινέας βεβαιότερον τετά-
72 ξεσθαι. Ξυνέβη οὖν αὐτῷ ἅτε ἐν αὐτῇ τῇ ἐφόδῳ καὶ ἐξ 1
ὀλίγου παραγγείλαντι τόν τε Ἀριστοκλέα καὶ τὸν Ἱππο-
νοΐδαν μὴ θελῆσαι παρελθεῖν, ἀλλὰ καὶ διὰ τοῦτο τὸ
αἰτίαμα ὕστερον φεύγειν ἐκ Σπάρτης δόξαντας μαλακι-
5 σθῆναι, καὶ τοὺς πολεμίους φθάσαι τῇ προσμίξει, καὶ
κελεύσαντος αὐτοῦ, ἐπὶ τοὺς Σκιρίτας ὡς οὐ παρῆλθον
οἱ λόχοι, πάλιν αὖ σφίσι προσμῖξαι, μὴ δυνηθῆναι ἔτι
μηδὲ τούτους ξυγκλῆσαι. ἀλλὰ μάλιστα δὴ κατὰ πάντα 2

to the *Mantineans*, i.e. the left wing, which was formed by the Sciritae. See on 4. — **βεβαιότερον τετάξεσθαι**: ἐν ἀσφαλείᾳ ἔσεσθαι, ὡς ἂν μὴ δυνάμενον κυκλωθῆναι, Schol.
72. *This order is disobeyed, consequently the left wing is defeated, but the centre and right wing gain a decisive victory.*
1. ξυνέβη κτἑ.: the two clauses τόν τε Ἀριστοκλέα . . . μὴ θελῆσαι παρελθεῖν and καὶ τοὺς πολεμίους φθάσαι τῇ προσμίξει depend upon ξυνέβη. Between these is inserted a third clause, ἀλλὰ καὶ . . . μαλακισθῆναι, which is really parenthetical, but is formally dependent upon ξυνέβη because it is attracted by its surroundings into the acc. and inf. See on c. 48. 3. St. would like to read ἔφευγον and δόξαντες, but it is more likely that Thuc. employed this peculiar form of attraction than that it crept in as a later corruption. — **ἅτε**: const. with παραγγείλαντι, for ἅτε is always joined with partics. in Thuc. *Cf.* iv. 94. 7; 130. 25; vii. 44. 30; 58. 20; 85. 15; viii. 52. 13. The two adv. expressions, ἐν αὐτῇ τῇ ἐφόδῳ and ἐξ ὀλίγου (*at short notice*) mutually explain one another. — **4. φεύγειν**: *they were exiled*, doubtless after a trial. *Cf.* c.

26. 24. — **δόξαντας μαλακισθῆναι**: *because they were considered* (either by the people or by their judges) *to have acted like cowards*. — **5. φθάσαι τῇ προσμίξει**: equiv. to προσμίσγοντας φθάσαι, *they got ahead of them with their attack*, i.e. they attacked them before the movement was carried out. The verb προσμιγνύναι in the sense of attack occurs in i. 111. 13; ii. 39. 17; iv. 96. 6. The use of the dat. is peculiar. St. compares Dem. XXI. 38, ὀργῇ καὶ τρόπου προπετείᾳ φθάσαι τὸν λογισμόν. See App. — **6. ἐπὶ τοὺς Σκιρίτας**: this stands before the conj. ὡς for emphasis. *Cf.* i. 19. 2; ii. 64. 17; iii. 56. 26; iv. 27. 2. As the two lochi did not move to fill the space left vacant (τὸ διάκενον τοῦτο) by the departure of the Sciritae, Agis commanded the latter to return to the main body of the army (σφίσι like ἀπὸ σφῶν in 17, and προσμῖξαι as in c. 58. 3 and iii. 106. 14). This, however, they were unable to do, because the enemy were already between them and their friends. See App. — **8. ξυγκλῆσαι**: intr. as in iv. 35. 2.
8. ἀλλὰ μάλιστα δή: the force of this is the same as that of μάλιστα δή of c. 66. 6, except that it is strengthened by ἀλλά. — **9. ἐμπειρίᾳ**: the

τῇ ἐμπειρίᾳ Λακεδαιμόνιοι ἐλασσωθέντες τότε τῇ ἀνδρίᾳ
10 ἔδειξαν οὐχ ἧσσον περιγενόμενοι. ἐπειδὴ γὰρ ἐν χερσὶν 3
ἐγίγνοντο τοῖς ἐναντίοις, τὸ μὲν τῶν Μαντινέων δεξιὸν
τρέπει αὐτῶν τοὺς Σκιρίτας καὶ τοὺς Βρασιδείους, καὶ
ἐσπεσόντες οἱ Μαντινῆς καὶ οἱ ξύμμαχοι αὐτῶν καὶ τῶν
Ἀργείων οἱ χίλιοι λογάδες κατὰ τὸ διάκενον καὶ οὐ ξυγ-
15 κλῃσθὲν τοὺς Λακεδαιμονίους διέφθειρον, καὶ κυκλωσάμενοι ἔτρεψαν καὶ ἐξέωσαν ἐς τὰς ἁμάξας καὶ τῶν
πρεσβυτέρων τῶν ἐπιτεταγμένων ἀπέκτεινάν τινας. καὶ 4
ταύτῃ μὲν ἡσσῶντο οἱ Λακεδαιμόνιοι· τῷ δ᾽ ἄλλῳ στρατοπέδῳ, καὶ μάλιστα τῷ μέσῳ, ᾗπερ ὁ βασιλεὺς Ἆγις ἦν
20 καὶ περὶ αὐτὸν οἱ τριακόσιοι ἱππῆς καλούμενοι, προσ-

experience and the ease and accuracy in the execution of manoeuvres which result from experience. In this the Lacedaemonians were inferior throughout (κατὰ πάντα ἐλασσωθέντες). Indeed, this was the first great battle upon open ground in which they had engaged for many years (see Müller-Strübing, *Thuc. Forsch.* p. 12 f.), and at the very beginning of the battle they did not succeed in carrying out the movements commanded by Agis. Nevertheless they proved that they were superior in courage, and thereby won the victory. ἔδειξαν περιγενόμενοι, *showed by the result that they were superior* (const. as in c. 9. 40 and iv. 73. 8), is the expression of one who regards the battle from a later point of view; hence the aor.(not περιγιγνόμενοι with Poppo and St.). The account of the actual events is introduced by the following γάρ. See App.

12. αὐτῶν: *i.e.* τῶν Λακεδαιμονίων. The gen. of the pron. stands first as in i. 30. 14; iv. 199. 2. — 14. οἱ χίλιοι λογάδες: *cf.* c. 67. 13. — οὐ ξυγκλῃσθέν: *cf.* μὴ δυνηθῆναι ξυγκλῇσαι, 7. —

15. τοὺς Λακεδαιμονίους: *i.e.* those who, acc. to c. 67. 5 f., had been placed next to (ἐξῆς) the Sciritae and Brasideans, but had been separated from them by their movement toward the left (c. 71. § 3). The enemy now came in between the Sciritae and the Lacedaemonians, and attacked the flank of the latter. — διέφθειρον: impf., "they inflicted great losses upon them." *Cf.* iii. 98. 12. — κυκλωσάμενοι: since they had advanced into the διάκενον. — 16. ἐς τὰς ἁμάξας: ἔσω τῶν ἁμαξῶν, Schol. Among the baggage-wagons which stood behind the army. Near these the πρεσβύτεροι were drawn up in reserve, ἐπιτεταγμένοι.

20. οἱ τριακόσιοι ἱππῆς καλούμενοι: *cf.* Hdt. viii. 124. 13, τριηκόσιοι Σπαρτιητέων λογάδες, οὗτοι οἵπερ ἱππέες καλέονται (perhaps Kr., followed by St. and v. Herwerden, is right in inserting οἱ before ἱππῆς). These men who 'were chosen from the flower of the Spartan youth, served as a royal body-guard as well on foot as on horse-back.' Hermann, *Griech. Staatsalt.*

πεσόντες τῶν Ἀργείων τοῖς πρεσβυτέροις καὶ πέντε λόχοις ὠνομασμένοις καὶ Κλεωναίοις καὶ Ὀρνεάταις καὶ
Ἀθηναίων τοῖς παρατεταγμένοις ἔτρεψαν οὐδὲ ἐς χεῖρας
τοὺς πολλοὺς ὑπομείναντας, ἀλλ᾽ ὡς ἐπῆσαν οἱ Λακε-
25 δαιμόνιοι, εὐθὺς ἐνδόντας καὶ ἔστιν οὓς καὶ καταπατη-
73 θέντας τοῦ μὴ φθῆναι τὴν ἐγκατάληψιν. ὡς δὲ ταύτῃ 1
ἐνεδεδώκει τὸ τῶν Ἀργείων καὶ ξυμμάχων στράτευμα,
παρερρήγνυντο ἤδη ἅμα καὶ ἐφ᾽ ἑκάτερα, καὶ ἅμα τὸ

§ 29. 15 ff. They certainly served on foot, but of their use as cavalry there is no proof. See Gilbert, *Griech. Staatsalt.* I. p. 77. — 21. τῶν Ἀργείων: see App. — τοῖς πρεσβυτέροις καὶ πέντε λόχοις ὠνομασμένοις: ἅμα ἀναγνωστέον πεντελόχοις. Schol. Nothing is known of the relation of these divisions of the Argive troops to one another, or to the χίλιοι λογάδες of 14, and c. 67. 13. ὠνομασμένοις indicates that πέντε λόχοι or πεντέλοχοι was the conventional name of a division of troops, which seems, in conjunction with the πρεσβύτεροι, to be identical with the ἄλλοι Ἀργεῖοι of c. 67. 15. See Arnold's note on this passage. — 23. Ἀθηναίων τοῖς παρατεταγμένοις: this is that part of the Attic contingent (*cf.* c. 61. 1; 67. 17) which stood next the Orneatae, furthest toward the right. The fortunes of the main body of the Athenians are related in c. 73. 4 ff. — οὐδὲ ἐς χεῖρας ὑπομείναντας: i.e. οὐδὲ μέχρι τοῦ ἐς χεῖρας ἐλθεῖν ὑπομείναντας: "not waiting until they came to close quarters." Similarly, μήτε ἐς ἀλκὴν ὑπομεῖναι, iii. 108. 5. — 25. καταπατηθέντας: *sc.* ὑπ᾽ ἀλλήλων, as Grote, VI. c. 56, p. 356 f., has shown. — 26. τὴν ἐγκατάληψιν: correctly explained by Grote as subj. of μὴ φθῆναι. This is equiv. to τοῦ τοὺς Λακεδαιμονίους μὴ φθῆναι ἐγκαταλαβόντας αὐτούς. In their panic they fell under the feet of their own comrades, running away, that the enemy might not catch them before they could escape. ἐγκατάληψιν is very expressive : "the holding fast, while still on the spot" (ἐν); Grote translates: "the actual grasp of the Lacedaemonians." — 26. τοῦ μή: with inf. expressing purpose. See on i. 4. 6, τοῦ τὰς προσόδους μᾶλλον ἰέναι αὐτῷ. GMT. 95, 1; H. 960.

73. *The Athenians were saved from excessive losses by the assistance of their cavalry : nor did the Lacedaemonians pursue their defeated opponents very far.*

3. παρερρήγνυντο, ἐκυκλοῦτο: the two impfs., each with ἅμα, indicate the moment of the greatest peril. "The (defeated) Argives and their allies were on the point of being entirely severed from the rest of the army, and at the same time the right wing of the enemy was on the point of surrounding the Athenians." Among the allies the body of Athenians mentioned in c. 72. 23 is included. οἱ Ἀργεῖοι καὶ ξύμμαχοι is to be supplied as subj. of παρερρήγνυντο. *Cf.* iv. 96. 25; vi. 70. 10. — ἐφ᾽ ἑκάτερα: they were separated on the right from the victorious Mantineans, who were pressing forward, and on the left

δεξιὸν τῶν Λακεδαιμονίων καὶ Τεγεατῶν ἐκυκλοῦτο τῷ περιέχοντι σφῶν τοὺς Ἀθηναίους, καὶ ἀμφοτέρωθεν αὐτοὺς κίνδυνος περιειστήκει, τῇ μὲν κυκλουμένους, τῇ δὲ ἤδη ἡσσημένους. καὶ μάλιστ᾽ ἂν τοῦ στρατεύματος ἐταλαιπώρησαν, εἰ μὴ οἱ ἱππῆς παρόντες αὐτοῖς ὠφέλιμοι ἦσαν. καὶ ξυνέβη τὸν Ἆγιν, ὡς ᾔσθετο τὸ εὐώνυμον 2 σφῶν πονοῦν τὸ κατὰ τοὺς Μαντινέας καὶ τῶν Ἀργείων τοὺς χιλίους, παραγγεῖλαι παντὶ τῷ στρατεύματι χωρῆσαι ἐπὶ τὸ νικώμενον. καὶ γενομένου τούτου οἱ μὲν Ἀθη- 3 ναῖοι ἐν τούτῳ, ὡς παρῆλθε καὶ ἐξέκλινεν ἀπὸ σφῶν τὸ στράτευμα, καθ᾽ ἡσυχίαν ἐσώθησαν καὶ τῶν Ἀργείων μετ᾽ αὐτῶν τὸ ἡσσηθέν. οἱ δὲ Μαντινῆς καὶ οἱ ξύμμαχοι καὶ τῶν Ἀργείων οἱ λογάδες οὐκέτι πρὸς τὸ ἐγκεῖσθαι τοῖς ἐναντίοις τὴν γνώμην εἶχον, ἀλλ᾽ ὁρῶντες τούς τε σφετέρους νενικημένους καὶ τοὺς Λακεδαιμονίους ἐπιφερομένους ἐς φυγὴν ἐτράποντο. καὶ τῶν μὲν 4 Μαντινέων καὶ πλείους διεφθάρησαν, τῶν δὲ Ἀργείων

from the main body of the Athenians, who composed the extreme left wing (see c. 67. 17), and were now in danger of being surrounded by the right wing of the Lacedaemonians and Tegeans. — 4. τῷ περιέχοντι σφῶν: cf. c. 71. 13. — 6. αὐτούς: sc. τοὺς Ἀθηναίους, refers to them all, so that their two divisions are designated in their situation at the moment, the one as κυκλούμενοι (pres. pass. *on the point of being surrounded*), the other as ἡσσημένοι acc. to c. 72.23 ff. — 8. οἱ ἱππῆς: *i.e.* the three hundred of c. 61. 2 and 67. 18. — παρόντες: *by their presence*, because the enemy dared not come near them; or possibly we should read παριόντες, *by advancing* to protect the foot-force.

9. καὶ ξυνέβη: *then it happened.* — τὸ εὐώνυμον σφῶν: cf. c. 71. 15. — 11.

παραγγεῖλαι: see on c. 71. 17. — χωρῆσαι ἐπὶ τὸ νικώμενον: *to go to* (assist) *the defeated part of the army* (the left wing). This movement is described in the following παρῆλθε καὶ ἐξέκλινε ἀπὸ σφῶν (τῶν Ἀθηναίων) τὸ στράτευμα: they turned toward the left and moved away from the Athenians. This intr. use of ἐκκλίνειν does not occur elsewhere.

15. τὸ ἡσσηθέν: *i.e.* the part of the Argives which had been defeated in c. 72. 21. The aor. is used in reference to the action there described; the pf. ἡσσημένους (7), in reference to the condition resulting from that action. — 16. πρὸς τὸ ἐγκεῖσθαι: cf. c. 72. 16 ff. — 19. ἐπιφερομένους: this results from the χωρῆσαι ἐπὶ τὸ νικώμενον of 11.

20. καὶ πλείους: these words are opp.

λογάδων τὸ πολὺ ἐσώθη. ἡ μέντοι φυγὴ καὶ ἀποχώρησις οὐ βίαιος οὐδὲ μακρὰ ἦν· οἱ γὰρ Λακεδαιμόνιοι μέχρι μὲν τοῦ τρέψαι χρονίους τὰς μάχας καὶ βεβαίους τῷ μένειν ποιοῦνται, τρέψαντες δὲ βραχείας καὶ οὐκ ἐπὶ
25 πολὺ τὰς διώξεις.
74 Καὶ ἡ μὲν μάχη τοιαύτη καὶ ὅτι ἐγγύτατα τούτων 1 ἐγένετο, πλείστου δὴ χρόνου μεγίστη δὴ τῶν Ἑλληνικῶν καὶ ὑπὸ ἀξιολογωτάτων πόλεων ξυνελθοῦσα. οἱ δὲ Λα- 2 κεδαιμόνιοι προθέμενοι τῶν πολεμίων νεκρῶν τὰ ὅπλα
5 τροπαῖον εὐθὺς ἵστασαν καὶ τοὺς νεκροὺς ἐσκύλευον καὶ τοὺς αὑτῶν ἀνείλοντο καὶ ἀπήγαγον ἐς Τεγέαν, οὗπερ ἐτάφησαν, καὶ τοὺς τῶν πολεμίων ὑποσπόνδους ἀπέδοσαν.

to the following τῶν Ἀργείων λογάδων τὸ πολὺ ἐσώθη. Of these only a few fell, while a greater number of the Mantineans were cut down. καί is emphatic; not only did they take to flight, but a considerable number were killed (more than of the λογάδες; 200, acc. to c. 74. 9). See App. — 22. οὐ βίαιος: "not hotly pursued." *Cf.* iv. 31. 15. — οὐδὲ μακρά: correctly explained by the Schol. as referring to distance: οὐδὲ ἐπὶ πολὺ διάστημα. — 23. χρονίους (in i. 12. 3, with fem. ending χρονία) καὶ βεβαίους: these are pred. adjs. with τὰς μάχας ποιοῦνται, corresponding to advs. with μάχεσθαι. So βραχείας (temporal) belongs with τὰς διώξεις, sc. ποιοῦνται. Plut. *Lyc.* 22 makes a similar statement concerning the Lacedaemonian manner of fighting.

74. *The number of slain on both sides.*

1. τοιαύτη καὶ ὅτι ἐγγύτατα τούτων: *cf.* i. 22. 17, τοιούτων καὶ παραπλησίων; vii. 42. 10, ἴσον καὶ παραπλήσιον. Slightly different is vii. 86. 23, τοιαύτη ἢ ὅτι ἐγγύτατα τούτων αἰτίᾳ. — 2. πλείστου δὴ χρόνου μεγίστη δή: δή is repeated with the sups. on account of the special emphasis. On the gen. of time, see Kr. *Spr.* 47, 2, 3. — 3. ξυνελθοῦσα: see App.

4. προθέμενοι τῶν πολεμίων νεκρῶν τὸ ὅπλα: *i.e.* πρὸ τῶν πολεμίων νεκρῶν τὰ ὅπλα θέμενοι (see on ii. 2. 22): "they halted in front of the enemy's dead." So const. by Haase, *Lucubr. Thuc.* p. 7. Herbst, Jahrbb. 1858, p. 693, shows, by comparison of this passage with Xen. *Ages.* ii. 15, that this was done 'because then the enemy would certainly be compelled to ask for their dead,' and thus own themselves defeated. — 5. ἵστασαν: impf. The erection of the τροπαῖον was not perfected until after the enemy owned their defeat. This they did ὑποσπόνδους τοὺς νεκροὺς κομιζόμενοι (*cf.* ii. 79. 29) or ἀναιρούμενοι (*cf.* vii. 5. 10), which corresponds to the ἀποδιδόναι of the victors. — ἐσκύλευον: the remark of Aelian *V.H.* vi. 6, οὐκ ἐξῆν ἀνδρὶ Λάκωνι οὐδὲ σκυλεῦσαι τὸν πολέμιον applies, then, only to the time of the actual battle.

ἀπέθανον δὲ Ἀργείων μὲν καὶ Ὀρνεατῶν καὶ Κλεωναίων 3
ἑπτακόσιοι, Μαντινέων δὲ διακόσιοι, καὶ Ἀθηναίων ξὺν
10 Αἰγινήταις διακόσιοι καὶ οἱ στρατηγοὶ ἀμφότεροι. Λακεδαιμονίων δὲ οἱ μὲν ξύμμαχοι οὐκ ἐταλαιπώρησαν
ὥστε καὶ ἀξιόλογόν τι ἀπογενέσθαι· αὐτῶν δὲ χαλεπὸν
μὲν ἦν τὴν ἀλήθειαν πυθέσθαι, ἐλέγοντο δὲ περὶ τρια-
75 κοσίους ἀποθανεῖν. τῆς δὲ μάχης μελλούσης ἔσεσθαι 1
καὶ Πλειστοάναξ ὁ ἕτερος βασιλεὺς ἔχων τούς τε πρεσβυτέρους καὶ νεωτέρους ἐβοήθησε· καὶ μέχρι μὲν Τεγέας ἀφίκετο, πυθόμενος δὲ τὴν νίκην ἀπεχώρησε. καὶ 2
5 τοὺς ἀπὸ Κορίνθου καὶ ἔξω ἰσθμοῦ ξυμμάχους ἀπέστρεψαν πέμψαντες οἱ Λακεδαιμόνιοι, καὶ αὐτοὶ ἀναχωρήσαντες καὶ τοὺς ξυμμάχους ἀφέντες (* Κάρνεια γὰρ
αὐτοῖς ἐτύγχανον ὄντα) τὴν ἑορτὴν ἦγον. καὶ τὴν ὑπὸ 3
τῶν Ἑλλήνων τότε ἐπιφερομένην αἰτίαν ἔς τε μαλακίαν

9. **ξὺν Αἰγινήταις**: this shows that Cleruchi from Aegina (see ii. 27. 5 ff.) had also been called out. — 10. **οἱ στρατηγοὶ ἀμφότεροι**: Laches and Nicostratus. *Cf.* c. 61. 2. — 11. **οἱ ξύμμαχοι**: *i.e.* the allies from Arcadia, who are not mentioned in the account of the battle; hence οὐκ ἐταλαιπώρησαν, they had not been exposed and had not suffered any considerable losses. — 12. **ὥστε καὶ ἀξιόλογόν τι ἀπογενέσθαι**: καί has the effect of adding to the assurance that something in itself improbable nevertheless really happened. See on i. 15. 7; iv. 48. 25. ἀπογίγνεσθαι, *be missing, die*, occurs also in ii. 34. 4; 51. 22; 98. 10.

75. *Remarks on the battle of Mantinea. The hostilities between Epidaurus and Argos are renewed.*

1. **τῆς δὲ μάχης μελλούσης κτἑ.**: the epexegetical δέ introduces the following aors. (ἐβοήθησε and ἀφίκετο, to be translated by the English plpf.), which go back to the time before the battle. — 2. **ὁ ἕτερος βασιλεύς**: either the law mentioned by Hdt. v. 75. 9 f., μὴ ἐξεῖναι ἔπεσθαι ἀμφοτέρους τοὺς βασιλέας ἐξιούσης στρατιῆς, was neglected in this instance, or it did not apply to the sending of reinforcements. — **τούς τε πρεσβυτέρους καὶ νεωτέρους**: *cf.* c. 64. 10 ff. — 3. **καὶ . . . ἀπέστρεψαν**: the narrative of the events succeeding the battle is resumed.

5. **τοὺς ἀπὸ Κορίνθου κτἑ.**: see c. 64. 15. — **ἀπέστρεψαν**: *they caused them to turn back. Cf.* iv. 97. 7. — 7. **Κάρνεια**: on the time of this festival, see on c. 54. 8. — 8. **ἐτύγχανον ὄντα**: on the pl., see on ἐπῆλθον Ὀλύμπια, i. 126. 13.

8. **καὶ . . . ἀπελύσαντο**: "and so by this one deed they had done away with the accusation which was commonly brought against them at that time." — 9. **τότε**: taken in connexion

διὰ τὴν ἐν τῇ νήσῳ ξυμφορὰν καὶ ἐς τὴν ἄλλην ἀβουλίαν τε καὶ βραδυτῆτα ἑνὶ ἔργῳ τούτῳ ἀπελύσαντο, τύχῃ μὲν ὡς ἐδόκουν κακιζόμενοι, γνώμῃ δὲ οἱ αὐτοὶ ἔτι ὄντες. Τῇ δὲ προτέρᾳ ἡμέρᾳ ξυνέβη τῆς μάχης ταύτης 4 καὶ τοὺς Ἐπιδαυρίους πανδημεὶ ἐσβαλεῖν ἐς τὴν Ἀργείαν ὡς ἐρῆμον οὖσαν καὶ τοὺς ὑπολοίπους φύλακας τῶν Ἀργείων ἐξελθόντων αὐτῶν διαφθεῖραι πολλούς. καὶ 5 Ἠλείων τρισχιλίων ὁπλιτῶν βοηθησάντων Μαντινεῦσιν ὕστερον τῆς μάχης καὶ Ἀθηναίων χιλίων πρὸς τοῖς προτέροις, ἐστράτευσαν ἅπαντες οἱ ξύμμαχοι οὗτοι εὐθὺς ἐπὶ Ἐπίδαυρον, ἕως οἱ Λακεδαιμόνιοι Κάρνεια ἦγον, καὶ διελόμενοι τὴν πόλιν περιετείχιζον. καὶ οἱ μὲν ἄλλοι 6 ἐξεπαύσαντο, Ἀθηναῖοι δὲ ὥσπερ προσετάχθησαν τὴν

with τὴν ἐν τῇ νήσῳ ξυμφοράν, evidently refers to the whole period since the capture of Sphacteria in 425 B.C. — ἐπιφερομένην αἰτίαν: cf. αἰτίαν ἐπιφέρειν, iii. 46. 26. — ἐς μαλακίαν: cf. viii. 88. 8, ἐς τὴν φιλίαν διαβάλλειν. — 10. ἐς τὴν ἄλλην ἀβουλίαν: *general stupidity*. On this use of ἄλλος, see on i. 128. 21; ii. 14. 2. — 12. κακιζόμενοι: *being ill-spoken of, having incurred disgrace*. This is in accordance with the use of this word elsewhere in Thuc. (cf. i. 105. 26; ii. 21. 23) and with ὑπὸ τῶν Ἑλλήνων ἐπιφερομένην αἰτίαν above. The dat. τύχῃ must then be taken to mean "by a mishap," "through unfortunate circumstances." (The explanation "hardly used by fortune" would be appropriate as regards the sense, but is not in accordance with the use of κακίζεσθαι.) A similar idea is expressed in ii. 87. 7 ff.

14. προτέρᾳ: see App. — τῆς μάχης: depends upon the comp. προτέρᾳ

as, 19, upon ὕστερον. — 16. ὡς ἐρῆμον οὖσαν: τοῦ στρατεύματος, Schol. This is retaliation for the attack mentioned in c. 56. § 5. — 16. τῶν Ἀργείων: const. with φύλακας. — 17. ἐξελθόντων αὐτῶν: "since the citizens fit for military service had gone away." St. strikes out αὐτῶν and takes τῶν Ἀργείων ἐξελθόντων together. — 17. πολλούς: const. as pred. *in great numbers*.

18. Ἠλείων: the Eleans had delayed for a time on account of anger. See c. 62. 5. — 19. τοῖς προτέροις: cf. c. 61. 1 ff. Thuc. does not tell what general or generals took the command of the Athenian troops in place of those who had fallen (see c. 61. 2 ; 74. 10). Müller-Strübing, *Aristoph. und die hist. Krit.* p. 447 ff., suggests Demosthenes. This seems, in view of c. 80. 16, not improbable (though Cl. thinks otherwise). — 22. διελόμενοι: used of like operations in ii. 75. 11; 78. 4; iv. 69. 10; vii. 19. 6.

23. ἐξεπαύσαντο: ἀπέκαμον τοῦ περι-

ἄκραν τὸ Ἡραῖον εὐθὺς ἐξειργάσαντο. καὶ ἐν τούτῳ
25 ξυγκαταλιπόντες ἅπαντες τῷ τειχίσματι φρουρὰν ἀνεχώρησαν κατὰ πόλεις ἕκαστοι. καὶ τὸ θέρος ἐτελεύτα.
76 Τοῦ δ' ἐπιγιγνομένου χειμῶνος ἀρχομένου * εὐ- 1
θὺς οἱ Λακεδαιμόνιοι [ἐπειδὴ τὰ Κάρνεια ἤγαγον] ἐξεστράτευσαν, καὶ ἀφικόμενοι ἐς Τεγέαν λόγους προύπεμπον ἐς τὸ Ἄργος ξυμβατηρίους. ἦσαν δὲ αὐτοῖς πρότερόν 2
5 τε ἄνδρες ἐπιτήδειοι καὶ βουλόμενοι τὸν δῆμον τὸν ἐν
Ἄργει καταλῦσαι, καὶ ἐπειδὴ ἡ μάχη ἐγεγένητο, πολλῷ
μᾶλλον ἐδύναντο πείθειν τοὺς πολλοὺς ἐς τὴν ὁμολογίαν. ἐβούλοντο δὲ πρῶτον σπονδὰς ποιήσαντες πρὸς
τοὺς Λακεδαιμονίους αὖθις ὕστερον καὶ ξυμμαχίαν, καὶ
10 οὕτως ἤδη τῷ δήμῳ ἐπιτίθεσθαι. καὶ ἀφικνεῖται πρόξε- 3
νος ὢν Ἀργείων Λίχας ὁ Ἀρκεσιλάου παρὰ τῶν Λακεδαιμονίων δύο λόγω φέρων ἐς τὸ Ἄργος, τὸν μὲν καθ'

τειχίζειν. Schol. The mid. in Thuc. occurs here only; ἐκπαύσω in Eur. *Ion*, 144. — τὴν ἄκραν τὸ Ἡραῖον: appos. 'The Heraeum by the harbour, the site of which can be found on the small rocky height.' Curtius, *Pelopon.* II. p. 428. *Cf.* Paus. ii. 29. 1, τὸ δὲ πρὸς τῷ λιμένι ἐπὶ ἄκρας ἀνεχούσης ἐς θάλασσαν λέγουσιν Ἥρας εἶναι. — 24. ἐξειργάσαντο: on this side the Athenians finished the wall of circumvallation which, with the outworks which may have belonged to it, formed the τείχισμα of 25.
76. *In Argos the oligarchical party gains the upper hand, and brings about a peace with Sparta.*
1. εὐθύς: const. with ἀρχομένου. *Cf.* c. 13. 2; iv. 52. 1. — 2. [ἐπειδὴ τὰ Κάρνεια ἤγαγον]: see App. — 3. λόγους ξυμβατηρίους: *proposals of peace*. Not found elsewhere in Att. writers; later freq. used, esp. by Dion H. (ii. 45, *etc.*).

4. αὐτοῖς: const. grammatically with ἐπιτήδειοι, but its position at the beginning of the sent. points to a general relation: "there had always been partizans of theirs there." — 5. τὸν δῆμον: τὴν δημοκρατίαν. Schol. *Cf.* iii. 81. 20. — 7. τοὺς πολλούς: *the many, the people* (Cl. renders, *a great number*, and cites iv. 6. 6, which does not apply). — ἐς τὴν ὁμολογίαν: a rare const. with πείθειν which is defined by the Schol. ἤγουν καταπεῖσαι ὁμολογῆσαι καὶ συνθέσθαι. — 8. σπονδὰς ποιήσαντες: *after they had first made a truce (cf.* c. 30. 26; ii. 29. 24); with ξυμμαχίαν, 9, we must supply ποιῆσαι (*cf.* c. 30. 26; ii. 29. 24; viii. 6. 10), depending, like the following ἐπιτίθεσθαι, upon ἐβούλοντο. — 9. αὖθις: denotes progress after πρῶτον or πρότερον. *Cf.* c. 36. 11; 78. 5; iv. 73. 26; vi. 90. 5.
11. Λίχας ὁ Ἀρκεσιλάου: see on c. 50. 14. — 12. καθ' ὅ τι, ὡς: the ellip-

ὅ τι εἰ βούλονται πολεμεῖν, τὸν δ᾽ ὡς εἰ εἰρήνην ἄγειν. καὶ γενομένης πολλῆς ἀντιλογίας (ἔτυχε γὰρ καὶ ὁ Ἀλκι-
15 βιάδης παρών) οἱ ἄνδρες οἱ τοῖς Λακεδαιμονίοις πράσ-
σοντες, ἤδη καὶ ἐκ τοῦ φανεροῦ τολμῶντες, ἔπεισαν τοὺς
Ἀργείους προσδέξασθαι τὸν ξυμβατήριον λόγον. ἔστι
δὲ ὅδε·

77   "Καττάδε δοκεῖ τᾷ ἐκκλησίᾳ τῶν Λακεδαιμονίων
ξυμβαλέσθαι ποττὼς Ἀργείως, ἀποδιδόντας τὼς παῖδας
τοῖς Ὀρχομενίοις καὶ τὼς ἄνδρας τοῖς Μαιναλίοις, καὶ
τὼς ἄνδρας τὼς ἐν Μαντινείᾳ τοῖς Λακεδαιμονίοις ἀποδι-
5 δόντας, καὶ ἐξ Ἐπιδαύρω ἐκβῶντας καὶ τὸ τεῖχος ἀναι-

sis in these brief expressions (as in Lat. quaestio an or quomodo, etc.) cannot be supplied with certainty (πολεμήσουσι with καθ᾽ ὅ τι and εἰρήνην ἄξουσι with ὡς would do). In case the Argives preferred war, the λόγος probably contained threats, and in case of an agreement, the proposal of the terms given in c. 77. — 14. ἔτυχε... παρών: he was already present in c. 61. 8. — 15. τοῖς Λακεδαιμονίοις: the dat. of advantage with πράσσειν as in iii. 4. 21; iv. 106. 10. — 16. ἐκ τοῦ φανεροῦ: equiv. to φανερῶς. Cf. iv. 79. 10; 106. 11. — τολμῶντες: abs. Cf. ii. 43. 11.
77. *The terms of the treaty of peace between the Lacedaemonians and the Argives.*
1. καττάδε δοκεῖ κτέ.: the Dor. dialect in the two documents given in c. 77 and 79 does not agree in all respects with the rules laid down by Ahrens (*de dial. Dor.* p. 480 ff.). Still, it does not seem best to depart from the reading of the Mss. in an attempt to reconstruct the original language of these chaps. See App. — καττάδε: Att. κατὰ τάδε; 2. ποττώς: Att. πρὸς

τούς; 5. ἐκβῶντας: Att. ἐκβαίνοντας; 6. αἱ δέ κα μὴ εἴκωντι: Att. ἐὰν δὲ μὴ εἴκωσι; 7. εἴμεν: Att. εἶναι; 10. ἔχοντι: Att. ἔχουσι; ἀποδόμεν: Att. ἀποδοῦναι; πολίεσσι: Att. πόλεσι; τῷ σιῷ σύματος: Att. τοῦ θεοῦ θύματος; 11. αἰ μὲν λῆν: Att. εἰ μὲν βούλεσθαι; 15. ἀλεξέμεναι: Att. ἀλέξειν; 18. ἐντι: Att. εἰσι; ἐσσοῦνται: Att. ἔσονται; 22. ἀπιδάλλην: Att. ἀποπέμπειν. For details, see the notes in St.'s edit. — τᾷ ἐκκλησίᾳ: acc. to Hdt. vii. 134. 9, the proper designation of the popular assembly at Sparta is ἀλία, which Ahrens wished to insert in the text; but it seems more likely that this assembly was properly called ἀπέλλα. See Gilbert, *Griech. Staatsalt.* I. p. 53 f. — 2. τὼς παῖδας: *i.e.* the hostages mentioned in c. 61. 22. — 3. τὼς ἄνδρας: these must be the ὅμηροι ἐκ τῆς Ἀρκαδίας αὐτόθι ὑπὸ Λακεδαιμονίων κείμενοι of c. 61. 18, although no mention of the Maenalians is made there. Why the distinction between παῖδες and ἄνδρες is made is not clear. παῖς seems to be used here and in 9 to designate those who are not of military age. — 5. τὸ τεῖχος: the τείχισμα of c. 75. 25.

ροῦντας. αἰ δέ κα μὴ εἴκωντι τοὶ Ἀθηναῖοι ἐξ Ἐπιδαύρω, 2
πολεμίως εἶμεν τοῖς Ἀργείοις καὶ τοῖς Λακεδαιμονίοις
καὶ τοῖς τῶν Λακεδαιμονίων ξυμμάχοις καὶ τοῖς τῶν
Ἀργείων ξυμμάχοις. καὶ αἴ τινα τοὶ Λακεδαιμόνιοι παῖδα 3
ἔχοντι, ἀποδόμεν ταῖς πολίεσσι πάσαις. περὶ δὲ τῶ σιῶ 4
σύματος, αἰ μὲν λῆν, τοῖς Ἐπιδαυρίοις ὅρκον δόμεν, αἰ δέ,
αὐτὼς ὀμόσαι. τὰς δὲ πόλιας τὰς ἐν Πελοποννάσῳ, 5
καὶ μικρὰς καὶ μεγάλας, αὐτονόμως εἶμεν πάσας καττὰ
πάτρια. αἰ δέ κα τῶν ἐκτὸς Πελοποννάσω τις ἐπὶ τὰν 6
Πελοπόννασον γᾶν ἴῃ ἐπὶ κακῷ, ἀλεξέμεναι ἀμόθι βου-
λευσαμένως, ὅπᾳ κα δικαιότατα δοκῇ τοῖς Πελοποννα-
σίοις. ὅσσοι δ' ἐκτὸς Πελοποννάσω τῶν Λακεδαιμονίων
ξύμμαχοί ἐντι, ἐν τῷ αὐτῷ ἐσσοῦνται ἐν τῷπερ καὶ τοὶ
τῶν Λακεδαιμονίων καὶ τοὶ τῶν Ἀργείων ξύμμαχοί ἐντι,
τὰν αὐτῶν ἔχοντες. ἐπιδείξαντας δὲ τοῖς ξυμμάχοις ξυμ- 7

6. τοὶ Ἀθηναῖοι: the Athenians had been most active in the operations against Epidaurus. *Cf.* c. 75. 25.
10. περὶ τῶ σιῶ σύματος: on the forms, see above. This refers to the cause of the quarrel between Argos and Epidaurus. See c. 53. 2 f. τῶ σιῶ, *i.e.* τοῦ Ἀπόλλωνος τοῦ Πυθαέως. Perhaps van Herwerden is right in inserting τῶ (*i.e.* τοῦ) before σύματος, though the omission of the art. may be explained on account of the preceding gen. — 11. αἰ μὲν λῆν, τοῖς Ἐπιδαυρίοις ὅρκον δόμεν, αἰ δέ, κτέ.: *if they wish, they shall impose an oath upon the Epidaurians; but if not, they shall swear it themselves.* λῆν is inf. The inf. after εἰ occurs also in iv. 98. 12, καὶ αὐτοὶ εἰ μὲν ἐπὶ πλέον δυνηθῆναι τῆς ἐκείνων κρατῆσαι, τοῦτ' ἂν ἔχειν. This is not unlike the inf. in rel. clauses. *Cf.* c. 28. 4; 46. 17. αἰ δέ is for εἰ δὲ μή. *Cf.* Plat. *Conv.* 212 c, εἰ μὲν βούλει, ὡς ἐγκώμιον εἰς Ἔρωτα νόμισον εἰρῆσθαι, εἰ δέ, ὅ τι καὶ ὅπῃ χαίρεις ὀνομάζων, τοῦτο ὀνόμαζε. See App.
13. αὐτονόμως εἶμεν πάσας: the Lacedaemonians always endeavoured to prevent other cities from establishing empires or hegemonies.
15. ἀμόθι: is another Dor. form for ἀμᾷ, *i.e.* κοινῇ. See App. — 16. ὅπᾳ κα: equiv. to ὡς ἂν with subjv.
18. ἐσσοῦνται: see App. — 19. ἐντι κτέ.: see App.
20. ξυμβαλέσθαι: this repeats the ξυμβαλέσθαι of 2 with the added conditions ἐπιδείξαντας τοῖς ξυμμάχοις and αἴ κα αὐτοῖς δοκῇ: "they were to communicate (the conditions) to their allies, and then conclude the peace if they (the Argives and Lacedaemonians) thought best." (Cl. takes αὐτοῖς to refer to the allies. But in that case there is no distinction between

βαλέσθαι, αἴ κα αὐτοῖς δοκῇ. αἰ δέ τι δοκῇ τοῖς ξυμμάχοις, οἴκαδ' ἀπιάλλην."

78 Τοῦτον μὲν τὸν λόγον προσεδέξαντο πρῶτον οἱ 1 Ἀργεῖοι, καὶ τῶν Λακεδαιμονίων τὸ στράτευμα ἀνεχώρησεν ἐκ τῆς Τεγέας ἐπ' οἴκου· μετὰ δὲ τοῦτο ἐπιμιξίας οὔσης ἤδη παρ' ἀλλήλους, * οὐ πολλῷ ὕστερον ἔπραξαν
5 αὖθις οἱ αὐτοὶ ἄνδρες ὥστε τὴν Μαντινέων καὶ Ἠλείων καὶ τὴν Ἀθηναίων ξυμμαχίαν ἀφέντας Ἀργείους σπονδὰς καὶ ξυμμαχίαν ποιήσασθαι πρὸς Λακεδαιμονίους· καὶ ἐγένοντο αἵδε·

79 " Καττάδε ἔδοξε τοῖς Λακεδαιμονίοις καὶ Ἀργείοις 1 σπονδὰς καὶ ξυμμαχίαν εἶμεν πεντήκοντα ἔτη, ἐπὶ τοῖς ἴσοις καὶ ὁμοίοις δίκας διδόντας καττὰ πάτρια· ταὶ δὲ ἄλλαι πόλιες ταὶ ἐν Πελοποννάσῳ κοινανεόντων τᾶν
5 σπονδᾶν καὶ τᾶς ξυμμαχίας αὐτόνομοι καὶ αὐτοπόλιες τὰν αὐτῶν ἔχοντες, καττὰ πάτρια δίκας διδόντες τὰς ἴσας καὶ ὁμοίας. ὅσσοι δὲ ἔξω Πελοποννάσω Λακεδαιμονίοις 2

αἴ κα αὐτοῖς δοκῇ and the following αἰ δέ τι δοκῇ τοῖς ξυμμάχοις). Then follows αἰ δέ τι δοκῇ (subj. after the simple αἰ as in c. 79. 11 and 13) without ἄλλο (which only the inferior Mss. offer): "if the allies saw fit, they might send the treaty home" (οἴκαδ' ἀπιάλλην), i.e. refer it to the governing bodies of their respective cities.

78. *Soon after the oligarchical party at Argos induces the Argives to relinquish their previous alliances and make an alliance with Sparta.*

1. πρῶτον: pred. agreeing with λόγον. πρῶτον is in contradistinction to μετὰ δὲ τοῦτο κτέ. in 3. — 3. ἐπιμιξίας: cf. c. 35. 3. — 4. παρ' ἀλλήλους: const. with ἐπιμιξίας οὔσης, as with the verb ἐπιμίσγειν in i. 13. 19. — ἔπραξαν: aor. This expresses the result of πράσσοντες in c. 76. 15. — 6. σπονδὰς καὶ ξυμμαχίαν: see App. on c. 27. 2. The same reading must be adopted in c. 79. 2 and 80. 1.

79. *The terms of the treaty of alliance between the Lacedaemonians and the Argives.*

2. ἐπὶ τοῖς ἴσοις καὶ ὁμοίοις: cf. c. 27. 12. — 3. διδόντας: as if τοὺς Λακεδαιμονίους κτέ. preceded instead of the dat. Cf. i. 31. 9; 53. 1; 72. 3, ἔδοξεν αὐτοῖς παριτητέα ἐς τοὺς Λακεδαιμονίους εἶναι, τῶν μὲν ἐγκλημάτων πέρι μηδὲν ἀπολογησομένους κτέ. — 4. κοινανεόντων: Att. κοινωνούντων. An excellent emendation of Valckenaer for κοινὰν or κοινᾶν ἐόντων of the Mss. — 5. τᾶς ξυμμαχίας: the Mss. give τὰν ξυμμαχιᾶν (or more freq. ξυμμαχίαν). See App. on c. 27. 2. — αὐτοπόλιες: this does not occur elsewhere. Cf. αὐτοπολῖται, Xen. Hell. v. 2. 14. It cor-

ξύμμαχοί ἐντι, ἐν τοῖς αὐτοῖς ἐσσοῦνται τοῖσπερ καὶ τοὶ Λακεδαιμόνιοι· καὶ τοὶ τῶν Ἀργείων ξύμμαχοι ἐν τῷ αὐτῷ ἐσσοῦνται τῷπερ καὶ τοὶ Ἀργεῖοι, τὰν αὐτῶν ἔχοντες. αἰ δέ ποι σρατείας δέῃ κοινᾶς, βουλεύεσθαι Λακεδαιμονίως καὶ Ἀργείως ὅπα κα δικαιότατα κρίναντας τοῖς ξυμμάχοις. αἰ δέ τινι τᾶν πολίων ᾖ ἀμφίλογα, ἢ τᾶν ἐντὸς ἢ τᾶν ἐκτὸς Πελοποννάσω, αἴτε περὶ ὅρων αἴτε περὶ ἄλλου τινός, διακριθῆμεν. αἰ δέ τις τῶν ξυμμάχων πόλις πόλει ἐρίζοι, ἐς πόλιν ἐλθεῖν, ἄν τινα ἴσαν ἀμφοῖν ταῖς πολίεσσι δοκείοι. τὼς δὲ ἔτας κἀττὰ πάτρια δικάζεσθαι."

80 Αἱ μὲν σπονδαὶ καὶ ἡ ξυμμαχία αὕτη ἐγεγένητο,

responds to αὐτοτελεῖς καὶ αὐτόδικοι of c. 18. 7.

8. τοῖς αὐτοῖς: it is difficult to see why this is pl. Cf. c. 77. 18. Kirchhoff (Sitzungsber. d. Berl. Akad. 1883, p. 860) may be right in reading τῷ αὐτῷ and τῷπερ. — τοῖσπερ: (or τῷπερ) is used without the repetition of ἐν. Cf. c. 42. 2.

11. στρατείας: so Portus for στρατιᾶς of the Mss. — **12. ὅπα κα**: sc. κρίνωντι. Cf. c. 77. 16. — **κρίναντας τοῖς ξυμμάχοις**: adjudging (i.e. allotting) to the allies what part of the burden of the war each shall bear. The aor. partic. may refer to time preceding the execution of the plan expressed in βουλεύεσθαι. GMT. 24, n. 3; Madvig, Philol. Suppl. Vol. 2, p. 46. Perhaps, as Kr. suggests, Thuc. wrote κρίνωντι.

13. ἀμφίλογα: neut. pl. Cf. ἀντίπαλα, c. 8. 6; ἀδύνατα, iii. 88. 4; ἑτοῖμα, ii. 3. 15. — **15. διακριθῆμεν**: like all the preceding infs. this and the two which follow depend upon ἔδοξε: they shall come to an agreement about it. This accounts for the opts. ἐρίζοι

and δοκείοι. GMT. 77; H. 937. The sent. αἰ δέ τις τῶν ξυμμάχων πόλις πόλει ἐρίζοι does not introduce new subjs., but assumes that there has been a failure to come to an agreement: "but if one of the allied cities should get into a (real and open) quarrel with another," they shall have recourse to arbitration. — **16. ἴσαν**: aequam, fair, impartial. — **17. δοκείοι**: (Kirchhoff, δοκίοι) Dor. for the Att. δοκοίη. — **τὼς δὲ ἔτας**: (Poppo and St. for τοῖς δὲ ἔταις of the Mss.) τοὺς δὲ πολιτευομένους ἐν μιᾷ ἑκάστῃ πόλει δι' ἀλλήλων λύειν τὰ διάφορα, Schol. Acc. to Hesych. ἔται are ἑταῖροι, συνήθεις πολῖται, δημόται, and in an inscription from Olympia (Corp. Inscr. Gr. I. p. 30 f.) they are opp. to the τελεσταῖς, i.e. to τοῖς ἐν τέλει. The sense of the passage then is: "the citizens (i.e. private individuals as opp. to the cities) shall conduct their legal business according to the laws of their respective states." See App.

80. The Lacedaemonians and Argives acting together induce Perdiccas and the Chalcidian cities to join their

καὶ ὁπόσα ἀλλήλων πολέμῳ ἢ εἴ τι ἄλλο εἶχον, διελύσαντο. κοινῇ δὲ ἤδη τὰ πράγματα τιθέμενοι ἐψηφίσαντο κήρυκα καὶ πρεσβείαν παρ' Ἀθηναίων μὴ προσδέχεσθαι, ἢν μὴ ἐκ Πελοποννήσου ἐξίωσι τὰ τείχη ἐκλιπόντες, καὶ μὴ ξυμβαίνειν τῳ μηδὲ πολεμεῖν ἀλλ' ἢ ἅμα. καὶ τά τε ἄλλα θυμῷ ἔφερον καὶ ἐς τὰ ἐπὶ Θρᾴκης χωρία καὶ ὡς Περδίκκαν ἔπεμψαν ἀμφότεροι πρέσβεις καὶ ἀνέπεισαν Περδίκκαν ξυνομόσαι σφίσιν. οὐ μέντοι εὐθύς γε ἀπέστη τῶν Ἀθηναίων, ἀλλὰ διενοεῖτο, ὅτι καὶ τοὺς Ἀργείους ἑώρα· ἦν δὲ καὶ αὐτὸς τὸ ἀρχαῖον ἐξ Ἄργους. καὶ τοῖς Χαλκιδεῦσι τούς τε παλαιοὺς ὅρκους ἀνενεώσαντο καὶ ἄλλους ὤμοσαν. ἔπεμψαν δὲ καὶ παρὰ τοὺς Ἀθηναίους οἱ Ἀργεῖοι πρέσβεις, τὸ ἐξ Ἐπιδαύρου τεῖχος κελεύοντες ἐκλιπεῖν. οἱ δ' ὁρῶντες ὀλίγοι πρὸς πλείους ὄντες τοὺς ξυμφύλακας ἔπεμψαν Δημοσθένην τοὺς σφετέρους ἐξ-

alliance. The Athenians evacuate Epidaurus.

2. ἢ εἴ τι ἄλλο εἶχον: with the indefinite sense, *or whatever else they had* to find fault with in their relations with one another, and in accordance with this the expression διελύσαντο is chosen; *they came to an agreement* about it. From this we must suply ἀπέδοσαν with ὁπόσα ἀλλήλων πολέμῳ (sc. εἶχον). Cf. c. 17. 12. — 3. τιθέμενοι: διατιθέμενοι, διοικονομοῦντες, Schol. See on i. 25. 2. — 5. τὰ τείχη: *i.e.* the τείχισμα at the Heraeum near Epidaurus. See c. 75. 25; 77. 5. Perhaps Pylos also is meant (cf. c. 39. 6 and 14; 56. 11), as the pl. τείχη would naturally include all fortifications held by the Athenians in Peloponnesus.
7. θυμῷ ἔφερον: "they were very energetic." Cf. i. 31. 2, ὀργῇ φέροντες.
10. διενοεῖτο: sc. ἀποστῆναι. See on i. 1. 7. — 11. ἑώρα: sc. ἀφεστηκότας. See on i. 78. 10; 80. 2. — τὸ ἀρχαῖον

ἐξ Ἄργους: cf. iii. 99. 8, where his family is said to be Τημενίδαι. The oldest account of this relation is given by Hdt. viii. 137. ff. — 12. τοὺς παλαιοὺς ὅρκους: cf. c. 31. 26 as regards the Argives. The Chalcidians had doubtless had treaties of some kind with the Lacedaemonians ever since they left the Athenian alliance. See i. 58. 10.
14. τὸ ἐξ Ἐπιδαύρου τεῖχος: the proleptic use of ἐξ (see on i. 8. 9) is here admitted with ἐκλιπεῖν. Cf. i. 105. 19, τῶν δ' ἐκ τῆς πόλεως ὑπολοίπων.
— 15. ὀλίγοι ὄντες: corrected by Abresch for ὄντας of the Mss. This is opp. to πρὸς πλείους τοὺς ξυμφύλακας, *i.e.* the Argives, Eleans, and Mantineans, who far outnumbered the 1000 Athenians. Cf. c. 75. § 5 and 6. See App. — 16. Δημοσθένην: this form of the acc. seems to have the best authority. This Demosthenes is the well-known general. See iii. 91. 2;

ἄξοντα. ὁ δὲ ἀφικόμενος καὶ ἀγῶνά τινα πρόφασιν γυμνικὸν ἔξω τοῦ φρουρίου ποιήσας, ὡς ἐξῆλθε τὸ ἄλλο φρούριον, ἀπέκλῃσε τὰς πύλας. καὶ ὕστερον Ἐπιδαυρίοις 20 ἀνανεωσάμενοι τὰς σπονδὰς αὐτοὶ οἱ Ἀθηναῖοι ἀπέδοσαν 81 τὸ τείχισμα. μετὰ δὲ τὴν τῶν Ἀργείων ἀπόστασιν ἐκ τῆς 1 ξυμμαχίας καὶ οἱ Μαντινῆς, τὸ μὲν πρῶτον ἀντέχοντες, ἔπειτ᾽ οὐ δυνάμενοι ἄνευ τῶν Ἀργείων, ξυνέβησαν καὶ αὐτοὶ τοῖς Λακεδαιμονίοις καὶ τὴν ἀρχὴν ἀφεῖσαν τῶν 5 πόλεων. καὶ Λακεδαιμόνιοι καὶ Ἀργεῖοι, χίλιοι ἑκάτεροι, 2 ξυστρατεύσαντες, τά τ᾽ ἐν Σικυῶνι ἐς ὀλίγους μᾶλλον κατέστησαν αὐτοὶ οἱ Λακεδαιμόνιοι ἐλθόντες, καὶ μετ᾽ ἐκεῖνα ξυναμφότεροι ἤδη καὶ τὸν ἐν Ἄργει δῆμον κατέλυσαν, καὶ ὀλιγαρχία ἐπιτηδεία τοῖς Λακεδαιμονίοις

iv. 3. 8; 66. 14.—17. πρόφασιν: see on c. 53. 2. ὑποκρίνας (read ὑποκρινάμενος) ποιεῖν ἀγῶνά τινα γυμνικόν, Schol. Under this pretence he enticed the garrison out of the fortification, and prevented their return (ἀπέκλῃσε τὰς πύλας). Afterwards he surrendered the place to the Epidaurians.— 19. φρούριον: this word, which is found in the most and best Mss., must be used in the sense of φρουρά. *Cf.* c. 75. 25. St. cites (besides some doubtful passages of Aesch.) Xen. *An.* i. 4. 15, ὑμῖν χρήσεται καὶ εἰς φρούρια καὶ εἰς λοχαγίας. See App.— 20. ἀνανεωσάμενοι: see App.

81. *Mantinea joins the Lacedaemonian alliance. Oligarchies are established at Sicyon and Argos.*

1. ἀπόστασιν ἐκ τῆς ξυμμαχίας: *i.e.* ἀπὸ τῶν Ἀθηναίων.— 3. οὐ δυνάμενοι: sc. ἀντέχειν.— 4. τὴν ἀρχὴν ἀφεῖσαν τῶν πόλεων: some of these cities had been subject to them before they joined the Argive alliance (see c. 29. 3); and they had extended their power since that time. See c. 33. 3 and 10; 62. 1. They were obliged to give up their sovereignty in compliance with the provision of the treaty in c. 79. 3 ff., ταὶ δὲ πόλιες κοινανεόντων τᾶν σπονδᾶν καὶ τᾶς ξυμμαχίας αὐτόνομοι καὶ αὐτοπόλιες κτέ.

5. Λακεδαιμόνιοι καὶ Ἀργεῖοι, αὐτοὶ οἱ Λακεδαιμόνιοι, ξυναμφότεροι: the subj. changes from the whole to one of its parts and back again to the whole within the same period. *Cf.* c. 10. 47 ff.— 6. ἐς ὀλίγους: this is Thuc.'s regular expression for an oligarchy. *Cf.* viii. 53. 22; 89. 18, and see on ii. 37. 2; viii. 38. 11.— μᾶλλον: *i.e.* μᾶλλον ἢ πρότερον, intimating that the Sicyonian government was not thoroughly democratic before. — 8. κατέλυσαν: *cf.* c. 76. 6. Diod. xii. 80. 42 reports that this revolution was not accomplished without bloodshed: συλλαβόντες τοὺς δημαγωγεῖν εἰωθότας ἀπέκτειναν.— 9. ἐπιτήδεια τοῖς Λακεδαιμονίοις: *cf.* i. 19. 1, καὶ οἱ μὲν Λακεδαιμόνιοι οὐχ ὑποτελεῖς ἔχοντες φόρον

10 κατέστη. * καὶ πρὸς ἔαρ ἤδη ταῦτα ἦν τοῦ χειμῶνος λήγοντος, καὶ τέταρτον καὶ δέκατον ἔτος τῷ πολέμῳ ἐτελεύτα.

82 Τοῦ δ' ἐπιγιγνομένου θέρους Διῆς τε οἱ ἐν Ἄθῳ 1 ἀπέστησαν Ἀθηναίων πρὸς Χαλκιδέας, καὶ Λακεδαιμόνιοι τὰ ἐν Ἀχαΐᾳ οὐκ ἐπιτηδείως πρότερον ἔχοντα καθίσταντο. καὶ Ἀργείων ὁ δῆμος κατ' ὀλίγον ξυνιστάμενός τε 2
5 καὶ ἀναθαρσήσας ἐπέθεντο τοῖς ὀλίγοις, τηρήσαντες αὐτὰς τὰς γυμνοπαιδίας τῶν Λακεδαιμονίων. καὶ μάχης γενομένης ἐν τῇ πόλει ἐπεκράτησεν ὁ δῆμος, καὶ τοὺς

τοὺς ξυμμάχους ἡγοῦντο, κατ' ὀλιγαρχίαν δὲ σφίσιν αὐτοῖς μόνον ἐπιτηδείως ὅπως πολιτεύσουσι θεραπεύοντες.

82. But the next summer the democratic party comes again into power at Argos, and tries to secure itself by making an alliance with Athens and building long walls to the sea.

1. Διῆς: they were the inhabitants of the town of Dium (see iv. 109. 10), the same who had already (see c. 35. 1) engaged in hostilities toward Athens, and who now openly joined her enemies. Here, as in c. 35. 2, some inferior Mss. read Δικτιδῆς.—
3. τὰ ἐν Ἀχαΐᾳ οὐκ ἐπιτηδείως πρότερον ἔχοντα: cf. i. 19. 1 ff. At the beginning of the war only the Pelleneans were on the side of the Lacedaemonians. See ii. 9. 6. — καθίσταντο: sc. ἐπιτηδειότερον or ἐπὶ τὸ σφίσιν ὠφέλιμον. Cf. i. 76. 2.
4. ὁ δῆμος ἀναθαρσήσας ἐπέθεντο: δῆμος with adjs. in the sing. and the verb in the pl. occurs also in iii. 80. 1 f. G. 135, 3; II. 609. — κατ' ὀλίγον ξυνιστάμενός τε καὶ ἀναθαρσήσας: the oligarchy which was established in Argos πρὸς ἔαρ, say in March (see c. 81. 10), lasted until the time of the gymnopaediae, a period of about five

months, since this festival took place in Hecatombaeum (about July; see Schoemann, *Griech. Alt.* II. p. 460. Diod., xii. 80. 45, wrongly says that the oligarchy lasted eight months). During this period the secret meetings and deliberations (ξυνίστασθαι, as in ii. 88. 4; iii. 70. 24; viii. 65. 6) of the popular party were held, until sufficient confidence for a rising had been gained (ἀναθαρσήσας in the aor. denotes the conclusion of the deliberations expressed by the pres. ξυνιστάμενος). — κατ' ὀλίγον: *gradually*, in continuous progress toward completion. Cf. i. 61. 18; 69. 13. (Cl. now adopts this explanation by St.) Paus., ii. 20. 2, says that this fierce insurrection broke out because the leader of the χίλιοι λογάδες (cf. c. 67. 13; 72. 14) outraged the betrothed bride of a man of the common people, and this may have been the immediate occasion of the outbreak. — 6. τὰς γυμνοπαιδίας: 'this was a festival somewhat resembling the Lupercalia at Rome, in which boys and men danced naked, each arranged in distinct chori, the movements expressing warlike and gymnastic contests; while at the same time coarse and licentious

μὲν ἀπέκτεινε, τοὺς δὲ ἐξήλασεν. οἱ δὲ Λακεδαιμόνιοι, 3
ἕως μὲν αὐτοὺς μετεπέμποντο οἱ φίλοι, οὐκ ἦλθον ἐκ
πλείονος, ἀναβαλόμενοι δὲ τὰς γυμνοπαιδίας ἐβοήθουν.
καὶ ἐν Τεγέᾳ πυθόμενοι ὅτι νενίκηνται οἱ ὀλίγοι, προελθεῖν μὲν οὐκέτι ἠθέλησαν δεομένων τῶν διαπεφευγότων,
ἀναχωρήσαντες δὲ ἐπ' οἴκου τὰς γυμνοπαιδίας ἦγον.
καὶ ὕστερον ἐλθόντων πρέσβεων ἀπό τε τῶν ἐν τῇ πόλει 4
καὶ ἀγγέλων τῶν ἔξω Ἀργείων, παρόντων τε τῶν ξυμμάχων καὶ ῥηθέντων πολλῶν ἀφ'. ἑκατέρων ἔγνωσαν μὲν
ἀδικεῖν τοὺς ἐν τῇ πόλει καὶ ἔδοξεν αὐτοῖς στρατεύειν
ἐς Ἄργος, διατριβαὶ δὲ καὶ μελλήσεις ἐγίγνοντο. ὁ δὲ 5
δῆμος τῶν Ἀργείων ἐν τούτῳ, φοβούμενος τοὺς Λακεδαιμονίους καὶ τὴν τῶν Ἀθηναίων ξυμμαχίαν πάλιν προσαγόμενός τε καὶ νομίζων μέγιστον ἂν σφᾶς ὠφελήσειν,

language was interchanged, as in the Roman triumphs.' Arnold. The festival was mainly in honour of Apollo. See Schoemann, *Griech. Alt.* II. p. 460.

9. οὐκ ἦλθον ἐκ πλείονος: the sense of this passage evidently is: "while their friends were sending for them, they failed to come for a very long (or too long) time; but at last they postponed the festival and started on the march" (ἐβοήθουν impf.). The fact that they only went as far as Tegea before hearing of the revolution at Argos seems to show that they were in no great hurry. See App. — 11. προελθεῖν μέν, ἀναχωρήσαντες δέ: the opposition of these two parts of the sent. is very effective: "as to advancing, they had no idea of such a thing (οὐκ ἠθέλησαν); on the contrary, they went home and celebrated their festival." — 12. τῶν διαπεφευγότων: i.e. the members of the oligarchical party of Argos.

15. καὶ ἀγγέλλων: see App. — 16.

ἀφ' ἑκατέρων: see on iii. 36. 24. This prep. is freq. used with λέγεσθαι and similar words. In these speeches each party doubtless tried to justify itself and make its opponents seem completely in the wrong.

19. φοβούμενος, προσαγόμενος, νομίζων: these parties. all interpret τειχίζει μακρὰ τείχη. The chief reason is expressed in φοβούμενος τοὺς Λακεδαιμονίους, which is further enlarged by πάλιν προσαγόμενος τὴν τῶν Ἀθηναίων ξυμμαχίαν and νομίζων μέγιστον ἂν σφᾶς ὠφελήσειν, these two expressions being closely connected by τε and καί. "The Argives undertook the building of long walls because they were afraid of the Lacedaemonians and (therefore) embraced the alliance of Athens and thought they should be greatly the gainers." — 20. προσαγόμενος: οἰκειούμενος, Schol. This act was a declaration in favour of the Athenian policy (and political ideas) and therefore in itself a renewal of the alliance

τειχίζει μακρὰ τείχη ἐς θάλασσαν, ὅπως, ἢν τῆς γῆς εἴργωνται, ἡ κατὰ θάλασσαν σφᾶς μετὰ τῶν Ἀθηναίων ἐπαγωγὴ τῶν ἐπιτηδείων ὠφελῇ. ξυνῄδεσαν δὲ τὸν τει- 6
25 χισμὸν καὶ τῶν ἐν Πελοποννήσῳ τινὲς πόλεων. καὶ οἱ μὲν Ἀργεῖοι πανδημεί, καὶ αὐτοὶ καὶ γυναῖκες καὶ οἰκέται, ἐτείχιζον· καὶ ἐκ τῶν Ἀθηνῶν αὐτοῖς ἦλθον τέκτονες καὶ λιθουργοί. καὶ τὸ θέρος ἐτελεύτα.*

83 Τοῦ δ' ἐπιγιγνομένου χειμῶνος Λακεδαιμόνιοι ὡς 1 ᾔσθοντο τειχιζόντων, ἐστράτευσαν ἐς τὸ Ἄργος αὐτοί τε καὶ οἱ ξύμμαχοι πλὴν Κορινθίων· ὑπῆρχε δέ τι αὐτοῖς καὶ ἐκ τοῦ Ἄργους αὐτόθεν πρασσόμενον. ἦγε δὲ τὴν
5 στρατιὰν Ἆγις ὁ Ἀρχιδάμου, Λακεδαιμονίων βασιλεύς.

with Athens, which remained in force from this time. — 21. **ὠφελήσειν**: the subj. is not τὴν τῶν Ἀθηναίων ξυμμαχίαν, but is, as Herbst (*Hamburg Progr.* 1867, p. 32 f.) rightly observes, to be supplied from the following τειχίζει μακρὰ τείχη. This is further explained in ὅπως ... ὠφελῇ: for ἡ κατὰ θάλασσαν ἐπαγωγὴ τῶν ἐπιτηδείων is the advantage derived from the long walls. μετὰ τῶν Ἀθηναίων is a secondary and necessary consequence. ἂν ὠφελήσειν is equiv. to ὅτι ὠφελήσει ἄν with the suppressed prot. ἢν τοῦτο γένηται. GMT. 37, 2; 53; H. 845; 861; 946. Cf. ii. 80. 40; vi. 66. 4; viii. 25. 28; and 71. 12 with App. See App.
24. **ξυνῄδεσαν τὸν τειχισμόν**: if this reading is correct, the knowing about or being privy to this project shows an inclination toward the philo-Athenian policy of Argos which was exhibited by the building of the long walls. See App. — 25. **τινές**: interposed between the gens., as in i. 45. 8, ἐς τῶν ἐκείνων τι χωρίων. — 28. **λιθουργοί**: so masons had been brought

from Athens to assist in the circumvallation of Nisaea. See iv. 69. 6.

83. *The Lacedaemonians attack the Argives, take and tear down the long walls, and take Hysiae. The Argives make an incursion into the territory of Phlius. The Athenians blockade the coast of Macedonia.*

2. **ὡς ᾔσθοντο τειχιζόντων**: the gen. with αἰσθάνεσθαι occurs also in i. 57. 14; 72. 3; ii. 81. 31; iv. 108. 31, the partic. in the gen. here only, but freq. in the acc. Cf. c. 37. 15; i. 47. 1. The Lacedaemonians must have heard at once of the doings at Argos; so that ὡς ᾔσθοντο must not be taken too strictly. — 3. **ὑπῆρχέ τι αὐτοῖς πρασσόμενον**: the use of πράσσειν in καί τι αὐτῷ ἐπράσσετο ἐς τὰς πόλεις (iv. 121. 12) is here combined with that of ὑπάρχειν in ἀσφάλειάν τινα ὑπάρχουσάν οἱ in vi. 59. 7, "there was also a party acting from Argos itself in their interest." — 4. **ἐκ τοῦ Ἄργους αὐτόθεν**: an emphatic combination. Cf. ii. 25. 18, αὐτόθεν ἐκ τῆς περιοικίδος Ἠλείων. See Herbst, *gegen Cobet*, p. 58 ff.

καὶ τὰ μὲν ἐκ τῆς πόλεως δοκοῦντα προϋπάρχειν οὐ 2
προυχώρησεν ἔτι· τὰ δὲ οἰκοδομούμενα τείχη ἑλόντες
καὶ καταβαλόντες καὶ Ὑσιὰς χωρίον τῆς Ἀργείας λαβόντες καὶ τοὺς ἐλευθέρους ἅπαντας οὓς ἔλαβον ἀποκτεί-
ναντες ἀνεχώρησαν καὶ διελύθησαν κατὰ πόλεις. ἐστρά- 3
τευσαν δὲ μετὰ τοῦτο καὶ Ἀργεῖοι ἐς τὴν Φλιασίαν, καὶ
δηώσαντες ἀπῆλθον, ὅτι σφῶν τοὺς φυγάδας ὑπεδέχον-
το· οἱ γὰρ πολλοὶ αὐτῶν ἐνταῦθα κατῴκηντο. κατέκλη- 4
σαν δὲ τοῦ αὐτοῦ χειμῶνος καὶ Μακεδόνας Ἀθηναῖοι,
Περδίκκᾳ ἐπικαλοῦντες τήν τε πρὸς Ἀργείους καὶ Λακεδαιμονίους γενομένην ξυνωμοσίαν καὶ ὅτι παρασκευα-
σαμένων αὐτῶν στρατιὰν ἄγειν ἐπὶ Χαλκιδέας τοὺς ἐπὶ
Θρᾴκης καὶ Ἀμφίπολιν Νικίου τοῦ Νικηράτου στρατη-
γοῦντος ἔψευστο τὴν ξυμμαχίαν καὶ ἡ στρατεία μάλιστα
διελύθη ἐκείνου ἀπάραντος· πολέμιος οὖν ἦν. καὶ ὁ χειμὼν ἐτελεύτα οὗτος, καὶ πέμπτον καὶ δέκατον ἔτος τῷ
πολέμῳ ἐτελεύτα.

84   Τοῦ δ' ἐπιγιγνομένου θέρους * Ἀλκιβιάδης τε πλεύ- 1

6. **οὐ προυχώρησεν ἔτι**: it made no further progress, it failed them. — 7. **τὰ οἰκοδομούμενα τείχη**: the walls which were building, not τὰ κατεσκευασμένα, as Diod. (xii. 81. 76) wrongly says. — 8. **Ὑσίας**: Hysiae was near the Arcadian frontier on the road from Argos to Tegea, where its ruins may still be seen. See Curtius, *Pelopon.* II. p. 367.

12. **ὅτι σφῶν τοὺς φυγάδας ὑπεδέχοντο**: const. with ἐστράτευσαν and δηώσαντες, not with ἀπῆλθον. σφῶν stands before τοὺς φυγάδας with almost the effect of the ethical dat. See on ἐπεὶ σφῶν οἱ ξύμμαχοι ἐπόνουν, i. 30. 14.

14. **Μακεδόνας, Περδίκκᾳ**: see App. — 15. **τὴν ξυνωμοσίαν**: cf. c. 80. 9. — 19. **ἔψευστο**: *violated*, "did not preserve." Cf. iii. 66. 17, τὴν μὴ κτείνειν ψευσθεῖσαν ὑπόσχεσιν. — ἡ **στρατεία**: see App. — **μάλιστα**: implies that there were also other reasons. — 20. **διελύθη**: as in iii. 114. 21, διέλυσαν τὸν πόλεμον. — **ἀπάραντος**: this reading of the Mss. is certainly wrong. For emendations, see App.

84. *Alcibiades places three hundred Argives of the oligarchical party under custody upon the neighbouring islands. The Athenians send an expedition against the island of Melos, but try negotiations before proceeding to actual hostilities.*

1. **Ἀλκιβιάδης τε, καὶ ἐπὶ Μῆλον**: the doings of Alcibiades at Argos and the expedition against Melos are thus (by τε and καί) brought together as the two most important events of

σας ἐς Ἄργος ναυσὶν εἴκοσιν Ἀργείων τοὺς δοκοῦντας ἔτι ὑπόπτους εἶναι καὶ τὰ Λακεδαιμονίων φρονεῖν ἔλαβε, τριακοσίους ἄνδρας, καὶ κατέθεντο αὐτοὺς Ἀθηναῖοι ἐς τὰς ἐγγὺς νήσους ὧν ἦρχον· καὶ ἐπὶ Μῆλον τὴν νῆσον Ἀθηναῖοι ἐστράτευσαν ναυσὶν ἑαυτῶν μὲν τριάκοντα, Χίαις δὲ ἕξ, Λεσβίαιν δὲ δυοῖν, καὶ ὁπλίταις ἑαυτῶν μὲν διακοσίοις καὶ χιλίοις καὶ τοξόταις τριακοσίοις καὶ ἱπποτοξόταις εἴκοσι, τῶν δὲ ξυμμάχων καὶ νησιωτῶν ὁπλίταις μάλιστα πεντακοσίοις καὶ χιλίοις. οἱ δὲ Μήλιοι 2 Λακεδαιμονίων μέν εἰσιν ἄποικοι, τῶν δ' Ἀθηναίων οὐκ ἤθελον ὑπακούειν ὥσπερ οἱ ἄλλοι νησιῶται, ἀλλὰ τὸ μὲν πρῶτον οὐδετέρων ὄντες ἡσύχαζον, ἔπειτα ὡς αὐτοὺς ἠνάγκαζον οἱ Ἀθηναῖοι δῃοῦντες τὴν γῆν, ἐς πόλεμον

the summer. — 3. ἔτι: still, after τοὺς μὲν ἀπέκτειναν, τοὺς δὲ ἐξήλασαν, as mentioned in c. 82. 7. — τὰ Λακεδαιμονίων φρονεῖν: cf. iii. 68. 18: vi. 51. 7; viii. 31. 7. — 4. κατέθεντο: deposited. The mid. is always used in the sense of "place under custody." See on iii. 72. 2. — 5. ἐς τὰς ἐγγὺς νήσους: so they had once before confined the suspected Corcyreans on Aegina. See iii. 72. 1 ff. — ἐπὶ Μῆλον: a previous attempt under Nicias to subjugate the island had been unsuccessful. See iii. 91. § 1 f. and 94. 2. Yet from Ol. 88, 3 (426 B.C.) on, the Melians are found, and the amount of their tribute is specified, on the lists of tributaries of Athens. See U. Köhler, zur Geschichte des delisch-attischen Bundes in Abhh. d. Berl. Akad. 1869, p. 146. — 7. Λεσβίαιν: these were ships of the Methymnaeans, for the rest of Lesbos was now held by Athenian Cleruchs to whom the Lesbians paid rent in lieu of tribute. See iii. 50. 5 ff.; vi. 85. 8. Wecklein, cur. epigr. p. 16, shows from inscriptions that this reading is preferable to Λεσβίαις of most Mss. — 9. ξυμμάχων καὶ νησιωτῶν: cf. vi. 85. 6 ff., καὶ γὰρ τοῖς ἐκεῖ ξυμμάχοις ὡς ἕκαστοι χρήσιμοι ἐξηγούμεθα, Χίους μὲν καὶ Μηθυμναίους νεῶν παροκωχῇ αὐτονόμους, τοὺς δὲ πολλοὺς χρημάτων βιαιότερον φορᾷ, ἄλλους δὲ καὶ πάνυ ἐλευθέρως ξυμμαχοῦντας, καίπερ νησιώτας ὄντας καὶ εὐλήπτους, διότι ἐν χωρίοις ἐπικαίροις εἰσὶ περὶ τὴν Πελοπόννησον. From this it appears, as Herbst (Philol. 42, p. 724) observes, that the "islanders" here mentioned are different from the ξύμμαχοι. Cf. vii. 57. 32 ff., where Cephallenians and Zacynthians are mentioned as νησιῶται and αὐτόνομοι.

11. Λακεδαιμονίων ἄποικοι: see Hdt. viii. 48. 3. — 13. οὐδετέρων ὄντες: γράφεται μεθ' ἑτέρων, Schol. This means οὐδὲ μεθ' ἑτέρων. Thuc. uses, however, both forms. Cf. ξυμμάχους μηδετέρων, c. 94. 2; μηδετέρων ὄντας, i. 35. 2; τοὺς μηδὲ μεθ' ἑτέρων, ii. 67. 34; ἔστε μηδὲ μεθ' ἑτέρων, ii. 72. 11. — 14. ἐς πόλεμον φανερὸν κατέστησαν: so also in c. 25. 15.

15 φανερὸν κατέστησαν. στρατοπεδευσάμενοι οὖν ἐς τὴν 3
γῆν αὐτῶν τῇ παρασκευῇ ταύτῃ οἱ στρατηγοὶ Κλεομήδης
τε ὁ Λυκομήδους καὶ Τισίας ὁ Τισιμάχου, πρὶν ἀδικεῖν
τι τῆς γῆς, λόγους πρῶτον ποιησομένους ἔπεμψαν πρέσβεις. οὓς οἱ Μήλιοι πρὸς μὲν τὸ πλῆθος οὐκ ἤγαγον,
20 ἐν δὲ ταῖς ἀρχαῖς καὶ τοῖς ὀλίγοις λέγειν ἐκέλευον περὶ
ὧν ἥκουσιν. οἱ δὲ τῶν Ἀθηναίων πρέσβεις ἔλεγον τοιάδε·
85 "Ἐπειδὴ οὐ πρὸς τὸ πλῆθος οἱ λόγοι γίγνονται, 1
ὅπως δὴ μὴ ξυνεχεῖ ῥήσει οἱ πολλοὶ ἐπαγωγὰ καὶ ἀνέλεγκτα ἐς ἅπαξ ἀκούσαντες ἡμῶν ἀπατηθῶσι (γιγνώσκο-
μεν γὰρ ὅτι τοῦτο φρονεῖ ὑμῶν ἡ ἐς τοὺς ὀλίγους ἀγωγή),
5 ὑμεῖς οἱ καθήμενοι ἔτι ἀσφαλέστερον ποιήσατε· καθ'
ἕκαστον γὰρ καὶ μηδ' ὑμεῖς ἑνὶ λόγῳ, ἀλλά, πρὸς τὸ μὴ
δοκοῦν ἐπιτηδείως λέγεσθαι εὐθὺς ὑπολαμβάνοντες κρίνετε. καὶ πρῶτον εἰ ἀρέσκει ὡς λέγομεν, εἴπατε."

15. στρατοπεδευσάμενοι ἐς τὴν γῆν: is elliptical for ἐσβαλόντες ἐς τὴν γῆν καὶ στρατοπεδευσάμενοι. — 17. Τισίας ὁ Τισιμάχου: see App. — 20. τοῖς ὀλίγοις: the ὀλίγοι appear here and in c. 85. 4 as the chief governing body, a small senate or assembly, to which the holders of important offices (αἱ ἀρχαί, cf. c. 28. 2; 47. 52 and 55; i. 90. 27) belong.

NEGOTIATIONS BETWEEN THE ENVOYS OF THE ATHENIANS AND THE COUNCIL OF THE MELIANS. Chaps. 85–113.

(On the course of the dialogue, see App. fin.)

85. 2. ὅπως δή: evidently in order that. Cf. vii. 18. 5. — ῥήσει: cf. c. 111. 15, ῥήματος. These words occur in Thuc. only in these two places. — ἀνέλεγκτα: untested, "against which no argument is advanced." In vi. 53. 14,

ἀνέλεγκτον, used of a person, means "not subjected to trial." — 4. φρονεῖ: βούλεται, Schol. δύνασθαι is elsewhere (cf. i. 141. 5; vi. 36. 9) used in this sense of mean, have for its object. — ὑμῶν: subj. gen. with ἀγωγή. St., followed by Cl., writes ἡμῶν as obj. gen. — 5. οἱ καθήμενοι: who are sitting there to listen to us. This has a slight shade of mockery. Cf. iii. 38. 32, σοφιστῶν θεαταῖς ἐοικότες καθημένοις μᾶλλον ἢ περὶ πόλεως βουλευομένοις, and vi. 13. 2. — ἔτι ἀσφαλέστερον ποιήσατε: act in a still safer way. ἀσφαλέστερον is adv. — 6. ἑνὶ λόγῳ: the only correct reading for ἐν ὀλίγῳ of most Mss. The meaning is the same as that of ξυνεχεῖ ῥήσει. "As you feared that the πολλοί would be misled by a ξυνεχὴς ῥῆσις, do not you either (μηδ' ὑμεῖς) form your judgment from one speech." — 7. ὑπολαμβάνοντες: cf. c. 49. 17. — κρίνετε: "form (and deliver) your judicial

86   Οἱ δὲ τῶν Μηλίων ξύνεδροι ἀπεκρίναντο· "ἡ μὲν 1
ἐπιείκεια τοῦ διδάσκειν καθ' ἡσυχίαν ἀλλήλους οὐ ψέγεται, τὰ δὲ τοῦ πολέμου παρόντα ἤδη καὶ οὐ μέλλοντα διαφέροντα αὐτοῦ φαίνεται. ὁρῶμεν γὰρ αὐτούς τε
5 κριτὰς ἥκοντας ὑμᾶς τῶν λεχθησομένων, καὶ τὴν τελευ-
τὴν ἐξ αὐτοῦ κατὰ τὸ εἰκὸς περιγενομένοις μὲν τῷ δικαίῳ
καὶ δι' αὐτὸ μὴ ἐνδοῦσι πόλεμον ἡμῖν φέρουσαν, πει-
σθεῖσι δὲ δουλείαν."
87   ΑΘ. Εἰ μὲν τοίνυν ὑπονοίας τῶν μελλόντων λο- 1
γιούμενοι ἢ ἄλλο τι ξυνήκετε ἢ ἐκ τῶν παρόντων καὶ ὧν
ὁρᾶτε περὶ σωτηρίας βουλεύσοντες τῇ πόλει, παυοίμεθ'
ἄν· εἰ δ' ἐπὶ τοῦτο, λέγοιμεν ἄν.
88   ΜΗΛ. Εἰκὸς μὲν καὶ ξυγγνώμη ἐν τῷ τοιῷδε καθ- 1
εστῶτας ἐπὶ πολλὰ καὶ λέγοντας καὶ δοκοῦντας τρέ-

decision." — 8. ὡς λέγομεν: as we propose.
86. 2. ἐπιείκεια: esp. consideration on the part of the powerful for subjects or inferiors, as opp. to ὕβρις; *equity* with a touch of clemency. See on iii. 40. 7. — 4. αὐτοῦ: i.e. τοῦ διδάσκειν καθ' ἡσυχίαν ἀλλήλους. — φαίνεται: see App. — 6. ἐξ αὐτοῦ: this refers again to τοῦ διδάσκειν καθ' ἡσυχίαν ἀλλήλους. "If this is agreed to, then the result brings to us," etc. — περιγενομένοις: "if we prove ourselves to be in the right." — τῷ δικαίῳ: "by the justice of our cause."
87. 1. τοίνυν: forms a vigorous and almost impatient beginning: *well, then, if you, etc.* τοίνυν occurs in Thuc. only in direct address. Cf. c. 89. 1; 105. 1; iii. 45. 14; viii. 53. 20. — ὑπονοίας λογιούμενοι: used somewhat ironically: *to consider hidden thoughts*, and hence *to argue from suspicious fancies about the future*. — 2. ἄλλο τι ἤ: cf. iii. 85. 13, ὅπως ἀπόγνοια ᾖ τοῦ ἄλλο τι ἢ κρατεῖν τῆς γῆς, where the Schol. supplies πρᾶξαι after ἄλλο τι. A similar expression is τί ἄλλο ἤ in iii. 39. 10 and 58. 24. — ὧν ὁρᾶτε: this is still dependent upon ἐκ. Cf. c. 42. 2. Here, however, the rel. is attracted into the case of an omitted indef. antec. — 4. ἐπὶ τοῦτο: sc. ξυνήκετε.
88. 1. εἰκὸς καὶ ξυγγνώμη: like δίκαια καὶ πρέποντα ἅμα in i. 144. 16, this alludes to both the objective and the subjective aspect of the matter, to its intrinsic naturalness and propriety as well as to the judgment of others respecting it. — ξυγγνώμη: (sc. ἐστι) occurs with inf. in iv. 61. 17, with εἰ in i. 32. 24. — καθεστῶτας: the expression is a general one: "men in such a position." — 2. ἐπὶ πολλὰ τρέπεσθαι: cf. i. 20. 21, ἐπὶ τὰ ἑτοῖμα τρέπονται, and iv. 104. 6, ἐφ' ἁρπαγὴν τραπέσθαι. — καὶ λέγοντας καὶ δοκοῦντας: "in words as well as thoughts." δοκοῦντας is a less invidious expression than ὑπονοίας, which the Athenians

πεσθαι· ἡ μέντοι ξύνοδος καὶ περὶ σωτηρίας ἥδε πάρεστι καὶ ὁ λόγος ᾧ προκαλεῖσθε τρόπῳ, εἰ δοκεῖ, γιγνέσθω.

89 ΑΘ. Ἡμεῖς τοίνυν οὔτε αὐτοὶ μετ' ὀνομάτων κα- 1
λῶν, ὡς ἢ δικαίως τὸν Μῆδον καταλύσαντες ἄρχομεν ἢ
ἀδικούμενοι νῦν ἐπεξερχόμεθα, λόγων μῆκος ἄπιστον
παρέξομεν, οὔθ' ὑμᾶς ἀξιοῦμεν ἢ ὅτι Λακεδαιμονίων
5 ἄποικοι ὄντες οὐ ξυνεστρατεύσατε ἢ ὡς ἡμᾶς οὐδὲν ἠδικήκατε λέγοντας οἴεσθαι πείσειν, τὰ δυνατὰ δ' ἐξ ὧν ἑκάτεροι ἀληθῶς φρονοῦμεν διαπράσσεσθαι, ἐπισταμένους
πρὸς εἰδότας ὅτι δίκαια μὲν ἐν τῷ ἀνθρωπείῳ λόγῳ ἀπὸ

used in c. 87. 1.— 3. μέντοι: forms the transition from their excuse to the question in hand: "but we admit that."— καὶ περὶ σωτηρίας: these words admit the right of the Athenians to remind them of their position, and the following words καὶ ὁ λόγος ... γιγνέσθω express their reluctant assent to the proposal of the Athenians. — 4. ᾧ προκαλεῖσθε τρόπῳ: i.e. τούτῳ τῷ τρόπῳ ᾧ τὸν λόγον γίγνεσθαι προκαλεῖσθε.

89. 1. τοίνυν: here again this particle urges the point at issue: "very well; but let us both give up fine words."— 2. δικαίως: const. with ἄρχομεν.— 3. ἀδικούμενοι, οὐδὲν ἠδικήκατε: these words express the meaning of the ὀνόματα καλά which are to be given up.— ἐπεξερχόμεθα: "press our just right," "insist upon punishment," as in vi. 38. 10. — λόγων μῆκος: equiv. to πολλοὺς καὶ μακροὺς λόγους, and with this is joined ἄπιστον, "not carrying conviction." — 4. οὔθ' ὑμᾶς ἀξιοῦμεν κτέ.: const. οὐκ ἀξιοῦμεν ὑμᾶς οἴεσθαι πείσειν λέγοντας, upon which ὅτι ... οὐ ξυνεστρατεύσατε and ὡς ... ἠδικήκατε depend. — 5. οὐ ξυνεστρατεύσατε: sc. ἡμῖν. "That you did not join with us in the war because you as colonists of the Lacedaemonians were under no obligation to do so." — 6. τὰ δυνατὰ δὲ ... διαπράσσεσθαι: this also depends upon ἀξιοῦμεν, the meaning of which is somewhat modified: "we think it right (for both of us) to aim at accomplishing what is possible according to the real opinion (i.e. without any misleading fine phrases) of both of us." The subj. of διαπράσσεσθαι is no longer ὑμᾶς, but ἑκατέρους, the expression of which is rendered needless by the presence of ἑκάτεροι. — 7. ἐπισταμένους πρὸς εἰδότας: "since we both equally know," ἐπισταμένων καὶ ὑμῶν καὶ ἡμῶν, Schol. — 8. τῷ ἀνθρωπείῳ λόγῳ: the Schol. explains this by ἀνθρώπινος λογισμός. This is not philosophical speculation, but the reasoning of practical life, in which, acc. to the thoroughly realistic point of view here adopted, justice is regarded (κρίνεται) only when the pressure of necessity is the same on both parties. If that is not the case, the only thing to be considered is what is possible, and this the stronger party accomplishes, while the weaker party must make the best of it. — 9.

τῆς ἴσης ἀνάγκης κρίνεται, δυνατὰ δὲ οἱ προύχοντες
10 πράσσουσι καὶ οἱ ἀσθενεῖς ξυγχωροῦσιν.
90 ΜΗΛ. Ἦι μὲν δὴ νομίζομέν γε, χρήσιμον (ἀνάγ- 1
κη γάρ, ἐπειδὴ ὑμεῖς οὕτω παρὰ τὸ δίκαιον τὸ ξυμφέρον λέγειν ὑπέθεσθε) μὴ καταλύειν ὑμᾶς τὸ κοινὸν ἀγαθόν, ἀλλὰ τῷ ἀεὶ ἐν κινδύνῳ γιγνομένῳ εἶναι τὰ εἰκότα
5 δίκαια, καί τι καὶ ἐντὸς τοῦ ἀκριβοῦς πείσαντά τινα ὠφε-
ληθῆναι· καὶ πρὸς ὑμῶν οὐχ ἧσσον τοῦτο, ὅσῳ καὶ ἐπὶ

δυνατά: stands first for emphasis. It is the obj. of πράσσουσι and also of ξυγχωροῦσιν in accordance with the free use of neut. adjs. and prons., as in c. 41. 11 and 20; viii. 45. 21. Cobet, *V. L.* p. 271 and 454, proposes (after Dobree) προστάσσουσι for πράσσουσι. 90. 1. ᾗ μὲν δὴ νομίζομέν γε: these words introduce in an almost timid way an attempt to aid the cause of the weaker party by saving the δίκαιον in the form of the εἰκός. γε after νομίζομεν has its full force, *as we think at any rate*. See App. — 2. ἀνάγκη γάρ: *sc.* τὸ ξυμφέρον λέγειν. — οὕτω ... λέγειν: is the obj. of ὑπέθεσθε: "to talk so (as you have just been doing) not about justice, but about what is advantageous." — 3. ὑπέθεσθε: *i.e.* ὑπόθεσιν ἐποιήσασθε, "you have made it the foundation (or the starting-point) of the discussion." This use occurs in Thuc. only here, but freq. in Plat. (*e.g. Charm.* 171 d, ὃ ἐξ ἀρχῆς ὑπετιθέμεθα; *Rep.* iv. 437 a) and later writers. A similar use with added dat. is found in Hdt. i. 156. 2, ταῦτά οἱ ὑπετίθετο; iv. 135. 12; v. 98. 10; vii. 237. 10. — τὸ κοινὸν ἀγαθόν: what is meant is τὸ δίκαιον as the foundation of human society (see on c. 104. 4), which has, however, been excluded from the discussion. — ἀλλὰ τῷ κτέ.: "yet it is expedient (χρήσιμον embraces

τῷ ἀεὶ ... δίκαια as well as the other infs.) that to every one in peril what is reasonable be accounted right"; *i.e.* even if we must not call it a right (δίκαιον), still it should have the effect of a right. St. strikes out δίκαια in 5, but by so doing he loses the point of the subtle and artificial argumentation of the Melians by which, as they dare not openly oppose the Athenians, they try to substitute εἰκότα for δίκαια. (καί, which some Mss. insert before δίκαια, is inappropriate.) — 5. ἐντὸς τοῦ ἀκριβοῦς πείσαντα: the aor. for πείσοντα of most Mss. seems necessary; for it must refer to time antecedent to ὠφεληθῆναι, "even if one has not entirely proved his point, even if one has not attained to the ἀκριβές (ἐντός, like Lat. citra and sometimes intra, denotes that a missile has fallen short of the mark), still it is expedient (χρήσιμον) that one derive some advantage." See App. — 6. πρὸς ὑμῶν: *in your interest*. *Cf.* ii. 86. 19; iii. 38. 3. The reason for this is very cautiously expressed. Instead of saying: your contempt of justice will sometime cost you dear; for if those whom you now oppress ever come into power, they will take such revenge upon you that your fate will be a warning example to other ruling states, the Melians express

μεγίστῃ τιμωρίᾳ σφαλέντες ἂν τοῖς ἄλλοις παράδειγμα
γένοισθε.

91   ΑΘ. Ἡμεῖς δὲ τῆς ἡμετέρας ἀρχῆς, ἢν καὶ παυ- 1
θῇ, οὐκ ἀθυμοῦμεν τὴν τελευτήν· οὐ γὰρ οἱ ἄρχοντες
ἄλλων, ὥσπερ καὶ Λακεδαιμόνιοι, οὗτοι δεινοὶ τοῖς νι-
κηθεῖσιν (ἔστι δὲ οὐ πρὸς Λακεδαιμονίους ἡμῖν ὁ ἀγών),
5 ἀλλ' ἢν οἱ ὑπήκοοί που τῶν ἀρξάντων αὐτοὶ ἐπιθέμενοι
κρατήσωσι· καὶ περὶ μὲν τούτου ἡμῖν ἀφείσθω κινδυ- 2
νεύεσθαι· ὡς δὲ ἐπ' ὠφελίᾳ τε πάρεσμεν τῆς ἡμετέρας
ἀρχῆς καὶ ἐπὶ σωτηρίᾳ νῦν τοὺς λόγους ἐροῦμεν τῆς ὑμετέρας πόλεως, ταῦτα δηλώσομεν, βουλόμενοι ἀπόνως μὲν
10 ὑμῶν ἄρξαι, χρησίμως δ' ὑμᾶς ἀμφοτέροις σωθῆναι.

92   ΜΗΛ. Καὶ πῶς χρήσιμον ἂν ξυμβαίη ἡμῖν δου- 1
λεῦσαι, ὥσπερ καὶ ὑμῖν ἄρξαι;

the same idea in the intentionally obscure form, *inasmuch as you, if you should ever fall, would, by the heaviest vengeance* (which you will then incur), *be a* (warning) *example to others.* — ἐπὶ μεγίστῃ τιμωρίᾳ: the prep. prop. denotes the accompanying circumstances or conditions. *Cf.* ἐπὶ τοῖς δεινοῖς εὐέλπιδες, i. 70. 10; 143. 8; iii. 67. 33; iv. 22. 13.
91. 1. παυθῇ: καταλυθῇ, Schol. —
2. οὐκ ἀθυμοῦμεν τὴν τελευτήν: *we do not look forward to the end with dismay.* The adv. acc. is used with ἀθυμεῖν as in c. 40. 13 with ἀπορεῖν. Elsewhere we find the dat. (*cf.* vii. 60. 27) or πρός (*cf.* ii. 88. 11). — 3. ὥσπερ καί: *cf.* c. 44. 9; i. 74. 25; ii. 55. 7. — οὗτοι: on the emphatic repetition of a preceding word by οὗτος, see on iv. 44. 15. — 4. ἔστι δὲ κτέ.: "with the Lacedaemonians, however, we are not contending." This parenthetical remark, introduced by the adversative δέ, is directed against the implied meaning of the last part of c. 90. —
5. ἀλλ' ἢν ... κρατήσωσι: *sc.* οὗτοι δεινοί εἰσι. — αὐτοὶ ἐπιθέμενοι: the unexpected or surprising nature of such an attack is indicated by αὐτοί. Those very ones who had been oppressed now assume the offensive themselves.
6. ἀφείσθω: "it may be left to us"; imv. pf. pass. *Cf.* εἰρήσθω, Xen. *Mem.* iv. 2. 19; Isocr. iv. 14. — κινδυνεύεσθαι: "to support this peril," impers. pass. *Cf.* i. 73. 15, καὶ γὰρ ὅτε ἐδρῶμεν, ἐπ' ὠφελίᾳ ἐκινδυνεύετο. — 8. τοὺς λόγους: *i.e.* the proposals or conditions to be offered. — 9. ἀπόνως: *without trouble.* They hoped to induce the Melians to come to terms without resorting to force. — 10. ἄρξαι: aor., *to acquire dominion.* — χρησίμως: followed by the dat. ἀμφοτέροις. This expresses the result of σωθῆναι; "so that it will be advantageous to both of us."

92. 1. χρήσιμον ἂν ξυμβαίη: like γίγνεσθαι, ξυμβαίνειν is sometimes

93 ΑΘ. Ὅτι ὑμῖν μὲν πρὸ τοῦ τὰ δεινότατα παθεῖν ὑπακοῦσαι ἂν γένοιτο, ἡμεῖς δὲ μὴ διαφθείραντες ὑμᾶς κερδαίνοιμεν ἄν.

94 ΜΗΛ. Ὥστε δὲ ἡσυχίαν ἄγοντας ἡμᾶς φίλους μὲν εἶναι ἀντὶ πολεμίων, ξυμμάχους δὲ μηδετέρων, οὐκ ἂν δέξαισθε;

95 ΑΘ. Οὐ γὰρ τοσοῦτον ἡμᾶς βλάπτει ἡ ἔχθρα ὑμῶν ὅσον ἡ φιλία μὲν ἀσθενείας, τὸ δὲ μῖσος δυνάμεως παράδειγμα τοῖς ἀρχομένοις δηλούμενον.

96 ΜΗΛ. Σκοποῦσι δ' ὑμῶν οὕτως οἱ ὑπήκοοι τὸ εἰκός, ὥστε τούς τε μὴ προσήκοντας καὶ ὅσοι ἄποικοι ὄντες οἱ πολλοὶ καὶ ἀποστάντες τινὲς κεχείρωνται ἐς τὸ αὐτὸ τιθέασιν;

const. with adjs. *Cf.* i. 74. 1, τοιούτου μέντοι ξυμβάντος τούτου; vi. 34. 60; 90. 1; vii. 30. 21. — δουλεῦσαι: like ἄρξαι (c. 91. 10), denotes the beginning of the relation.—2. καὶ ὑμῖν: *cf.* c. 91. 3.
93. 1. πρὸ τοῦ ... παθεῖν: *before suffering the worst*. *Cf.* c. 100. 4. — 2. ὑπακοῦσαι: this is the voluntary act which would lead to subjection, and is therefore substituted as a milder word for δουλεῦσαι in c. 92. — μὴ διαφθείραντες ὑμᾶς: *i.e.* by not robbing ourselves of the strength you would bring us.
94. 1. ὥστε δέ: see App. — 3. δέξαισθε: see App.
95. 1. γάρ: this introduces the reason for the unexpressed denial, equiv. to οὐκ ἂν δεξαίμεθα· οὐ γάρ. *Cf.* c. 97. 1; 99. 1. — 2. ὅσον ἡ φιλία ... δηλούμενον: the simple expression ἡ φιλία (opp. to ἡ ἔχθρα) is developed, by the addition of the reasons for the assertion that the friendship of the Melians is worse than their enmity, into an ungrammatical form of sent. which is inadmissible in English. This complex expression is equiv. to two independent clauses: "your hostility does not injure us so much as your friendship; for your friendship appears to our subjects a proof of our weakness, whereas your hostility seems to them a proof of our power."
96. 1. οἱ ὑπήκοοι: *i.e.* the ἀρχόμενοι of c. 95. It has just been stated that they would regard the friendship of the Melians as a proof of weakness on the part of Athens. In reply to this, the question is asked whether the subjects of Athens regard all relations between stronger and weaker states in the same way; whether a small state which has no special connexion with a more powerful one could not remain on friendly terms with it, and yet preserve its own independence. " Do your subjects really look at equity in this way so that they put all in the same category?" — 2. ὅσοι: these fall naturally under the two categories: that of simple ἄποικοι (these are the majority, οἱ πολλοί) and that of those who have revolted

97 · ΑΘ. Δικαιώματι γὰρ οὐδετέρους ἐλλείπειν ἡγοῦν- 1
ται, κατὰ δύναμιν δὲ τοὺς μὲν περιγίγνεσθαι, ἡμᾶς δὲ
φόβῳ οὐκ ἐπιέναι· ὥστε ἔξω καὶ τοῦ πλεόνων ἄρξαι καὶ
τὸ ἀσφαλὲς ἡμῖν διὰ τὸ καταστραφῆναι ἂν παράσχοιτε,
5 ἄλλως τε καὶ νησιῶται ναυκρατόρων καὶ ἀσθενέστεροι
ἑτέρων ὄντες εἰ μὴ περιγένοισθε.

98   ΜΗΛ. Ἐν δ' ἐκείνῳ οὐ νομίζετε ἀσφάλειαν; (δεῖ 1
γὰρ αὖ καὶ ἐνταῦθα, ὥσπερ ὑμεῖς τῶν δικαίων λόγων
ἡμᾶς ἐκβιάσαντες τῷ ὑμετέρῳ ξυμφόρῳ ὑπακούειν πεί-
θετε, καὶ ἡμᾶς τὸ ἡμῖν χρήσιμον διδάσκοντας, εἰ τυγχά-
5 νει καὶ ὑμῖν τὸ αὐτὸ ξυμβαῖνον, πειρᾶσθαι πείθειν). ὅσοι

and been subdued (τινες, e.g. the Lesbians). The parts are in the same case as the whole. Cf. c. 10. 47 ff.
97. 1. δικαιώματι: a claim based upon justice, as in i. 41. 1. — **γάρ**: this introduces the reason for the unexpressed affirmative answer, as in c. 99. 1 for the neg. — **οὐδετέρους**: i.e. neither τοὺς μὴ προσήκοντας nor τοὺς ἀποίκους ὄντας καὶ ἀποστάντας. — 2. **τοὺς μέν**: i.e. τοὺς μὴ προσήκοντας, who should, acc. to the opinion just expressed by the Melians, be allowed to retain their independence; and this is the meaning of περιγίγνεσθαι. — 4. **τὸ ἀσφαλὲς ἂν παράσχοιτε**: because our subjects will no longer believe that we are afraid of you. The expression, "you will, by the loss of your independence, increase our security," is not without a sort of bitter irony, which is still sharper in **ἄλλως τε καὶ ... εἰ μὴ περιγένοισθε**. Just because you are islanders, and insignificant islanders at that, you have all the less reason for claiming the right to retain your independence. — 5. **ναυκρατόρων**: the gen. depends upon περιγένοισθε. Cf. i. 55. 10, Κέρκυρα περιγίγνεται τῷ πολέμῳ τῶν Κορινθίων.

G. 175, 2; H. 749. — 6. **ἑτέρων**: than others, i.e. other islanders.
98. 1. ἐν ἐκείνῳ: i.e. in the relation proposed in c. 94, ὥστε ἡσυχίαν ... μηδετέρων, or, as the Schol. explains, ἐν τῷ μὴ πειρᾶσθαι τοὺς μὴ προσήκοντας καταστρέφεσθαι. The chief emphasis of the interr. sent. rests upon **ἐν ἐκείνῳ. ἀσφάλειαν** refers back to τὸ ἀσφαλές in c. 97. 4. The Melians ask, "doesn't that proposal of ours seem to you to be a safe one?" The following sent., **δεῖ γὰρ πειρᾶσθαι ... πείθειν**, is inserted parenthetically (with αὖ καὶ ἐνταῦθα referring to c. 90. 1), to give a reason for recurring to the proposal which the Athenians have already rejected in c. 95. The argument in support of this proposal is contained in the next sent., **ὅσοι γάρ ... αὐτοὺς κτέ.**, where it is expressed in negative form: "if you do not follow our advice, you will make enemies of all who are now neutral." — 3. **ἐκβιάσαντες**: force out. See App. — τῷ ὑμετέρῳ ξυμφόρῳ, τὸ ἡμῖν χρήσιμον: "what is for your interest, what is for ours." The Melians hope to make their own interest acceptable to the Athenians (**πείθειν**) only if it coin-

γὰρ νῦν μηδετέροις ξυμμαχοῦσι, πῶς οὐ πολεμώσεσθε αὐτούς, ὅταν ἐς τάδε βλέψαντες ἡγήσωνταί ποτε ὑμᾶς καὶ ἐπὶ σφᾶς ἥξειν; κἂν τούτῳ τί ἄλλο ἢ τοὺς μὲν ὑπάρχοντας πολεμίους μεγαλύνετε, τοὺς δὲ μηδὲ μελλήσαντας γε-
10 νέσθαι ἄκοντας ἐπάγεσθε;

99   ΑΘ. Οὐ γὰρ νομίζομεν ἡμῖν τούτους δεινοτέρους, 1 ὅσοι ἠπειρῶταί που ὄντες τῷ ἐλευθέρῳ πολλὴν τὴν διαμέλλησιν τῆς πρὸς ἡμᾶς φυλακῆς ποιήσονται, ἀλλὰ τοὺς νησιώτας τέ που ἀνάρκτους, ὥσπερ ὑμᾶς, καὶ τοὺς
5 ἤδη τῆς ἀρχῆς τῷ ἀναγκαίῳ παροξυνομένους. οὗτοι γὰρ πλεῖστ' ἂν τῷ ἀλογίστῳ ἐπιτρέψαντες σφᾶς τε αὐτοὺς καὶ ἡμᾶς ἐς προῦπτον κίνδυνον καταστήσειαν.

100   ΜΗΛ. Ἦ που ἄρα, εἰ τοσαύτην γε ὑμεῖς τε μὴ 1

cides (τυγχάνει ξυμβαῖνον, sc. τὸ ἡμῖν χρήσιμον) with that of the Athenians themselves.— 6. πολεμώσεσθε: mid., *make enemies of.* The pass. of this occurs in i. 36. 10; 57. 5, 6.— 7. ἐς τάδε: *at this* which is going on here, *i.e.* at our fate.— 8. κἂν τούτῳ: opp. to ἐν ἐκείνῳ of 1. — τί ἄλλο ἢ: *cf.* c. 87. 2; ii. 16. 10; iii. 39. 10. — 9. μελλήσαντας: see App.
99. 1. οὐ γὰρ: see on c. 97. 1. — 2. ὅσοι ἠπειρῶται ποιήσονται, τοὺς νησιώτας παροξυνομένους: the inhabitants of the mainland are opp. to the islanders. The Athenians wish to show that they are in danger not so much from the former as from the latter. "The people of the mainland will in their freedom (the dat. τῷ ἐλευθέρῳ denotes not so much cause as merely an attendant circumstance, and is nearly equiv. to ἐλεύθεροι ὄντες) defer indefinitely any measures of precaution they may take against us, which is not the case with the islanders, whether they are, like you, free from restraint, or irritated by the

necessity of submission to our rule." For other explanations, see App. — 6. τῷ ἀλογίστῳ: *rash* or *ill-considered action*, in consequence of παροξύνεσθαι. — 7. ἐς κίνδυνον καταστήσειαν: so also in ii. 100. 25. Similarly ἐς ἀπορίαν, ii. 81. 37; vii. 75. 14; ἐς ταραχήν, iv. 75. 10; ἐς ἔκπληξιν, vi. 36. 7. The Schol. explains this chap. as follows: οὐ γὰρ νομίζομεν τοὺς ἐλευθέρους τῶν ἠπειρωτῶν ἡμῖν ἔσεσθαι πολεμίους· μὴ δεδιότες γὰρ ἡμᾶς, ὡς ἂν κατὰ γῆν οὐ μέλλοντας αὐτοῖς ἐπιστρατεύειν, πολλὴν μέλλησιν τοῦ φυλάττεσθαί τε ἡμᾶς καὶ πολεμεῖν ποιήσονται. τοὺς δὲ ἐν ταῖς νήσοις ἐλευθέρους ὥσπερ ὑμᾶς, καὶ τοὺς ὑπακούοντας μὲν ἤδη, διὰ δὲ τὸ ἐξ ἀνάγκης καὶ μὴ ἑκοντὶ ὑπακούειν παροξυνομένους καὶ ταραττομένους τούτους ἡγούμεθα, εἰ περιίδοιμεν ὑμᾶς ἐλευθέρους (so Cl. for ἡμᾶς: "if we should permit you to be free"), ἐπαρθέντας ἀλογίστως καὶ ἀντιστάντας ἡμῖν αὐτούς τε καὶ ἡμᾶς αὐτοὺς ἐς κίνδυνον καταστήσειν.
100. 1. ἦ που ἄρα: *surely then.* An emphatic asseveration followed by a confident conclusion. Both belong

παυθῆναι ἀρχῆς καὶ οἱ δουλεύοντες ἤδη ἀπαλλαγῆναι τὴν
παρακινδύνευσιν ποιοῦνται, ἡμῖν γε τοῖς ἔτι ἐλευθέροις
πολλὴ κακότης καὶ δειλία μὴ πᾶν πρὸ τοῦ δουλεῦσαι
ἐπεξελθεῖν.

101 ΑΘ. Οὐκ, ἤν γε σωφρόνως βουλεύησθε· οὐ γὰρ
περὶ ἀνδραγαθίας ὁ ἀγὼν ἀπὸ τοῦ ἴσου ὑμῖν μὴ αἰσχύνην ὀφλεῖν, περὶ δὲ σωτηρίας μᾶλλον ἡ βουλὴ πρὸς
τοὺς κρείσσονας πολλῷ μὴ ἀνθίστασθαι.

102 ΜΗΛ. Ἀλλ' ἐπιστάμεθα τὰ τῶν πολέμων ἔστιν
ὅτε κοινοτέρας τὰς τύχας λαμβάνοντα ἢ κατὰ τὸ διαφέρον
ἑκατέρων πλῆθος. καὶ ἡμῖν τὸ μὲν εἶξαι εὐθὺς ἀνέλπι-
στον, μετὰ δὲ τοῦ δρωμένου ἔτι καὶ στῆναι ἐλπὶς ὀρθῶς.

103 ΑΘ. Ἐλπὶς δὲ κινδύνῳ παραμύθιον οὖσα τοὺς

with πολλὴ κακότης, sc. ἂν εἴη. — 3. παρακινδύνευσιν ποιοῦνται: equiv. to παρακινδυνεύουσι (cf. iii. 36. 11), with the emphatic signification of παρα- implying excess. See on iii. 32. 15. The aor. infs. παυθῆναι and ἀπαλλαγῆναι, both const. with ἀρχῆς, express the purpose of παρακινδύνευσιν ποιοῦν- ται. — 4. πρὸ τοῦ δουλεῦσαι: cf. c. 93. 1. — πᾶν ἐπεξελθεῖν: try (cf. c. 9. 41) everything (cf. iii. 45. 20), even the most extreme measures.

101. 1. οὔκ: this refers, not to any particular words, but to the whole idea of what precedes; equiv. to οὐ ποιήσετε τοῦτο. Cf. iii. 66. 19. — 2. ἀπὸ τοῦ ἴσου: this belongs with ὁ ἀγών, and is opp. to πρὸς τοὺς κρείσσονας πολλῷ: "with equal forces." See on i. 77. 8. — 3. ὀφλεῖν: with Bekker and others against the authority of the Mss., which read ὀφλεῖν. The sense ("not to fall into disgrace") demands the aor. (of pres. ὀφλισκάνω). — ἡ βουλή: this is substituted for ὁ ἀγών as if to exclude the notion of a decision by violence.

102. 1. ἀλλά: this does not, like δέ, introduce an objection or direct reply, but a new observation or point of view. Cf. c. 108. 1. — πολέμων: see App. — 2. κοινοτέρας: this is to be explained from the meaning of κοινός, impartial (cf. iii. 53. 8; 68. 7), "the fortunes of war sometimes turn out more impartially (i.e. more in accordance with justice) than the difference in the forces on the two sides would lead one to expect." — τὰς τύχας λαμβάνοντα: cf. ὅταν καιρὸν λά- βωσιν, vi. 86. 13. — ἢ κατά: cf. i. 76. 17; ii. 50. 2. — 4. τοῦ δρωμένου: this is, as in c. 66. 18, prop. pass., but since it refers directly to the agent, it is used here and in vi. 16. 12 as a general expression for independent action. On the use of the partic. for the inf., see on c. 9. 18. — ἔτι: const. with ἐλπίς, and ὀρθῶς with στῆναι. So Polyb.,xxxiii. 12. 3, has ὀρθῶς ἵσταντο. Van Herwerden's proposal, ὀρθοῖς, is needless. Cf. also Soph. O. T. 50, στάντες τ' ἐς ὀρθόν.

103. 1. ἐλπὶς δέ: in introducing a reply, δέ throws special emphasis

μὲν ἀπὸ περιουσίας χρωμένους αὐτῇ, κἂν βλάψῃ, οὐ καθεῖλε· τοῖς δ' ἐς ἅπαν τὸ ὑπάρχον ἀναρριπτοῦσι (δάπανος γὰρ φύσει) ἅμα τε γιγνώσκεται σφαλέντων καὶ ἐν 5 ὅτῳ ἔτι φυλάξεταί τις αὐτὴν γνωρισθεῖσαν οὐκ ἐλλείπει. ὃ ὑμεῖς ἀσθενεῖς τε καὶ ἐπὶ ῥοπῆς μιᾶς ὄντες μὴ βούλεσθε παθεῖν, μηδὲ ὁμοιωθῆναι τοῖς πολλοῖς, οἷς παρὸν ἀνθρωπείως ἔτι σῴζεσθαι, ἐπειδὰν πιεζομένους αὐτοὺς ἐπιλίπωσιν αἱ φανεραὶ ἐλπίδες, ἐπὶ τὰς ἀφανεῖς καθ10 ίστανται, μαντικήν τε καὶ χρησμοὺς καὶ ὅσα τοιαῦτα μετ' ἐλπίδων λυμαίνεται.

104 ΜΗΛ. Χαλεπὸν μὲν καὶ ἡμεῖς, εὖ ἴστε, νομίζομεν 1

upon one word, whether it be (as here; c. 91. 1; 96. 1; 106. 1) the preceding or (as in c. 94. 1; 98. 1; 109. 1) the following word.— παραμύθιον: the concrete means of παραμυθία. The two are not so entirely equiv. as Lobeck (ad *Phryn.* p. 517) thinks, but differ as do the Lat. nouns in -mentum and -io.— 2. ἀπὸ περιουσίας: cf. ἐκ τοῦ περισσεύοντος, *of their abundance*, St. Mark, XII. 44.— οὐ καθεῖλε: the gnomic aor., drawing a general inference from special cases. Cf. i. 69. 31. GMT. 30, 1; H. 840; Kühn. 386, 7.— 3. τοῖς δ' ἐς ἅπαν τὸ ὑπάρχον ἀναρριπτοῦσι: *those who cast* (the die) *for all their possessions*. With ἀναρριπτοῦσι supply κίνδυνον, i.e. the die. Cf. iv. 85. 13; 95. 5; vi. 13. 8. ἐς ἅπαν τὸ ὑπάρχον must be taken together. Those who, on account of their poverty, are obliged to risk their all are opp. to those who, like rich men buying lottery tickets, risk only what they can afford to lose. See App.— 4. ἅμα: const. with γιγνώσκεται σφαλέντων. "When misfortune has come upon them the true nature of Hope is recognized; but then she does not leave

(οὐκ ἐλλείπει, trans.; cf. Eur. *El.* 609) anything in which (i.e. in respect to which) one can be on his guard against her now that she is known." — 6. ὅ: *but this*, expressing a strong opposition. Cf. c. 107. 3; 109. 3, and see on iv. 17. 18.— ἐπὶ ῥοπῆς μιᾶς: this is a stronger expression than ἐπὶ ῥοπῆς μικρᾶς in Eur. *Hipp.* 1163. The meaning is not "only a little is needed to turn the scale," but, corresponding to ἐς ἅπαν τὸ ὑπάρχον ἀναρριπτοῦσι, "everything is at the mercy of a single turn." — μὴ βούλεσθε: this resembles the Lat. nolite, but partakes of the nature of a benevolent warning: "pray do not be willing." Thuc. uses this expression in one other place, iv. 10. 2, μηδεὶς ξυνετὸς βουλέσθω δοκεῖν εἶναι.— 7. οἷς παρόν, καθίστανται: the rel. pron. stands in the dependent clause, but must be supplied as subj. of the main verb.— ἀνθρωπείως: *by human means*.— 9. ἐπιλίπωσιν: *deficiant, fail.* Cf. ii. 70. 4, ὁ σῖτος ἐπελελοίπει.— ἀφανεῖς: sc. ἐλπίδας, *hopes with no visible foundation*. The explanation, which is added in appos., mentions such unstable objects of

πρὸς δύναμίν τε τὴν ὑμετέραν καὶ τὴν τύχην, εἰ μὴ ἀπὸ
τοῦ ἴσου ἔσται, ἀγωνίζεσθαι· ὅμως δὲ πιστεύομεν τῇ
μὲν τύχῃ ἐκ τοῦ θείου μὴ ἐλασσώσεσθαι, ὅτι ὅσιοι πρὸς
5 οὐ δικαίους ἱστάμεθα, τῆς δὲ δυνάμεως τῷ ἐλλείποντι
τὴν Λακεδαιμονίων ἡμῖν ξυμμαχίαν προσέσεσθαι, ἀνάγκην ἔχουσαν, καὶ εἰ μή του ἄλλου, τῆς γε ξυγγενείας
ἕνεκα καὶ αἰσχύνῃ βοηθεῖν. καὶ οὐ παντάπασιν οὕτως
ἀλόγως θρασυνόμεθα.
105   ΛΘ. Τῆς μὲν τοίνυν πρὸς τὸ θεῖον εὐμενείας οὐδ' 1
ἡμεῖς οἰόμεθα λελείψεσθαι. οὐδὲν γὰρ ἔξω τῆς ἀνθρωπείας τῶν μὲν ἐς τὸ θεῖον νομίσεως τῶν δ' ἐς σφᾶς

hope, which, in conjunction μετ' ἐλπίδων, effect men's ruin.
104. 2. τὴν τύχην: this is the ruling power which affects men's lives without their own action, and is believed by the pious to be dependent upon τὸ θεῖον. Its special manifestations are the τύχαι. *Cf.* c. 102. 2. See Introd. to Book I., p. 29. What is, in c. 102. 2, expressed by κοιναί in connexion with τύχαι is here, with τύχη itself, denoted by ἀπὸ τοῦ ἴσου: "not preferring either of the contending parties." — **4.** ἐκ τοῦ θείου: *cf.* c. 112. 7. — ὅσιοι: this is the only instance of the pers. use of this word in Thuc., *god-fearing, observant of the divine ordinances* (the ὅσια of i. 71. 25; ii. 52. 11, and the ὅσιον of iii. 84. 14) upon which human society is based, and the chief of which is the δίκαιον which the Melians have called (in c. 90. 3) τὸ κοινὸν ἀγαθόν. The opposites of the ὅσιοι are therefore plainly called οὐ δίκαιοι, although the Athenians are not mentioned by name. — **5.** ἱστάμεθα: this word is used esp. of warlike opposition. *Cf.* i. 33. 22; 53. 6; iii. 39. 13. — τῷ ἐλλεί-ποντι: const. with προσέσεσθαι, and take ἡμῖν as dat. of interest, nearly equiv. to the possessive gen., "their alliance will supplement our deficiency." — **8.** αἰσχύνη: *from a feeling of honour*. *Cf.* iv. 19. 15. — οὐ παντάπασιν οὕτως ἀλόγως: "not altogether so foolish as you may suppose." See on c. 59. 17 and ii. 11. 24.
105. 1. τοίνυν: see on c. 87. 1. — πρὸς τὸ θεῖον: this in conjunction with εὐμένεια denotes a good relation in the widest sense; not only that the Athenians hope for the favour of the gods, but also that they fulfil their obligations toward them. It is an indirect reply to the ὅσιοι πρὸς οὐ δικαίους of the Melians. πρὸς τὸ θεῖον is not to be changed with Kr. to πρὸς τοῦ θείου, nor with Meincke to περὶ τὸ θεῖον. — **2.** λελείψεσθαι: equiv. to ἐλασσώσεσθαι of 12, "that we shall be inferior therein." — τῆς ἀνθρωπείας: this belongs to both the following substs. (νομίσεως and βουλήσεως), and is therefore placed before both in the sent. *Cf.* ii. 44. 4. — **3.** νομίσεως: this is here used not so much of opinion or belief as of the exercise of religious customs and cer-

αὐτοὺς βουλήσεως δικαιοῦμεν ἢ πράσσομεν. ἡγούμεθα 2
γὰρ τό τε θεῖον δόξῃ, τὸ ἀνθρώπειόν τε σαφῶς διὰ παντὸς ὑπὸ φύσεως ἀναγκαίας, οὗ ἂν κρατῇ, ἄρχειν. καὶ ἡμεῖς οὔτε θέντες τὸν νόμον οὔτε κειμένῳ πρῶτοι χρησάμενοι, ὄντα δὲ παραλαβόντες καὶ ἐσόμενον ἐς ἀεὶ καταλείψοντες χρώμεθα αὐτῷ, εἰδότες καὶ ὑμᾶς ἂν καὶ ἄλλους ἐν τῇ αὐτῇ δυνάμει ἡμῖν γενομένους δρῶντας ἂν ταὐτό. καὶ πρὸς μὲν τὸ θεῖον οὕτως ἐκ τοῦ εἰκότος οὐ 3
φοβούμεθα ἐλασσώσεσθαι· τῆς δὲ ἐς Λακεδαιμονίους δόξης, ἣν διὰ τὸ αἰσχρὸν δὴ βοηθήσειν ὑμῖν πιστεύετε αὐτούς, μακαρίσαντες ὑμῶν τὸ ἀπειρόκακον οὐ ζηλοῦμεν

emonies, τὰ νενομισμένα, τὰ εἰθισμένα περὶ τοὺς θεούς, Schol. — ἐς σφᾶς αὐτοὺς βουλήσεως: i.e. ἐς τοὺς ἀνθρώπους, which is suggested by the preceding ἀνθρωπείας. Like Lat. voluntas, βούλησις denotes one's state of mind toward others. — 4. δικαιοῦμεν, πράσσομεν: the first refers to βουλήσεως: "we put forward no unwarranted pretensions," the second to both νομίσεως and βουλήσεως.

5. δόξῃ, σαφῶς: these words, placed respectively after the substs. τὸ θεῖον and τὸ ἀνθρώπειον, denote the degree of certainty of ἡγούμεθα as applied to these substs., and are not to be const. with ἄρχειν: "for of the gods we believe, and of men we know, that by a law of their nature, wherever they have power (i.e. throughout the realm of their power), they always rule." Greater stress is laid upon ἀνθρώπειον, as is evident from its position before τε. — διὰ παντός: this is temporal, as usual. See on i. 38. 2. Like ὑπὸ φύσεως ἀναγκαίας, it belongs with ἄρχειν. The Athenians leave it to the Melians to give the general proposition τὸ ἀνθρώπειον οὗ ἂν κρατῇ ἄρχειν its application to the case in hand: οὕτω καὶ τοῖς Ἀθηναίοις προσήκειν ὡς κατὰ θάλασσαν κρατοῦντας ὑμῶν νησιωτῶν ὄντων ἄρχειν. But the proposition itself, ἄρχειν τινὰ οὗ ἂν κρατῇ, or "might makes right," is the νόμος to which reference is made in the subsequent words. — 9. ὑμᾶς ἄν, δρῶντας ἄν: the repetition of ἄν with subj. and verb adds clearness as well as emphasis. Cf. c. 9. 16. — 11. ταὐτό: see App. — ἐκ τοῦ εἰκότος: in accordance with probability. This refers to the statement of 2, οὐδὲν ἔξω τῆς ἀνθρωπείας ἐς τὸ θεῖον νομίσεως πράσσομεν.

12. φοβούμεθα: is here followed by the fut. inf. on account of the implied notion of indir. disc. GMT. 46, n. 6 (b); II. 948 a. — τῆς δόξης: const. with τὸ ἀπειρόκακον, 14, and τὸ ἄφρον, 15. — ἐς Λακεδαιμονίους: cf. iii. 14. 1, τὰς ἐς ὑμᾶς ἐλπίδας, and iv. 81. 12, ἐπιθυμία ἐς τοὺς Λακεδαιμονίους. — 13. ἥν: cognate acc. with πιστεύετε, since δόξῃ is here nearly equiv. to πίστις. See App. — διὰ τὸ αἰσχρόν: equiv. to αἰσχύνῃ of c. 104. 8. αἰσχρὸν νομίζοντας τοὺς ἀποίκους πολεμουμένους, Schol. — 14. ὑμῶν τὸ ἀπειρόκακον: your simplicity, which arises from inexperience of evil.

15 τὸ ἄφρον. Λακεδαιμόνιοι γὰρ πρὸς σφᾶς μὲν αὐτοὺς 4
καὶ τὰ ἐπιχώρια νόμιμα πλεῖστα ἀρετῇ χρῶνται· πρὸς δὲ
τοὺς ἄλλους πολλὰ ἄν τις ἔχων εἰπεῖν ὡς προσφέρονται,
ξυνελὼν μάλιστ' ἂν δηλώσειεν ὅτι ἐπιφανέστατα ὧν
ἴσμεν τὰ μὲν ἡδέα καλὰ νομίζουσι, τὰ δὲ ξυμφέροντα
20 δίκαια. καίτοι οὐ πρὸς τῆς ὑμετέρας νῦν ἀλόγου σωτηρίας ἡ τοιαύτη διάνοια.

106 ΜΗΛ. Ἡμεῖς δὲ κατ' αὐτὸ τοῦτο ἤδη καὶ μάλι- 1
στα πιστεύομεν τῷ ξυμφέροντι αὐτῶν Μηλίους ἀποίκους
ὄντας μὴ βουλήσεσθαι προδόντας τοῖς μὲν εὔνοις τῶν
Ἑλλήνων ἀπίστους καταστῆναι, τοῖς δὲ πολεμίοις ὠφε-
5 λίμους.

107 ΑΘ. Οὐκ οὖν οἴεσθε τὸ ξυμφέρον μὲν μετὰ ἀσφα- 1
λείας εἶναι, τὸ δὲ δίκαιον καὶ καλὸν μετὰ κινδύνου
δρᾶσθαι; ὃ Λακεδαιμόνιοι ἥκιστα ὡς ἐπὶ τὸ πολὺ τολμῶσιν.

16. πλεῖστα: adv. See on i. 3. 23.
— 17. πολλὰ ὄν τις ἔχων εἰπεῖν: a common rhetorical expression. Cf. Dem. III. 27; VIII. 52. — 18. ξυνελών: freq. used by Thuc. to introduce a brief summing up, esp. in speeches. Cf. ii. 41. 1; iii. 40. 16; vi. 80. 14. — 20. καίτοι: and yet (see on ii. 60. 16; iv. 18. 5) this selfish character of the Lacedaemonians is not favourable to the fulfilment of your present foolish hope of deliverance. The ἄλογος σωτηρία is here intentionally opp. to the οὐκ ἀλόγως θρασυνόμεθα of c. 104. 9.

106. 1. κατ' αὐτὸ τοῦτο: precisely because the Lacedaemonians νομίζουσι τὰ ξυμφέροντα δίκαια. — 2. τῷ ξυμφέροντι αὐτῶν: const. with μὴ βουλήσεσθαι (not with πιστεύομεν). διὰ τὸ ἴδιον ξυμφέρον, Schol. We should, as St. observes, expect τῷ αὐτῶν ξυμφέροντι or τῷ αὐτῶν ξυμφέροντι, but αὐτῶν, even in the position in which it stands here, may have the sense of ἴδιον (Lat. ipsorum). Still we should naturally translate it of them (Lat. eorum, i.e. of some other people), which is here plainly impossible. See App. — 4. καταστῆναι: an emphatic γενέσθαι. Cf. i. 70. 3; iii. 102. 26; iv. 92. 15; vi. 82. 13.

107. 1. οὐκ οὖν κτέ.: this is the ordinary neg. introduction of a question expecting an affirmative answer: don't you think then? i.e. "of course you understand." This sense would appear more plainly if we were to read οὐκ οὖν ἴστε instead of οἴεσθε, as the Schol. may perhaps have done, who explains: ἀλλ' οὖν, ὥσπερ ἴστε, συμφέρει κτέ. — 3. δρᾶσθαι: see App. — ὅ: "but just that." Cf. c. 103. 6; 109. 3.

108 ΜΗΛ. Ἀλλὰ καὶ τοὺς κινδύνους τε ἡμῶν ἕνεκα 1
μᾶλλον ἡγούμεθ' ἂν ἐγχειρίσασθαι αὐτούς, καὶ βεβαιοτέρους ἢ ἐς ἄλλους νομιεῖν, ὅσῳ πρὸς μὲν τὰ ἔργα τῆς
Πελοποννήσου ἐγγὺς κείμεθα, τῆς δὲ γνώμης τῷ ξυγγενεῖ
5 πιστότεροι ἑτέρων ἐσμέν.

109 ΑΘ. Τὸ δ' ἐχυρόν γε τοῖς ξυναγωνιουμένοις οὐ 1
τὸ εὔνουν τῶν ἐπικαλεσαμένων φαίνεται, ἀλλ' ἢν τῶν
ἔργων τις δυνάμει πολὺ προύχῃ· ὃ Λακεδαιμόνιοι καὶ
πλεῖόν τι τῶν ἄλλων σκοποῦσι. τῆς γοῦν οἰκείας παρα-
5 σκευῆς ἀπιστίᾳ καὶ μετὰ ξυμμάχων πολλῶν τοῖς πέλας
ἐπέρχονται· ὥστε οὐκ εἰκὸς ἐς νῆσόν γε αὐτοὺς ἡμῶν
ναυκρατόρων ὄντων περαιωθῆναι.

110 ΜΗΛ. Οἱ δὲ καὶ ἄλλους ἂν ἔχοιεν πέμψαι· πολὺ 1

108. 1. καὶ τοὺς κινδύνους: the dangers which are connected with the δίκαιον and καλόν. "The Lacedaemonians will be more ready to face them for our sake, and will consider them less dangerous (βεβαιοτέρους with κινδύνους; cf. iii. 39. 5, τὸν μετὰ τῶν ὀλίγων κίνδυνον ἡγησάμενοι βεβαιότερον) than in relation to others (ἐς ἄλλους)," *i.e.* than if they were to face them for the sake of others. ἐς expresses a general relation, as in c. 105. 12. — τε: const. not with κινδύνους alone, but as the connective of the first clause, ἀλλά ... ἐγχειρίσασθαι αὐτούς with the second, καὶ βεβαιοτέρους νομιεῖν. — 2. ἐγχειρίσασθαι: the mid. does not occur elsewhere in Attic Greek. — 3. ὅσῳ: *inasmuch as*. — πρὸς τὰ ἔργα: adres gerendas, "when anything is to be done." Melos is so near the coast of Peloponnesus that it could easily send troops or supplies to the Lacedaemonians. — 4. κείμεθα: equiv. to ἡ ἡμετέρα νῆσος κεῖται. The application of the word is transferred from the island to its inhabitants. — **τῆς γνώμης τῷ ξυγγενεῖ**: "on account of the likeness of our views which arises from our relationship." This is indirectly an explanation of τῆς ξυγγενείας ἕνεκα, of c. 104. 7. γνώμη is used of views on political matters, as in i. 113. 10; iii. 70. 27; iv. 56. 17. — 5. ἑτέρων: *than any others*. See on i. 84. 7.

109. 1. τὸ ἐχυρόν: stands in the relation of pred. to τὸ εὔνουν after φαίνεται, and the art. is added to emphasize the subst. use of ἐχυρόν (*cf.* ii. 43. 22 f.) : " the thing which inspires confidence is not the good will," *etc.*; the positive side is then expressed by the cond. sent. ἀλλ' ἢν τις προύχῃ. — 5. **καὶ μετὰ ξυμμάχων πολλῶν**: a similar idea is expressed in ii. 39. § 2. — 6. **οὐκ εἰκὸς αὐτοὺς περαιωθῆναι**: εἰκός regularly takes the inf. aor. (never the fut.) where the probability of the occurrence of a fut. action is to be expressed. See on i. 81. 13.

110. 1. καὶ ἄλλους: *i.e.* the allies, a list of whom is given in ii. 9. § 2. The Corinthians would be esp. fitted

δὲ τὸ Κρητικὸν πέλαγος, δι' οὗ τῶν κρατούντων ἀπορώτερος ἡ λῆψις ἢ τῶν λαθεῖν βουλομένων ἡ σωτηρία.
καὶ εἰ τοῦδε σφάλλοιντο, τράποιντ' ἂν καὶ ἐς τὴν γῆν 2
ὑμῶν καὶ ἐπὶ τοὺς λοιποὺς τῶν ξυμμάχων, ὅσους μὴ
Βρασίδας ἐπῆλθε· καὶ οὐ περὶ τῆς μὴ προσηκούσης μᾶλλον ἢ τῆς οἰκειοτέρας ξυμμαχίδος τε καὶ γῆς ὁ πόνος
ὑμῖν ἔσται.

111 ΑΘ. Τούτων μὲν καὶ πεπειραμένοις ἄν τι γένοιτο 1

for such service. — πολύ: cf. πολλὴ ἡ Σικελία, vii. 13. 16. — 2. τὸ Κρητικὸν πέλαγος: the sea to the south and southeast from Peloponnesus. See on iv. 53. 13. — δι' οὗ: per quod, i.e. on account of its greatness. — τῶν κρατούντων, τῶν βουλομένων: subjective gens. — ἀπορώτερος: on the masc. ending in the comp. of compound adjs., see on iii. 89. 21 and iv. 31. 15. Kr. Spr. § 23, 1, Rem. — 3. λῆψις: in the sense of λαμβάνειν, as in c. 115. 5; vii. 25. 16.
4. τοῦδε: sc. τοῦ κατὰ θάλασσαν βοηθῆσαι ἡμῖν. — 5. τοὺς λοιποὺς τῶν ξυμμάχων: esp. those on the Thracian coast. This, as the most important part of the Athenian empire, may be particularly referred to in τῆς οἰκειοτέρας ξυμμαχίδος of 7. — ὅσους μὴ ἐπῆλθε: such as he did not reach. The cond. rel. (with μή, not οὐ) is equiv. to εἴ τινας μὴ ἐπῆλθε. GMT. 61, 1; H. 913. — 6. οὐ μᾶλλον ἤ: not so much as. See on i. 73. 17. — 7. οἰκειοτέρας: this is opp. to τῆς μὴ προσηκούσης (not τῆς οὐ προσηκούσης, and therefore a general expression applicable to other places besides Melos; G. 283, 4; H. 1025 a), and belongs with both ξυμμαχίδος and γῆς. With προσηκούσης we should supply ξυμμαχίδος rather than γῆς, for it was as ξυμμαχίς that new territory was added to the Athe-

nian empire. γῆς is then added as an afterthought: "not about territory which you hope to add to your empire without any right, but about your own empire and, for that matter, your own country." Cl. supplies γῆς with μὴ προσηκούσης, and cites i. 13. 18; ii. 11. 20; 20. 17. Cf. also c. 111. 20. There is no difficulty in supplying γῆς, but the above explanation seems better. See App.
111. 1. τούτων μὲν καὶ πεπειραμένοις κτέ.: the point of this reply to the threatening language of the Melians lies in the proud assurance that such a double attack was nothing new for the Athenians. It is, therefore, certain that, as St. observes, πεπειραμένοις refers to the Athenians only. In the litotes (οὐκ ἀνεπιστήμοσιν, i.e. εὖ εἰδόσιν) the Athenians express with self-conscious irony the confident belief that "the fame of our campaigns has probably come to your ears." The effect of τούτων τι is somewhat similar: "some of these things (with which you threaten us) would not come upon us without our having experienced the like before," i.e. "nothing of all this is new to us." On the pers. const. of πεπειραμένοις, see on ii. 3. 9. This const. occurs with γίγνεσθαι also in ii. 60. 1. See App.

ἡμῖν, καὶ ὑμῖν οὐκ ἀνεπιστήμοσιν ὅτι οὐδ' ἀπὸ μιᾶς πώποτε πολιορκίας Ἀθηναῖοι δι' ἄλλων φόβον ἀπεχώρησαν. ἐνθυμούμεθα δὲ ὅτι φήσαντες περὶ σωτηρίας 2 βουλεύσειν οὐδὲν ἐν τοσούτῳ λόγῳ εἰρήκατε ᾧ ἄνθρωποι ἂν πιστεύσαντες νομίσειαν σωθήσεσθαι, ἀλλ' ὑμῶν τὰ μὲν ἰσχυρότατα ἐλπιζόμενα μέλλεται, τὰ δ' ὑπάρχοντα βραχέα πρὸς τὰ ἤδη ἀντιτεταγμένα περιγίγνεσθαι. πολλήν τε ἀλογίαν τῆς διανοίας παρέχετε, εἰ μὴ μεταστησάμενοι ἔτι ἡμᾶς ἄλλο τι τῶνδε σωφρονέστερον γνώσεσθε. οὐ γὰρ δὴ ἐπί γε τὴν ἐν τοῖς αἰσχροῖς καὶ προύπτοις 3 κινδύνοις πλεῖστα διαφθείρουσαν ἀνθρώπους αἰσχύνην τρέψεσθε. πολλοῖς γὰρ προορωμένοις ἔτι ἐς οἷα φερον-

4. ἐνθυμούμεθα: in the freq. occurring sense of sympathetic interest (cf. c. 32. 5); here "we observe with regret."—φήσαντες: see c. 87; 88.—5. ἄνθρωποι: is used with reference to what is said in c. 105. 4 ff. about the θεῖον and the ἀνθρώπειον.— 6. νομίσειαν: see App.—ὑμῶν τὰ ἰσχυρότατα ἐλπιζόμενα μέλλεται: your strongest (grounds of confidence), being (mere) hopes, are held in abeyance. τὰ μὲν ἰσχυρότατα ὑμῶν ἐλπίδες εἰσὶ μέλλουσαι, Schol. The sense is expressed in a characteristic manner by the pass. μέλλεται (in Xen. An. iii. 1. 47 it is different, where μέλλεσθαι means be put off).—8. βραχέα: const. περιγίγνεσθαι with this. Cf. i. 50. 25, ὀλίγαι ἀμύνειν; ii. 61. 12, ταπεινή ἐγκαρτερεῖν.—πολλήν τε: a final conclusion: "and so you exhibit great want of sense."—9. μεταστησάμενοι: causing to withdraw. See on i. 79. 3, and compare with this trans. aor. partic. the corresponding intrans. μεταστάντων in 25.—10. γνώσεσθε: come to a conclusion. Cf. c. 36. 10; i. 70. 7; ii. 61. 12; iii. 40. 18.

11. οὐ γὰρ δή . . . τρέψεσθε: a similar expression is used in i. 122. 23, οὐ γὰρ δὴ πεφευγότες ταῦτα ἐπὶ τὴν πλείστους δὴ βλάψασαν καταφρόνησιν κεχωρήκατε. In both passages an urgent warning is expressed; but here the danger is in the future, and therefore may still be avoided, while in the other case the fault is regarded as already committed.—13. πολλοῖς γάρ κτέ.: this sent. contains, in chiastic order, an explanation of the two epithets in the preceding sent.: προορωμένοις ἔτι (ἔτι with προ-, while it is still time to avoid them) corresponds to προύπτοις κινδύνοις and τὸ αἰσχρὸν καλούμενον to αἰσχροῖς. This explains the unusual αἰσχροῖς κινδύνοις (for which ἐσχάτοις, ἄκροις, ἰσχυροῖς have been proposed), i.e. "in dangers which threaten disgrace," by which the loss of political independence is here meant. The Schol. renders: τὸ ἀπρεπὲς τοῦ ὀνόματος, and adds: τουτέστι τὸ ὑπακούειν ἔχον τι ποιητικὸν αἰσχύνης. Cf. Dem. xviii. 178, μὴ δεῖσθαι Θηβαίων μηδέν· αἰσχρὸς γὰρ ὁ καιρός, "it would bring you disgrace."—14. ἀπα-

ται τὸ αἰσχρὸν καλούμενον ὀνόματος ἐπαγωγοῦ δυνάμει
15 ἐπεσπάσατο ἡσσηθεῖσι τοῦ ῥήματος ἔργῳ ξυμφοραῖς
ἀνηκέστοις ἑκόντας περιπεσεῖν καὶ αἰσχύνην αἰσχίω μετὰ
ἀνοίας ἢ τύχης προσλαβεῖν. ὃ ὑμεῖς, ἢν εὖ βουλεύησθε, 4
φυλάξεσθε καὶ οὐκ ἀπρεπὲς νομιεῖτε πόλεώς τε τῆς μεγίστης ἡσσᾶσθαι μέτρια προκαλουμένης, ξυμμάχους γε-
20 νέσθαι ἔχοντας τὴν ὑμετέραν αὐτῶν ὑποτελεῖς, καὶ δοθείσης αἱρέσεως πολέμου πέρι καὶ ἀσφαλείας μὴ τὰ
χείρω φιλονικῆσαι· ὡς οἵτινες τοῖς μὲν ἴσοις μὴ εἴκουσι,
τοῖς δὲ κρείσσοσι καλῶς προσφέρονται, πρὸς δὲ τοὺς
ἥσσους μέτριοί εἰσι, πλεῖστ' ἂν ὀρθοῖντο. σκοπεῖτε οὖν 5
25 καὶ μεταστάντων ἡμῶν καὶ ἐνθυμεῖσθε πολλάκις ὅτι
περὶ πατρίδος βουλεύεσθε, * ἢν μιᾶς πέρι καὶ ἐς μίαν
βουλὴν τυχοῦσάν τε καὶ μὴ κατορθώσασαν ἔσται.

γωγοῦ: *seductive, misleading. Cf.* c. 85. 2; vi. 8. 7. — 15. ἐπεσπάσατο: aor. as in c. 103. 3. The mid. of this verb is used in iii. 44. 16; it is therefore not necessary to write, with v. Herwerden, *Stud. Thuc.* p. 80, ἐπέσπασε τό. Even without the art., περιπεσεῖν (16) and προσλαβεῖν (17) contain the obj. of πολλοῖς ἐπεσπάσατο: "so-called baseness by the power of a seductive word brings upon many (the misfortune) to fall into real troubles," etc. — ῥήματος ἔργῳ: the juxtaposition makes the opposition in meaning all the more noticeable. — 16. ἑκόντας: acc. as subj. of περιπεσεῖν in spite of the preceding dats. πολλοῖς, προορωμένοις, and ἡσσηθεῖσι. — αἰσχύνην αἰσχίω μετὰ ἀνοίας ἢ τύχης: *a disgrace which is more disgraceful when incurred through folly than* (it would be if incurred through) *fortune*. See App. — 17. προσλαβεῖν: "incur disgrace *in addition to* their misfortunes." *Cf.* iii. 82. 50.

18. πόλεως τῆς μεγίστης: the order is like that in ii. 61. 17; iv. 10. 7; 86. 2 and 8, with emphasis upon the adj. placed after the subst. and art. — 19. μέτρια προκαλουμένης: *cf.* c. 37. 23, τὰ εἰρημένα προκαλούμενοι. The substance of these proposals follows in the inf. γενέσθαι κτέ. — 20. ὑποτελεῖς: sc. φόρου (*cf.* i. 19. 1; 80. 14). With the exception of the few αὐτόνομοι (*cf.* i. 97. 1) this was the regular condition of the Athenian ξύμμαχοι, in which respect they differed from those of the Lacedaemonians, acc. to i. 19. 1. — 21. καί... φιλονικῆσαι: const. with οὐκ ἀπρεπὲς νομιεῖτε. φιλονικῆσαι (on the spelling, see St. *Quaest. Gram.* p. 13) with the neut. obj. τὰ χείρω as in Plat. *Prot.* 360 e. — 23. καλῶς προσφέρονται: *behave properly;* a euphemism for *submit*.

25. ἐνθυμεῖσθε: *consider earnestly. Cf.* 4. — 26. ἢν μιᾶς πέρι . . . ἔσται: the explanation of the Schol. πολλάκις πρὸ ὀφθαλμῶν λάβετε ὅτι περὶ πατρίδος ἡ σκέψις μιᾶς οὔσης, περὶ ἧς ἐν μιᾷ βου-

112 Καὶ οἱ μὲν Ἀθηναῖοι μετεχώρησαν ἐκ τῶν λόγων· οἱ δὲ Μήλιοι κατὰ σφᾶς αὐτοὺς γενόμενοι, ὡς ἔδοξεν αὐτοῖς παραπλήσια καὶ ἀντέλεγον, ἀπεκρίναντο τάδε· "Οὔτε ἄλλα δοκεῖ ἡμῖν ἢ ἅπερ καὶ τὸ πρῶτον, ὦ Ἀθηναῖοι, οὔτ᾽ ἐν ὀλίγῳ χρόνῳ πόλεως ἑπτακόσια ἔτη ἤδη οἰκουμένης τὴν ἐλευθερίαν ἀφαιρησόμεθα, ἀλλὰ τῇ τε μέχρι τοῦδε σῳζούσῃ τύχῃ ἐκ τοῦ θείου αὐτὴν καὶ τῇ ἀπὸ τῶν ἀνθρώπων καὶ Λακεδαιμονίων τιμωρίᾳ πιστεύοντες πειρασόμεθα σῴζεσθαι. προκαλούμεθα δὲ ὑμᾶς φίλοι μὲν εἶναι, πολέμιοι δὲ μηδετέροις, καὶ ἐκ τῆς γῆς ἡμῶν ἀναχωρῆσαι σπονδὰς ποιησαμένους αἵτινες δοκοῦσιν ἐπιτήδειοι εἶναι ἀμφοτέροις."

113 Οἱ μὲν δὴ Μήλιοι τοσαῦτα ἀπεκρίναντο· οἱ δὲ Ἀθη-

λῇ ἢ κατορθώσετε ἢ σφαλήσεσθε undoubtedly gives the meaning intended; but the sent. is certainly corrupt, and the difficulties are not overcome by the various emendations proposed. See App. — 27. τυχοῦσάν τε καὶ κατορθώσασαν: the alternatives are expressed in the same way, as in ii. 35. 8, εὖ τε καὶ χεῖρον εἰπόντι.

112. 1. μετεχώρησαν: corresponds to μεταστάντων of c. 111. 25. — 2. κατὰ σφᾶς αὐτούς: by themselves alone; κατά as in ii. 39. 11. — 3. παραπλήσια καί: similia atque: about the same as. Cf. ii. 60. 20; iii. 14. 2. — ἀντέλεγον: the impf. because the negotiations were not yet at an end. We should, however, use the plpf. in English.

4. οὔτε ἄλλα δοκεῖ ἡμῖν, οὔτε ἀφαιρησόμεθα: "neither our opinion nor our intention has changed." The theoretical and the practical aspects of the affair are placed side by side. — ἅπερ καί: see on c. 13. 7, ὧν κἀκεῖνος ἐπενόει. — 5. ἑπτακόσια ἔτη: this statement, which is evidently not intended to be exact, carries us back to the time of the Dorian invasion. Conon, narrat. 36, mentions the Spartan Philonomus as founder of Melos soon after the Dorians took possession of Sparta. See Müller, Orchomenos, p. 317. — 7. ἐκ τοῦ θείου: opp. to ἀπὸ τῶν ἀνθρώπων, with reference to c. 105. 5 ff.; 11 ff. τὸ θεῖον is further explained by τύχη, and οἱ ἄνθρωποι by Λακεδαιμόνιοι, the whole being arranged in chiastic order. καὶ Λακεδαιμονίων, which St. rejects, should therefore be retained. καί introduces the specification of ἀνθρώπων, and is equiv. to et — quidem.

9. παρακαλούμεθα κτέ.: first comes the proposal of the Melians as it affects themselves (φίλοι . . . μηδετέροις), then as it affects the Athenians. This is equiv. to ἡμῶν φίλων ὄντων ὑμῖν, πολεμίων δὲ μηδετέροις, ὑμᾶς ἐκ τῆς γῆς ἡμῶν ἀναχωρῆσαι. — 10. φίλοι: nom. referring to the subj. of προκαλούμεθα. G. 136, N. 3 (a); H. 940. — 12. ἐπιτήδειοι: elsewhere this adj. has three terminations. Cf. c. 21. 7; 81. 9; viii. 11. 12.

ναῖοι διαλυόμενοι ἤδη ἐκ τῶν λόγων ἔφασαν· "'Αλλ' οὖν μόνοι γε ἀπὸ τούτων τῶν βουλευμάτων, ὡς ἡμῖν δοκεῖτε, τὰ μὲν μέλλοντα τῶν ὁρωμένων σαφέστερα κρίνετε, τὰ δὲ ἀφανῆ τῷ βούλεσθαι ὡς γιγνόμενα ἤδη θεᾶσθε, καὶ Λακεδαιμονίοις καὶ τύχῃ καὶ ἐλπίσι πλεῖστον δὴ παραβεβλημένοι καὶ πιστεύσαντες πλεῖστον καὶ σφαλήσεσθε."

114 Καὶ οἱ μὲν 'Αθηναίων πρέσβεις ἀνεχώρησαν ἐς 1 τὸ στράτευμα· οἱ δὲ στρατηγοὶ αὐτῶν, ὡς οὐδὲν ὑπήκουον οἱ Μήλιοι, πρὸς πόλεμον εὐθὺς ἐτρέποντο καὶ διελόμενοι κατὰ πόλεις περιετείχισαν κύκλῳ τοὺς Μηλίους. καὶ ὕστερον φυλακὴν σφῶν τε αὐτῶν καὶ τῶν ξυμμάχων 2 καταλιπόντες οἱ 'Αθηναῖοι καὶ κατὰ γῆν καὶ κατὰ θάλασ-

113. 2. διαλυόμενοι ἤδη: as they were on the point of leaving. διαλύεσθαι as in ii. 12. 13; vi. 41. 16, διελύθησαν ἐκ τοῦ ξυλλόγου. ἐκ τῶν λόγων (cf. c. 112. 1) is the opposite of ἐς λόγους (cf. iii. 8. 6; iv. 38. 4; 73. 33). — ἀλλ' οὖν: well then. This introduces the final summing up of the result of the conference. — 3. ἀπὸ τούτων τῶν βουλευμάτων: judging from the conclusion at which you have arrived. — 4. τὰ ὁρώμενα: that which lies before your eyes. Cf. ii. 42. 21; iii. 45. 23. — 5. τῷ βούλεσθαι: equiv. to βουλήσει ἀσαφεῖ in iv. 108. 21. — 6. παραβεβλημένοι καὶ πιστεύσαντες: with these words πλεῖστον (6) is to be taken adv. being most entirely given over to (the Lacedaemonians, etc.) and having trusted them most entirely. παραβεβλημένοι is pass., as in Ar. Pl. 243, πόρναισι καὶ κύβοισι παραβεβλημένος. The pf. partic. is used because this expresses a trait of the character of the Melians; the aor. partic. πιστεύσαντες is used to refer to the action of the Melians in putting their faith in the Lacedaemonians, etc., in this particular instance. Cf. ἐλθόντας καὶ κεκτημένους, vii. 66. 6. Kr. Spr. § 56, 14. This explanation of St. makes it unnecessary to strike out either καὶ πιστεύσαντες (with v. Herwerden) or καί (with Cl., who takes παραβεβλημένοι as mid., having risked, with πλεῖστον as its obj.).

114. After the conference has come to an end, the Athenians invest the town, and begin the siege with part of their army.

2. οὐδὲν ὑπήκουον: a common expression. Cf. i. 26. 16; 29. 1. — 3. ἐτρέποντο: the impf. denoting the beginning of the new course of action is the reading of the best Mss. though many editt. read ἐτράποντο. Cf. vii. 71. 13. In i. 5. 4 and ii. 52. 11, ἐτράποντο denotes also the accomplishment; hence the aor. — διελόμενοι περιετείχισαν: cf. c. 75. 22, where the impf. περιετείχιζον is used because the building of the wall was a work of some time, and was, in fact, never finished. — 5. φυλακὴν καταλιπόντες ... ἀνεχώρησαν: so also in ii. 78. 6 ff.

σαν ἀνεχώρησαν τῷ πλείονι τοῦ στρατοῦ, οἱ δὲ λειπόμενοι παραμένοντες ἐπολιόρκουν τὸ χωρίον.

115 Καὶ Ἀργεῖοι κατὰ τὸν χρόνον τὸν αὐτὸν ἐσβαλόντες ἐς τὴν Φλιασίαν καὶ λοχισθέντες ὑπό τε Φλιασίων καὶ τῶν σφετέρων φυγάδων διεφθάρησαν ὡς ὀγδοήκοντα, καὶ οἱ ἐκ τῆς Πύλου Ἀθηναῖοι Λακεδαιμονίων πολ-
5 λὴν λείαν ἔλαβον. καὶ Λακεδαιμόνιοι δι' αὐτὸ τὰς μὲν 2 σπονδὰς οὐδ' ὣς ἀφέντες ἐπολέμουν αὐτοῖς, ἐκήρυξαν δὲ εἴ τις βούλεται παρὰ σφῶν Ἀθηναίους λῄζεσθαι. καὶ 3 Κορίνθιοι ἐπολέμησαν ἰδίων τινῶν διαφορῶν ἕνεκα τοῖς Ἀθηναίοις· οἱ δ' ἄλλοι Πελοποννήσιοι ἡσύχαζον. εἷλον 4
10 δὲ καὶ οἱ Μήλιοι τῶν Ἀθηναίων τοῦ περιτειχίσματος τὸ κατὰ τὴν ἀγορὰν προσβαλόντες νυκτός, καὶ ἄνδρας τε ἀπέκτειναν καὶ ἐσενεγκάμενοι σῖτόν τε καὶ ὅσα πλεῖστα ἐδύναντο χρήσιμα ἀναχωρήσαντες ἡσύχαζον· καὶ οἱ Ἀθηναῖοι ἄμεινον τὴν φυλακὴν τὸ ἔπειτα παρεσκευάζοντο,
15 * καὶ τὸ θέρος ἐτελεύτα.

— 6. καὶ κατὰ γῆν καὶ κατὰ θάλασσαν: const. with φυλακὴν καταλιπόντες.
115. *Hostilities in various parts of Peloponnesus. The Melians make a successful sally against the Athenians.*
1. καὶ Ἀργεῖοι κτέ.: they had done the same thing the previous year. See c. 83. 10 ff. — τὸν χρόνον τὸν αὐτόν: the order of words as in τῇ ἐπιχειρήσει τῇ αὐτῇ, vii. 39. 2. — 2. λοχισθέντες: *falling into an ambuscade*, pass. of λοχίζειν, the act. of which is used in iii. 107. 18, where, however, the troops employed in the ambush are the dir. obj. of the action of the verb.
— 3. διεφθάρησαν ὡς ὀγδοήκοντα: the general subj. Ἀργεῖοι is limited in the course of the period. *Cf.* c. 10. 47 ff.; 59. 1 ff.
4. οἱ ἐκ τῆς Πύλου Ἀθηναῖοι: *cf.* c.

56. 11, where the sending of fresh forces is mentioned. — 6. ἀφέντες τὰς σπονδάς: *cf.* ἀφέντες τὴν ξυμμαχίαν, c. 78. 6; i. 102. 19. — οὐδ' ὥς: const. with ἐπολέμουν, not merely with ἀφέντες. There was as yet no renewal of the war, for this is not recorded until vi. 105. 5. — 7. εἴ τις βούλεται ... λῄζεσθαι: on the ellipsis, see on i. 27. 4; iii. 52. 11; iv. 37. 8. — παρὰ σφῶν: *cf.* ii. 41. 3.
8. διαφορῶν: see App.
10. τὸ κατὰ τὴν ἀγοράν: this must refer to that part of the Athenian camp which was used as a market. *Cf.* i. 62. 4; iii. 6. 12. — 12. ἐσενεγκάμενοι: equiv. to ἐσκομισάμενοι. *Cf.* i. 117. 5; vi. 22. 6. — 13. χρήσιμα: see App. — 14. τὸ ἔπειτα: *after this. Cf.* iv. 54. 14; 170. 2.

116 Τοῦ δ' ἐπιγιγνομένου χειμῶνος Λακεδαιμόνιοι μελ- 1
λήσαντες ἐς τὴν Ἀργείαν στρατεύειν, ὡς αὐτοῖς τὰ διαβατήρια ἱερὰ ἐν τοῖς ὁρίοις οὐκ ἐγίγνετο, ἀνεχώρησαν.
καὶ Ἀργεῖοι διὰ τὴν ἐκείνων μέλλησιν τῶν ἐν τῇ πόλει
5 τινὰς ὑποπτεύσαντες τοὺς μὲν ξυνέλαβον, οἱ δ' αὐτοὺς
καὶ διέφυγον. καὶ οἱ Μήλιοι περὶ τοὺς αὐτοὺς χρόνους 2
αὖθις καθ' ἕτερόν τι τοῦ περιτειχίσματος εἷλον τῶν Ἀθηναίων, παρόντων οὐ πολλῶν τῶν φυλάκων. καὶ ἐλθού- 3
σης στρατιᾶς ὕστερον ἐκ τῶν Ἀθηνῶν ἄλλης, [ὡς ταῦτα
10 ἐγίγνετο], ἧς ἦρχε Φιλοκράτης ὁ Δημέου, καὶ κατὰ κράτος ἤδη πολιορκούμενοι, γενομένης καὶ προδοσίας τινὸς
ἀφ' ἑαυτῶν, ξυνεχώρησαν τοῖς Ἀθηναίοις ὥστ' ἐκείνους
περὶ αὐτῶν βουλεῦσαι. οἱ δὲ ἀπέκτειναν Μηλίων ὅσους 4
ἡβῶντας ἔλαβον, παῖδας δὲ καὶ γυναῖκας ἠνδραπόδισαν.
15 τὸ δὲ χωρίον αὐτοὶ ᾤκισαν, ἀποίκους ὕστερον πεντακοσίους πέμψαντες.

116. *Prosecutions at Argos for political reasons. The Melians make another sally, but the Athenians, having received reinforcements, oblige the town to surrender, and treat the inhabitants with great severity.*

2. μελλήσαντες: aor., *when they had prepared everything* for the expedition. *Cf.* i. 134. 16; viii. 23. 28. — 3. ἱερὰ ἐν τοῖς ὁρίοις: see App. — 4. διὰ τὴν ἐκείνων μέλλησιν: this corresponds to μελλήσαντες of 2, "because of this plan of the Lacedaemonians, of which they had heard." See Grote, VI. c. 56, p. 372. — 5. ὑποπτεύσαντες: see App.

7. καθ' ἕτερόν τι: *at another point* (than that κατὰ τὴν ἀγοράν; *cf.* c. 115. 11). τι is limited by τοῦ περτειχίσματος.

9. ὡς ταῦτα ἐγίγνετο: this is a superfluous and awkward addition, and Cl. and others are prob. right in rejecting it. — 11. γενομένης καὶ προδοσίας: *when treason had also made its appearance. Cf.* iv. 103. 20, ἅμα τῆς προδοσίας οὔσης. — 12. ἀφ' ἑαυτῶν: *from among themselves.* — 12. ὥστε: *on condition that.* See on i. 28. 18; 29. 22. GMT. 98, 2; H. 953 b.

12. ἀπέκτειναν: at the instigation of Alcibiades, acc. to Andoc. iv. 22 and Plut. *Alc.* 16, who uses the expression ἀποσφαγῆναι, *i.e.* they were killed by the sword. So Diod. xii. 80. 55 says ἀποσφάξαι. — 15. ᾤκισαν: with good Mss. instead of ᾤκησαν. For such a new settlement ᾤκισαν is the proper expression. See on i. 98. 4; ii. 70. 21.

APPENDIX.

1. 1. αἱ μὲν ἐνιαύσιοι σπονδαὶ διελέλυντο μέχρι Πυθίων. The difficulty of this passage arises from the fact that whereas the truce had, acc. to iv. 118. 48, been ended since the 14th of Elaphebolion (about the end of March) and the plpf. διελέλυντο refers to past time, a temporal limitation, *until the Pythian games*, is added which refers to the future. The sense is: "In the following summer there was a period (after the 14th of Elaphebolion) when the year's truce had expired (which period lasted) until the Pythian games. And in the ἐκεχειρία (at the very end of this period) the Athenians removed the Delians," *etc.* In c. 2 the narrative proceeds: "but Cleon," *etc.* Here δέ corresponds to μέν in c. 1. 1. This is essentially the explanation offered by Herbst, Philol. 42, p. 662 ff. and adopted in the main by Schütz, Ztschr. f. d. Gymn. Wesen, 31, p. 246.

Cl. offers two explanations. According to the first, Thuc. originally intended to write: "The truce had, to be sure, come to an end in March, but not until August did Cleon finish the necessary preparations and set out with the expedition for Thrace." Into this simple account he may, then, have inserted the mention of the second purification of Delos, for which the sacred truce of the Pythian games was the time chosen. Being led in this way to mention the games, he connected them loosely with what precedes by the expression μέχρι Πυθίων, and then, with reference to the games, gave the needful clear statement of time by ἐν τῇ ἐκεχειρίᾳ and, c. 2. 2, μετὰ τὴν ἐκεχειρίαν. Without this addition, which may have been made at a later time, the passage would read: τοῦ δ' ἐπιγιγνομένου θέρους αἱ μὲν ἐνιαύσιοι σπονδαὶ διελέλυντο · Κλέων δὲ 'Αθηναίους πείσας μεσοῦντος ἤδη τοῦ θέρους ἐς τὰ ἐπὶ Θράκης χωρία ἐξέπλευσεν.

In his second explanation, Cl. proposes to take μέχρι in the sense of "with the exception of," for which he cites Plat. *Legg.* vi. 772 a; γυμνοὺς καὶ μέχρι περ αἰδοῦς σώφρονος, *naked, all but* ("bis auf"), *etc.*, and a fragment of the comic poet Machon in Athen. xiii. p. 581 f. verse 40, ἄνθρωπον ἄχρι τοῦ στόματος ἠσβολωμένον, *a man blackened with soot up to* ("bis auf") *his mouth.* Then the passage under discussion would mean: "The truce for one year had come to an end (on the 14th of Elaphebolion), and there was war again with the exception of (the time of) the Pythian games." The words καὶ ἐν τῇ ἐκεχειρίᾳ serve to explain the unusual expression μέχρι Πυθίων: "and it was just in the time of the truce resulting from this festival that the Athenians undertook the purification of Delos," which, as a religious act, presupposes a condition of peace.

168   APPENDIX.

Müller-Strübing, *Aristophanes und die hist. Krit.*, p. 392, note, thinks something has been lost, and proposes to supply ἀναβολὴ δὲ ἦν (or ἐγένετο) τοῦ πολέμου, or words to that effect, after διελέλυντο. Philippi, Rhein. Mus. 36, p. 254, proposes to read διελέλυντο, καὶ ἐν τῇ μέχρι Πυθίων (ἔτι) ἐκεχειρίᾳ Ἀθηναῖοι κτλ. This would assist St.'s explanation which follows.

St., in his note on this passage, says: αἱ ἐνιαύσιοι σπονδαὶ διελέλυντο μέχρι Πυθίων idem valet quod τῶν ἐνιαυσίων σπονδῶν διάλυσις ἦν μέχρι Πυθίων pariter atque iv. 16. § 2, ἐσπείσθαι δὲ αὐτὰς μέχρι οὗ ἐπανέλθωσιν nihil aliud est quam εἶναι δὲ τὰς σπονδὰς μέχρι οὗ ἐπανέλθωσιν. Est autem διάλυσις τῶν σπονδῶν is rerum status quo foedus exiit needum bellum renovatum est, qui medius inter bellum et pacem status deinde ἐκεχειρία dicitur. To this Cl. observes that Thuc. always (*i.e.* in iv. 58. 2; 117. 2, 15; 118. 46; 119. 11; 122. 3; 123. 3; 134. 2; v. 15. 10; 26. 14; 32. 22; 49. 14; vi. 26. 9) uses ἐκεχειρία to denote a truce based upon special treaty or religious agreement, and that the preps. ἐν (τῇ ἐκεχειρίᾳ) and μετά (τὴν ἐκεχειρίαν) seem to indicate that the time referred to was clearly defined. The word cannot, therefore, be used of a "state between war and peace." οἱ before Ἀθηναῖοι is the reading of Vat.

Kirchhoff (Monatsberichte d. Berlin Akad. 1864, p. 129 ff.) has proved by the testimony of an inscription from Delphi, that the Pythian games were held in the Delphic month Bucatius, and therefore in the Attic month Metageitnion. (This was the opinion of Krüger, Weissenborn, and Grote. Boeckh and Clinton wrongly placed the Pythian games in the Attic month Munychion.)

1. 5. ᾗ πρότερόν μοι δεδήλωται. Cl. puts a comma after δεδήλωται, making these words a parenthetical clause with which he supplies Δῆλον καθαρθῆναι. In support of this understanding of the passage, he cites iii. 104. He adds that ᾗ ... δεδήλωται would be simpler. Then ὡς ἀνελόντες ... ποιῆσαι would recapitulate the manner of the purification. The explanation given in the note is that of Kr.

2. 7. Κωφὸν λιμένα. A sure emendation of Pluygers after Strabo vii. frg. 32. The Mss. give Κολοφωνίων λιμένα.

2. 10. ἐς τὴν πόλιν. Cobet, Mnem. 14, p. 3, proposes ἐπὶ τὴν πόλιν.

2. 11. ἐς τὸν λιμένα. Rightly corrected by Bekker for τὸν λιμένα, as is seen from c. 3. 4.

3. 4. περιέπλεον περιπεμφθεῖσαι. Cl., following Haacke, inserts αἱ after περιέπλεον. This would be more regular, but is not necessary, esp. as περιπεμφθεῖσαι is not necessarily attrib.

4. 9. Συρακοσίοις, Συρακούσας: these forms of the names of the city and its inhabitants are those adopted by most editt., though the spelling in the Mss. is far from uniform. The Vat. has usually Συρακοῦσαι and Συρακούσσιοι. See Buttmann, *Ausf. Sprachl.* § 21, N. 9.

4. 24. αἰσθόμενος. Cobet, Mnem. 14, p. 4, proposes οἰόμενος, which may be correct, as αἰσθόμενος is rarely const. with the inf. But see Kühn. 484, 4. *Cf.* iii. 38. 27; vi. 59. 10; Plat. *Phaedr.* 235 c.

5. 8. [τοῖς κομιζομένοις]. Cl. brackets these words; other editt. reject only τοῖς. These Locrians were on the way home, and perhaps instead of omitting τοῖς κομιζομένοις, it would be simpler to read (with Cobet, Mnem. 14, p. 4) ἐπ' οἴκου κομιζομένοις.
5. 13. Ἰπωνιέας καὶ Μεδμαίους. The Mss. give Ἰτωνέας καὶ Μελαίους. Weidner (see Rhein. Mus. 9, p. 141) recognized the places referred to in Strabo, vi. 5, and corrected to Ἱππωνιάτας καὶ Μεδμαίους. Beloch (Jahrbb. 1881, p. 392), with the help of coins of Hipponium, corrects to the form given in the text.
7. 6. ξυνῆλθον. Dobree, Ullrich, and Cl. read ξυνεξῆλθον. But the repetition of ἐξ seems in this case hardly necessary.
7. 7. καὶ οὐ βουλόμενος, αὐτοὺς διὰ τὸ ἐν τῷ αὐτῷ καθημένους βαρύνεσθαι ἀναλαβὼν ἦγε. Cl. punctuates with a comma after βαρύνεσθαι, with no comma after βουλόμενος. He explains: "not wishing them to be depressed by remaining in inactivity." διὰ τὸ ἐν τῷ αὐτῷ καθημένους is, according to this view (which is also held by Jowett), equiv. to διὰ τὸ ἐν τῷ αὐτῷ καθῆσθαι. This use of the partic. might be adopted here if anywhere because of the awkwardness which the two infs. καθῆσθαι βαρύνεσθαι would present. Cl. gives two other examples of the same const. in Thuc.: iv. 63. 2, διὰ τὸ ἤδη φοβεροὺς παρόντας Ἀθηναίους, and viii. 105. 10, διὰ τὸ κρατήσαντες ἀδεῶς. In his App. on iv. 63. 2, he explains the use of the partic. (for the inf.) in these three passages, as a result of the nature of the partic., which, as a part of speech, stands midway between verb and noun, and compares it with other uses of the partic. (such as those mentioned in GMT. 108, n. 4). Although Thuc. may have employed the partic. as Cl. thinks, for the syntax of Thuc. is sometimes tentative and hence not unnaturally at variance with that of later writers, it may be better to adopt St.'s explanation and punctuate after βουλόμενος: "although he did not wish it, he put his forces in motion because they were being depressed by remaining too long inactive." This involves the necessity of taking καὶ οὐ βουλόμενος in a concessive sense: "although he did not wish it"; but there is no objection to this. That οὐ βουλόμενος in this sense does not occur elsewhere in Thuc. is doubtless merely the result of chance.
A. von Velsen (sched. crit. p. 13 ff.) regards διὰ τὸ ἐν τῷ αὐτῷ καθημένους βαρύνεσθαι not as the obj. of οὐ βουλόμενος, but as a repetition of the idea expressed in τῶν στρατιωτῶν ἀχθομένων τῇ ἕδρᾳ, and thinks a second inf. ἀτολμοτέρους γίγνεσθαι, belonging to αὐτούς, is needed after βαρύνεσθαι. Thuc. may well have been guilty of such an omission, for the verb to be supplied for αὐτούς would naturally seem almost like a repetition of βαρύνεσθαι.
7. 20. οὐκ ἀνῆλθεν. Corrected by Haacke for οὐ κατῆλθεν of the Mss.
9. 5. ἵνα μή τῳ τὸ κατ' ὀλίγον ... ἀτολμίαν παράσχῃ. Most Mss. and the best ones read: ἵνα μὴ τῷ τε κατ' ὀλίγον κτέ. Bekker, Kr., and Poppo, feeling the need of a subj. for φαινόμενον παράσχῃ, wrote μὴ τό τε. Cl., as well as Bekker, saw that since κατ' ὀλίγον and μὴ απαντας express the same idea, they cannot be connected by τε, καί (Böhme cites ii. 2. 19 against this view,

but there ἐν εἰρήνῃ denotes the condition or circumstances, while τοῦ πολέμου μήπω φανεροῦ καθεστῶτος denotes the time). Consequently Cl. adopts Poppo's conjecture, and writes ἵνα μή τῳ τὸ κατ' ὀλίγον. When once the indef. pron. τῳ had been misunderstood and its place taken by the art., the change of the following τό to τε was very natural. The reading μή τῳ τό is eminently satisfactory; for (1) we are not obliged to supply from ἐπιχείρησιν some word like ἐπιχειρεῖν as subj. of ἐνδεὲς φαινόμενον ἀτολμίαν παράσχῃ instead of the natural and simple subj. τό ... κινδυνεύειν, and (2) by means of the indef. pron. τῳ both φαινόμενον and παράσχῃ receive a personal application which is almost necessary in a lively speech like that of Brasidas. Similar expressions in giving admonition or advice occur freq. in other speeches. *Cf.* i. 33. 17; ii. 63. 7; vi. 33. 16; and in Brasidas's former speech, iv. 86. 9.

9. 20. ξυνταθῆναι. Krüger followed by St. and Cl. for Mss. ξυνταχθῆναι, since the real opposition to τὸ ἀνειμένον appears only in ξυντείνεσθαι, not in ξυντάττεσθαι, and the same expression occurs in Xen. *Oec.* 2. 18, συντεταμένῃ γνώμῃ.

9. 31. νομίσατε τρία εἶναι τοῦ καλῶς πολεμεῖν. The Mss. omit τρία. St. (followed by Cl.) is undoubtedly right in restoring τρία from Stob. *Flor.* II. p. 326, ed. Meineke. The Schol., too, says: ὅτι ἐκ τριῶν γίγνεται τὸ καλῶς πολεμεῖν. Nothing is more easily lost in Mss. than numerals. Besides, as St. shows, Thuc. likes numerical expressions in sententious remarks. *Cf.* i. 33. 23; 74. 3; 122. 22; iii. 40. 6; iv. 64. 19. It is also necessary that the three infs. which follow should form parallel expressions, *i.e.* that they should all have the art. or all be without it. If the first and second infs. have the art., and the third does not, we should have only two alternatives, the first expressed by τὸ ἐθέλειν, the second by τὸ αἰσχύνεσθαι καὶ πείθεσθαι. St. and Cl. therefore insert τό before τοῖς ἄρχουσι πείθεσθαι. The loss of τό before τοῖς is easily explained.

9. 37. καὶ δουλείαν. Schütz, Ztschr. f. d. Gymn. Wesen 31, p. 249, following Böhme, thinks ὑπάρχειν must be supplied with δουλείαν to complete a chiastic arrangement by which δουλείαν is opp. to ἐλευθερίαν and Ἀθηναίων δούλοις to Λακεδαιμονίων ξυμμάχοις. Then κεκλῆσθαι must be understood with Ἀθηναίων δούλοις.

10. 9. ὑπὸ τὰς πύλας ἵππων τε πόδες πολλοὶ καὶ ἀνθρώπων ὡς ἐξιόντων ὑποφαίνονται. Naber, Mnem. 14, p. 316, calls attention to the fact that this spying under the gate is unnecessary, not to say absurd, in view of 1. 5, ἐν τῇ πόλει ἐπιφανεῖ οὔσῃ ἔξωθεν περὶ τὸ ἱερὸν τῆς Ἀθηνᾶς θυομένου (sc. Βρασίδου), which Grote, VI. c. 54, p. 248, renders: "so conspicuous was the interior of the city to spectators without, that the temple of Athênê, and Brasidas with its ministers around him, performing the ceremony of sacrifice, was distinctly recognized." If the interior of the city was so conspicuous, why should the scouts expose themselves to useless danger by spying under the gates? Naber proposes σποδὸς πολλὴ ... ὑποφαίνεται for πόδες πολλοὶ ... ὑποφαίνονται. This cloud of dust could be seen from any point from which

the interior of the city was visible. Though this conjecture may be incorrect, the explanation (of Cl.) given in the note does not seem entirely satisfactory.

10. 16. σχολῇ, with Kr., St., and Böhme for σχολή (*cf.* i. 142. 2; iii. 46. 10). The subj. of γίγνεσθαι (what he has commanded) must be supplied from the preceding words, as often with παρεσκεύαστο. *Cf.* i. 46. 1; iv. 67. 2.

10. 39. τὸ δὲ δεξιὸν τῶν Ἀθηναίων ... αὐτοὺς ἔτρεψαν. For a proper appreciation of this passage, a clear understanding of the narrative is necessary. Thuc., who doubtless possessed most accurate information concerning the details of the events at Amphipolis, inasmuch as his Thracian property was in the immediate neighbourhood, certainly ascribes the defeat of the Athenians in great measure to Cleon's foolishness and bad generalship. Cleon's conduct, from the moment when he is first opposed to Brasidas, lacks firmness and method. He sets his forces in motion merely to appease the discontent of his men, and always takes up his position with the intention of avoiding a battle (ἀπιέναι ἐνόμιζε, ὁπόταν βούληται, ἀμαχεί, c. 7. 17). Brasidas succeeds by a well-planned and well-executed attack in throwing the Athenian troops on both wings into confusion; but the left wing, which was already retreating, is able to escape and continue the retreat. The right wing, on the contrary, against which Brasidas himself charged (and was mortally wounded) stood its ground longer. Cleon, to be sure, ran away as he had all along intended to do, and was presently killed by a Myrcinian peltast; but the hoplites on the right wing, who had formed in close array at this point, defended themselves bravely for some time, until the constant attacks of the enemy's cavalry forced them at last to take to flight.

In this account a form of expression which is often used in narration occurs twice, — a general statement is followed by a more particular statement of details, the parts of which are introduced by καί — μέν — δέ. So after ξυνέβη τοὺς Ἀθηναίους θορυβηθῆναι in 33, the two parts follow: καὶ τὸ μὲν εὐώνυμον κέρας ... ἀπορραγὲν ἔφυγε (34–36) and τὸ δὲ δεξιὸν ... ἔμενε (39), and again after this general statement: καὶ ὁ μὲν Κλέων ... ἀποθνῄσκει (40–42) and οἱ δὲ ... ἔτρεψαν (42–46). This careful and elaborate structure of the period makes it prob. that the clearly expressed subj. καὶ ὁ μὲν Κλέων is opposed to an equally clearly expressed substantive subj. οἱ δὲ αὐτοῦ ξυστραφέντες ὁπλῖται. St., who rejects Cl.'s explanation as given above, strikes out ὁπλῖται, taking οἱ αὐτοῦ in the sense of sui, like τοῖς ἑαυτῶν in viii. 45. 14. He then takes ξυστραφέντες as pred. with ἐπὶ τὸν λόφον, which he explains by reference to c. 7. 15. This explanation is, on the whole, less satisfactory than Cl.'s.

10. 47. οὕτω δή. This is the only proper introduction for the ultimate consequence instead of οὕτω δέ of the Mss. *Cf.* iv. 30. 7; 73. 27, and the numerous dependent clauses introduced by οὕτω δή, *e.g.* i. 131. 8; ii. 12. 16, etc.

11. 4. περιέρξαντες. The reading of the best Mss. (*cf.* Soph. *Aj.* 593, ξυνέρξετε), although we find in Thuc. εἴργειν and εἰρχθῆναι, iv. 63. 5; v. 49. 3; ἀπείρξει, iii. 45. 9, and ἀπεῖρξαν, iv. 37. 4.

172   APPENDIX.

11. 5. ἥρῳ. More correct than ἥρωι acc. to Hdn. ii. 714: τὴν δοτικὴν εἰς ι ἀνεκφώνητον ποιοῦσιν οἱ Ἀττικοὶ οἷον τῷ ἥρῳ.

14. 19. ἐδεδίεσαν. Lobeck, *ad Phryn.* p. 181, thinks that here and in iv. 55. 18, the only correct form is ἐδέδισαν. But this is not found in the best Mss. See v. Bamberg. Ztschr. f. d. Gymn. Wesen, 1874, p. 36.

14. 23. ὥστ' ἀδύνατα εἶναι ἐφαίνετο Ἀργείοις καὶ Ἀθηναίοις ἅμα πολεμεῖν. The introduction of this sent. by ὥστε is hard to explain. St., omitting ὥστε and inserting δέ, regards the whole clause as a parenthesis. The clause is thus to be understood as expressing the result of all which precedes. This is also Kr.'s explanation. Cl. thinks this is no great improvement, and suggests ὅλως τ' ἀδύνατα εἶναι ἐφαίνετο, and *it was evidently utterly impossible* (cf. ἁπλῶς τε in iii. 45. 29). Thuc. does not elsewhere use ὅλως, but Cl. thinks it is so common in Plato and the orators that there is no objection to it here.

15. 5. πρῶτοί τε καὶ ὁμοίως σφίσι ξυγγενεῖς. That this reading of the Mss. (which is also that of the Schol. on Ar. *Pax*, 479) is in some way corrupt, is generally acknowledged (Jowett explains ὁμοίως ξυγγενεῖς as meaning either that they were all *equally related* to the first men of the state, or that they were all of the first rank, and *accordingly were related* to the governing body). The trouble has generally been sought in ὁμοίως, which has accordingly been changed to ὁμοίων (Reiske) or ὁμοίοις (Bekker). Herbst, Philol. 16, p. 310, and Steup, Rhein. Mus. 25, p. 304, defend ὁμοίοις. Herbst explains: "for the Spartans among them were the first men of the state, and related to them, who were Homoei"; Steup: "and related to them their peers" (*i.e.* belonging like them to the first and most respected families). Neither of these explanations is thoroughly satisfactory. Steup very properly compares the passage of Plut. *Nic.* 10, οἱ γὰρ ἐκ Πύλου κομισθέντες ἦσαν ἐξ οἴκων τε πρώτων τῆς Σπάρτης καὶ φίλους καὶ ξυγγενεῖς τοὺς δυνατοὺς ἔχοντες. Cl. suggests πρῶτοί τε καὶ οἴκοις ἐπιφανέσι ξυγγενεῖς, and since Steup, p. 287, is certainly right in saying that the 120 Spartans who were captured at Sphacteria could not all belong to the first families, Cl. further suggests that we might read ἦσαν γὰρ οἱ Σπαρτιᾶται αὐτῶν κτέ.: "for there were among them some Spartans of the first rank and related to the most distinguished families." This agrees very well with ἤδη καὶ ἀρχάς τινας ἔχοντας in c. 34. 11. St. accepts Rauchenstein's conjecture (Philol. 36, p. 234) ὅμοιοι σφίσι ξυγγενεῖς, and explains: Spartiatae captivi cum homoei essent, homoeis Lacedaemoniis, qui rei publicae administrationem habebant, cognati erant. On the Homoei, see Schoemann, *Opusc. Acad.* I. p. 108; Gilbert, *Griech. Staatsalt.* I. p. 41; Lachmann, *Spartan. Staatsverf.* p. 222 ff.; Hermann, *Griech. Alterth.* I. § 25, 12 ff.

15. 7. οὔπως. This reading of the best Mss. for οὔπω does not occur elsewhere in Thuc., but Photius and Suid. testify to its use: οὔπως, οὐδένα τρόπον καὶ Θουκιδίδης ἐν ε' καὶ Ὅμηρος. Still, as the corruptions of the Mss. are very old, the reading οὔπως is perhaps somewhat doubtful. See Cobet, Mnem. 14 (1886), p. 6.

APPENDIX. 173

15. 9. ἐνδεξαμένους. St.'s reading, though supported only by a few Mss. and the quotation of Thomas Mag. p. 616, 6, is better than the fut. ἐνδεξομένους. ἂν ἐνδεξαμένους is equiv. to ὅτι ἂν ἐνδέξαιντο; then ἂν ἐνδεξομένους would be equiv. to ὅτι ἂν ἐνδέξοιντο (or ἐνδέξονται); but the fut. opt. (or fut. ind.) in apod. with ἄν is, to say the least, of very doubtful propriety. GMT. 37, 2, N. 1, and 41, 4. Herbst, *Hamburg Progr.* 1867, p. 37 f., thinks differently.

16. 6. τότε δέ. Since all the Mss. read τότε δέ, not δή, it seems best to judge of this case after the analogy of i. 11. 4 and 18. 1. See on i. 11. 4. There is a certain opposition to the previous state of things under Brasidas and Cleon, and this justifies the use of δέ. Kühn. 533, 1. However common the use of τότε δή and οὕτω δή to introduce explanatory and additional clauses may be in Thuc., the present case does not exactly correspond to this usage, since here the description of a gradual influence (σπεύδοντες ... προεθυμοῦντο) is introduced, not of a definite event as in i. 49. 30; 58. 9; ii. 12. 16; iii. 98. 6. St., in his note *ad. loc.*, takes the opposite view.

16. 6. ἑκατέρᾳ τῇ πόλει σπεύδοντες τὰ μάλιστ' αὐτήν. (The vulgate has οἱ ἐν ἑκατέρᾳ τῇ πόλει σπεύδοντες τὰ μάλιστα τὴν ἡγεμονίαν.) So St. restores this passage. σπεύδειν τί τινι is rare, but not unparalled (*cf.* Eur. *Iph. T.* 579), and is supported by general analogy. The corruptions of this passage are of early origin, and have given rise to many attempts at emendation. Now, however, the passage is perfectly clear, and the genesis of the corruptions in the Mss. can be distinctly traced. It begins with the common mistake of μάλιστα τήν for μάλιστ' αὐτήν (*cf.* c. 38. 17). Then the art. was utterly senseless without a subst., and some copyist supplied from what he understood of the context ἡγεμονίαν, thinking this would be properly used in connexion with the men who stood at the head of their respective states. Some one else, who thought personal leadership, not the hegemony of the state was meant, inserted οἱ ἐν before ἑκατέρᾳ in order to define the position of Pleistoanax and Nicias, and this reading, which is that of some Mss., was accepted by some editt. before Bekker. That this is wrong, is generally recognized by recent editt., and various emendations for ἡγεμονίαν have been proposed, such as ἡσυχίαν, ὁμόνοιαν, ὁμολογίαν, and ἠρεμίαν, but all in vain. By removing the additions arising from the original mistake, St. has in all probability restored the passage to its original form. Now the partic. σπεύδοντες clearly expresses the common motive of Nicias and Pleistoanax, and πολλῷ δὴ μᾶλλον προεθυμοῦντο, standing at the end of the passage, shows the effect of the events recorded in the preceding chaps. Müller-Strübing, *Aristoph. und die hist. Krit.* p. 634, proposes to read διαβάλλων, ἄλλως τε καὶ ἑκατέρᾳ τῇ πόλει σπεύδοντες τὰ μάλιστα τὴν ἡγεμονίαν· τότε δὴ Πλειστοάναξ ὁ Παυσανίου βασιλεὺς Λακεδαιμονίων κτέ. This sounds well, but there is no reason to think that Thuc. wrote it.

16. 18. ἐνθυμίαν. Cobet, Mnem. 14, p. 7, is probably right in changing ἐνθυμίαν to ἐνθύμιον, a word of much more frequent occurrence.

16. 23. ἀδελφοῦ. Cobet, Mnem. 14, p 8, suggests Δελφοῦ. These two words are freq. confused. So the modern inhabitants of the site of Delphi imagined a story about some brothers (ἀδελφοί) to account for the name Δελφοί applied by travellers to the place.

16. 28. δοκοῦσαν. The reading δοκοῦσαν seems to be assured by the agreement of the best Mss. It is more doubtful whether Thuc. wrote the concise expression μετὰ δώρων in the sense of "bribery." All the Mss. collated by Bekker insert ἕως after δοκοῦσαν, but this gives no sense. We must therefore recognize in ἕως the remnant of some word which was early corrupted. Perhaps the original reading was: διὰ τὴν ἐκ τῆς Ἀττικῆς ποτὲ μετὰ δωροδοκήσεως (not δωροδόκησιν, as others following Suid. s.v. δώρων δόκησιν, have suggested) δοκοῦσαν ἀναχώρησιν. The various corruptions of the Mss. arise from the juxtaposition of -δοκήσεως and δοκοῦσαν both beginning with the same letters. St. now reads μετὰ δώρων δοκήσεως ἀναχώρησιν. None of the various conjectures seem certain.

17. 6. καὶ τόν τε χειμῶνα τοῦτον ἦσαν ἐς λόγους. Julius Steup has subjected the text from c. 13 to this point to careful investigation and criticism (Rhein. Mus. 25, p. 273–305). He tries to prove that there are a number of interpolations, and after removing these from c. 13–17, he comes to the conclusion that the original and genuine narrative of Thuc. consists of the following words: τοῦ δ' ἐπιγιγνομένου χειμῶνος εὐθὺς μέχρι μὲν Πιερίου τῆς Θεσσαλίας διῆλθον οἱ περὶ τὸν Ῥαμφίαν, κωλυόντων δὲ τῶν Θεσσαλῶν, καὶ ἅμα Βρασίδου τεθνεῶτος ᾧπερ ἦγον τὴν στρατιάν, ἀπετράποντο ἐπ' οἴκου. ξυνέβη τε εὐθὺς μετὰ τὴν ἐν Ἀμφιπόλει μάχην καὶ τὴν Ῥαμφίου ἀναχώρησιν ἐκ Θεσσαλίας ὥστε πολέμου μὲν μηδὲν ἔτι ἅψασθαι μηδετέρους, πρὸς δὲ τὴν εἰρήνην μᾶλλον τὴν γνώμην εἶχον, οἱ μὲν Ἀθηναῖοι πληγέντες ἐπὶ τῷ Δηλίῳ καὶ δι' ὀλίγου αὖθις ἐν Ἀμφιπόλει καὶ οὐκ ἔχοντες τὴν ἐλπίδα τῆς ῥώμης πιστὴν ἔτι, ᾗπερ οὐ προσεδέχοντο πρότερον τὰς σπονδάς, δοκοῦντες τῇ παρούσῃ εὐτυχίᾳ καθυπέρτεροι γενήσεσθαι. οἱ δ' αὖ Λακεδαιμόνιοι (or καὶ οὐχ ἧσσον οἱ Λακεδαιμόνιοι) ἐπιθυμίᾳ τῶν ἀνδρῶν τῶν ἐκ τῆς νήσου κομίσασθαι. ξυνέβαινε δὲ καὶ πρὸς τοὺς Ἀργείους αὐτοῖς τὰς τριακονταέτεις σπονδὰς ἐπ' ἐξόδῳ εἶναι, καὶ ἄλλας οὐκ ἤθελον σπένδεσθαι οἱ Ἀργεῖοι, εἰ μή τις αὐτοῖς τὴν Κυνοσουρίαν γῆν ἀποδώσει, ὥστε ἄφυκτα (conjecture for ἀδύνατα) εἶναι ἐφαίνετο Ἀργείοις καὶ Ἀθηναίοις ἅμα πολεμεῖν.

The notes on c. 13. 7; 14. 1 and 4; 24. 12, and those on c. 15, 16, and 17 explain the passages which Steup rejects, and show their connexion with the rest of the narrative. We must not lose sight of the evident purpose of Thuc. to show how internal relations and the feelings which prevailed at Sparta and Athens paved the way for peace. It is therefore natural that a detailed exposition of these relations and feelings should form the transition from the account of the last warlike undertakings (the battle of Amphipolis and the march of the 900 hoplites under Rhamphias) to the description of the negotiations for peace. Seen in this light, the fact that the author recurs to what he has previously told, and that he gives various reasons for the same thought regarded from different sides, is not so remarkable as it appears

APPENDIX. 175

to Steup (p. 279 f). It cannot be denied that several passages in the chapters in question contain corruptions of early origin. Such are esp. c. 14. 23; 15. 4, 5; 16. 7 and 28, which have been discussed above. Steup rightly observes (p. 301) that in the four or five chapters in question four words occur which are not found elsewhere in Thuc.; but this is not a strong argument against the genuineness of our text, for it is well known that hardly any writer has more ἅπαξ εἰρημένα than Thuc.; and the four words, διαγίγνεσθαι, ἐνθυμία (ἐνθύμιον?) ἀνεπίληπτος and οὕπως (possibly οὕπω!) are in themselves unobjectionable. On the other hand, οὕπως in c. 15. 7 is expressly cited by Photius, Suid. (Θουκιδίδης ἐν ε´); Plut. de Pyth. orac. 403 B, mentions the oracle of c. 16. 26; and the Schol. on Ar. Pax, 479, gives a long quotation from c. 15. § 1. These are such strong arguments for the genuineness of our text, that only the most urgent necessity would justify us in overruling them by the assumption of a far earlier interpolation (Steup, p. 303).

17. 7. ἦσαν. This form is preferable to ᾖσαν or ᾔεσαν of most Mss. See App. on i. 1. 5.

17. 9. ὡς ἐς ἐπιτειχισμόν. Poppo's conjecture, adopted by St. and Cl., for ὡς ἐπὶ τειχισμόν. The Schol. explains correctly: ὡς μελλόντων φρούρια ἐπιτειχίσειν ἐν τῇ Ἀττικῇ τῶν Λακεδαιμονίων, which would not be sufficiently expressed by τειχισμόν.

17. 12. ὥστε ἃ ἑκάτεροι . . . , τὴν Νίσαιαν. Steup, Stud. I. p. 55–59, comes to the conclusion that these words, which do not accord with the following treaty of peace, are not part of the account of Thuc., but an interpolation.

18. 1. Σπονδὰς ἐποιήσαντο κτέ. J. Steup, in the first number of his Thukydideische Studien, p. 29–72, and A. Kirchhoff in the Sitzungsberichte der Preussischen Akademie d. Wissenschaften, 1882, p. 909–940, have discussed this document with great care and acuteness. To both of these essays reference has been made in the notes (1. 3, 18, 28, 45, etc.). Steup suggests many considerable changes in the text, which he thinks are necessary to make it thoroughly comprehensible, but it is not safe to depart so widely from the Mss., although some of the changes proposed by Steup are perhaps improvements. As proposals of Steup which demand consideration, Cl. mentions the following: in 21 Steup reads τάσδε τὰς πόλεις, and in 25 he construes ἐπειδὴ αἱ σπονδαὶ ἐγένοντο with ἀποδόντων, explaining σπονδαί as "state of peace." In 34 he punctuates with a period after Ἀταλάντην, after which he changes the order of two parts of the sent., and reads: καὶ τοὺς ἐν Σκιώνῃ πολιορκουμένους Πελοποννησίων (Ἀθηναίους) ἀφεῖναι καὶ τοὺς ἄλλους ὅσοι Λακεδαιμονίων ξύμμαχοι ἐν Σκιώνῃ εἰσὶ καὶ ὅσους Βρασίδας ἐσέπεμψε καὶ τοὺς ἄνδρας ὅσοι εἰσὶ Λακεδαιμονίων ἐν τῷ δημοσίῳ τῷ Ἀθηναίων ἢ ἄλλοθί που ὅσης Ἀθηναῖοι ἄρχουσιν ἐν δημοσίῳ, ἀποδόντων δὲ καὶ Λακεδαιμόνιοι καὶ ξύμμαχοι οὕστινας ἔχουσιν Ἀθηναίων καὶ τῶν ξυμμάχων κατὰ ταὐτά. In 46 he reads περὶ for περί, and gives 47 ff. in the following form: ὅρκους δὲ ποιήσασθαι Ἀθηναίους πρὸς Λακεδαιμονίους καὶ τοὺς ξυμμάχους· ὁ δ' ὅρκος ἔστω ὅδε· "ἐμμενῶ ταῖς

ξυνθήκαις καὶ ταῖς σπονδαῖς ταῖσδε δικαίως καὶ ἀδόλως." ἔστω δὲ Λακεδαιμονίοις καὶ τοῖς ξυμμάχοις κατὰ ταὐτὰ ὅρκος πρὸς Ἀθηναίους κατὰ πόλεις, ὀμνύντων δὲ τὸν ἐπιχώριον ὅρκον ἑκάτεροι τὸν μέγιστον, ἑπτακαίδεκα ἐξ ἑκάστης πόλεως· τὸν δὲ ὅρκον ἀνανεοῦσθαι κατ' ἐνιαυτὸν ἀμφοτέρους.

The most important changes proposed by Kirchhoff are mentioned elsewhere. The others are mainly in the forms of words, as θάλαττα for θάλασσα and ἐάν for ἤν. These changes are made in order to make the language of this document agree with that of similar documents found in inscriptions of this date. One such inscription has preserved to us part of the document given by Thuc. in c. 47. A comparison of c. 47 with the inscription shows that the copy furnished us in the Mss. of Thuc. is by no means accurate, and in the chapter now under discussion the inaccuracies seem to be still greater than in c. 47. Cl., in his preface to Book VIII. p. xxvi., and Jowett in his note on c. 47, think that the discrepancies between the inscription and the text of Thuc. are of little account, and should not affect our estimate of the trustworthiness of the Mss. They somewhat underrate the importance of the discrepancies in question, but they are right in thinking that we should not attempt to restore the text of Thuc. to agree with the inscription even in c. 47, where part of the inscription corresponding to the chapter of Thuc. is preserved, and much less here where we have not the stone as a guide. Whether we accept Cl.'s view, and believe that Thuc. wrote this part of his history during his absence from Athens, and therefore owed his copy of the document to the kindness of some friend, or follow Kirchhoff in assuming that the copy was not made until after the historian returned to Athens, we have no means of knowing how accurate that copy was. Since, then, our object must be to give the text of Thuc. as nearly as possible as he wrote it (not as he ought to have written it), we ought not to depart widely from the reading of the Mss., and adopt the language of the inscriptions, so long as there is any uncertainty in regard to the accuracy with which Thuc. (or the person whom he employed) copied the documents in question. It seems, therefore, inadvisable to adopt many of the formal changes proposed by Steup and Kirchhoff, though their labours, as well as St.'s, in restoring the text to a form which expresses the proper meaning are deserving of high praise and grateful recognition.

18. 3. ἐξεῖναι. Kirchhoff's conjecture (Sitzungsber. d. Berl. Akad., 1882, p. 911) for καὶ ἰέναι. St. and Cl. bracket καὶ ἰέναι, which could be understood only as an amplification and explanation of θεωρεῖν, unless ἰέναι without καί were placed after βουλόμενον; in either case it would be superfluous.

18. 16. ἤν. Only the form ἐάν is found in Attic inscriptions before the Macedonian period, but Thuc. has the form ἤν in all documents cited by him excepting iv. 118. 13, and v. 47. 68. See St.'s note ad loc.

18. 18. ἀποδόντων δέ κτέ. St., who considers Cl.'s explanation of this passage as given in the note inadmissible, conjectures that a considerable gap occurs after Ἀμφίπολιν. This he would fill out as follows: ὅσαι δὲ πόλεις τῶν ἐπὶ Θράκης ἀποστᾶσαι Ἀθηναίων Λακεδαιμονίοις προσεχώρησαν παραδοῦναι Λακεδαιμονίους Ἀθηναίοις. Steup, p. 33, would supply καὶ Οἰσύμην καὶ Θυσσὸν καὶ εἴ τινα ἄλλην ἔχουσιν ἐν τῇ Ἀθωίδι Ἀκτῇ πόλιν. The best explanation is perhaps that proposed by Kirchhoff, Sitzungsber. d. Berl. Akad. 1882, p. 917, who reads in 19 παρέλαβον for παρέδοσαν, for the Lacedaemonians had taken cities, but had certainly not restored any. If this reading be accepted, the comma in 20 must be placed before Ἀθηναίοις, and perhaps we should read Ἀθηναίους.

18. 28. βουλομένας ταύτας. St. rejects βουλομένας ταύτας as an interpolation added to explain αὐτούς. The punctuation adopted in the text is that proposed by Steup, *Stud.* I. p. 39 (with reference to Xen. *Anab.* v. 1. 14, and *Hell.* vi. 1. 18), and Kirchhoff. Sitzungsber. d. Berl. Akad. 1882, p. 916. Cl. places the comma before βουλομένας, and explains that βουλομένας ταύτας being used almost abs., the reference to the cities is repeated in αὐτούς for the sake of clearness.

18. 34. St. and Kirchhoff write Μέθανα with Strabo viii. 15, and inscriptions.

18. 46. βουλεύεσθαι περὶ αὐτῶν κτἑ. Perhaps Kirchhoff, *l.c.* p. 929, and others are right in rejecting αὐτῶν καὶ τῶν ἄλλων πόλεων and writing πέρι. The reading of the text is certainly at variance with the usage of Attic official documents.

18. 50. (ἑπτακαίδεκα ἐξ ἑκάστης πόλεως.) The Mss. give simply ἐξ ἑκάστης πόλεως. Ullrich, *Beitr.*, 1862, p. 15, suggests that ἐξ is a mistake for ιζ΄, observing that in c. 19 and 24 the oath is taken by seventeen delegates. But ἐξ is necessary after ἑπτακαίδεκα; hence St. and Cl. assume that ιζ΄ has fallen out of the Mss., and give the above reading. Kirchhoff, *l.c.* p. 932, observes that the number seventeen is probably the result of chance, and could not have been determined beforehand. He therefore brackets ἑπτακαίδεκα ... πόλεως as an interpolation added by some one after reading c. 19 and 24. He suggests, however (p. 935), the possibility that this number may have arisen from the combination of the Spartan kings and ephors (2 + 5) with ten other delegates. See on c. 19. 8.

18. 55. Ἀθήνησι. The correct reading suggested by v. Herwerden for Ἀθήναις. The ἐν before Ἀθήναις is wanting in the best Mss.

19. 5. Πλειστοάναξ, Ἆγις. Both names are wanting in all Mss. (evidently on account of the identical beginning of the following name), but have very properly been added by all modern editt. from c. 24. 2.

20. 3. ἡμερῶν ὀλίγων παρενεγκουσῶν κτἑ. Cl., in his notes on c. 19. 1 and this passage, thinks that two dates are referred to,—the middle of April in c. 19. 1, and the first of April here. But the attack upon Plataea occurred the first of April, so that ten years and a few days after that would be so near the middle of April that one can hardly avoid regarding this date as identical with that of c. 19. 1. ἐκ Διονυσίων εὐθύς (2) must, then, not be taken too strictly. One might say in English, "just after the Christmas holidays," though the day referred to fell about the middle of January. St., with Müller, de temp. quo bell. Pelop. init. ceperit, p. 14, thinks the words ἡ ἐσβολὴ ἡ ἐς τὴν Ἀττικήν are a clumsy interpolation.

20. 6. καὶ μὴ τὴν ἀπαρίθμησιν τῶν ὀνομάτων τῶν ἑκασταχοῦ ἢ ἀρχόντων ἢ ἀπὸ τιμῆς τινος [ἐς] τὰ προγεγενημένα σημαινόντων. This is the reading proposed by Cl., whose explanation is given in the notes. [ἐς] has come into the text through a misunderstanding. As οἷς, in 9, explains ἀρχόντων ἢ ἀπὸ τιμῆς τινος, the words οὐ γὰρ ἀκριβές ἐστιν must be isolated by punctuation so that the force of οἷς passes over them to the preceding words. This explanation at least makes the text comprehensible, and gives it in a form which is in accordance with Greek usage. The Mss. give the words in the following order: καὶ μὴ τῶν ἑκασταχοῦ ἢ ἀρχόντων ἢ ἀπὸ τιμῆς τινος τὴν ἀπαρίθμησιν τῶν ὀνομάτων ἐς τὰ προγεγενημένα σημαινόντων. But this cannot be understood except by means of a forced and artificial interpretation. Göller and Arnold saw the necessity of a change in the order; and St. follows Arnold in reading: καὶ μὴ τῶν ἑκασταχοῦ ἢ ἀρχόντων ἢ ἀπὸ τιμῆς τινος ἐς τὰ προγεγενημένα σημαινόντων τὴν ἀπαρίθμησιν τῶν ὀνομάτων. This gives the proper sense, but the order is still very awkward, since τὴν ἀπαρίθμησιν must be taken with κατά at the beginning of the sentence. (Schlitz, Ztschr. f. d. Gymn. Wesen, 1877, p. 251, proposes to read τῇ ἀπαριθμήσει.) The order proposed by Cl. is simpler, and the omission of ἐς before τὰ προγεγενημένα makes the const. much easier. οἱ σημαίνοντες τὰ προγεγενημένα, "those who give events their designation," are those from whose names events are designated, i.e. the ἐπώνυμοι τοῖς ἔτεσι γεγενημένοι, as the Schol. says.

21. 11. ἀπολογησόμενος. The fut. is necessary, though the most and best Mss. read ἀπολογησάμενος.

21. 14. κατειλημμένους. So Cl., with Kr., Haase, and St. for κατειλημμένας of the Mss. καταλαμβάνειν in the sense of *confirm* or *bind* is used by Thuc. with a pers. obj. only. *Cf.* i. 9. 2; iv. 86. 2. We must supply τοὺς Λακεδαιμονίους.

22. 1. αὐτοῦ ἔτυχον ὄντες. The Mss. read αὐτοί, but Kr.'s emendation αὐτοῦ is necessary in consideration of c. 17. 17. παρακαλέσαντες τοὺς ἑαυτῶν ξυμμάχους (the same idea is repeated in c. 27. 3). The allies, although they had not all shared in the negotiations for the peace, were still present in Sparta. αὐτοῦ ἔτι ἔτυχον ὄντες (which St. writes) would be still clearer.

22. 4. δέξασθαι. St. writes δέξεσθαι, referring to his *Quaest. Gramm.* 1872, p. 6. The fut. would be more regular, but there is no Ms. authority for it, and the aor. inf. may be admissible when reference to particular circumstances (as here to the expressed condition) is intended. See on c. 1. 7, and App. on ii. 3. 7. Here οὐκ ἔφασαν meaning *refused* may not introduce indir. disc. at all.

22. 6. αὐτοὶ δέ πρὸς τοὺς Ἀθηναίους κτέ. The translation of this passage given in the note is substantially in accordance with the explanation of Arnold. He says: 'Few sentences in Thuc. exhibit a more extraordinary specimen of anacoluthon than this. The clause νομίζοντες ... Ἀργείους is repeated after the

parenthetical clause ἐπειδὴ ... ἐπισπένδεσθαι, but in different words, νομίσαντες ... οὐ δεινοὺς εἶναι: and the parenthetical clause itself refers only to the name of the Argives, explaining the reason why they in particular had been separately mentioned. In order to make the construction grammatical, the words νομίσαντες αὐτοὺς and the negative οὐ must be omitted. The sense is as follows: Thinking that the Argives, whose hostile intentions were manifested by their late refusal to renew the truce, would cease to be formidable if deprived of the aid of Athens; and that the other states of Peloponnesus would, from the same cause, be most disposed to remain quiet; as the Athenian alliance would thus be closed against them, under which they would otherwise have ranged themselves.' The same explanation is adopted by Bekker, Kr., Poppo. Bloomfield, and Jowett, and is the only one possible if the text is to be preserved unchanged. But it is almost incredible that Thuc. wrote such an obscure, confused, and ungrammatical sent. The repetition of νομίζοντες by νομίσαντες makes the former partic. entirely superfluous, and οὐ is written without regard to the preceding ἥκιστα. Then, too, the clause πρὸς γὰρ ἄν ... χωρεῖν is quite out of place after ἡσυχάζειν, and can only be explained as an afterthought.

Many emendations have been proposed. Böhme suggests μόλις ἄν for μάλιστ' ἄν, and bases a new explanation upon this change; J. Steup, Rhein. Mus. 25, p. 282, strikes out νομίσαντες ... εἶναι and πρὸς γάρ ... χωρεῖν "as awkward explanations of an interpolator"; Madvig, *Adverss. Crit.* l. p. 324, reads: νομίζοντες ἥκιστ' ἄν σφίσι τούς τε Ἀργείους ἐπιτίθεσθαι (ἐπειδὴ ... οὐ δεινοὺς εἶναι) καὶ τὴν ἄλλην Πελοπόννησον μάλιστ' ἄν ἡσυχάζειν. St. strikes out νομίσαντες ... οὐ, and puts the parenthetical clause πρὸς γὰρ ἄν ... χωρεῖν after δεινοὺς εἶναι. He thinks the words which he rejects are part of an explanation or marginal note νομίσαντες αὐτοὺς ἄνευ Ἀθηναίων οὐ δεινοὺς εἶναι. This does not, however, seem very probable, and until the manner in which these words came into the text is more satisfactorily explained, we must regard them as a part of the original narrative of Thuc.

Cl. brackets νομίζοντες ἥκιστα ἄν σφίσι, and changes Ἀθηναίους of 12 to Ἀργείους. He observes that νομίσαντες ... οὐ cannot be an interpolation, because αὐτοὺς ἄνευ Ἀθηναίων is necessary as a contrast to ἅμα in c. 14. 24, and he explains the insertion of νομίζοντες ἥκιστα ἄν σφίσι by supposing that some copyist took αὐτούς as subj. of εἶναι, not as a pred. modification of τοὺς Ἀργείους, and therefore added νομίζοντες ἥκιστα ἄν αὐτούς to form a grammatical connexion for τοὺς Ἀργείους. He explains the change of Ἀθηναίους in 12 to Ἀργείους by comparison with c. 14. § 4. But an alliance of Sparta with Athens would not necessarily keep the Peloponnesian states from joining Argos, while it would prevent them from looking to Athens for assistance. Still, as the Peloponnesian states were not likely to join the Athenians, the change to Ἀργείους is almost necessary if πρὸς γὰρ ἄν ... χωρεῖν is taken to refer to the Peloponnesian states and not to the Argives themselves. These changes seem, however, rather violent, and Cl.'s arguments are not conclusive.

Philippi, Rhein. Mus. 36, p. 254, brackets νομίζοντες in 7 and οὐ in 10, construing ἥκιστα ἄν with δεινοὺς εἶναι, and taking αὑτούς as pred. modification of τοὺς Ἀργείους. He further considers πρὸς γὰρ ἄν ... χωρεῖν a gloss, in which he may be right; but certainly if these words belong in the text, they must be placed (with St.) after δεινοὺς εἶναι, for the Argives were likely to join with the Athenians, while the other states of Peloponnesus were not. But some other change besides the transposition of πρὸς γὰρ ἄν ... χωρεῖν seems to be necessary. Perhaps the following reading may commend itself: omitting τε of 8 punctuate with a comma after ἐλθόντον and with a colon after ἐπισπένδεσθαι. Then νομίσαντες must be changed to ἐνόμισαν γάρ (the partic. might possibly stand in a causal sense, but this would be harsh). The passage then reads: αὐτοὶ δὲ πρὸς τοὺς Ἀθηναίους ξυμμαχίαν ἐποιοῦντο, νομίζοντες ἥκιστα ἄν σφίσι τοὺς Ἀργείους, ἐπειδὴ οὐκ ἤθελον Ἀμπελίδου καὶ Λίχου ἐλθόντων, ἐπισπένδεσθαι· ἐνόμισαν γὰρ αὐτοὺς ἄνευ Ἀθηναίων οὐ δεινοὺς εἶναι (πρὸς γὰρ ἄν τοὺς Ἀθηναίους, εἰ ἐξῆν, χωρεῖν) καὶ τὴν ἄλλην Πελοπόννησον μάλιστ' ἄν ἡσυχάζειν. "But they themselves were about to make an alliance with the Athenians, thinking that the Argives would certainly not renew the treaty with them, since they had refused when Ampelidas and Lichas came to them (for that purpose); for they thought that they were not dangerous without the Athenians (for they supposed they would be joining the Athenians if they were able) and that the rest of Peloponnesus would be most likely to keep quiet." Before they concluded even a peace with Athens, the Lacedaemonians had tried in vain to renew their treaty with Argos (see c. 14. § 4). They were now, therefore, sure that a treaty with Argos was impossible. They were, moreover, afraid that the Argives would make an alliance with Athens (πρὸς γὰρ ἄν τοὺς Ἀθηναίους ... χωρεῖν), which would at once give power to Argos, and endanger the stability of the new peace which the Lacedaemonians and Athenians had just concluded. Besides, they thought that if they made an alliance with Athens, even the disaffected states of Peloponnesus would be afraid to move. νομίζοντες ... ἐπισπένδεσθαι gives as the reason for making the alliance the impossibility of renewing the treaty with Argos, and the rest of the passage shows why the impossibility of a treaty with Argos had the effect of driving the Lacedaemonians into the arms of the Athenians. This explanation seems to meet the exigencies of the case, and the emendations proposed are not violent. Even if πρὸς γὰρ ἄν ... χωρεῖν is not a gloss, it is easy for a clause to be shifted from its proper place; the change from ἐνόμισαν γάρ to νομίσαντες is not great, and when that had once taken place, the insertion of τε in τούς τε Ἀργείους to correspond to καὶ τὴν ἄλλην Πελοπόννησον was very natural.

23. 1. (καὶ Ἀθηναῖοι). These words are wanting in the Mss., but are indispensable. καὶ Ἀθηναίοις, 24, is also omitted in some Mss. It is also necessary to read with Böhme ἤν τινες, 2, for ἤν δέ τινες of the Mss. Kirchhoff (Sitzungsber. d. Berl. Akad. 1883, p. 830) writes Ἀθηναῖοι καὶ Λακεδαιμόνιοι, but there is no fixed order for these words in this document. St. and v. Her-

werden assume that after Λακεδαιμόνιοι, not καὶ 'Αθηναῖοι, but a number of other words have been lost, which they supply to correspond to c. 39. 12, and 46. 15. Steup, *Stud.* I. p. 73-83, in a careful discussion of the question, arrives at the conclusion that interpolations have crept into the text in the two last-mentioned passages. Kirchhoff adopts the same conclusion in a modified form. See App. on c. 39. 12.

23. 17. 'Αθηναίους. Acc. to Müller-Strübing, *Aristophanes und die hist. Krit.* p. 281, the Ms. in the British Museum, No. 11,727 (St.'s *M*, but he does not mention this variation) reads 'Αθηναίοις, and he suggests that the original reading may have been: 'Αθηναίοις Λακεδαιμονίοις καὶ 'Αθηναίους Λακεδαιμονίοις; but as a servile insurrection was not one of the dangers the Athenians had to fear, they may well have promised to aid the Lacedaemonians without exacting a similar promise in return.

25. 3. δεκαετῆ. St., *Quaest. Gramm.* p. 15, recommends the form δεκέτη which he has accepted in his text here and in c. 26. 15 (and in i. 112. 2, πεντέτεις). The Mss. vary in this and similar forms, but all give δεκαετῆ here.

25. 11. καὶ ἐπὶ ἓξ ἔτη μὲν καὶ δέκα μῆνας. Ullrich, in a learned and careful discussion of this passage (in his *Beiträge zur Erklärung des Thuc.* p. 153-168), comes to the conclusion that Thuc. thought of the beginning of the Sicilian expedition as the beginning of the second war, and proposes therefore to read ἓξ ἔτη καὶ τέσσαρας (δ') μῆνας, six years and four months, from the conclusion of the peace, early in the spring of 421 B.C., to the departure of the great fleet in the middle of summer, 415 B.C. He sees in the Sicilian expedition the most important division of the whole war, and feels the lack of any mention of such an important event in the description (in c. 26. § 2) of the intervening period (the διὰ μέσου ξύμβασις). But Thuc. mentions as the end of the middle period ἐπὶ τὴν ἑκατέρων γῆν στρατεῦσαι, which does not apply to the Sicilian expedition. This expedition is referred to, however, in c. 25. 12 ff., ἔξωθεν ... ἔβλαπτον ἀλλήλους τὰ μάλιστα, and also in c. 26. 12, ἐς ἄλλα ἀμφοτέροις ἁμαρτήματα ἐγένοντο (with which *cf.* ἐς Σικελίαν πλοῦς mentioned as an ἁμάρτημα in ii. 65. 45). Thuc. also refers to the second war as τὸν χρόνῳ ὕστερον μετὰ τὰ ἐκ Σικελίας πόλεμον in iv. 81. 9. Böhme thinks that the end of the time of peace is marked by the plan which the Lacedaemonians had for the invasion of Attica in the middle of the seventeenth year of the war (see vi. 93. 1 ff.), and defends the reading ἓξ ἔτη καὶ δέκα μῆνας upon this ground. But this assumption is incompatible with μὴ ... στρατεῦσαι. Duker and those who think that the end of the διὰ μέσου ξύμβασις is marked by the Athenian plundering expedition along the coast of Laconia in the summer of 414 B.C. (see vi. 105. 11 ff.), propose ἑπτὰ ἔτη καὶ δύο μῆνας. But this explanation (by reference to an attack from one side) leaves ἑκατέρων unexplained. Therefore Kr. (on Clinton's *Fasti* for the year 414 B.C.), who thinks that the condition ἐπὶ τὴν ἑκατέρων γῆν στρατεῦσαι is not fulfilled before the occupation of Decelea (early in the spring of 413 B.C., *cf.* vii. 19. 1 ff.) conjectures ἑπτὰ ἔτη καὶ τέσσαρας μῆνας. The words αὖθις ἐς πόλιμὸν φανερὸν κατέστησαν (in c. 25. 15) seem also to refer to this event. Still, the inroad upon Laconia (see vi. 105) is certainly στρατεῦσαι ἐπὶ τὴν γῆν, though only from one side, not ἑκατέρων, and the date of the ξυμμαχία μετὰ τὰς σπονδάς cannot be exactly determined; consequently it is best to follow Cl. in leaving the reading of the Mss. unchanged, though without vouching for its correctness. Schütz, Ztschr. f. d. Gymn.-Wesen, 31, p. 243 ff., thinks that the appointment of Gylippus (see vi. 93. 8 ff.) agrees best with the words ἓξ ἔτη καὶ δέκα μῆνας. L. Herbst, Philol. 1881, p. 357 ff., thinks Thuc. considered the decision of the assembly at Sparta (see vi. 93) the end of the peace, and Steup, Thukyd. Studien, I. p. 87 note, thinks the descent of the thirty Attic ships upon the coast of Laconia (see vi. 105) marks the renewal of the war. W. Jerusalem, Wiener Studien, 3, p. 287, thinks that the emphatic distinction made between the summer of 421 B.C. as a time of peace, and the following winter as the time when covert hostilities began (see c. 35. 1, and 36. 1), shows that Thuc. regarded not the σπονδαί nor the ξυμμαχία, but the beginning of the following winter, as the beginning of the six years and ten months. This agrees with the fact that the descent of the Athenians upon the coast of Laconia (see vi. 105) took place in the middle of summer, 414 B.C., i.e. six years and ten months later.

25. 13. ἀνοκωχῆς. St., Quaest. Gramm. p. 14, has shown that this is the proper reading for the usual ἀνακωχῆς here as well as in i. 40. 16; 66. 9; iii. 4. 12; iv. 38. 4; 117. 7.

26. 8. διῄρηται. Böhme understands τὰ ἔργα as subj.: "according to the acts as they have been recounted by me," but then we should certainly expect τὰ ἔργα as obj. of ἀθρείτω, and could dispense with τοῖς ἔργοις. Kr. explains: "how the peace is separated by the facts from the preceding and succeeding war." Others take διαιρεῖν in the sense of "define"; but none of these explanations is satisfactory. Perhaps the passage is corrupt. Some Mss. give διείρηται.

26. 10. οὔτ' ἀπεδέξαντο. Bekker's proposal to read οὐδ' is inadmissible. ἀπέδοσαν and ἀπεδέξαντο are both in the closest connexion with their common obj. πάντα.

26. 11. ἔξω τε τούτων. Cl. says that ἔξω τε τούτων is opp. to τοῖς τε ἔργοις (8). St. rightly observes that the events introduced by ἔξω τε τούτων are quite as much ἔργα as anything which precedes. He accordingly brackets τε (8), reading τοῖς γὰρ ἔργοις. Prob. Thuc. wrote τε intending to introduce something to correspond to it, but eventually finished the period in a different way.

26. 13. οἱ ἐπὶ Θρᾴκης ... ἐκεχειρίαν δεχήμερον ἦγον. Steup, Stud. I. p. 86 note, thinks these words were not written by Thuc. because the account of the διὰ μέσου ξύμβασις herein contained is neither complete nor accurate; but completeness and accuracy could not be expected in so brief a summary.

26. 14. ἐκεχειρίαν δεχήμερνο. Grote and others explain: "a truce terminable at ten days' notice." Certainly a truce which must be renewed every ten

APPENDIX. 183

days would be very inconvenient; but δεχήμεροι σπονδαί are always mentioned as the most unstable kind of truce, and in c. 32. 17 the expression δεχημέρους ἐπισπονδάς occurs. This can hardly mean anything else than a truce renewed every ten days. *Cf.* ἐπισπένδεσθαι, *renew a treaty*. Cobet, Mnem. 14, p. 10, proposes to emend ἐπισπονδάς to σπονδάς, but this avoids instead of explaining the difficulty.

26. 28. αἴσθεσθαι. St. refuses to recognize this pres. inf. here and in ii. 93. 17; iii. 83. 13; vii. 75. 8, but the accentuation of most of the Mss. can hardly be the result of chance, esp. as the pres. inf. would, owing to the general nature of the impressions to which reference is made, be in all these cases more natural than the aor. Buttmann, *Ausf. Spr.* II. p. 68, has pointed out other traces (among them Plat. *Rep.* x. 608 a) of this lost usage. The preservation of the short form of the pres. αἴσθεσθαι by the side of αἰσθάνεσθαι is the more easily explained, because, in being lengthened by the addition of -αν, the stem could not introduce a nasal before σ nor undergo a shortening of the stem vowel, as λήβω, λαμβάνω, τεύχω, τυγχάνω. See on the whole question G. Curtius, *das Verbum der griech. Spr.* II. 2 f.

27. 2. καὶ ὕστερον ἡ ξυμμαχία κτέ. St. considers the form of expression as explained in the note too awkward, but it is comprehensible and grammatical. If this is the proper understanding of the passage, the reason which led Campe, Philol. 11, p. 52, and St. to omit καί before οἱ μὲν ἄλλοι (4) and begin the main clause at that point, loses its force. The clause beginning καὶ αἱ ἀπὸ τῆς Πελοποννήσου πρεσβεῖαι repeats more in detail the statement of c. 22. 6, ἐκείνους μὲν ἀπέπεμψαν. The introductory impf. ἀνεχώρουν is then particularized acc. to common usage (by means of the introductory particles καί, μέν, δέ, see on i. 19. 1), and its parts expressed by the aor. ἀπῆλθον and the pres. ποιοῦνται. The reading ἡ ξυμμαχία for αἱ ξυμμαχίαι of the Mss., first proposed by Cobet and opposed by Herbst, *gegen Cobet*, p. 6, is adopted by Cl. This treaty of alliance between Athens and Sparta was a distinctly separate agreement (*cf.* 22. 6, αὐτοὶ δὲ πρὸς τοὺς Ἀθηναίους), and is elsewhere (c. 23. 25; 24. 9; 25. 2; 27. 8) invariably mentioned in the sing. The close proximity of the pls. αἱ σπονδαί and αἱ πρεσβεῖαι led the copyist to write the pl. αἱ ξυμμαχίαι, which is freq. employed where the circumstances warrant it. Similarly, in iii. 65. 2, ἱερομηνίαις for ἱερομηνίᾳ is wrongly written after σπονδαῖς.

27. 14. ἀρχήν. Philippi, Rhein. Mus. 36, p. 255, suggests that ἀρχήν is a gloss on αὐτοκράτορας which has crept into the text. The plenipotentiaries are, then, explained by the gloss as an 'ρχή or magistracy.

27. 15. τοῦ μὴ καταφανεῖς γίγνεσθαι. Cl. quotes the Schol., ἵνα μὴ φωραθῶσιν ὑπὸ τῶν Λακεδαιμονίων οἱ συνθέμενοι τοῖς Ἀργείοις. He explains: 'in order that those among them who might eventually fail in persuading the communities to which they belonged to join the alliance against Sparta, might not,' *etc.*, making τὸ πλῆθος refer, not to the Argives, but to the other states. This explanation is possible, but that given in the note is simpler.

31. 2. ἐποιήσαντο. This reading of the best Mss. is easily explained after the collective subst. πρεσβεία. G. 135, 3; II. 609. ἐποιήσατο of some Mss. is a needless correction.

31. 9. καὶ λυσάντων τὸν πόλεμον. Kr. reads καταλυσάντων without καί, and takes καταλυσάντων as a cond. partic., "if they put an end to the war." But then, as Cl. observes, the fulfilment of the condition is wanting. Cl. therefore reads καὶ καταλυσάντων, but St. calls attention to Strabo xiii. 1. 38, where λύειν πόλεμον occurs, and returns to the reading of the Mss. Elsewhere we find καταλύειν, or more rarely διαλύειν, but the analogy of λύειν σπονδάς is strong enough, even without the passage in Strabo, to justify us in retaining the reading of all the Mss.

31. 21. τὴν ξυνθήκην προφέροντες ἐν ᾗ εἴρητο κτέ. Steup, *Stud.* I. p. 62, thinks the words ἐν ᾗ εἴρητο ... καὶ ἐξελθεῖν are an interpolation by a 'reader who did not understand that τὴν ξυνθήκην referred to the treaty between Sparta and the other Peloponnesians.'

31. 28. περιορώμενοι [ὑπὸ τῶν Λακεδαιμονίων]. The words in brackets must have been inserted by some reader who thought περιορώμενοι was pass. Their omission was proposed by Dobree. The common reading forces us to take περιορώμενοι as pass. It is then understood by some to mean *neglected* (Grote VI. p. 287: 'left to themselves by the Lacedaemonians'), by others *carefully watched* (Jowett, 'jealously watched by,' etc.). Both are unsatisfactory. Müller-Strübing, *Pol. Beitr.* p. 27, proposes: ἡσύχαζον καὶ περιορώμενοι ὑπὸ τῶν Λακεδαιμονίων, νομίζοντες κτέ., with καί in the sense of *although*, and περιορώμενοι in that of *treated with neglect*.

32. 3. παῖδας καὶ γυναῖκας ἠνδραπόδισαν. Müller-Strübing, *Aristoph. und die hist. Krit.* p. 45, observes that this passage does not agree with the statement of iv. 123. 15, that Brasidas had removed the women and children of the Scioneans and Mendeans to Olynthus two years before. He discusses also the similar statement in regard to the Plataeans. Thuc. (in iii. 68. 15) says that when Plataea was taken (in the summer of 427 B.C.), the Lacedaemonians γυναῖκας ἠνδραπόδισαν, although he had previously informed us (in ii. 6. 15 ff.) that the Athenians τῶν ἀνθρώπων τοὺς ἀχρειοτάτους ξὺν γυναιξὶ καὶ παισὶν ἐξεκόμισαν, in the spring of 431 B.C. Cl. thinks that in the case of Plataea the words γυναῖκας (not παῖδας καὶ γυναῖκας) ἠνδραπόδισαν (iii. 68. 15) are an indication that the 110 women left behind as σιτοποιοί (*cf.* ii. 78. 13 f.) were not slaves; and that in the case of Scione the removal of the women and children by Brasidas (*cf.* iv. 123. 15), not being compulsory, was not completely carried out. Müller-Strübing, *Thukydideische Forschungen*, p. 142 ff., maintains his previous opinion. He rejects von Velsen's explanation (Philol. Anz. 1876, p. 373) that the σιτοποιοί at Plataea were slaves, and that Thuc. uses ἠνδραπόδισαν only in contradistinction to διέφθειραν (equiv. to ἀπέκτανον) in iii. 68. 13 (διέφθειραν Πλαταιῶν οὐκ ἐλάσσους διακοσίων κτέ.), and proposes to omit τοὺς ἡβῶντας, παῖδας δὲ καὶ γυναῖκας ἠνδραπόδισαν (in v. 32. 3) as an interpolation. There certainly must have been σιτοποιοί in

Scione as well as in Plataea, but this would not account for the παῖδες if the removal of the women and children was as complete as the character of Brasidas would lead us to expect ; but it is possible that something may have interfered with the thorough execution of his plan. St. suggests that the narrative is defective concerning this point.

32. 18. [τούτων] τῶν πεντηκοντουτίδων. Dobree, followed by Cl., St., and others, rejects τούτων. The form πεντηκοντουτίδων, after the analogy of τριακοντουτίδων in i. 87. 19, is better than πεντηκονταετίδων.

32. 21. ὥσπερ Βοιωτοὶ εἶχον. St. brackets these words (which were not in Valla's text) as superfluous. Perhaps, however, they refer to some provisions of the truce which are not specified.

35. 1. ἐν τῇ "Αθῳ Ἀκτῇ Διῇς. This reading is that of Didot and Bergk (*Hall. Progr.* 1859) for ἐν τῇ "Αθῳ Δικτιδιῆς of the Mss. The Διῆς (also in c. 82. 1 acc. to the best Mss.), from the town of Δῖον (*cf.* iv. 109. 10, 16), appear repeatedly in the tribute-lists of the Delian confederacy (Boeckh, *Staatshaushalt*, II. p. 438; U. Köhler, Abhandlgn. d. Berl. Akad. 1869, p. 76; *Corp. Inscr. Att.* I. 226 ff.) as Διῆς ἐξ "Αθω, and in company with them are the Θύσσιοι. The Ἀκτή is mentioned in iv. 109. 4. A name Δικτιδιῆς is unknown, and must be a mistake for Ἀκτῇ Διῆς. Poppo conjectured Χαλκιδῆς. Meineke prefers ἐν τῇ Ἀθωΐδι Ἀκτῇ. v. Herwerden reads ἐν τῇ "Αθῳ Διῆς.

35. 31. καὶ τοὺς ἄλλους [Εἵλωτάς τε καὶ] ὅσοι. Cl. brackets only τε. The reading of the text is that of St. Cl. thinks that besides the Helots some of the Perioeci may have deserted to Pylos, but the passage he cites in support of this view (iv. 41. 11 ff., τῶν τε Εἱλώτων αὐτομολούντων καὶ φοβούμενοι (*sc.* οἱ Λακεδαιμόνιοι) μὴ καὶ ἐπὶ μακρότερον σφίσι τι νεωτερισθῇ τῶν κατὰ τὴν χώραν) seems to refer esp. to the Helots, and this is made more evident by v. 14. 17 ff. Desertions on the part of the Perioeci are nowhere mentioned. Kr. omits only τε καί. The words Εἵλωτάς τε καί may possibly have arisen from a marginal gloss Εἵλωτάς τε καὶ Μεσσηνίους, as St. suggests.

36. 3. σπονδαῖς. The Mss. have no art. before σπονδαῖς, thereby seeming to show that these men were opposed not only to the peace which had lately been concluded, but to any peace with Athens. *Cf.* iv. 21. 3. Cl., following Steup, inserts ταῖς on the ground that since the peace had been concluded there could be no opposition to *treaties* with Athens, but only to *the treaty* then in force. The reading of the Mss. seems, however, to be preferable, for though the opponents of treaties in general would, of course, be opposed to *the treaty* in particular, the existence of the treaty would not change their general attitude, but they would still be opposed to *treaties*.

36. 7. Ξενάρης. This is the reading of the best Mss. here and in c. 37; 38; 46; not Ξενάρκης which Bekker adopts.

36. 11. μετὰ Βοιωτῶν κτέ. If Cl.'s interpretation of this passage as given in the note is correct, it is not necessary to read (with Ullrich, *Beitr.* 1846, p. 37 ff.) μετὰ Κορινθίων for μετὰ Βοιωτῶν, nor to adopt the changes proposed by St., who omits Βοιωτῶν Ἀργείους and ξυμμάχους, and reads αὖθις μετὰ τούτων. These readings are simpler than that given in the text, but depart too widely from the Mss.

36. 13. ἥκιστ' ἄν. The Mss. read ἥκιστα, but ἄν (which could easily be lost before ἀναγκασθῆναι) seems indispensable, and its force also affects ἑλέσθαι.

36. 14. ἑλέσθαι γὰρ Λακεδαιμονίους πρὸ τῆς 'Αθηναίων ἔχθρας κτέ. St. brackets 'Αθηναίων, and refers ἔχθρας καὶ διαλύσεως τῶν σπονδῶν to the Argives and the treaty of peace with them, which was nearing its end (see c. 14. 20; 22. 8; 28. 8), but Cl.'s explanation given in the note is more satisfactory. Jowett translates: "for the Lacedaemonians would prefer the friendship and alliance of Argos to anything which they might lose by the enmity of Athens and the dissolution of the treaty." This is also Kr.'s understanding of the passage. But to obtain this sense one would naturally write not ἔχθρας καὶ διαλύσεως σπονδῶν, but rather φιλίας καὶ σπονδῶν.

36. 18. ἡγουμένους. So St. for ἡγούμενοι. The nom. may have come into the Mss. through a mistaken idea that the word referred to the subj. of ἠπίσταντο.

36. 20. ἐδέοντο κτέ. This passage is evidently corrupt, for the acc. Βοιωτοὺς and ὅπως cannot both stand after ἐδέοντο. Herbst, Philol. 24, p. 653, tries to defend the reading of the Mss. Schütz, Ztschr. f. d. Gymn. Wesen, 31, p. 256, proposes to omit Βοιωτούς. The Schol. explains, ἐδέοντο Βοιωτοὺς οὕτω ποιῆσαι ὅπως παραδώσουσι, and St. therefore makes a gap in the text. Some word is wanted in place of ἐδέοντο, which shall signify ἐδέοντο οὕτω ποιῆσαι. Kr. suggests ᾐτοῦντο, Cl. ἐπήγοντο with reference to c. 41. 11. Cl. suggests, however, that the similarity of this passage to c. 39. § 2 is such as to awaken the suspicion that some copyist, thinking that Panactum might prob. have been mentioned in these negotiations, inserted at this point a clumsy imitation of c. 39. § 2. St. rejects this suggestion on the ground that c. 39. § 2 is not exactly a repetition of this passage, and remarks that we have no reason for calling the passage spurious because it is corrupt.

39. 12. εἰρημένον ἄνευ ἀλλήλων μήτε σπένδεσθαί τῳ μήτε πολεμεῖν. St., in his note on c. 23. 1, and Steup, *Thuk. Stud.* I. p. 73-83, have proved conclusively that the provision of the treaty to which reference is made here and in c. 46. 15 (εἴρητο ἄνευ ἀλλήλων μηδενὶ ξυμβαίνειν) is not contained in the treaty as it is given in c. 23. St. tries to bring about an agreement by filling the gap in c. 23. 1, as follows: κατὰ τάδε ξύμμαχοι ἔσονται Λακεδαιμόνιοι (καὶ 'Αθηναῖοι ἐπὶ τοῖς ἴσοις καὶ ὁμοίοις, μήτε σπένδεσθαί τῳ ἄνευ κοινῆς γνώμης μήτε πολεμεῖν· εἶναι δὲ τὴν ξυμμαχίαν) πεντήκοντα ἔτη. Steup, on the other hand, after a careful and thorough discussion of the whole account of the negotiations with which we are here concerned, comes to the conclusion that the words εἰρημένον ... πολεμεῖν in c. 39. 12 f., as well as εἴρητο ... ξυμβαίνειν in c. 46. 15 f., are interpolated. He thinks these words may have been inserted by the same reader to whom he ascribes the interpolations in c. 17. 13 ff. and c. 31. 21 ff. In cases of this kind, certainty is always hard to attain, and in this book harder than elsewhere. Cl.'s caution in leaving the text

APPENDIX. 187

unchanged is therefore to be commended, though the present condition of the text is far from satisfactory.

40. 3. ἦκον. The Mss. read ἴκοντο and ἤκοντο, but Thuc. cannot have used the simple verb ἵκεσθαι, which is not Att. The reading of the Mss. prob. arose from careless repetition of the following τό.

40. 10. πρότερον ἐλπίζοντες ἐκ τῶν διαφορῶν, εἰ μὴ μείνειαν αὐταῖς αἱ πρὸς Λακεδαιμονίους σπονδαί, τοῖς γοῦν Ἀθηναίοις ξύμμαχοι ἔσεσθαι. Cwiklinski, Hermes, 1877, p. 84 ff., maintains that these words are an interpolation. Cl.'s explanation, however, as given in the notes, is satisfactory. Thuc. explains clearly and with some irony the unpleasant position in which the Argives were placed by their foolish confidence in the representations of Cleobulus and Xenares (see c. 36). They were ill-informed concerning the events which had taken place, and did not find out until too late that the Boeotians, whom they had hoped to win over to their side, had concluded a treaty with Sparta. Meanwhile the alliance between Athens and Sparta had been formed, so that the Argives had now lost their former advantageous position between the rival powers, **πρότερον ἐλπίζοντες ἐκ τῶν διαφορῶν ... τοῖς γοῦν Ἀθηναίοις ξύμμαχοι ἔσεσθαι,** "whereas they had formerly (even after the peace of Nicias) hoped (pres. part. expressing continuance) that if their treaty with the Lacedaemonians did not last (ἐπ' ἐξόδῳ γὰρ πρὸς αὐτοὺς αἱ σπονδαὶ ἦσαν, c. 28. 8), *i.e.* should not be renewed, they could make an alliance with the Athenians at any rate." **γοῦν** with **Ἀθηναίοις,** to which Cwiklinski (p. 86) objects, seems to be peculiarly expressive and appropriate.

42. 3. Ἀνδρομένης. The best Mss. (followed by Bekker and Cl.) read **Ἀνδρομέδης.** But St. has shown that the masc. name corresponding to Andromeda is **Ἀνδρομέδων.** The common reading **Ἀνδρομένης** is therefore preferable.

43. 7. οὐ μέντοι ἀλλά. Chrysosthenes Balassides, Ἀθήναιον, 1880, p. 221-227, discusses the origin and use of this and the corresponding neg. expression **οὐ μέντοι οὐδέ.** He explains the ellipsis by reference to what follows, thinking that the opposite of the following idea should be supplied, whereas it is usually explained by reference to what precedes: *this, however, is not all, but,* etc. Kühn. 535, 7. In this passage, Balassides supplies **οὐ μέντοι ταύτῃ γε μόνον τῇ δόξῃ ἐπῄρετο** (or **προήγετο**) **ἀλλὰ κτέ.**

43. 9. ἑαυτόν. This reading of the better Mss. (some give ἑαυτῶν, which amounts to the same thing) is more emphatic than **αὑτόν,** which Bekker and Kr. adopt.

44. 10. τὴν κατὰ θάλασσαν. St. and v. Herwerden bracket these words, but it is natural that the Argives should lay most stress upon the powerful navy of Athens since they were themselves weak in that respect. See Müller-Strübing, *Pol. Beitr.* p. 26.

45. 2. ἦν καί. Poppo and Kr. for **καὶ ἦν** of the Mss. which Cl. defends. But the passages he cites (i. 120. 9; iii. 5. 11; iv. 63. 13) offer no sufficient analogy. **καί** belongs evidently with **ἐς τὸν δῆμον,** and must therefore stand after ἦν. St. and others take καί with ἐπαγάγωνται and read μὴ καί, ἢν κτέ., citing Plut. Nic. 10, μὴ καὶ τὸν δῆμον ἀπὸ τῶν αὐτῶν λόγων ἐπαγάγωνται.

45. 4. ταὐτά. St. for ταῦτα. Rightly, both in view of the connexion, and with reference to Plut. Nic. 10, τῶν αὐτῶν λόγων.

45. 5. μηχανᾶται δέ. This reading of the Mss. is entirely satisfactory. δέ introduces the sent. and at the same time marks a slight opposition between Alcibiades's conduct and that of the envoys. Cl. changes δέ to δή, and compares vi. 64. 13, τοιόνδε τι οὖν μηχανῶνται, but the change is needless.

46. 1. τῶν Λακεδαιμονίων αὐτῶν ἠπατημένων. St. and v. Herwerden (*Stud. Thuc.* p. 75) consider these words an interpolation. v. Herwerden omits also περὶ τοῦ ... ἥκειν. Müller-Strübing, *Pol. Beitr.* p. 29, changes ἠπατημένων to ἠπατηκότων. But no change is needed. Both perf. partics. express the successful result of Alcibiades's trick of c. 45. § 3, which deceived both Nicias and the Lacedaemonian envoys. Alcibiades deceived the Lacedaemonians, who, being themselves deceived, in turn deceived Nicias, and he, though he had himself been deceived, nevertheless urged the cause of the Lacedaemonians. So, since the deception of Nicias is a result of that of the envoys, we have τῶν Λακεδαιμονίων αὐτῶν ἠπατημένων placed before καὶ αὐτὸς (*likewise*; see on i. 50. 18) ἐξηπατημένος. The hopes of Nicias had been raised by the envoys who had declared the day before in the senate that they had full powers to conclude a treaty, and now that they, being themselves deceived by Alcibiades, contradicted their former statement, Nicias was doubly deceived (ἐξηπατημένος more emphatic than the simple ἠπατημένος; cf. iii. 43. 10; viii. 56. 24). Thuc. lays great stress upon Alcibiades's trick and its success. So also Plut. *Comp. Alc. et Coriol.* 2, μάλιστα δὲ κατηγοροῦσιν αὐτοῦ κακοήθειαν καὶ ἀπάτην, ᾗ τοὺς Λακεδαιμονίων πρέσβεις παρακρουσάμενος, ὡς Θουκιδίδης ἱστόρηκε, τὴν εἰρήνην ἔλυσεν.

47. 1. Σπονδὰς ἐποιήσαντο κτέ. A fragment of the official document recording this treaty was found by the Archaeological Society at Athens, in the spring of 1877, upon a marble slab on the southern slope of the Acropolis. This was published by Kumanudes, 'Αθήναιον 5, p. 313, and discussed by Kirchhoff, Hermes 12, p. 368 ff., who published it, *C. I. A.*, IV. p. 15 f., No. 46 b, with some remarks by Foucart (see also Schöne, Hermes 12, p. 472 ff., and St. in his note and appendix). Kirchhoff devotes another discussion to this treaty in the Sitzungsber. d. Berl. Akad. 1883, p. 839 ff. The fragment contains the last letters of the right-hand side of the first half of the entire inscription. Each line originally consisted of 76 or 77 letters. The fragment contains 12 or 13 letters of each of the first 12 lines, and a gradually decreasing number of the next 14 lines, the last letters being the end of the 25th line, ὅσαι δ of ὀμόσαι δέ in l. 44 of our text. The reading of the inscription differs from that of our Mss. in the following cases (the variations in orthography due to the difference between the Att. and Ion. alphabets are not taken into account) : —

1. 2, after 'Ηλεῖοι the inscription reads πρὸς ἀλλήλους.

APPENDIX.

l. 8 and 11, for Ἠλείους καὶ Μαντινέας: Μαντινέας καὶ Ἠλείους.
l. 21 f., for τὴν Ἠλείων ἤ: τὴν Ἀργείων ἤ.
l. 28, for ἤν: ἐάν.
l. 41, for μεταπεμψαμένη τήν: μεταπεμψαμέ ΝΕΤΕΙΣ, prob. μεταπεμψαμένη τῇ στρατιᾷ.
l. 42, the inscription has before ταῖς the letters ΙΣ, prob. from a preceding ἁπάσαις.

The text of the inscription has been completed and restored by Kirchhoff, Schöne, Foucart, and St. with no material disagreement. Assuming that the text as given by Kirchhoff is correct (and but few points admit of a possible doubt), there are 31 variations between the inscription and our text of Thuc. Of these thirteen are merely orthographical (ἐάν for ἤν nine times, θάλατταν for θάλασσαν twice, ἁπασῶν for πασῶν and ἁπάσαις for πάσαις). In three cases the order of the names 'Eleans, Mantineans, Argives,' is reversed. In four cases words which do not occur in our text are inserted in the inscription. Once our text inserts ταῖς πόλεσιν in l. 29. In eight cases the variations depend upon conjectures which are not absolutely certain, and may therefore be passed over. The two remaining variations are ἐς τὴν γῆν in l. 12 for ἐπὶ τὴν γῆν and ὧν ἂν ἄρχωσιν in l. 31 for ὧν ἄρχουσι. None of these are of any importance so far as the substance of the document is concerned, but it is at the first glance surprising and somewhat alarming that so many variations, slight though they may be, exist between the inscription and the text of Thuc. The importance of these variations depends, however, entirely upon the manner in which they arose. Kirchhoff, Schöne, St., and others believe that the variations are due to the writer or writers of that Ms. from which all the extant Mss. of Thuc. are derived; in other words, they believe that the copy inserted by Thuc. into his history was correct in every particular, and agreed exactly with the inscription. According to this view, there are in this one chapter thirty or more cases in which our Mss. depart from the text as written by Thuc. But there is no reason for assuming more corrupt readings at this point than elsewhere; and though the variations here do not much affect the sense, the same cannot safely be assumed to be the case throughout the work. If, then, the differences between our text in this chapter and the inscription are all due to corruptions in our Mss., but very little confidence can be placed in the Mss., nor can we rely implicitly upon any statement contained in a book which has come down to us in such a corrupt form. But it is by no means necessary to assume that Thuc. originally gave an absolutely correct copy of the document part of which is preserved to us in the inscription. Thuc. wrote at a time when the demands made by the public upon the historian were not such as we are justified in making now, and even now mistakes in the copying of official documents are not entirely banished from our histories. Even if we believe with Kirchhoff, that this part of his work was composed by Thuc. after his return to Athens, when he had access to the public archives, or at any rate to the Acropolis where a copy of this document was placed (cf.

c. 47. 65), it is no discredit to Thuc. if he contented himself with an accurate rendering of the sense and general form of the treaty without taking pains to make a literal copy. If, however (and this is not positively disproved), Thuc. obtained his copy of the treaty during his absence from Athens, the chance that the variations from the text of the inscription date from the very origin of his work is still further increased. In view of these considerations Cl. is justified in giving this chapter of the history as it is preserved in the Mss., leaving for others the task of establishing the text of the inscription and the original form of the treaty. That Thuc. obtained his copy of the treaty from Athens can, however, not be doubted. Gilbert, Philol. 1879, p. 265, suggests that the variations may be fully accounted for by supposing that Thuc. copied the document in Olympia (see c. 47. 10), but as Kirchhoff (*l.c.* p. 848) observes, Thuc. would in that case have given the treaty in the dialect of Elis.

47. 68. ἐὰν δοκῇ ... τοῦτο κύριον εἶναι. This formula corresponds so closely to that of c. 23 *fin.* that Bekker is certainly right in reading ὅτι ἂν δοκῇ for ὅτι δ' ἂν δόξῃ of the Mss. On the form ἐάν, see on c. 18. 10.

49. 5. ἐν τῷ ... νόμῳ. Naber, Mnem. 14, p. 320, proposes ἐκ τοῦ ... νόμου, *according to the law.* But ἐν τῷ νόμῳ seems to emphasize the fact that they imposed a fine within the law, *i.e.* not exceeding the limits prescribed by it. *Cf.* i. 77. 2 (ἐν δικασταῖς οὐκ ἐν ἄλλοις, in iii. 53. 3, is different).

49. 6. σφᾶς. This need not be changed (with Dobree, Göller, and others) to σφῶν nor (with St.) to σφίσι. Kühn. 555, 5, N. 8. It seems rather that the reference to the Lacedaemonians is made more emphatic by the unusual σφᾶς (a similar case is vi. 61. 27, where Bekker and St. read σφίσι). Nor is it likely that the same relation would be expressed once by σφῶν, the second time by αὐτῶν. For that matter, σφῶν would be unnecessary, for αὐτῶν is sufficient for both parts of the clause, since Φύρκον τεῖχος is contrasted with the more important Lepreum (see on c. 31. 6) and at the same time brought into relation with it by τε καί.

49. 7. αὐτῶν ὁπλίτας. Cl. inserts χιλίους between these words, remarking that the numeral (,α) might easily have been lost. He thinks 8 and 9 make the numeral necessary, but if the fine was 2000 minae at two minae for each man, it is evident that there were 1000 men, and the numeral is superfluous.

50. 5. ἐπομόσαι. With Cl. and St. for ἀπομόσαι, for the sense demands not an oath of negation, but the affirmative ἐπομόσαι as in ii. 5. 25.

51. 3. Μηλιᾶς. For Ms. Μηλιέας (with Cl.) after the analogy of Ἀλιᾶς (i. 105. 1), Δωριᾶς (i. 107. 4), Ἑστιαιᾶς (i. 114. 6).

54. 9. ἱερομηνία. So St. and v. Herwerden (with two Mss.) for ἱερομήνια of most Mss. The neut. pl. is generally explained (so Cl.) by reference to the fact that besides the Carneia several other festivals occurred in this month, while in iii. 56. 4 and 65. 2, ἱερομηνία is used to designate a particular point within the month, not the whole month. But the neut. pl. must come from an adj. ἱερομήνιος which occurs nowhere, and Schol. Pind. Nem. iii. 4, uses ἱερομηνία of the entire month.

55. 18. πυθόμενοι [δέ] τοὺς Λακεδαιμονίους. The omission of δέ was first proposed by Portus. δέ was doubtless inserted because πυθόμενοι was wrongly const. with ἀπῆλθον instead of with ἐβοήθησαν. Then ἐξεστρατεῦσθαι was taken to mean *had finished their campaign* ('the Lacedaemonian campaign was over,' Jowett), without regard to the fact that in 13, ἐξεστράτευσαν is used in its usual sense, *marched out*.

57. 10. Φλιοῦντα. St. writes Φλειοῦντα and, 13, Φλειάσιοι from inscriptions.

58. 1. Ἀργεῖοι δὲ προαισθόμενοι κτέ. The explanation given in the note is that of St., who, following Heilmann, writes τό τε (1) as two words. Cl. writes τότε in 1 as one word, and strikes out καί in 2. He translates: 'after the Argives had, to be sure, been informed at the beginning concerning the warlike preparations of the Lacedaemonians, nevertheless they did not move until (τότε δή, see on i. 49. 30) the enemy started for Phlius to join the others.' The chief reason for these changes is the desire to avoid the necessity of supplying αἰσθόμενοι καὶ τοῦτο or a similar expression with ἐπειδή ... ἐνχώρου; but St.'s explanation does away with any such presumed necessity, and though the const. as explained by St. is undoubtedly loose, it is not more so than in many other cases in Thuc. To Cl.'s reading St. justly objects that τότε πρῶτον does not mean "at the beginning," but "not until then (tum primum)," and that whereas τότε of 1 must refer to c. 57. 5 (ἐστράτευον), the second τότε in the same sent. (3) refers to another and later time (ἐχώρουν, 3). Müller-Strübing, *Thuk. Forsch.* p. 101. thinks we should read τό τε and insert παρεκάλεσαν τοὺς ξυμμάχους or words to that effect after τῶν Λακεδαιμονίων. He discusses this and the following chapters with great liveliness in *Aristoph. u. d. Hist. Krit.* p. 401 ff. A. Philippi, Rhein. Mus. 1881, p. 255 f., discusses the movements of the troops as here described, and finds that they are impossible. He thinks the narrative is incomplete or imperfect, and that the movements described in this and the following chapter must have taken a day longer than appears from our text.

58. 3. προσμίξαι. Cl. in his App. on ii. 84. 34, cites Apoll. Dysc., Hdn., and later grammarians, as authority for writing προσμῖξαι. The Mss. and most editt. read προσμίξαι. See v. Bamberg, Ztschr. f. d. Gymn. Wesen, 1874, p. 10 ff.

58. 21. ἐκάθηντο. After the analogy of c. 6. 22; iii. 97. 11; iv. 44. 14, for καθῆντο of nearly all Mss.

59. 22. προσελθόντε. With Vat. The inferior Mss. read προσελθόντες.

60. 2. εἰπόντες [τῶν Ἀργείων]. Cl. renders: "since they made these declarations from the Argives," *i.e.* "in the name of the Argives," and adds that τῶν Ἀργείων, which is dependent upon ταῦτα, refers expressly to ἑτοίμους γάρ εἶναί Ἀργείους above. It is better with St. and v. Herwerden, *Stud. Thuc.* p. 76, to omit τῶν Ἀργείων, which may be a mistaken gloss on ἑαυτῶν or a marginal explanation of τοῦ πλήθους.

60. 20. ἀλλὰ καὶ ἄλλῃ ἔτι προσγενομένῃ. So the Mss. The allies thought ἀξιόμαχοί ἐσμεν οὐ τῇ Ἀργείων μόνον ξυμμαχίᾳ, ἀλλὰ καὶ ἄλλῃ προσγενο-

μένη (*i.e.* ἐὰν ἄλλη προσγένηται καὶ ταύτῃ ἀξιόμαχοί ἐσμεν). If this idea were expressed in indir. disc. without the use of a partic., we should have καὶ ἄλλῃ εἰ προσγένοιτο without ἄν in the prot. or the apod. Bekker, followed by Cl. and others, reads κἂν ἄλλῃ for καὶ ἄλλῃ, on the ground that προσγενομένῃ is equiv. to εἰ προσγένοιτο (or προσεγένετο), and requires an apod. ἀξιόμαχοι ἂν εἴημεν (or ἦμεν). The allied forces might have thought εἰ ἄλλη προσγένοιτο ἀξιόμαχοι ἂν εἴημεν or εἰ ἄλλη προσεγένετο ἀξιόμαχοι ἂν ἦμεν, and either would be expressed by κἂν ἄλλῃ προσγενομένῃ; but if they thought ἐὰν ἄλλη προσγένηται, this would be expressed by καὶ ἄλλῃ προσγενομένῃ, and the omission of ὄν shows that this is the thought attributed to them by Thuc. δοκοῦντες may be taken in the sense of *seeming* (to the spectator) instead of that of *thinking*, but this would not affect the const. of the dependent clause.

61. 8. παρόντος κτέ. St. reads παριόντος, because, as he says, there is no doubt that Alcibiades was not only present, but came forward to speak (*cf.* i. 67. 12; vi. 15. 1; 19. 3), and spoke in behalf of the Athenians. If he was present at all, he doubtless spoke, so that παρόντος really answers the same purpose as παριόντος, and St.'s emendation is unnecessary. πρεσβευτὴν παρόντος shows clearly enough that Alcibiades, who had been στρατηγός in the preceding autumn (see c. 55. 17) now conducted these negotiations as a private individual (ἰδιώτης ὤν, Diod. xii. 79). Nevertheless, as he spoke in behalf of the Athenians, οἱ Ἀθηναῖοι is the subj. of the sent.

61. 9. ταῦτα. Cl. changes this reading of the Mss. to ταὐτά on the ground that ταῦτα referring to what follows is superfluous, and that the same things were said to the Argives and their allies. But there is no sufficient reason for Cl.'s assumption that the allies could not have been present in the same assembly with the Argives (Jowett renders, 'told the Argives in the presence of the rest,' and Grote, VI. c. 66, p. 345, says, 'an assembly was therefore convened, in which these allies took part along with the Argeians'), and if they were, ταὐτά is worse than superfluous. That the discussion was carried on in a joint assembly of Argives and allies is indicated by ἔν τε τοῖς Ἀργείοις καὶ ξυμμάχοις; for if the allies were not with the Argives, we should expect ἔν τε τοῖς Ἀργείοις καὶ τοῖς ξυμμάχοις.

62. 8. [Τεγεα]τῶν. St. rightly brackets Τεγεα, leaving only the art. Τεγεατῶν would have to stand after πόλει unless it were itself followed by the art. The reading of the Mss. may have arisen from a gloss (Τεγέᾳ) on πόλει.

63. 4. ὡς οὔπω πρότερον αὐτοὶ ἐνόμιζον. The explanation given in the note seems satisfactory. Cl. accepts Herlein's proposal (*Wertheimer Progr.* 1862) to insert a comma and ὡς after πρότερον. Kr., Badham, and Cobet strike out αὐτοὶ ἐνόμιζον.

63. 11. στρατευσάμενος. So some Mss., though most give στρατευσόμενος. St., after v. Herwerden, reads στρατευόμενος. But the aor. partic. seems admissible, being equiv. to ἐπειδὰν στρατεύσηται.

65. 9. βουλομένην. Cl. and St. after v. Herwerden and Meineke read βουλόμενον because δηλῶν introduces an explanation of διανοεῖται, which

they think is best given by the pers. use of βουλόμενον. The Schol. (νῦν ἀκαίρως αὐτὴν προθυμεῖσθαι ἀναλαβεῖν καὶ ἐπανορθῶσαι τὴν τότε γενομένην ἁμαρτίαν) seems to have read βουλόμενον, and Plut., *Mor.* 797 c, does so read. But βουλομένην, the reading of the Mss., can be explained by a somewhat unusual use of βούλεσθαι (*cf.* Plat. *Crat.* 414 a), and there is no subj. for βουλόμενον.

65. 10. ἢ κατὰ τὸ αὐτό. In spite of Kr.'s explanation given in the note, these words are at best a troublesome addition. Dobree prefers to omit them. St. omits only ἤ, and renders κατὰ τὸ αὐτό by eadem ratione (as in viii. 5. 36; 66. 16), making ratio refer to πρὸς χωρίον καρτερὸν ἰόντας σφᾶς. This is reasonable, but not certain.

65. 20. ἐξ ὀλίγου. In c. 64. 17. ἐξ ὀλίγου is used in the sense of *suddenly*. Perhaps, then, it is here a gloss on αἰφνιδίῳ or *vice versa*. Arnold marks αἰφνιδίῳ as spurious, for the Schol.'s gloss on ἐξ ὀλίγου, viz., καιροῦ δηλονότι, would be nonsense if his text contained αἰφνιδίῳ.

66. 6. μάλιστα δὴ Λακεδαιμόνιοι κτέ. The sense which must be contained in these words is indicated in the note, but it is hardly contained in the text. Meineke (Hermes 3, p. 356) therefore approves Campe's conjecture ἐξεφάνησαν for ἐξεπλάγησαν and explains: "the Lacedaemonians, when (ὡς ὁρῶσι) they saw the enemy advance from the hill, showed themselves upon this occasion more than ever Lacedaemonians." But St. is justly suspicious of this use of ἐκφαίνεσθαι. Rauchenstein, Philol. 36, p. 237, proposes διεφάνησαν in the same sense. Madvig (*Adverss. Crit.* I. p. 325) suggests: μάλιστα δὴ Λακεδαιμονίους ... ἐξεπλάγησαν, using ἐξεπλάγησαν in the sense of "wondered at"; but it is difficult to find a subj. for this verb, since the Argives who are mentioned some lines above, being already drawn up in line of battle, have no reason ἐκπλαγῆναι (unless we take this verb to mean simply "admire," for which there is no precedent), and they were not so surprised or astonished as to prevent them from attacking the Lacedaemonians with great energy (see c. 70. 1 f.). St. thinks there is a gap before ἐξεπλάγησαν, and suggests that the passage may originally have read μάλιστα δὲ Λακεδαιμόνιοι ἐς ὃ ἐμέμνηντο ἐν τούτῳ τῷ καιρῷ ἐξαναγκασθέντες εὐθὺς ἐκ πορείας μάχεσθαι οὐδ' ὡς ἐξεπλάγησαν or something to that effect. He formerly supplied ὅμως δὲ διὰ τάχους ὡς ἐς μάχην ἀντικατέστησαν after ἐξεπλάγησαν. Cl. suggests that ἐξεπλάγησαν may mean "excited admiration" or "caused astonishment," but of this use there is no known example. He also suggests that we might read ἐξηλλάγησαν for ἐξεπλάγησαν: "they were different from all others," and therefore "they excelled all others," and cites Eur. *Iph. Aul.* 564, τάν τ' ἐξαλλάσσουσαν χάριν as well as the use of ἐξηλλαγμένος in late authors. But these words are not used to mean more than simply "unusual," so that the use of ἐξηλλάγησαν in the sense of "excelled" is unparalleled. Müller-Strübing, *Thuk. Forsch.* p. 39, proposes to change the order and read: μάλιστα δὴ Λακεδαιμόνιοι ἐς ὃ ἐμέμνηντο ἐν τούτῳ τῷ καιρῷ ἐξεπλάγησαν. καὶ εὐθὺς ἀπὸ σπουδῆς —διὰ βραχέως γὰρ μελλήσεως ἡ παρασκευὴ αὐτοῖς ἐγίγνετο — καθίσταντο ἐς

κόσμον κτέ. This still leaves the astonishment of the Lacedaemonians unexplained, and the introduction by means of δή is not quite satisfactory (St. reads μάλιστα δέ, and Cl. suggests μάλιστα δὲ δή), but perhaps the Argives had advanced further than the Lacedaemonians expected, or, as Schütz, Ztschr. f. d. Gymn.-W. 1877, p. 200 f., suggests, the momentary panic of the Lacedaemonians may have been due to the fact that the enemy were drawn up in battle array, while they were themselves unprepared for battle.

68. 4. οὐκ ἂν ἐδυνάμην. St.'s note on these words reads: οὐκ ἂν δυναίμην pro codd. scriptura nunc emendavimus. Haec enim, licet el ἐβουλόμην subaudiatur, falsa est, cum contrarii affirmationem ei tribuere sententia vetemur. Nudum ἐδυνάμην Thuc. scribere poterat, non ἂν ἐδυνάμην. Cl. agrees with St., and asks 'how can εἰ ἐπεχείρουν or εἰ ἐβουλόμην be supplied when no reason for not wishing or trying can be imagined?' Müller-Strübing, *Thuk. Forsch.* p. 41, thinks the reason was that Thuc. did not wish to make an indiscreet use of the confidential statements of his Lacedaemonian friends. This is somewhat fanciful, but why is any definite reason necessary? Thuc. says: "It would now be impossible for me to give the exact numbers (if I were trying to do so; and knowing this beforehand, or not thinking the matter of sufficient importance to warrant troublesome investigations, I do not try)."

68. 6. τῶν δ' αὖ διὰ τὸ ἀνθρώπειον κομπῶδες ἐς τὰ οἰκεῖα [πλήθη] ἠπιστεῖτο. The numbers of the Lacedaemonians could not be given accurately on account of their habitual secrecy concerning affairs of state, and those of the others were open to suspicion διὰ τὸ ἀνθρώπειον κομπῶδες ἐς τὰ οἰκεῖα, *on account of the boastfulness which is natural to men in speaking of their own affairs* (not the boastfulness which is natural to men in speaking of their own affairs (not in speaking of their own numbers, πλήθη, any more than of other things). πλήθη evidently does not belong with οἰκεῖα. Cl. accordingly inserts τά before πλήθη, making τὰ πλήθη the subj. of ἠπιστεῖτο. But this is an unnecessary repetition of πλῆθος from 5, and besides, Thuc. uses the pl. πλήθη nowhere else. If the word were necessary to the sense, we might retain it; for, as Cl. says, the occasions for the use of the pl. are not freq., and it occurs in Dem. vi. 24 and Aeschin. iii. 134, but, inasmuch as it is quite superfluous, it is better to follow Kr., Meineke, and St. in omitting it.

69. 16. καθ' ἑκάστους τε. Perhaps St. is right in marking a gap in the text after these words. This gap he proposes to fill by τῶν ξυμμάχων βραχείᾳ παραινέσει or words to that effect. Schütz strikes out τε, and takes καί before μετά in the sense of *also*.

69. 18. * ἀγαθοῖς οὖσιν. In the explanation of this much discussed passage given in the note, the words ἀγαθοῖς οὖσιν are disregarded. Nor should we feel any lack if they were omitted. If we follow Haack, Poppo, and Böhme in connecting these words with ἐν σφίσιν αὐτοῖς, we get no clear expression of a thought, certainly not unless we insert ὡς. Kr. proposes ἀγαθοῖς ἀγαθὴν οὖσαν and translates: "they made their exhortation of those things concerning which they knew that the exhortation to the memory of them was useful to brave men," παρακέλευσιν being supplied with ἐποιοῦντο. Jowett translates: "but the Lacedaemonians, both in their war songs and in the words which a man spoke to his comrade, did but remind one another of what their brave spirits knew already," from which it does not appear clearly how he understands the passage, though he seems on the whole to follow Haack, *etc.* St. proposes ὧν ἠπίσταντο [τὴν] παρακέλευσιν τὴν μνήμην ἀγαθοῖς οὖσαν ἐποιοῦντο, mentionem eorum faciebant, quorum mentionem viris fortibus adhortationem esse sciebant or, as an alternative, ἐν σφίσιν αὐτοῖς τὴν παρακέλευσιν ὧν ἠπίσταντο τῇ μνήμῃ (ὡς) ἀγαθοῖς οὖσιν ἐποιοῦντο, apud se ipsos earum rerum quarum periti erant (*sc.* δι' ἔργων ἐκ πολλοῦ μελέτης) mentione adhortationem (sibi) ut viris strenuis (πειρασαμένοις, 5) faciebant. He compares the similar passage in iv. 95. 1 ff., δι' ὀλίγου μὲν ἡ παραίνεσις γίγνεται, τὸ ἴσον δὲ πρός γε τοὺς ἀγαθοὺς ἄνδρας δύναται καὶ ὑπόμνησιν μᾶλλον ἔχει ἢ ἐπικέλευσιν. Cl. conjectures that ἀγαθοῖς οὖσιν belongs in 19 after σώζουσαν, and translates: "they were thoroughly convinced, that practice continued through actual exertion from early youth (ἐκ πολλοῦ as in c. 67. 14), if one is of a good character, does more good than any eloquent exhortations." ἀγαθοῖς οὖσιν is then opp. to καλῶς ῥηθεῖσαν. St., however, justly objects to this use of σῴζειν with the dat. in the sense of " do good " or " help." πλείω τινὶ σῴζειν naturally means "preserve (or save) more things for a person," which would be quite out of place here. None of these explanations are very satisfactory, and as the passage is corrupt, it may be impossible to explain it perfectly.

70. 3. ὑπὸ αὐλητῶν πολλῶν νόμῳ ἐγκαθεστώτων. This is the reading of A. Gellius, adopted by most editt. including St. The best Mss. (and Cl.) read νόμου, which must be const. with ὑπό: *to the music of, etc.* But this makes the order of words rather awkward, and the idea is sufficiently expressed by ὑπὸ αὐλητῶν.

70. 5. προέλθοιεν. St. follows Gellius in writing προσέλθοιεν, and compares ἐν ταῖς προσόδοις of 6. But though προσέλθοιεν is in itself unobjectionable, it seems unnecessary when followed so closely by προσόδοις.

71. 2. ποιεῖ μέν καὶ ἅπαντα τοῦτο. St. brackets these words, but though they may be unnecessary, it is rash to omit them, for they are not likely to have been added by a later hand than the author's.

71. 5. προσστέλλειν. On the spelling, see App. on i. 15. 3. This reading is necessary for προστέλλειν of the Mss. The dat. τῇ ἀσπίδι can be explained only by προσ-, not by προ-. Each man pressed his uncovered right side as closely as possible *toward* the shield of his right-hand neighbour. This passage is imitated by Dio C. xl. 23. 3, ταῖς τῶν παραστατῶν ἀσπίσι τὰς γυμνώσιες σφῶν προσστέλλειν (*vulg.* προστέλλειν).

72. 5. τῇ προσμίξει. Kr. and Philippi (Rhein. Mus. 36, p. 257) may be right in thinking this is corrupt, esp. as the verb προσμῖξαι is used in another sense two lines below.

72. 6. ἐπὶ τοὺς Σκιρίτας κτέ. Cl. changes τούτους in 8 to τούτοις, and explains as follows: 'Since the two lochi had not been able to join the Sciritae at the proper time to fill up their loosened ranks (τὸ διάκενον τοῦτο), the king commanded them to unite again with them (the Lacedaemonians on the right wing) from whom they had already moved away some distance; but they could no longer effect an union with them. τούτοις refers to the Lacedaemonians, the σφίσι of 7. The subj. of ξυγκλῇσαι is still οἱ λόχοι of 7; therefore the opposition indicated by μηδέ can only be found in those with whom the λόχοι are to unite, and these are, as opp. to the Sciritae, ἐφ' οὓς οὐ παρῆλθον, the Lacedaemonians of the right wing, here referred to by τούτοις.' St. objects to this, and his objections are well founded. In the first place τούτοις, referring to the same troops to whom σφίσι refers is awkward, and in the second place Thuc. expressly says that the commanders of the two lochi refused to move (μὴ θελῆσαι παρελθεῖν, 3), so that Cl.'s assumption that they made a vain attempt to reach the Sciritae is in no way justified. The opposition indicated by μηδέ is between τούτους (the Sciritae), subj. of μὴ δύνασθαι ξυγκλῇσαι, and the two lochi. Agis ordered the two lochi to fill the gap between the main body and the Sciritae, and when they did not obey he ordered the Sciritae to return to their former position, 'but he found that it was too late, and that neither could they now fill the vacant space' (Jowett).

72. 9. τῇ ἐμπειρίᾳ Λακεδαιμόνιοι ἐλασσωθέντες. Cl.'s explanation as given in the note takes ἐμπειρίᾳ ἐλασσωθέντες in the sense of "inferior in experience," giving ἐλασσωθέντες the force of an adj. with no verbal significance. Some commentators, wishing to preserve the verbal force of the partic., have changed ἐμπειρίᾳ to some word with an almost opposite meaning. So Kr. proposes ἀπορίᾳ, and Müller-Strübing, Thuk. Forsch. p. 13, ἀταξίᾳ, "having been beaten through want of discipline." This, is, however, unnecessary, as ἐλασσοῦσθαι with the dat. occurs elsewhere in the sense of "be inferior" in a quality. Cf. Plat. Alc. I. 121 b, ὅρα μὴ τῷ τε γένους ὄγκῳ ἐλαττώμεθα τῶν ἀνδρῶν καὶ τῇ ἄλλῃ τροφῇ, and Xen. Hell. vi. 2. 28, μεγάλη ζημία ἦν τό τε ἐλαττοῦσθαι πᾶσι τούτοις. Madvig, Adv. I. p. 325, advises the omission of ἐλασσωθέντες, and translates: Lacedaemonii, qui semper arte, tum non minus virtute se praestare ostenderunt.

72. 21. τῶν Ἀργείων. Some inferior Mss. have τε between τῶν and Ἀργείων, but as three names of peoples follow, each connected by καὶ with the preceding, τε is better omitted.

73. 20. καὶ τῶν μὲν Μαντινέων καὶ πλείους διεφθάρησαν. Three Mss. read Μαντινέων οἱ πλείους, which St. thinks points to an original reading Μαντινέων καὶ οἱ πλείους, which he adopts. But οἱ πλείους means *the majority*. Now in c. 74. 9, we are told that of the Mantineans 200 fell, and this cannot be a majority of the Mantineans engaged, for as the battle was fought in the immediate vicinity of Mantinea there is every reason to believe that the entire military force of the state (certainly then more than 400 men) was in the battle. καὶ πλείους is peculiar, though it can be explained as in the note.

Possibly, however, we should read Μαντινέων καὶ ξυμμάχων πλείους or something of the sort.

74. 3. ξυνελθοῦσα. This in connexion with μάχη is unusual, but cannot be omitted on account of the pred. modifiers (πλείστου χρόνου, etc.). The pass. signification of the expression ἡ μάχη ξύνεισι or ξυνίστᾳται (cf. Hdt. i. 74. 8) sufficiently explains ὑπό. It is therefore unnecessary to read (with Kr.) ἀπό, and wrong to read (with v. Herwerden) ξυνελθουσῶν.

75. 14. προτέρᾳ. This reading of the Mss. should not be changed (with Cobet) to προτεραίᾳ. See Herbst, *gegen Cobet*, p. 35.

76. 2. [ἐπειδὴ τὰ Κάρνεια ἤγαγον]. These words are prob. a gloss derived from c. 75. 21. Their omission is recommended by Kr., St., Cobet, and v. Herwerden. "Now that the Carnea were over," even if 'not intended as a mark of time' (Jowett) can hardly be said in connexion with an expedition undertaken at the beginning of winter (on the time of the χειμών, see Introd. to Book I. p. 40), *i.e.* six weeks (Cl.) or two months after the Carnea. See on c. 54. 8.

77. 1. Καττάδε δοκεῖ κτέ.: Kirchhoff, Sitzungsber. d. Berl. Akad. 1883, p. 850 ff., discusses this document, and decides that it is probably of Lacedaemonian origin, although on account of the change from the original alphabet to the Ionic, the orthography (σ for θ, *etc.*) does not decide the matter with certainty, for the peculiarly Laconian spelling of our Mss. may be due to the person who transcribed the document from the older to the later alphabet. It is therefore not impossible that the dialect of the document was originally Argive.

77. 11. αἱ μὲν λῆν, τοῖς Ἐπιδαυρίοις ὅρκον δόμεν, αἱ δέ, αὐτώς ὁμόσαι. The Mss. read ἐμενλῆν (Vat. ἐμέλην), which is joined in the inferior Mss. with the preceding σύματος in various ways, as συμβατόσαιθεν λῆν, συμβατόσαι μὲν λῆν, σύματος αἱμὲν λῆν, *etc.* The Mss. have no αἱ after δόμεν. The reading given in the text was proposed by Ahrens, who translates: de sacrificio Apollinis Argivi, si placet, iusiurandum in Epidaurios transferant, si minus, ipsi iurent. St. says he cannot see why the Argives should swear an oath about a sacrifice due from the Epidaurians, and asks, 'How could it please the Argives to take the oath themselves instead of the Epidaurians? What could they swear that they would do in this matter anyway? That they would force the Epidaurians to perform the sacrifice due?' Boehme says Ahrens thought the choice was given to the Epidaurians whether the oath should be sworn by them (that the sacrifice had been unjustly imposed upon them) or the Argives should swear (that they were bound to perform the sacrifice). St. objects to this on the ground that the Epidaurians would not be likely to allow the Argives to impose the sacrifice upon them by an oath, and that the interests of Apollo are not sufficiently consulted if the Epidaurians are permitted to get rid of the sacrifice due from them by means of an oath. He therefore reads: περὶ δὲ τῶ σιῶ σύματος μέλην τοῖς Ἐπιδαυρίοις, ὅρκον δόμεν δὲ αὐτώς (and brackets ὁμόσαι) translating dei sacrificium Epidauriis curae sit, iuramentum autem (de ea re, *i.e.* sacrificium sibi curae fore) praestent; *i.e.* the Epidaurians are to attend to the sacrifice, but must bind themselves by an oath to do so. The objection to this is that it necessitates the omission of ὀμόσαι and the change of ἐμενλῆν to μέλην (Att. μέλειν). Kirchhoff, Sitzungsber. d. Berl. Akad. 1883, p. 857, explains Ahrens' reading (which he adopts) as follows: 'Finally, the question which had furnished the ostensible cause of the feud between Argos and Epidaurus (*cf.* c. 53. 2 ff.) remains to be settled in some way for the sake of propriety, even if Argos has relinquished the idea of settling it by force. It is, accordingly, to be determined, not by the judgment of an umpire chosen and acknowledged by both parties, but simply by an oath, which the Argives are permitted either to swear themselves or to impose upon the Epidaurians, a method of procedure which was not infrequently employed in analogous cases. *Cf.* c. 18. 16 f., ἐὰν δέ τι διάφορον ἦ πρὸς ἀλλήλους, δικαίῳ χρήσθων καὶ ὅρκοις, a clause in the treaty of the peace of Nicias.' The Argives were to be allowed to make oath that the Epidaurians were bound to perform the sacrifice, and this oath was to be accepted as evidence, as was freq. done in private suits. If, however, the Argives preferred, they could propose to the Epidaurians to swear that they were not bound to perform the sacrifice. If the Epidaurians took this oath, they would then be free from the obligation of the sacrifice, their oath being taken as sufficient proof of their case. If they refused to take the oath, they thereby confessed themselves in the wrong, and if they still persisted in their refusal to perform the sacrifice, they could be coerced by the united arms of Argos and Sparta. Thus a perfunctory settlement of the original dispute was reached. Cl. objects to all emendations as yet proposed because the words δόμεν δέ αὐτὼς ὀμόσαι are not taken together. These words he translates: "but they must take an oath to give (the sacrifice)," and he thinks that ἐμεν λῆν must contain an inf. with the signification "impose," such as ἐπιθεῖναι or ἐπιτάξαι, so that the sense of the whole passage would be: "concerning the sacrifice of Apollo, an oath must be imposed upon the Epidaurians; but they must swear that they will perform it (*i.e.* the sacrifice)." In this case, however, the Epidaurians would be treated as if the question at issue had been already decided against them, which does not seem to agree with the spirit of the treaty and the relations of the states concerned, nor does any sufficient reason appear for wishing to connect the words δόμεν δέ αὐτὼς ὀμόσαι. Although the reading proposed by Ahrens is not altogether certain, it gives a satisfactory sense, and it is certainly better to adopt it than to retain the incomprehensible reading of the Mss.

77. 15. ἀμοθι. This is St.'s reading for ἀμοθεί, which Ahrens renders sine seditione et dissensione.

77. 18. ἐσσοῦνται. Ahrens writes, here and in c. 79. 8, 10, ἐσσίονται, which is certainly more in accordance with the peculiarities of the Dor. dialect.

77. 19. καὶ τοὶ τῶν Ἀργείων ξυμμαχοί εντι, τὰν αὐτῶν ἔχοντες. Kirchhoff, Sitzungsber. d. Berl. Akad. 1883, p. 855, reads καὶ τοὶ τῶν Ἀργείων ξύμμαχοι ἐν τῷ αὐτῷ ἐσσίονται ἐν τῷπερ καὶ τοὶ Ἀργεῖοι, τὰν αὐτῶν ἔχοντες, which he takes from the corresponding passage in c. 79. 9 f. This may well be correct, for one certainly feels the lack of any mention of the Argives in the text of the Mss.

79. 17. τὼς δὲ ἔτας. Cl. reads τοῖς δὲ ἔτας (the Mss. give τοῖς δὲ ἔταις) and translates: "but citizens of the town shall conduct the negotiations with them," etc.; i.e. the court to which the cities appeal shall consist of private citizens, not of officials or public judges. But he confesses that this use of δικάζεσθαι is unusual. The question of quarrels between states has been settled, and now a provision is made for private suits. These are to be conducted καττὰ πάτρια, i.e. the cities are to retain their ancient laws and customs. St. compares Cic. in Verr. Act. ii. 13. 32, Siculi hoc iure sunt, ut quod civis cum cive agat domi certet suis legibus, and ibid. 37. 90, ut cives inter se legibus suis agerent. This interpretation gives to δικάζεσθαι its regular signification.

80. 15. ὀλίγοι ὄντες. The reading ὀλίγους ὄντας is possible, referring to τοὺς σφετέρους; for the complete identification in ὀλίγοι ὄντες of the Athenians at home (οἱ δέ) with the 1000 who were sent to Epidaurus is somewhat forced. The acc. would, however, cause confusion with τοὺς ξυμφύλακας.

80. 19. φρούριον. Haack, Poppo, Kr., and Boehme write φρουρικόν with some inferior Mss., for which only one parallel, in Dio C. lvi. 42, is cited. Possibly φρουρίον in 18 should also be taken in the sense of φρουρά. In that case it should be const. with ἀγῶνα γυμνικόν. Philippi, Rhein. Mus. 36, p. 257, proposes to omit τοῦ φρουρίου.

80. 20. ἀνανεωσάμενοι. We have no knowledge of any previous treaty with the Epidaurians, nor is it probable that there was one. St. therefore strikes out Ἐπιδαυρίοις, and makes ἀνανεωσάμενοι τὰς σπονδάς refer to a renewal of the treaty with Argos. Cl. suggests that ἀνανεωσάμενοι τὰς σπονδάς may have come into the text through confusion with 12. Müller-Strübing, Aristoph. u. d. hist. Krit. p. 446 ff., discusses this passage in connexion with c. 74 and 75, but does not succeed in explaining it. Possibly Ἐπιδαυρίοις should stand after ἀπέδοσαν, and ἀνανεωσάμενοι κτέ. should be understood as referring to the treaty with Argos. But even then the passage is not clear, and seems to lack the final revision of the author.

82. 8. οἱ δὲ Λακεδαιμόνιοι, ἕως μὲν αὐτοὺς μετεπέμποντο οἱ φίλοι, οὐκ ἦλθον ἐκ πλείονος. This passage has given much trouble. Kr. thinks it is not genuine. St. (and van Herwerden) marks a gap after πλείονος, and remarks that the gap is indicated by the want of connexion in sense between ἦλθον and ἐκ πλείονος, and also by the fact that ἀναβαλόμενοι δέ is not prop. opp. to the preceding ἕως μὲν . . . οἱ φίλοι, to which the mention of some subsequent time ought to correspond. He offers as a possible reading: ἕως μὲν αὐτοὺς μετεπέμποντο οἱ φίλοι, οὐκ ἦλθον, ἐκ πλείονος δ' ἐπεὶ οὐ τυχόντες ἐπαύ-

σαντο (sc. μεταπεμπόμενοι), ἀναβαλόμενοι δὲ τὰς γυμνοπαιδίας ἐβοήθουν. The chief difficulty is evidently in ἐκ πλείονος, which does not seem appropriate. Cl. says that in all the six places where we find this expression in Thuc. (iv. 42. 15; 103. 13; 129. 22; this passage; viii. 88. 6; 91. 1), the explanation is more or less uncertain. In iv. 129. 22, it is taken in a local sense, "from a great distance," "by a long roundabout way," while elsewhere it is explained as a temporal expression: "a long time before," "for a long time." Everywhere, however, there is a marked opposition between the clause containing ἐκ πλείονος and some other clause. Cl. suggests, therefore, that ἐκ πλείονος may mean "with great zeal," and the passage under discussion would then mean: "the Lacedaemonians did not, to be sure, hurry to take the field with any particular eagerness as long as their friends were sending for them, still they did put off the Gymnopaediae," *etc.* To this St. justly objects that as far as we know ἐκ πλείονος always refers to distance in time or space, as do the similar expressions ἐκ πολλοῦ, ἐκ πλείστου, ἐξ ὀλίγου, ἐξ ἐλάσσονος, ἐξ ἐλαχίστου. Rauchenstein, Philol. 36, p. 298, proposes to read ἐκ πλείονος δὲ ἀναβαλόμενοι τὰς γυμνοπαιδίας ἐβοήθουν, but this would mean that they came long before, not long after. Jowett says: 'ἐκ πλείονος, sc. χρόνου, "did not come for a long time," not with μετεπέμποντο, "while their friends were sending for them for a long time," which the order of the words forbids.' This use of ἐκ πλείονος (though Jowett's explanation is the usual one) seems a little peculiar. If we could take ἐκ πλείονος with μετεπέμποντο, it would very prop. designate the moment from (ἐκ) which the repeated sending on the part of the φίλοι was counted; but if taken with οὐκ ἦλθον, it cannot denote any point from which, since the not-coming of the Lacedaemonians does not date from any particular point. Still, ἐκ πλείονος διεθρόει, in viii. 91. 1, is so much like this passage that the assumption of a defect in the text is hardly warranted.

82. 14. ἐλθόντων πρέσβεων ἀπό τε τῶν ἐν τῇ πόλει καὶ ἀγγέλων τῶν ἔξω Ἀργείων. So Müller-Strübing, *Pol. Beitr.* p. 32. The reading of the Mss. (ἀγγέλων καὶ) is evidently corrupt. Most editt. strike out ἀγγέλων, and understand: "envoys came to them both from the Argives in the city and from those outside." Müller-Strübing justly observes that the Argives outside the city were exiles, not a body politic, and could, therefore, not send πρέσβεις, but only ἄγγελοι, not *envoys*, but only *messengers* (he ascribes a similar suggestion to Arnold's first edit.; in his later editt. it is not to be found). Accordingly he proposes to read: ἐλθόντων πρέσβεών τε ἀπὸ τῶν ἐν τῇ πόλει καὶ ἀγγέλων τῶν ἔξω Ἀργείων. This is perfectly clear and good sense. Unquestionably, too, the change from πρέσβεων ἀπό τε to πρέσβεών τε ἀπό is necessary to bring about an exact correspondence between πρέσβεων and ἀγγέλων. It is, however, possible to have τε after ἀπό, because it seems not unlikely that ἀγγέλων may have been the result of an afterthought, so that Thuc. may have left τε where it would have been had ἀγγέλων been omitted. Still, when once the position of καὶ ἀγγέλων had been improperly reversed, it would be natural for πρέσβεών τε ἀπό to be changed to πρέσβεων ἀπό τε. Cl., following other com-

mentators, suggests that perhaps we should read ἀπό τε (position as in iv. 70. 4) τῶν ἐν τῇ πόλει Ἀργείων καὶ τῶν ἔξω.

82. 21. St. rejects as a gloss the words τε καὶ νομίζων μέγιστον ἂν σφᾶς ὠφελήσειν, because (as he explains, *Quaest. Gramm.* p. 10) the connexion of προσαγόμενός τε καὶ νομίζων is bad since the opinion indicated by νομίζων is the reason of the act denoted by προσαγόμενος. Cl. rightly says that this is no sufficient reason for rejecting these words. St. also objects to ἂν with the fut. inf. (which occurs acc. to the best Ms. authority five times in Thuc.); but even if this is to be avoided, it is better to write μέγιστα or μέγιστον δή (Meineke, Hermes 3. p. 371) for μέγιστον ἂν than to reject the whole passage.

82. 24. ξυνῄδεσαν. ξυνῄνεσαν (Kr.) would not much change the sense. Meineke proposes ξυνῄνυσαν with transposition of ξυνῄνυσαν ... πόλεων to a place after ἐτείχιζον. But this is inadmissible because the walls were never finished, for the Lacedaemonians τὰ οἰκοδούμενα τείχη εἷλον, c. 83. 7. St. strikes out τὸν τειχισμόν on the ground that the political tendencies of the Argives, not merely the building of the walls, were viewed with sympathy by the Peloponnesian states. But these tendencies found their expression in the τειχισμός. Müller-Strübing's change of ξυνῄδεσαν to ξυνετέλεσαν ἐς (*Thuk. Forsch.* p. 63) is unnecessary and unwarranted.

83. 14. κατέκλῃσαν ... Μακεδόνας Ἀθηναῖοι, Περδίκκᾳ ἐπικαλοῦντες. Goeller's emendation for Μακεδονίας and Περδίκκαν. The Schol. explains τοῦτ' ἔστι τῶν εἰσαγωγίμων τῆς θαλάσσης αὐτοὺς ἀπέκλῃσαν, which shows that his reading was that given in the text. St. compares i. 117. 6, (οἱ Σάμιοι) ἐλθόντος τοῦ Περικλέους κατεκλῄσθησαν, while just before ἐσεκομίσαντο καὶ ἐξεκομίσαντο ἃ ἐβούλοντο. The Athenians prevented the Macedonians from carrying on their coasting trade. Even if winter put an end to naval warfare, trade between neighbouring harbours was doubtless carried on whenever the weather permitted. Meineke doubts this, and proposes κατέλῃσαν, praedabantur, retaining Μακεδονίας. But an act. verb λῄζω does not occur even in composition.

83. 19. στρατεία. Cl. and St. for στρατιά of the Mss. (on the freq. confusion of these words, see App. on i. 10. 18). Here only an intended expedition can be meant, which was given up when the defection of Perdiccas became known. Jowett keeps the reading of the Mss., but is obliged to assume that the expedition was actually sent.

83. 20. ἀπάραντος. Thuc. uses ἀπαίρειν only of departing by sea, which would make no sense here. ἀναπεισθέντος, which the Schol. gives as an explanation, is taken from c. 80. 8, and is not adapted to the context here. Poppo suggested ἀποστάντος, which expresses the required meaning, and is not a violent change. St.'s ἀπαρνηθέντος hardly agrees with ἐψευστο; for Perdiccas is not likely to have given a plain refusal. ἀπατήσαντος and ἀποδράντος and οὐ παρόντος are suggested by Cl. as possible readings.

84. 17. Τισίας ὁ Τισιμάχου. Both names are spelled in inscriptions (*C. I. A.* I. 181, 299) Τεισίας, Τεισίμαχος, but, as Cl. says, the propriety of

changing the reading in Thuc. is doubtful. Not only would similar names (Tisamenes in iii. 92. 8, Tisander in iii. 100. 4) have to be changed, but consistency would require many other changes from the received orthography.

86. 4. διαφέροντα αὐτοῦ φαίνεται. Dion. H. *de Thuc. iud.* c. 37, finds fault with Thuc. for writing αὐτοῦ when he should have written αὐτῆς referring to ἐπιείκεια or αὐτά referring to τὰ τοῦ πολέμου. The first would be much less expressive, as αὐτοῦ refers very appropriately to τὸ διδάσκειν ἀλλήλους καθ' ἡσυχίαν, and αὐτά would make no sense, as a gen. after διαφέροντα is indispensable. Buecheler, Jahrbb. 1874, p. 691, concludes that Dion. H. must have read φαίνετε, drawing this conclusion from the words of Dion. τῷ πληθυντικῷ καὶ οὐδετέρῳ (καὶ) κατὰ τὴν αἰτιατικὴν ἐσχηματισμένῳ πτῶσιν which refer to τὰ τοῦ πολέμου; for if τὰ τοῦ πολέμου be neut. acc., φαίνεται is incomprehensible. Buecheler adds: nec quicquam ego morae habeo quo minus haec scriptura ipsi reddatur Thucydidi. (St. has taken φαίνετε into his text.) Cl. objects to this, urging that Thuc. nowhere uses φαίνειν (though he uses φαίνεσθαι more than ninety times); and further that the parallelism of the period (ἡ μὲν ἐπιείκεια ... οὐ ψέγεται, τὰ δὲ τοῦ πολέμου διαφέροντα αὐτοῦ φαίνεται), one of the most effective rhetorical devices of Thuc., is destroyed by the adoption of φαίνετε.

90. 1. ἦ μὲν δή. This reading has the best Mss. authority. ἡμεῖς μὲν δή and ἡμεῖς δή are adopted by Bekker, Kr., and St. on the authority of some Mss.

90. 5. πείσαντα. Cl. reports and rejects an explanation communicated orally by Bekker, that 'the fut. πείσοντα seems to refer to a presentiment of the speaker.' Jowett renders "although he may be destined to fail in making out a strict case, he should be profited." But it would be difficult to find examples for such a use of the fut., and the change to πείσαντα is very easy, and even supported by two Mss.

94. 1. ὥστε δέ. δέ is wanting in the majority of Mss., but it is more likely to have been dropped than inserted after ὥστε, and is freq. used in this dialogue to introduce a reply with some emphasis. *Cf.* c. 91. 1; 96. 1; 98. 1 (this is very like the case in question); 103. 1; 106. 1; 109. 1.

94. 3. δέξαισθε. This is the reading of two Mss. and Procop. p. 221 adopted by most editt. Herbst, *Hamburg Progr.* 1867, p. 26 f., and Cl. retain the reading of the most and best Mss., δέξοισθε, but the fut. opt. not in indir. disc. and with ἄν is unparalleled. See GMT. 26 and Rem.; Stahl, *Quaest. Gram.* p. 10.

98. 3. ἐκβιάσαντες. This (and ἐκβιάζοιεν in vi. 64. 6) is the reading of Vat. and others of the best Mss. for ἐκβιβάσαντες (and ἐκβιβάζοιεν). This is surely not accidental; and though the act. form ἐκβιάζω is found only in late writers (*e.g.* Plut. *Sympos.* iv. 662 a), still it is reasonable that an act. ἐκβιάζω, in which external force is opp. to the δίκαιον, should exist by the side of the mid. βιάζεσθαι, καταβιάζεσθαι, etc., in which the force (βία) proceeding from the subj. is most important. ἐκβιβάζειν in a figurative sense is also without parallel. (St. rejects ἐκβιάζειν in both passages.)

APPENDIX.

98. 9. μελλήσαντας. Reiske's emendation for μελλήσοντας of the Mss. is adopted also by Cl., St., and others. The Schol. explains, τοὺς μηδὲ διανοηθέντας ὑμῖν τὴν ἀρχὴν πολεμεῖν. The sense is οἳ μηδὲ ἐμέλλησαν (πολέμιοι) γενέσθαι, not οἳ μελλήσουσιν κτέ.

99. 2. ὅσοι ἠπειρῶταί που ὄντες κτέ. Cl. explains as follows: 'the intention of the Athenians is to prove that they are not so much in danger from the inhabitants of the Greek mainland as from the islanders. The reason lies in the ἐλεύθερον in the case of those on the mainland, in the ἀναγκαῖον τῆς ἀρχῆς in the case of the islanders. The ἐλεύθερον as a consequence of the ἠπειρῶται ὄντες is used here in the sense of freedom of motion (not without reference to the fundamental ἐλεύθω equiv. to εἶμι), in consequence of which the ἠπειρῶται could turn whithersoever they would for their defence, and could also call in others to their assistance. But for this very reason they were less likely to make warlike preparations against the more powerful state, whereas the islanders, even if they were as yet free from the ἀρχή, were nevertheless in constant anxiety on account of the inevitableness of it (τῆς ἀρχῆς τῷ ἀναγκαίῳ), and were therefore driven to acts of hostility.' Cl. is, however, unable to reconcile the τε after νησιώτας and the τούς before δήη (both in 4) with this explanation, and therefore strikes out these two words. St. changes τῷ ἐλευθέρῳ, in 2, to τῶν ἐλευθέρων, and cites the explanation of the Schol. τοὺς ἐλευθέρους τῶν ἠπειρωτῶν. He compares vii. 44. 44, ὅσοι ἦσαν τῶν προτέρων στρατιωτῶν. Rauchenstein, Philol. 36, p. 239, thinks that τῷ ἐλευθέρῳ means that the inhabitants of the mainland believed that there was less danger to their liberty (than to that of others) from the naval power of the Athenians. It is hard to see how this can all be contained in τῷ ἐλευθέρῳ.

102. 1. πολέμων. This is the only correct reading, though nearly all Mss. give πολεμίων. τὰ τῶν πολέμων occurs also in ii. 11. 16.

103. 3. τοῖς δ' ἐς ἅπαν τὸ ὑπάρχον ἀναρριπτοῦσι. The explanation given in the note is that of St. Cl. says: 'If Thuc. wrote this as it stands, the opposition to the ἀπὸ περιουσίας χρωμένοις is not exact; it should be τοῖς ὀλίγα κεκτημένοις. It is still more remarkable that the reason for the rash conduct of men is sought in the nature of hope, which is represented as inclined to extravagance. Both causes of offence are removed if we read ἀναρριπτοῦσα: then we understand by τοῖς δέ all except those who ἀπὸ περιουσίας τῇ ἐλπίδι χρῶνται ("but in the case of the others"), and it is said of Hope (personified) that in the case of these people she stakes all that they have upon a cast of the die, i.e. that she leads them on to ruinous rashness. ἐς ἅπαν τὸ ὑπάρχον is to be taken together: for the unexpressed κίνδυνον, which must be supplied with ἀναρριπτεῖν, makes their "whole property" appear as the stake for which the die is thrown.' Cl. adds that he does not see how δάπανος δὲ φύσει can be said of ἐλπίς unless her activity has already been expressed in ἀναρριπτοῦσα. He explains that he means the dat. τοῖς δέ to be const. with γιγνώσκεται, in the same way in which τοῖς δέ ἀναρριπτοῦσι is const. in the note. But there is no reason why τοῖς δέ should mean *all others*, and ἀναρριπτοῦσι is at least as easy to understand as Cl.'s ἀναρριπτοῦσα.

105. 11. ταὐτό. This reading for αὐτό of the Mss. was rightly adopted by St. from the explanation of the Schol. εἰδότες ὅτι καὶ ὑμεῖς καὶ ἄλλος ὁστισοῦν ἐν τῇ ὁμοίᾳ δυνάμει γενόμενος ἡμῖν τὸ αὐτὸ ἂν ἔπραττεν.

105. 13. ἥν. So Kr., Poppo, and St., with the best Mss. authority. Reiske proposes ᾗ, which would be like ᾧ πιστεύσαντες of c. 111. 5. Cl. approves of this, but suggests also καθ' ἥν.

106. 2. τῷ ξυμφέροντι αὐτῶν. St. strikes out these words as a gloss on κ'ατ αὐτὸ τοῦτο, being led to this by the unusual use of αὐτῶν. Certainly very little is lost by the omission, but ξυμφέρον of c. 107. 1 makes it prob. that ξυμφέροντι should be retained here.

107. 3. δρᾶσθαι. Nearly all Mss. give δρᾶσαι, but δρᾶσθαι is necessary, as the act. is incomprehensible.

110. 7. τῆς οἰκειοτέρας ξυμμαχίδος τε καὶ γῆς. All Mss. contain the words ξυμμαχίδος τε καὶ γῆς, and the Schol. explains περὶ τῆς τῶν ξυμμάχων καὶ τῆς ὑμετέρας, so that St. is not justified in rejecting these words. ξυμμαχὶς is here rather the country of the allies than equiv. to τὸ ξυμμαχικόν as in c. 36. 4.

111. 1. τούτων μὲν καὶ πεπειραμένοις. The next words in the Mss. are ἄν τι γένοιτο καὶ ὑμῖν καὶ οὐκ κτέ. To obtain the prop. sense, St. strikes out καί after ὑμῖν, and Cl. (who is followed in the text) also adds ἡμῖν after γένοιτο. This brings πεπειραμένοις ἡμῖν into the necessary opposition to ὑμῖν οὐκ ἀνεπιστήμοσιν. The Schol. evidently had the common reading, for he explains: τούτων μὲν καὶ ὑμεῖς πεπείρασθε καὶ οὐκ ἀνεπιστήμονές ἐστε. But this cannot be right, since the Melians had not experienced these things.

111. 6. νομίσειαν. This is the form of the third pers. pl. aor. opt. always used by Thuc. It must therefore be adopted here, though the Mss. read νομίσαιεν. See on iii. 49. 10; St. Quaest. Gram. p. 18. (So the third pers. sing. should, as St. observes, be written -σειε, not -σαι, in ii. 49. 11; 84. 8.)

111. 17. τύχης. St., following the Schol., reads τύχῃ, but there is no real objection to the reading of the text.

111. 26. ἣν μιᾶς πέρι... ἔσται. St. proposes ἧς μιᾶς πέρι with the comment: 'intellege ἧς μιᾶς πέρι καὶ ἐς μίαν βουλὴν... βουλεύσασθαι ἔσται· ἐς de effectu dictum ut vii. 87. 6; viii. 1. 25; 86. 30; cf. Hom. Il. B 379, ἔς γε μίαν βουλεύσομεν.' Other emendations are proposed by Rauchenstein, Philol. 36, p. 241; Schütz, Ztschr. f. d. Gymn.-Wesen, 31, p. 268; Bernadakis, Jahrbb. 23, p. 154. Prob. some words, in which the opposition between σῴζεσθαι and διαφθείρεσθαι was expressed, have been lost either before or after ἔσται. Until this loss is correctly restored, any conjectures concerning the form of the rel. pron. ἥν are uncertain.

115. 8. διαφορῶν. This form (from ἡ διαφορά) is, as the reading of the Mss., preferable to διαφόρων (from τὰ διάφορα). The meaning may be *quarrels* (διαφοραί) quite as well as *grounds of disagreement* (διάφορα). Cl., however, prefers διαφόρων.

115. 13. χρήσιμα. Cl. prefers χρήματα (see on vi. 49. 3), which may certainly mean *supplies* of any kind, not money only. The Mss. read χρήμασι, which is certainly corrupt, and the change from this to χρήσιμα, *useful things, necessaries*, is very slight. Valla renders quae ex usu forent.

116. 3. ἱερὰ ἐν τοῖς ὁρίοις. These words are not elsewhere (*cf.* c. 54. 6; 55. 14) added to διαβατήρια. Cobet therefore (*V. L.* p. 454, and *Nov. L.* p. 477) strikes them out. They certainly do look very like a gloss on διαβατήρια; still it is possible that they belong in the text.

116. 5. ὑποπτεύσαντες. So Meineke for ὑποτοπεύσαντες. ὑποτοπῆσαι (see on i. 20. 9) means only *surmise*, and is always (except in i. 56. 4) followed by the inf.

Summary of the Dialogue. Chaps. 85–113.

85 The Athenians suggest that the various points at issue be discussed
86 and settled one at a time. The Melians see the advantage of this course, but express their apprehension that the warlike movements of the Athenians may interfere with the freedom of discussion, and prevent argu-
87 ments from having their proper weight. The Athenians call upon them to give up all other thoughts and consider only the welfare of their city,
88 whereupon the Melians agree to conduct the deliberations in the way proposed.

89 The Athenians then bring to the front the practical point of view: that there is no use in talking of rights acquired or wrongs suffered, but only of what is attainable in view of the available resources, because in human affairs right has power only in proportion to the resources at its disposal; and in accordance with that which is attainable the powerful must act and the weak submit.

90 To this the Melians reply that, even if they may no longer advance arguments based upon right, still a regard for reasonable claims which do not rest solely upon brute force is not only for the benefit of the weak, but may also, in case of a change of fortune, prove to be advantageous
91 to the powerful. The Athenians refuse to consider this point; for they say there could be no danger to them unless it came from an uprising of their subjects, and against that they could protect themselves. They then undertake to show that the voluntary surrender of the Melians will
92 be advantageous to both parties alike. When the Melians question this
93 statement, the Athenians reply that the Melians would by surrendering escape a much harder but inevitable fate, while the Athenians would be the gainers by obtaining possession of the city with all its resources un-
94 impaired. "Is it not enough for you," the Melians ask, "if we maintain
95 friendly relations toward you, but preserve our neutrality?"—"No; for your friendship would be regarded by our subjects as a proof of our weakness (because they would think we were unable to reduce you to subjection), while the hatred you would feel toward us after your subjugation would be regarded as a proof of our power (inasmuch as it would
96 result from that power)."—"Will your subjects not regard our relations

to you, if you leave us our freedom, in a different light from those of
states which are chiefly your own colonies, and in some cases have revolted and been subdued by you? For we have never had anything to
97 do with you."—"No; for on the score of right and justice both would
have a good deal to say for themselves, but they will think that states
like yours have maintained their freedom by their own power, and that
we are afraid to reduce them by force of arms. Therefore your subjection would not only add to our power, but would increase the safety of
our position. Least of all must you, who are islanders, and insignifi-
98 cant ones besides, be allowed to retain your independence."—"But don't
you think the neutrality we propose is good for your safety? (For, since
you have forced us to discuss only the question of expediency, we must
try to show you that our interest is yours also.) For will not violence
toward us make all who are now neutrals your enemies? Will they
not fear a fate like ours? And are you not therefore strengthening the
enemies whom you already have, and exciting against you others who
99 never before thought of being your enemies?"—"We are not afraid of
that: for the people of the mainland in their freedom have nothing to
fear from us, and therefore put off all such preparations as might make
them dangerous to us. The islanders, both our subjects and those who
are as yet unsubdued, are our danger; for these are the ones whose reck-
lessness is most likely to bring ruin upon themselves and us."
100 The Melians say that it would be base and cowardly for them to yield,
101 to which the Athenians reply that the question is not one of baseness or
honour, but merely whether they shall risk their existence in a conflict
102 with a much more powerful enemy. When the Melians declare that,
since the fortunes of war are variable, there is still some hope for them
103 if they fight, the Athenians warn them that Hope is a great deceiver, and
is only detected when men, yielding to her blandishments, have staked
their all and been ruined. They add that only the foolish forsake the
natural means for saving themselves, and have recourse to supernatural
104 aid, from which only harm results. Still the Melians, with the confidence
of righteousness, refuse to give up their trust in the divine assistance,
and they also expect powerful aid from the Lacedaemonians, who cannot
105 with honour desert their kinsmen. The Athenians reply that trust in the
gods should not pass beyond the bounds of the external laws according to which the deity acts, and that it is better in human affairs to
rely upon human resources. From the Lacedaemonians, moreover, the
Melians must not expect much help, since they are notorious for act-
106 ing always in accordance with their own convenience and interest. But
their own interest would, the Melians suggest, induce the Lacedaemonians
to help them, since they would otherwise suffer a loss of reputation with
107 friends and foes.—The Lacedaemonians, however, would not risk any-
108 thing for the sake of a reputation for magnanimity.—But they might

need the aid of the Melians, whose geographical position and faithfulness
109 to their kinsmen make them of value. — "In war," the Athenians reply, "men regard not the good will, but the material power of their allies, and nobody does this more than the Lacedaemonians, who are not likely to run the risk of trying to protect an island against an overwhelming
110 naval force." — "On the other hand," the Melians say, "a naval war in the open Cretan sea offers other advantages, and the Lacedaemonians may attack you in Attica and in Thrace, so that you will need your strength
111 for your own preservation." — The Athenians reply that they have never yet retired from a siege through fear of a foe elsewhere. But all this discussion has not really touched upon the point to be considered, the best interest of Melos (*cf.* c. 87), whose existence is at stake. Therefore the Athenians call upon the Melians to consider the matter once more with a proper understanding of the true state of the case, without allowing uncertain hope or an unreasonable feeling of honour to mislead them, and to come to a wise decision. But the only wise decision would be to yield to the overwhelming power of Athens and become tributary. For there is no disgrace in yielding to those who are more mighty than ourselves, however disgraceful it may be to submit to our equals.
112 After consulting among themselves, the Melians still persevere in their decision, resolving not to give up the independence they had enjoyed for seven hundred years, but to put their trust in the gods and the Lacedaemonians and defend themselves to the last.
113 The Athenians then leave the conference, exclaiming: "If that is your decision, you are the only men we have ever met who consider the future more certain than the present, and regard that which is wrapped in obscurity as already existing; and so by casting yourselves upon the Lacedaemonians and fortune and hope, and trusting them entirely, you will bring down utter ruin upon yourselves."

GREEK INDEX.

[The references to the Greek text are by chapters and thirds of chapters; to the notes, by chapter and line of text annotated: *e.g.*, 18 a refers to the Greek text at the first third of c. 18; and 87. 2 refers to the note on line 8 of c. 67.]

ἀγώνισις, 50. 18.
αἴσθεσθαι, 26. 28 App.
αἰσθόμενος, ὑπό, 2. 8.
  with inf. 4. 24 App.
ἀλλά, 102. 1.
ἄλλο τι ἤ, 87. 2.
ἅλωσις, 15. 6.
ἄμιπποι, 57. 12.
ἀμόθι, 77. 15.
ἄν, repeated, 9. 16; 105. 9.
  with fut. inf. 82. 21.
ἀναγκαίαν οὖσαν, 8. 10.
ἀναδάσασθαι, 4. 5.
ἀναφέρειν, 28. 2.
ἀνοκωχή, 25. 13 App.; 32. 30.
ἀπό, proleptic, 65. 15.
  with ἐπιστέλλεσθαι, 37. 2.
ἀπάγειν, 53. 3; 63. 16.
ἀπέχειν, 3. 14.
ἀπογίγνεσθαι, 74. 12.
ἀποκρύπτειν, 65. 22.
τὰ ἄριστα, πράσσειν, 9. 36.
ἀρκείτω δεδηλωμένον, 9. 3.
αἱ ἀρχαί, 28. 2.
ἀρχήν, 27. 14.
αὐτός, τρίτος, 4. 1.
ταῦτα γιγνώσκειν, 36. 10.
τὸ αὐτὸ λέγειν, 31. 27;
  ποιεῖν, 38. 6.

αὐτοβοεί, 3. 9.
αὐτόδεκα, 20 2.
αὐτοδίκους, 18 a.
αὐτοπόλιες, 79. 5.
αὐτοτελεῖς, 18 a.

βίᾳ αἱρεῖν, 7. 14.

γνώμην ἔχειν πρός, 13 c; 14 a; 44. 7.
γράμμα, 29. 17.
γυμνά, 10. 17.

δέ, epexegetical, 10. 21; 30. 11.
  with ἔπειτα, 7. 1.
δεινὰ ποιεῖν, 42. 15.
δεκαετῆ, 25. 3.
δεχήμερος, 26. 14; 32. 17.
δημόσιον, 18. 35.
δι' ὀργῆς ἔχειν, 29. 13; 46. 32.
δι' ὀλίγου, 66. 4.
διὰ παντός, 69. 8; 105. 5.
διαβατήρια, 54. 6.
διαμάχεσθαι, 41. 14.
διελθεῖν, 20 a; 55. 20.
δικαίωμα, 97. 1.
δικαίωσις, 17. 11.

ἐγχειρίσασθαι, 108. 2.
αἱ δέ, for εἰ δὲ μή, 77. 11.
εἴ πως, 4. 17.

εἰκός, with aor. inf. 109. 6.
εἶναι, with advs. 23. 8.
ἐκ, with ἀπολιπεῖν, 4. 11.
  proleptic with ἐκλιπεῖν, 80. 14.
ἐκ πλείονος, 82. 9.
ἐξ ὀλίγου, 64. 17; 65. 20.
ἐκ τοῦ φανεροῦ, 76. 16.
ἐκεχειρία, 1. 2 ; 2 a; 49 b.
δεχήμερος, 26. 14 App.
ἐκπίπτειν, 5. 4.
ἐν, with κατοικίζειν, 35. 35.
ἐν αἰτίᾳ ἔχειν, 60. 10; 60 c; 63. 2; 65. 24.
ἐν βλάβῃ, 52. 16.
ἐν καλῷ, 46. 6; 50. 17; 60 b.
ἔνδημοι ἀρχαί, 47. 52.
ἐνέκειντο, 43. 3.
ἐξελεῖν, 43. 16.
ἐξορκοῦν, 47. 52.
ἐπὶ πολύ, 16. 23.
ἐπιλιπεῖν, 103. 9.
ἐπιπαριέναι, 10. 37.
ἐπισπένδεσθαι, 22. 9.
ἐπισπονδαί, 32. 17.
ἐπιτειχισμός, 17. 9 App.
ἐπιτρέπειν, 31. 14.
ἐπιφέρειν αἰτίαν ἐς, 75. 9.

GREEK INDEX.

ἐς, with ἔχειν, 2. 5.
  with πείθειν, 76. 5.
  with σπεύδειν, 37. 22.
  with χωρεῖν, 40. 6.
ἐς ὀλίγους, 81. 6.
ἔτας, 79. 17.
εὐθύς, 13. 2; 76. 1.

θῦμα, 53. 2; 77. 11.

ἱερὰ τέλεια, 47. 47.
ἱερομηνία, 54. 9 App.

καθαρόν, 8. 7.
καί, emphatic, 21. 16.
  proleptic, 45. 9.
  for ἤ, 74. 1.
κακὸν κακῷ ἰᾶσθαι, 65. 7.
κατ' ὀλίγον, 9. 5.
καταλαμβάνειν, 59. 7.
καθίστασθαι ἐς θροῦν, 29. 11.
καταλύειν, 23. 8.
κατατίθεσθαι, 84. 4.
κλέμματα, 9. 15.

λύειν, for καταλύειν, 31. 9 App.

μέντοι, 88. 3.
μέχρι Πυθίων, 1. 1 App.
μή, irregular, 60. 25.
  in hypothetical expression, 64. 17.

ξυγγνώμη, with inf. 88. 1.
ξυγγραφή, 35. 12.
ξυγχεῖν, 39. 15.
ξυγχωρῇ, impers. 40. 21.
ξυμβαίνειν, with adv. 92. 1.
ξύμβασιν, τὴν διὰ μέσου, 26. 7.

ξύν ὅπλοις, 50. 9.
ξυνελών, 105. 18.

ὁρᾶν, 27. 9.
ὅσιος, 104. 4.
ὅτι, explanatory, 9. 2.
  introducing a dir. quot. 10. 20.
  with μεταμέλεσθαι, 14. 10.
ὅτου, for ὁτουοῦν, 18. 57.
οὐ μέντοι ἀλλά, 43. 7 App.
οὐχ ἧσσον, 15. 3.
οὐκ οὖν, 30. 19; 107. 1.
οὐδ' ὑφ' ἑτέρων, 48. 3.
οὕπως, 15. 7 App.
ὀφλεῖν, 101. 3.

παράγγελσις, 66. 14.
παρακαλεῖν, 17. 17; 55. 3.
παρακινδύνευσιν ποιεῖσθαι, 100. 3.
παραμύθιον, 103. 1.
παρασχόν, impers. abs., 14. 11; 60. 25.
ἐν τῷ παρατυχόντι, 38. 3.
ἀπὸ περιουσίας, 103. 2.
περιορώμενοι, 31. 27.
περιτείχισμα, 2. 12.
ποιεῖν, like πάσχειν, 70. 7; 71. 2.
πόλεμος φανερός, 25. 15; 84. 14.
πολεμοῦσθαι, 98. 6.
πρᾶγμα, 4. 22.
πράσσειν, 15. 5; 32. 12.
προεπανασείειν, 17. 8.
προτίθεσθαι, 35. 11.
προσκαθέζεσθαι, with acc., 61. 15.
προσκεῖσθαι, 9. 23.

προσστέλλειν, 71. 5 App.
προστάττειν, 8. 14.
προτέρᾳ, for προτεραίᾳ, 75. 14.
πρῶτος πόλεμος, 20. 13; 24 c.

ῥαβδοῦχοι, 50. 15.
ἐπὶ ῥοπῆς μιᾶς, 103. 6.
ῥύεσθαι, 63. 11.

ἐτετάχατο, 6. 23.
τέ, introductory, 28. 7.
  between the art. and its noun, 30. 5.
  of alternative action, 39. 3.
τοίνυν, 87. 1; 89. 1; 105. 1.
τότε, 6. 1.
τότε δέ, 16. 6 App.
τοῦ μή, with inf. expressing purpose, 72. 26.
τρέπεσθαι κατά, 9. 10.
τρὶς ἐννέα, 26. 21.
τύχη, 104. 2.

ὑπὸ σπουδῆς, 66. 9.

φιλεῖ, solet, 70. 6.
φρονεῖν, with τά and the gen. 84. 3.
φρούριον, 80. 19.

ἐν χερσί, 3. 12.
ἐς χεῖρας, 72. 23.
χρηματίζειν, 5. 2.

ὥσπερ καί, 14 c; 29. 9; 44 b; 91. 3.
ὥστε, in emphatic transition, 14. 3.
  on condition that, 27. 13; 61. 21.

INDEX OF SUBJECTS.

Acanthus, provision respecting, in the treaty between Lacedaemon and Athens, 18 b.
Acanthus, a Lacedaemonian, 19 b; 24 a.
Accusative (abs.), 30. 9; 53. 3; 56. 5; 60. 25; 63 a; 65. 10; (adv.), 91. 2; (cognate), 105. 13; (instead of dat.), 79. 3; 111. 16; (with τρέπομαι), 58. 15.
Achaea, 82 a.
Acropolis of Athens, 18 c; 23 c; 47 c.
Adramyttium, 1 c.
Aegina, 53 c; 74 c.
Aenianians, 51 a.
Aeson, 40 c.
Agesippidas, 56 a.
Agis, 24 a; 54; 58; 59; 60; 63; 65 a, c; 66 a; 70–74; 83 a.
Agreement with pred. subst. 3. 14; 49. 9.
Agrigentum, 4 c.
Alcaeus, 19 a; 25 a.
Alcibiades, 43–46; 52 c; 53; 55; 56 b; 61 b; 76 b; 84 a.
Alcinidas, 19 b.
Alciphron, 59 c; 60 a.
Altar of Olympian Zeus, 50 a.
Ampelidas, 22 b.
Amphipolis, 10 a, b;

Amphipolis, 11 a; 12 c; 18 a; 21; 35; 46; 83 c; battle of, 6–11.
Amyclar, 18 c.
Anacoluthon, 41. 10.
Anactorium, 30 b.
Andromenes, 42 a.
Androsthenes, 49 a.
Anthene, 41 a.
Antimenidas, 42 a.
Antippus, 19 b; 24 a.
Aorist, gnomic, 103. 2; inceptive, 17. 12; 28. 7; 91. 10; 92. 1, 2; inf. without ἄν, 9. 27; 22. 4; partic. with αἰσθάνεσθαι, 10. 38; partic. referring to idea suggested by main verb, 79. 11.
Apollo, 18 a, c; 23 a; 53 a.
Apposition (partitive), 3. 23; 57. 3; 67. 10.
Arcadia, 29 a.
Arcadians, 57 b; 58 c; 60 b; 64; 67 b; 73 a.
Arcesilaus, 50 b; 76 b.
Archers (mounted), 84 b.
Argilus, 18 b.
Argives, 14 c; 22 b; 27; 28; 29; 31; 36–38; 40; 41; 43; 44; 46 c; 47; 50 b; 52 b; 53–56; 58–62; 64–67; 70–74; 76–84; 115 a; 116 a.

Argos, 27 a; 30 a; 31 a; 36 c; 37 c; 38 c; 41 b, c; 43 c; 47 a, c; 57 b; 58 b; 63 a; 65 a, c; 76 a, c; 80 b; 81 c; 82 b; 83 a; 84 a.
Aristides, 18 b.
Aristocles, 16 b.
Aristocrates, 19 c; 24 b.
Artemisium, 19 a.
Article, not repeated, 5. 1; 10. 31; omitted, 10. 55.
Artynae, 47 c.
Assimilation, 37. 13.
Atalante, 18. 34.
Athena, 10 a; 23 c.
Athenians, passim.
Athens, passim.
Athos, 3 c; 35 a; 82 a.
Autocharidas, 12 b.

Boeotarchs, 37 c; 38 b.
Boeotia, councils of, 38. 8.
Boeotians, 3 c; 17 c; 26 b; 31 c; 32 b, c; 35–39; 52 a; 57–60; 64 b.
Brasidas, 6–11; 16 a.
Brasideans, 34 a; 67 a; 71 c; 72 b.
Brycinniae, 4 b.

Carnea, 75 a; 76 a.
Carneus, 54. 8, 9.
Caryae, 55 b.

INDEX OF SUBJECTS. 211

Cephallenia, 35 c; 56 b.
Cerdylium, 6-10.
Chalcidians, 80 b; 82 a.
Chalcidice, 2-11; 18 b, c;
  21 b; 31 c; 80 b; 82 a.
Charadrus, 60 c.
Chians, 84 a.
Chiastic order, 16. 3;
  111. 13; 112. 17.
Chionis, 19 b; 24 a.
Clearidas, 6-11; 21 b;
  34 a.
Clinias, 43. 4.
Cleobulus, 36-38.
Cleomedes, 84 c.
Cleon, 2 a; 3 c; 6-11.
Cleonae, 67 c; 72 c; 74 b.
Cnidis, 51 c.
Comparatives with two
  terminations, 110. 2.
Construction changed,
  61. 10; 65. 25.
Corinth, 30 a, c; 50 c;
  53 b; 64 b.
Corinthians, 17 c; 25 a;
  27; 30-32; 35; 36; 38;
  48; 50 c; 52 c; 55 a;
  57 c; 58 c; 59 a; 60 b;
  64 b; 75 a; 83 a;
  115 b.
Coryphasium, 18. 33.
Council, of eighty at
  Argos, 47 c; four of
  Boeotia, 38. 8.
Cranii, 35 c; 56 b.
Cretan Sea, 110 a.
Cynuria, 14 c; 41 a.
Cythera, 14 b; 18. 33.

Damagetus, 19 b; 24 a.
Dative, of advantage, 76.
  15; of cause, 26. 22;
  of interest, 3. 21; 46.
  22; 57. 2; ethical, 44.

Dative,
  6; object for which
  coinciding with the
  limit of motion, 10.
  11; 13. 4; of person
  with respect to whom,
  10. 28; by continued
  force of a prep. 42. 2;
  with plpf. pass. 29. 3;
  with φθάσαι, 72. 5;
  with φιλία, 5. 3.
Delium, 14 a; 15 c.
Delos, 1; 32 a.
Delphi, 16 b; 18 a, c.
Demeas, 116 c.
Demiurgi, 47 c.
Demosthenes, 19 c; 24 b;
  80 c.
Dians, 35. 2; 82. 1.
Diathus, 19 b; 24 a.
Dionysia, 20. 2; 23. 20.
Dium, see Dians.
Dolopes, 51 a.
Dorians, 9 a; 54 b.
Doric dialect, 77; 79.
Drachma, Aeginetan,
  47. 40.

Earthquake, 45 c; 50 c.
Edonians, 6 b.
Eighty, council of, at
  Argos, 47 c.
Eion, 6-12.
Elaphebolion, 19 a.
Eleans, Elis, 17 c; 31 a, b;
  43 c; 44 b; 46 c; 47;
  49; 50; 58 a; 62; 75 c;
  78.
Ellipsis, 1. 8; 4. 8; 15.
  7; 76. 11; 84. 15;
  115. 7.
Empedias, 19 b; 24 a.
Emphasis, 89. 9; 98. 1.
Endius, 44 c.

Enomoty, 68. 9.
Ephors, 19 a; 36 a; 37 a.
Epicydidas, 12 a.
Epidaurians, Epidaurus,
  53-56; 75 b, c; 77 a, b;
  80 b, c.
Erasistratus, 4 a.
Euphamidas, 55 a.
Eustrophus, 40 c.
Euthydemus, 19 c; 24 b.
Expediency and justice,
  90; 98; 107.

Factions in Messene,
  5. 5.
Festivals, 23 c; 41 c;
  47 c; 54 b; 75 b; 76 a;
  82 a.
Fines, 49; 63.
Flute players, 70. 3.
Funeral, 11 a.
Future, inf. with ἄν,
  82. 21.

Galepsus, 6 a.
Games, 1 a; 47 c; 49;
  50.
Genitive (abs.), 56. 18;
  71. 1; (objective), 8.
  12; (subjunctive), 85.
  4; 110. 2; (partitive),
  37. 21; 52. 11; 71. 19;
  (predicate partitive),
  16. 29; (of price), 6.
  7; (of time), 14. 13;
  (with αἰσθάνεσθαι),
  83. 2; (with προτίθε-
  σθαι), 74. 4; (with
  ξυναίρεσθαι), 28. 13.
Gymnopaediae, 82. 6.

Hagnon, 11 a; 19 c;
  24 b.
Hegesippidas, 52 a.

Helots, 34 a; 35 c; 56 b.
Hera, temple of, 75 c.
Heraclea, 12 c; 51; 52.
Heracles, temple of, 64 c; 66 a.
Heraeans, 67. 7.
Hiponicans, 5 c.
Hipponoidas, 71 c; 72 a.
Hyacinthia, 23 c; 41 c.
Hysiae, 83 b.

Imbrians, 8 b.
Imperative pf. pass. 91. 6.
Indicative, in general protasis, 9. 12.
Infinitive, by attraction, 53. 8; 72. 1; of purpose, 69. 6; in dependent clauses, 28. 4; 46. 17; 77. 11; for imv., 9. 26; interchanging with finite moods, 18. 38; 23. 18; with περιόψεσθαι, 29. 6; aor. with εἰκός, 109 6.
Iolcius, 19 c; 24 b.
Ionians, 9 a.
Ischagoras, 19 a; 21; 24 a.
Isthmionicus, 19 c; 24 b.
Isthmus, 18 c.
Italy, 4; 5.

Justice, 89 c; 90; 98; 107.

Kings, Spartan, give all orders in battle, 66 b.
Knights, 72 c.

Lacedaemon, Lacedaemonians, *passim*; their

Lacedaemonians, military organization, 66; 68. 9. See Introd. p. 4.
Laches, 19 c; 24 b; 43 b; 61; 74 c.
Lamachus, 19 c; 24 b.
Lampon, 19 c; 24 b.
Laphilus, 19 b; 24 a.
Lemnians, 8 a.
Leon, a Lacedaemonian, 44 c.
Leon, an Athenian, 19 c; 24 b.
Leontini, 4 a, c.
Lepreum, 31; 34 b; 49 a; 50 a; 62.
Leuctra, 54 a.
Lichas, 22 b; 50 b; 76 b.
Litotes, 111. 1.
Locrians (Opuntian), 64 b.
Locrians (in Italy), 5 a, c.
Lot, 21 a.
Lycaeum, 16 c; 54 a.
Lycomedes, 84 c.

Macedonia, 80 b; 83 c.
Maenalia, 64 a; 67 b; 77 a.
Malians, 51 a.
Mantinea, Mantineans, 26 b; 29 b; 33; 43 c; 44; 46; 47; 50 b; 55 a; 58 a; 61; 62; 64 c; 65; 75 c; 78; 81 a; battle of, 66–74.
Mecyberna, 18. 29; 39 a.
Megara, Megarians, 17 c; 31 c; 38 a; 58 c; 59 b; 60 b.
Medmaeans, 5 c.
Melos, 84–116.

Menas, 19 b; 21; 24 a.
Mercenaries, 6 c.
Messene in Sicily, 5 a.
Messenians, 35 c; 56.
Metagenes, 19 b; 24 a.
Methone, 18 b.
Methydrium, 58 a.
Myrcinus, 6 c; 10 c.
Myrtilus, 19 c; 24 b.

Nemea, 58–60.
Neodamodes, 34 b; 67 a.
Niceratus, 16 a; 83 c.
Nicias, 16 a; 19 c; 24 b; 43 b; 46; 83 c.
Nicostratus, 61 a; 74 c.
Nisaea, 17 b.
Nominative, referring to the subj. of the main verb, 112. 10.

Obols, Aeginetan, 47 b.
Odomantians, 6 a.
Oecist, 12. 12.
Olympia, 18 c; 47 c; 49; 50; Zeus of, 31 b; 50 a.
Olynthus, 3 c; 18 b; 39 a.
Oracle, 16 b; 26 c; 32 a; 103 c.
Orchomenus, 61 b, c.
Orestheum, 64 a.
Oroeae, 67 c; 72 c; 74 b.

Panactum, 3 c; 18 b; 35 c; 36 c; 39 c; 42 a, c; 44 c; 46 b.
Panathenaea, 47 c.
Pancratium, 49 a.
Parrhasians, 33.
Participle, attributive, after its subst. 5. 4; 16. 21; predicate, 30. 2; supplementary, 69. 8; for infinitive, 9. 18; 66. 18; 102. 4.

INDEX OF SUBJECTS.

Pasitelidas, 3 b.
Patrae, 52 c.
Pay of soldiers, 47 b.
Peace, of Nicias, 18; 26; between Argos and Lacedaemon, 77.
Pellene, 58 c; 59 b; 60 b.
Pentecosty, 68.
Perdiccas, 6 a; 80 b; 83 c.
Perfect infinitive, 9. 35; 16. 12.
Phaedimus, 42 a.
Phaeax, 4; 5.
Pharnaces, 1 c.
Philocharidas, 19 b; 21; 24 a; 44 c.
Philocrates, 116 c.
Phlius, 57; 58 b; 59 b; 60 b; 83 b; 115 a.
Phocians, 32 a; 64 b.
Phyrcus, 49 a.
Pierium, 13 a.
Plataea, 17 b.
Plataeans, 32 a.
Pleistoanax, 16 b, c; 24 a; 33; 75 a.
Pleistolas, 19 b; 24 a; 25 a.
Plural verb with neut. subj. 26. 12; 75. 8.
Polemarchs, 47 c; 66 b.
Polles, 6 a.
Present infinitive for imperfect, 60. 27.
Prisoners of war, 18 b.
Procles, 19 c; 24 b.
Pteleum, 18 b.
Pylos, 7 b; 14; 18 b; 35 c; 36 c; 39 b; 44-46; 56 b; 115 a.
Pythian games, 1 a.
Pytho, 18 b.

Pythodorus, 19 c; 24 b.
Relative, not repeated, 2.14; conditional, 110. 5; with antecedent omitted, 103. 7.
Rhamphias, 12; 13.
Rhium, 52 c.

Samiuthus, 58 c.
Sane, 18 b.
Scione, 18 b; 32 a.
Sciritae, 67 a; 68 b; 71 b; 72 b.
Scritis, 33 b.
Scolus, 18 b.
Scyllaeum, 53 c.
Sermyle, 18 b.
Seventeen make oath, 19. 8; 18. 50 App.
Sicels, 4 c.
Sicily, 4; 5.
Sicyonians, 52 c; 58-60; 81 c.
Singaeans, 18 b.
Six Hundred at Elis, 47 c.
Sollium, 30 b.
Sparta, see Lacedaemon.
Spartolus, 18 b.
Speech of Brasidas, 9.
Stageirus, 6 a; 18 b.
Strymon, 7 c.
Subject, divided, 10. 47; changed, 61. 12; 64. 9; 81. 5; 115. 3; plural with sing. verb, 47. 35; singular with pl. verb, 47. 37; 60. 22; 82. 4.
Superstition, caused by earthquakes, 45 c; 50 c; causes expeditions to be given up, 54 b; 55 b; 116 a;

Superstition, in observance of festivals, 54 b; 75 a; 82 a.
Syracusans, 4.

Tegea, Tegeans, 32 a; 57 b; 62; 64 b; 65 b; 67-76; 78; 82 a.
Tellis, 19 b; 24 a.
Thasos, 6 a.
Theagenes, 19 c; 24 b.
Theori, 47 c.
Thessalians, 13; 51 a.
Thousand Argives, 67 c; 72 b; 73 c.
Thrace, 6 a, c; 10 c.
Thrasycles, 19 c; 24 b.
Thrasyllus, 59 c; 60 a, c.
Thucydides, 26 c.
Thyrea, 41 b.
Thyssus, 35 a.
Timocrates, 19 c; 24 b.
Tisias, 84 c.
Torone, 2; 3; 18 b.
Trachinians, see Heraclea.
Treaties, 18 f.; 23 f.; 47; 77; 79.
Tribute, 18 b.
Truce, ten days,' 26 b; 32 b.

Walls, long, of Patrae, 52 c; of Argos. 82; 83 a.

Xenares, 36-38; 46 c; another, 51 c.

Zeus, Olympian, 31 a; Lycaean, 16 c; temple of, at Mantinea, 50 a.
Zeuxidas, 19 b; 24 a.

www.ingramcontent.com/pod-product-compliance
Lightning Source LLC
Chambersburg PA
CBHW020827230426
43666CB00007B/1129